PSYCHOLOGICAL COUNSELING

The Century Psychology Series

Richard M. Elliott, Gardner Lindzey, and
Kenneth MacCorquodale, Editors

Psychological Counseling

Second Edition

EDWARD S. BORDIN
University of Michigan

New York

APPLETON-CENTURY-CROFTS

EDUCATIONAL DIVISION

MEREDITH CORPORATION

PRINTED IN THE UNITED STATES OF AMERICA

390-10775-1

PREFACE TO THE FIRST EDITION

The term *psychological counseling* is sufficiently new to require explanation. The choice of this term as a title was governed by a dual purpose: (1) to address counselors being trained to further individual personality development; (2) to treat counseling as a process based on psychological foundations. Counselors speak with many tongues and identify with many disciplines and professional groups. There are counseling disciplines rooted in education, psychology, psychiatry, sociology, and social work. Counselors are found among educators, social workers, lawyers, and ministers, as well as psychiatrists and psychologists. The dividing lines between these groups are vague and there is a great deal of overlap in concepts and functions. Just as psychology draws on the contributions of psychiatry, education, and social work, this description of counseling in psychological terms incorporates facts and concepts derived from these other sources. Whether or not a merging of all these kinds of counseling will evolve, clarification of their interrelationships should prove useful to the student of counseling and beneficial to his future clients.

The needs of students in didactic courses in counseling or psychotherapy have guided the organization of the text. It is intended primarily for graduate students in psychology, particularly those who plan to become counseling or clinical psychologists. For the most part, the discussion will assume that the reader possesses a broad familiarity with the facts and principles of psychology, especially those associated with personality theory and development, both normal and abnormal, and with theory and technique of psychological assessment.

I am convinced that the seeds of theory cannot take hold except in soil fertilized by direct observation. Those who study formal statements about counseling without an adequate observation of therapeutic situations are likely to acquire only a superficial understanding, one which may even block further growth. To avoid this difficulty, the section devoted to concepts and theories underlying therapeutic relationships is preceded by a reproduction and discussion of verbatim transcriptions of six recorded interviews between different client-counselor pairs. In this way I hope to establish some common foundation in the perception of actual interviews which can facilitate understanding. Similarly, examination of the many practical problems faced by the counselor as he goes about his task of aiding his clients to move toward greater maturity is accompanied by illustrative material in the form of interviews or portions of them. Since opportunities for detailed observation of the methods of other practitioners are so limited, it is hoped that counseling psychologists, social workers, and psychiatrists will also find useful the many illustrative interviews which have been included. Incidentally, the legions of part-time high school and college counselors may find in these same interviews and their accompanying analyses an effective aid toward identifying the limitations of their training and toward establishing a clearer sphere of function.

It is appropriate here to express my appreciation to the many clients and counselors who permitted an invasion of their privacy so that concrete evidences of the process of counseling might be available for research and teaching. The interviews found in this book have, with a few exceptions, been accumulated during my residence at the Universities of Minnesota and Michigan and at Washington State College. In all cases precautions have been taken to preserve anonymity by changing names and places.

That in writing this book I owe much to many need hardly be mentioned. It is commonplace for authors to call attention to the many colleagues who have contributed to their apperceptive store. Without shifting responsibility for its shortcomings, it seems enough to acknowledge that whatever contributions are contained herein owe much to the *Zeitgeist* at Michigan, Minnesota, and Washington State. Of the more specific contributors, I must mention Professor Richard M. Elliott. His warm interest and encouragement stimulated me to progress faster. His patient, thorough editing and wise advice materially raised the intelligibility level of the manuscript. My colleagues, Drs. Gerald S. Blum, Harold L.

Raush, and Stanley J. Segal, were kind enough to read portions of the text and give helpful suggestions.

For typing the manuscript in its many stages I am grateful to Marietta Nelson, who did most of it, and to Helen Davis and Elvi Fitzgerald.

Finally, I wish to acknowledge the courtesy of the following journals and publishers in allowing me to quote from their publications: *Journal of Clinical Psychology*; *The Psychoanalytic Quarterly*; The American Psychological Association; Houghton Mifflin Company; International Universities Press; W. W. Norton & Company; The Ronald Press Company; and the University of Chicago Press.

E.S.B.

PREFACE TO THE SECOND EDITION

In the life of every book the point is reached when it must face one of three fates: to be retired to the back shelves of intellectual history, to be reborn in the womb of its author's mind in a new second generation identity (often with a new title), or to be rejuvenated as a revision through up-to-date trappings and the infusion of current ideas. When the combination of the publisher's reports and Stanley J. Segal, student, colleague, and friend, questioning me, "when are you going to revise your book," made the first alternative seem untenable, I had to choose between the latter two. While my own thinking and developments in the field had not been static, the basic ideas which characterized this book and its organization remained unchanged. A revision was the choice open and four major developments were to be incorporated.

The first of the new developments is the crystallization of "community psychology." Since college counselors and student personnel workers had already evolved the spirit of this movement, although without the current generalized orientation and terminology, and since the first edition had already moved toward this generalization, it was an easy task to revise the first edition to bring it up to date. The reader will find the first chapter drastically revised and the rest of the chapters slightly modified. My aim remained to fit the individual processes of psychological counseling into the larger enterprise of a social program of prevention and the enhancement of individual development. I have not addressed myself to the details of theory and practice of the larger program.

A second development, the burst of interest in various versions of "behavior therapy," required some revision of the analysis of theories in Chapter 4. I found that these conceptions fitted in very neatly as extensions and, possibly, improvements over earlier positions attempting to apply learning theories. At the time when operating examples, as distinguished from experimental analogues, were offered, they seemed hardly distinguishable from illustrations based on earlier learning paradigms. As I write these words, some novel applications are beginning to appear.

In the period since the publication of the first edition, the greatest change both in my own ideas and in the field has occurred in the role of the therapist's personality in counseling and psychotherapy. My earlier Chapter 8 had to be almost completely replaced. So great is the momentum being built up both in theory and research on this theme that I am inclined to predict that a teacher using this book as a text will soon have to be supplementing it with a more up-to-date material.

Finally, although there are many examples of counseling clients, presenting problems of vocational choice, throughout the book and in the many transcripts of interviews, the burgeoning theory and research on the intimate connections between vocational and personality development required that a chapter on vocational counseling be added. A new conception of the process is offered which breaks from the earlier tradition but does not take the form of psychotherapy.

I am indebted to Miss Joan Rambo for typing the revised manuscripts and to Miss Charlene Becker for typing the index. I wish to acknowledge the courtesy of the following publishers in permitting me to add quotations required in the course of my revisions and additions: The Free Press; Harcourt, Brace & World, Inc.; John Wiley & Sons, Inc.

E.S.B.

CONTENTS

Preface to the First Edition   v

Preface to the Second Edition   ix

I. INTRODUCTION TO PSYCHOLOGICAL COUNSELING

1. The Goals of Psychological Counseling   3
2. Counseling and Interprofessional Relationships   27
3. Introduction to Counseling Interactions   47

II. THEORETICAL FOUNDATIONS

4. An Analysis of Theories   109
5. The Dimensions of Therapeutic Relationships: A Point of
    View   135
6. The Ambiguity Dimension of Therapeutic Relationships   149
7. The Cognitive and Conative Dimensions of Therapeutic Re-
    lationships   166
8. Personal Dimensions in Therapeutic Relationships   183

III. THE PROCESS OF PSYCHOLOGICAL COUNSELING

9. Initiating the Counseling Relationship   215
10. Analysis of Initial Interviews   232
11. Test Selection and Interpretation   295
12. Illustrations and Problems   313
13. The Process of Counseling: General Problems   366
14. The Process of Counseling: A Model for Vocational Coun-
    seling   423
15. Case Records   445

Bibliography   457
Index   467

Part I

INTRODUCTION TO PSYCHOLOGICAL COUNSELING

THE PURPOSE of this portion of the book is to acquaint the reader with the salient features of the activities of the psychological counselor. His goals are described and differentiated from those of other human relations workers, for example, psychotherapists, teachers, and other types of counselors. The responsibilities of the counselor to other workers in an organization or community are reviewed, along with professional responsibilities and ethics. Finally the reader will observe a representative sample of the kinds of demands clients make and the ways in which counselors meet them.

CHAPTER I

The Goals of Psychological Counseling

THROUGHOUT THEIR lives people seek the help of others when they find themselves unable to cope with the problems encountered. Both the problem and the help required may be either impersonal or personal. The aid received may range from offering specific scientific or technical knowledge such as how to repair a machine, construct a building, or fill out an income tax return to the kind of aid which involves caring about the person who faces such personal problems as confusion about his standards and religious beliefs, unhappiness and conflict in his family, or the experience of loss of self-control and alienation from reality. For problems of a more personal nature and where a personal relationship is desired, people turn to lawyers, physicians, teachers, psychiatrists, psychologists, social workers, and clergymen. All of these persons have used the term *counseling* to refer to the service they render. Therefore, this book about psychological counseling must start by differentiating this kind of counseling from others. In addition to differentiating psychological from nonpsychological counseling, we will need to distinguish it from another form of psychological aid, that of psychotherapy. This first chapter will consider the kinds of problems people bring to the psychological counselor and the ends that his interventions are designed to serve.

PERSONALITY DEVELOPMENT AND
PERSONALITY PROBLEMS

Personality and the course of its development represent the vantage point from which the psychological counselor views the individual's problems. We refer now to impulses and wishes, hopes and aspirations, anxieties and fears, all of which play a part in organizing behavior, developing special response apparatuscs, giving a persistently distinctive character to each person, and providing a basis for intraindividual coherence. At each stage of his development, the individual faces certain tasks and must meet certain requirements set by society, the specific persons with whom he associates, and by his own developing desires and needs. Often persons encounter difficulties in meeting those requirements that reside in themselves, e.g., conflicting motives, anxieties, distortions of perception, and largely unrecognized and uncontrollable self-defeating reactions. In the extreme, we see all forms of disturbed function associated with severe neurotic and psychotic states—extreme anxiety and inhibition, loss of contact with reality, or impulsive and aggressive actions directed toward the self or others.

Over the last two decades public awareness and concern about mental health[1] has been rising, particularly in the United States. A comprehensive national survey of the dimensions of the task of meeting mental-health needs has made clear the gap between the number of persons suffering from severe and crippling emotional disturbances and the number of professionals available or likely to be available to offer them service (Action for Mental Health, 1961; Albee, 1959). This state of affairs has stimulated the development of patterns of service aimed at identification of the emotionally disturbed when their conditions have not reached crisis proportions with the idea that help at this early stage will not be so time consuming and may forestall more serious difficul-

---

[1] The use of such terms as "mental health," "psychopathology," and "patient," are vestiges of a view of psychological problems as analogous to medical diseases, e.g., malaria or tuberculosis. Most psychologists and many psychiatrists, see Menninger, Mayman, & Pruyser (1965), for example, doubt the usefulness of this analogy. These terms will be used in this book where necessary for communication purposes but without intending to subscribe to the analogy.

ties. Even this approach, however, appears destined to be insufficient to deal with the manpower gap. Stimulated by the example
of preventive medicine, there has been an increasing turn toward
what has been called primary prevention (Caplan, 1961), which is
directed toward the elimination or the modification of the conditions conducive to the development of psychological problems.
Activities pointed toward this end can be carried on at many
levels. Efforts can be directed at broad social factors which influence personality development, such as laws and judicial decisions
and general economic conditions. These and similar elements in
our social organization set the climate in which the individual
develops, and influence the well-being of his immediate family,
thereby influencing him. These are the factors which determine
how nourishing his environment is and how his own development
is stimulated by it.

The contribution of the professional mental health worker
in this sphere is problematic because our basic knowledge of the
critical factors in personality development is all too inexact. When
given the opportunity to speak with authority on the influence
of various social conditions or various kinds of parental behavior
on the future personal development of children, we have distress-
ingly few hard facts on which to draw.[2] Too often the mental-
health expert is competing on even terms with the man on the
street. The result is that his suggestions cannot carry much weight,
especially when they are directed toward social issues which in
our society are traditionally decided by political methods.

In the case just referred to, the professional is trying to suggest the content of a social decision. In the absence of hard facts
regarding the issues involved, the professional may be able to
make a more significant contribution by influencing the decision-
making process rather than the content. The research and practical experience derived from group dynamics (Cartwright, &
Zander, 1960) can be applied to many levels of social decision-
making.

This book is being written with the view that, in contrast to
social levels of action, there is an individual level of professional

---

[2] One exception is in the influence of discrimination on the development of
children. The testimony of social and personality psychologists, along with sociologists
and others, played an important role in critical supreme court decisions. (Clark, 1953)

service which can promote the fuller development of the individual by intervening at certain critical points in his development. These are points where he and those close to him—it may be his parents and teachers at first, and eventually his wife, children, and associates at work—face changes arising in the natural course of maturation. His way of dealing with the strains arising from these changes will influence the richness, freedom, and even creativity of his emotional life. His dealing with those strains presupposes that intrapsychic conditions—that is, the particular organization of motivations and the developing apparatuses of thought and action which go with them—have an important influence on how effectively and constructively the individual responds to his physical and social environment. Increasingly, the individual is able to select and modify that environment as well as to adapt to it.

Psychological interventions and transitional stages

To understand how the professional mental-health worker offers aid to an individual, we must examine the conditions under which a person is willing and able to accept such help. It is intuitively clear from observation of ourselves and others that people have inhibitions about dealing with personal matters. There are certain aspects of our actions and experiences that are not readily shared with others and, indeed, are thought about only reluctantly even by ourselves. When problems and discomforts arise in the personal sphere, they must become fairly acute before we are willing and able to take the step of confiding in another, especially someone who we have been led to believe has the power to intervene in a significant way. To this must be added the feelings of personal inadequacy which surround such confiding—feelings which run counter to the self-sufficiency and adequacy which play such an important part in socialization for adulthood.

It has often been thought that reluctance to enter into psychotherapy or to seek any other psychological treatment is a part of the legacy of social superstitions surrounding insanity. Proponents of this view optimistically believed that wider awareness of the naturalness of psychological difficulties would result in a readiness to consult psychiatrists, psychologists, and social workers equal to the readiness to consult doctors, lawyers, or even accountants. Such increase of awareness has in fact occurred. Psychiatry and psychology are everyday phenomena and are in fact treated as a regular part of daily life. It is true that within certain small social groups, e.g., film actors and actresses and mental-health professionals, personal therapy has not only become accepted, but is even "in." Yet the average person continues to resist admitting to himself or others that he is experiencing emotional difficulties and is in need of professional help. In a national sample, less than half of those who admitted that at some time in the past they had felt that they were going to have a "nervous breakdown" reported that they had personal problems for which professional help would have been relevant (Gurin, Veroff, & Feld, 1960: p. 38) . While ignorance and superstition can and do play a part in the reluctance to acknowledge psychological difficulties and to seek professional help, it seems likely that there is a more ineradicable source of this reluctance which resides in the very nature of personality organization. A person's very struggle to maintain control over himself, especially when this control is not functioning well, involves the use of mechanisms of restricted self-observation. The very difficulties that would make him seek help as well as his desire for self-control, both of which he himself might use in the helping process, contribute to his reluctance to seek professional help.

Before a person finally takes the step of seeking psychotherapy or approaching any professional person or agency, the discomforts created by his plight must be severe enough for him to overcome his inhibition about seeing and acknowledging them and about approaching a helper. Psychological counseling is oriented toward offering aid to persons whose discomforts have not yet become that severe, or to persons who are at some critical stage in their development. The aim of psychological counseling is not satisfied with the forestalling of severe emotional disorganization and discomfort. It allies itself with the educational aim of realizing the potential development of the individual. Therefore, we shall be concerned with the modifications in the psychotherapeutic process required for interactions with a person who is not as disabled by emotional conflicts as a person involved in psychotherapy. We shall examine the process of helping someone who seeks to deal with derivatives of his psychological problems without directly acknowledging them as such, or without meeting his real problems head on.

The theoretical and technical issues arising in such an enterprise shall occupy us throughout the entire treatise. At this point, it will suffice to outline the points in persons' lives toward which psychological counseling might be oriented. The life cycle is characterized by periods of important transitions. Most of these periods occur within a narrow span of time and reflect a confluence of patterns of biological and psychological maturation with patterns of social organization. Socially instituted patterns of feeding and cleanliness interact with the developing capacities of the child. In our society and many others, a child's readiness to widen his horizons, to engage in more constructive activity, to experience accomplishment, is recognized by his movement from an area bounded exclusively by his family into the school. The biosocial changes marking puberty, the movement into adult economic roles, the establishment of the lasting, intimate relationships of marriage and parenthood, and, finally, the movement into that period when one becomes aware that one's life is almost over and confronts the prospect of dying, all represent significant periods of development. Erikson (1959) has defined eight stages of man, each of which represents a radical change of perspective, possessing the potential for providing for the development of different capacities and for becoming a crisis. In Chapter 5 we shall return to a further examination of these views and their implications.

Having stated a conception of the transitional stages which form the life cycle, we can return to our main question of how and when a person can accept psychological interventions without necessarily being in a state which would drive him into psychotherapy. The answer is that he is likely to accept help when the trials of a particular developmental task or of a particular normative crisis tap some important developmental deficit, placing him in a momentary state of tension and anxiety. This is not the unendurable tension and discomfort which characterize those who seek psychotherapy. It will probably wane of its own accord as the crisis passes or the developmental process continues, leaving without adequate resolution, some residue of accumulated conflict and further psychic formation which continues to interfere with fully effective functioning.

At the point that the individual feels anxious and not fully able to cope with the particular situation he faces, he is willing to accept help, providing it is clearly linked with that situation. The young man or woman who finds the decision to marry unusually difficult, or the youngster who, at puberty, feels shy and awkward in new social relationships, or the mother who feels bereft of identity when her children are grown up, are each ready to make an examination of what makes the decision so difficult or the new role so hard to realize. Entering into such a process need not be construed as an admission of helplessness or as a step committing oneself to a thorough examination of all of the details of one's life. It is true that in many cases this may be necessary, but that is a bridge to be crossed when required, not something to be decided in advance. This means that the decision to accept help can be more casual.

The foregoing discussions of the developmental goals of psychological counseling stimulate questions about the distinction between normality and abnormality (Jahoda, 1958). Neither the statistical nor the dichotomous views of normality and abnormality are acceptable. The dichotomous view treats abnormality as though it were indivisible; either the personality is "infected" or it is not, the person is either "sick" or "well." My view of the psychological origins of personality embeds it in experience which varies from one individual to another and generates a continuum of effectiveness. While containing some elements of truth, the statistical view is inadequate. It treats normality as the state of effectiveness and integration attained by the average person. Viability appears to be a much more meaningful referent of normality. By this I mean that the person is able to function without the need for special supports from others, such as social welfare or clinical aid. Large numbers of the members of any society (the proportions will vary with the culture and subculture) are able to function without clinical or other aid even though they are not able to realize their full potential in either achievement or satisfaction, and experience discomforts and anxieties beyond those that are the inescapable accompaniments to living.

The reader will find that most of the clinical examples we use deal with college students and the developmental problems associated with work and effort, the search for greater identity and for self-control which are indigenous to this period of late adolescence. Most of the writer's professional experience has been concentrated in this type of clinical work. Despite this, the theoretical orientation will be more general and the practical issues will be analyzed at a level relevant to other ages and transitions.

THE COUNSELING SITUATION

Our developmental orientation poses the question of what distinguishes the counseling experience from the many others which shape the individual's personality. In the course of living, many kinds of interpersonal experiences further personality growth. When one person interacts with another, the experience may either go according to plan or inadvertently play a role in the growth process. *Counseling, as well as psychotherapy, are terms which have been used to apply to interactions where one person, referred to as the counselor or the therapist, has taken the responsibility for making his role in the interaction process contribute positively to the other person's personality development.*

The task of this book might be conceived as clarifying for the prospective counselor those characteristics of interpersonal situations which have therapeutic value. For the most part, the book will speak to those who have already acquired a firm foundation in basic psychological facts, theories and concepts, personality theory, psychopathology, and psychological assessment. We must hasten to warn the student that this understanding of the therapeutic characteristics of interactions, even when erected upon so broad a base, will not be enough. Before he can function adequately in a therapeutic role he must also understand and be able to integrate the demands made by therapeutic interactions upon his own personality. What the effects of his own personality may be upon his contributions toward personality change in another can best be observed in supervised clinical practice. A supervisor who is a sensitive clinician can aid the student to become aware of himself as a factor in the counseling situation and to modify this influence whenever it appears necessary. Even this type of further training may not be enough. The source of interference with counseling effectiveness may be so resistent to change that only more formal therapeutic experience will lead to its modification.

The locale for counseling

We have already remarked that personality deficits become apparent when people face situations which bring their personal inadequacies to the fore, and that at such times the average person is most amenable to the kinds of therapeutic influence which lead to further emotional integration. It follows, then, that counseling can be most effective when a person seeks help in dealing with a specific personal problem. This means that the counseling service must be perceived by clients as a place where a person experiencing some situational difficulty may profitably seek help.[3]

If counseling services are to be positive and preventive, they must be available and prepared to offer people help with the typical problems they face at various stages of their development. This means that counseling services should define their functions to include helping families and pupils to respond to the challenges arising when the child first leaves home for schooling; helping adolescents with perplexities in educational and vocational choices, or with social and premarital problems; older adolescents and adults with problems of marital choice and conflict, problems of parenthood and of occupational dissatisfaction; and older adults with the social and occupational difficulties linked to physiological and social changes associated with later maturity. For maximum accessibility to each of the age ranges served, counseling services will need to be more widely distributed than they have been in the past.

The major past settings of counseling services have been the school or college, or the community family service agency. Under the influence of the Veterans Administration medical program the work of counselors in medical settings with persons who must

[3] See Ch. 2 for a discussion of the implications of this requirement for the interpretation of counseling service.

adapt to illness and disability has expanded considerably. President Johnson's anti-poverty program has focused attention upon the problems of culturally deprived youngsters, most often members of minority groups who are discriminated against, in learning and in making realistic and self-fulfilling choices. New kinds of service agencies and, perhaps, new kinds of definitions of counseling will be required (Gordon, 1965). Some kinds of services, especially those concerned with the older employed adult dealing with occupational dissatisfaction and social and personal changes associated with later maturity and retirement may best be placed in business and industrial settings.

We need to return to the fact that a wide range of persons offer the service which we define as psychological counseling. The three major sources of their training appear to be psychological, sociological, and medio-psychiatric; and thus differences in training and outlook distinguish psychologists, social workers, and psychiatrists. This book is written by a psychologist for psychologists, but there is a great deal of overlap in content and concepts among the books written primarily for each of the three types of training. Perhaps a time will come when one training program will have evolved out of the three.[4] But there still remains doubt whether our knowledge of the therapeutic process and its principles has progressed far enough beyond a state of primitive understanding and purely empirical action to make such an amalgamation desirable. From the point of view of public welfare it would seem best to avoid a premature union and to encourage each group to preserve the unique aspects of its own training while simultaneously fostering cooperative working relationships; and this is true whether or not all three groups offer services under the aegis of one agency.

Antecendents of psychological counseling

We have discussed counseling in the context of personality development and disturbance. We shall see that this kind of personal service has its roots in the activities designed to help

[4] At least one interdisciplinary conference (Holt, 1965) came to the conclusion that it was desirable to experiment with an interdisciplinary training program for psychotherapists.

persons with the specific difficulties they face without very much involvement with the long-term implications of the aid. The implications of this later concern with personality development reach much farther than is at first evident. They mean, for one thing, that when a troubled person comes to the psychological counselor, as he often does, with concrete decisions to be made, specific problems to be solved, or particular situations to be clarified, the counselor's *primary* goal is not to contribute to the resolution of these immediate situations. That major goal lies farther ahead. The primary goal requires understanding of the obstacles to further personality growth and development that are typified by this person's rather specific and temporarily limited difficulty. The counselor aims to contribute to the removal of these deeper lying personal obstacles and to bring about the reactivation of the psychological growth processes in that person. Thus, the solution of the immediate problem is one desired outcome, of course, but it alone is not a sufficient measure of the psychological counselor's usefulness to his client.

At this point it should be made clear that the goal of personality growth and development makes certain assumptions about the nature and organization of behavior. To assume that a contribution to growth and development is not necessarily identical with the resolution of a particular life situation is to assume that our behavior equipment is organized—and now we speak metaphorically—in a series of interdependent networks. It further assumes that these networks arrange themselves around certain nuclear attitudes, emotions, and impulse systems. From these affective nuclei flow much of the nourishment for the extension of the system of behavior and for its modification. Any lasting and pervasive modification of a particular system of behavior must act upon the system as a whole and particularly upon its nucleus.

This contrast between modifying specific behavior and modifying the dynamic organization which generates it is equivalent to the distinctions made between modifying symptoms and modifying personalities. In psychotherapy applied to abnormal behavior, the symptom orientation might be represented by inducing an alcoholic to give up drinking through the development of a conditioned response of nausea to alcohol. Where the alcoholic behavior functions as part of a nuclear behavior system involving particular attitudes and impulses, it would be expected that these motivating energies, blocked from expression through drinking, will find some other equivalent outlet, such as overeating or invalidism.

Murray (1938: pp. 6–11) has discussed this contrast in terms of a central versus a peripheral view of personality and behavior. Psychological theories have varied in the relative importance they have attached to central or peripheral aspects. Psychoanalytic personality theory has, of course, been a major source of emphasis on the central view of behavior organization, and counselors have been increasingly influenced by it. So much so that the prevailing emphasis in counseling, as in other psychotherapeutic endeavors, is upon dealing with the nuclear aspects of behavior. This emphasis does not, however, require the extreme assumption that all sets of behavior are involved in a closely bound dynamic organization. Our view is that behaviors vary in the intimacy of their relationship to the individual's dynamic system and consequently vary in their amenability to change independent of some underlying, more general behavioral organization.

This trend toward a more centralist approach to the client's problems can be seen more clearly when we examine the antecedents of psychological counseling. Counseling started as a service concerned with two major areas of people's lives, the educational and vocational development of adolescents, and the effective functioning of families. One was represented by educational and vocational counseling and the other by social work services which rendered financial and consultative aid to economically depressed families.

Vocational counseling, or vocational guidance as it was then and still is called in the schools, was offered by Parsons in a community-supported agency for young people (Allen, 1927: pp. 4–13).[5] From there it expanded to high schools, colleges, and universities where counselors tried to help the adolescent make a satisfactory vocational choice. Emphasis was placed on the adolescent's limited experience and the dangers of making decisions based on inadequate knowledge. Early vocational counselors placed a great deal of stress upon accumulating and trans-

[5] For a somewhat fuller account of the transition from vocational guidance to psychological counseling, see Super (1955).

mitting educational and occupational information. With the impetus toward psychological measurement dating from World War I, vocational counselors acquired another important resource for informing their clients. With psychological testing came the psychological point of view. Greater emphasis was placed on the analysis of the psychological demands of jobs and on relating the personal demands of occupations to the psychological characteristics of the individual (Dvorak, 1935; Patterson, & Darley, 1936). Although vocational counseling had previously made no unusual training demands on the counselor beyond an acquaintance with occupations and the sources of information about them, the newer approach now began to require technical psychological training. More psychological training either induced or speeded up a modification in the counselor's objectives. Where before counselors had emphasized aiding the client to make a satisfactory decision, they began to see the process of helping him make a decision as one that should also increase his capacity to make succeeding decisions. Vocational counselors began to be aware that their efforts to transmit information and to stimulate thinking things out were not enough to aid many of their clients. They began to be aware that many of their clients clung to unrealistic vocational ambitions no matter how much information the counselor piled up, loaded with threats of dire failure or of some other disaster. They found that their clients not only braved the storm signals but stubbornly maintained their aspirations after repeated experiences of failure.

Many counselors reacted by ascribing these resistances and rigidities to the perversity and obstinacy of their clients. So they set about demonstrating that their clients were being irrational, and at times openly lost their tempers. But gradually wiser counselors began to look beneath the surface of this irrational behavior. With greater attention to motivation and emotion, these behaviors became more understandable and even in a sense more rational, though still relatively self-defeating to the client. Consequently, counselors began to shift their attention and emphasis from the issue of what information they could give their clients to that of understanding their aspirations and impulses, their fears and their needs. They began to give more attention to how a client's problem-solving behavior was related to his persistent needs and

concentrated less exclusively on the question of which occupational choice would probably prove most satisfying. Today, to an
increasing degree, counselors are examining their clients' efforts
to solve vocational problems with a view toward understanding
what there is about an individual's personality that makes these
problems difficult for him to solve. Their efforts are turned
toward achieving a comprehensive understanding of their clients
as striving people. Their estimate of their value to a client is
based not only on the satisfactoriness of the decision made, but
also on the effect the process of resolution has on the attitudes and
motives that turned the making of such a decision into an almost
insuperable problem.

Social casework or family counseling has followed an
analogous development (Garrett, 1949). Early social workers
represented society's conscience and compassion for its economically less fortunate members. The social work movement at one
time placed chief emphasis upon its role as an agent of public or
private philanthropic efforts to alleviate the effects of poverty and
its concomitants of poor educational, recreational, and health
facilities. To the social workers who found families in great dis-
tress, it seemed a matter of being caught in a network of difficulty
which led to undernourishment, disease, and crime out of which
came malformed bodies and stunted emotional life.

Gradually social workers and, unfortunately more slowly,
society at large have come to realize that for many families the
roots of the difficulty were not economic. Too often economic
aid might slow down but not prevent the ultimate disintegration
of a family. Consequently, social workers turned to psychological
and psychiatric concepts as a basis for understanding the difficulties
of their clients and for trying to help them. Gradually they have
come to see that their analysis of socioeconomic factors must be
supplemented with another form of analysis, often more fundamental: that of the psychological characteristics of the family and
its members. Their study of a family in difficulty is an analysis
of its psychological and emotional resources. Similarly, they too
have come to measure the success of their efforts by the family's
progress after it gets beyond the particular problem situation
rather than by whether that difficulty was surmounted.

This concern with the resources that individuals bring to the predicaments in which they find themselves and the degree to which the predicament is of their own making should not, of course, blind us to instances when, in fact, the individual or the family is a victim of circumstances beyond his control. This "caveat" is particularly cogent at a time when we are much concerned with the fate of those whose poverty and all of its accompaniments are a function of factors out of their control, especially those of prejudice and discrimination. Even here the psychological counselor will be concerned with the persisting personal obstacles created by these adverse experiences. Removing poverty and other limiting circumstances may not in itself enable the individual to freely use his opportunities.

To the extent that these two types of counseling have shifted their goal toward contributing to personality development, they have become forms of psychological counseling. Psychological counseling has as its aim influencing the individual's maturation and integration at the profoundest level possible. How general and far-reaching the effect of a particular counseling relationship will be will depend, assuming fully competent counseling, upon the particular needs of the client and his readiness for growth.[6]

For a mature and well-integrated client, the problem of vocational choice may arise only out of misinformation or ignorance, and the counselor will function as the most available informational resource. Such a client may still have some emotional immaturities but these are not involved at the moment and therefore counseling will necessarily have a restricted effect on him. The information he receives will be useful in making the particular decision he faces but will not necessarily enhance his ability to deal with other aspects of his life except in a preventive sense. By preventive we mean here simply that he avoided, by the use of timely information, a poor choice that might have resulted in dissatisfaction which, in its turn, would have brought emotional immaturities to the fore and blocked growth in other areas of his life.

On the other hand, the process of aiding a client with a

[6] Tyler (1960), using the geometrical analogy of the ever increasing divergence of the sides of an acute angle as they are extended, presents an interesting argument to the effect that a small change in the direction of development becomes a large one as the line is extended in the growth process.

problem of vocational decision, perhaps arising from job dissatisfaction, may lead to a much more general change. This sort of aid may influence the client's ability to deal with his parents and other authority figures, his relationship with his wife and his children, and his ability to obtain satisfaction in a wide variety of interpersonal relationships.

Counseling and psychotherapy

The distinction between counseling and psychotherapy has already been touched tangentially in our preceding discussions of the preventive and developmental goals of psychological counseling. The immediately foregoing discussion of the potential breadth of counseling goals makes this the natural place for a more direct consideration of the two terms. In the mental health field, where terms are often vaguely defined and loosely used, the confusion between these two is particularly marked. There are at least three sources of this confusion: the efforts by representatives of the medical profession to blanket psychotherapy under the legal definition of the practice of medicine; the semantic characteristics of both words in referring to a wide range of activities and goals; and the primitive state of theory and fact regarding personality change. Many attempts at distinguishing psychotherapy from counseling have been made without results which completely dispel the confusion and earn general agreement (Bordin, 1950: pp. 8–12, Raimy, 1950: p. 149; Williamson, 1950; Patterson, 1954: chap. 1). I am convinced that one source of the difficulty will prove to be that the distinction is more quantitative than qualitative.

First, let us deal with the question of psychotherapy as a medical process. Those who take this position advance such facts as—when severely disturbed persons must be placed in a controlled environment, they are usually hospitalized, or somatic disturbance may be one of the accompaniments of emotional disturbance and vice versa. In the long run the larger community will decide the question of whether it is in its best interest to invest a single professional group with the responsibility for psychotherapy. Their own interests aside, psychologists have argued that society's best interest will be served by avoiding the dangers of stultifying the intellectual contributions of other mental health disciplines and creating rigidifying influences against fullest manpower utilization which come with placing these other disciplines in an ancillary status to medicine. Meantime, some psychologists have sought to temporize with the problem by using the term counseling to denote those instances of psychotherapy where the presently defined responsibilities of hospitalization and the treatment of concurrent somatic conditions are not involved. This is hardly a lasting and constructive solution. Most psychologists favor the development of patterns of interprofessional collaboration appropriate to those instances where uniquely medical functions are required. Certainly, a counselor or a nonmedical psychotherapist will wish to maintain close working relations with an appropriate medical practitioner when his client's emotional difficulties are intimately associated with physical ailments. He may even refer the client to a practitioner who is able to deal with the intimately related medical and psychological symptoms. In all cases, the counselor owes it to his client not to undertake more responsibility than he is willing and prepared to accept.

Until we have gone more thoroughly into theoretical issues we shall only be able to make a start at discussing the semantic and theoretical bases for differentiating between counseling and psychotherapy. The counseling relationship is characterized by much less intensity of emotional expression and relatively more emphasis upon cognitive and rational factors than is the relationship in psychotherapy. It is this difference that makes it possible for the counselor to play an important supportive role with severely disturbed persons who are at that moment not amenable to psychotherapy. This is the basis for the frequently stated definition of counseling as being concerned with the essentially normal individual—a person who, by and large, sees the world and his place in it for what they are.

A word might be said here also about the relationship between clinical psychologists and psychological counselors. Psychological counseling is one type of psychological function which might be performed by a clinical psychologist, when the term *clinical psychologist,* is used in its broadest meaning to refer to applied psychological practice oriented to the needs and problems of individuals.

The convention of using the title with "psychologist," in it to refer to those who have obtained the Ph. D. degree, has been adopted as approved professional practice (APA, 1948: p. 188; Raimy, 1950: p. 37) and has been followed in licensing and certifying legislation. On the other hand, the volume of services contemplated in psychological counseling could be beyond our economic capacity to support if all but doctorally trained psychologists were excluded even were it possible to find the necessary manpower. It remains to be seen whether less than doctoral training such as that described by Rioch, Elkes, and Flint (1963) or that evolved in social work and in the training of school counselors (Bordin, 1950; Wrenn, 1961) can prove adequate for counselors who will be under the supervision of psychologists trained at the doctoral level.

Counseling in its earlier forms has been thought of as much simpler and less demanding than psychotherapy, and this belief has been transferred to psychological counseling. Experience at the University of Michigan, where doctoral level students in clinical psychology receive experience in psychological counseling as well as in other forms of psychotherapy, suggests otherwise. In the early stages of learning psychotherapy the student seems much occupied with the question of whether he will be personally adequate enough to be helpful to another and is also prone to make many errors in the process of relating. The typical client of psychological counseling, with a much more limited commitment than the person who seeks psychotherapy, will be turned aside by the student's necessary mistakes. The nature of the counseling situation requires a much more active early role than that of other psychotherapy. Usually the client in other psychotherapies has a longer story to tell. Further, decisions must be made much more quickly in counseling. All of this is too demanding for the self-consciousness that accompanies the student's early experiences. We find that he can overcome these obstacles more quickly and with less interference with his usefulness to his client in situations where those who come for help are already heavily committed by their desperation. After he has gained more confidence, the student is ready to operate more effectively in the more active role requiring more rapid clinical decisions which characterizes counseling.

RELATION OF PSYCHOLOGICAL COUNSELING TO OTHER TYPES OF COUNSELING

Let us now examine other common meanings of the term *counseling* with which psychological counseling may overlap.

Educational and remedial counseling

As education has become more individualized in its treatment of the student, educators have become more concerned with special learning problems. Consequently, provision is made for special individualized help in improving such various kinds of skills as reading, spelling, arithmetic, and well-articulated speech, and in removing blocks to learning. Specialists vary in the amount of attention they devote to emotional factors in these difficulties. There is relatively little tendency to deny that these emotional factors are present; the big question is the extent to which these emotional and motivational factors are the roots of the difficulties and not simply their concomitants. There seems to be no real need to choose between these two views of the role of emotion and motivation. One can assume that persons with these learning difficulties will distribute themselves from the one extreme where the difficulty arises primarily from mechanical sources or cognitive defects, to the other extreme where the difficulty arises because the particular skill has become invested with certain emotional conflicts of the individual. To the extent that remedial work is aimed at rectifying what must be defects in the learning sequences by which a skill was acquired, remedial counseling moves away from psychological counseling and is closer to teaching. To the extent that remedial work deals with emotional motivational factors as sources of difficulty, it moves closer to psychological counseling.

A simpler form of educational counseling is the aid given by teachers in educational planning. Educational counseling which is not primarily psychological is aimed primarily at giving the student information about such matters as sequences of courses, requirements for job entry or acceptance on a new level of educational training, for example, moving from junior high school to high school, from high school to college, from undergraduate to professional or graduate school. However, good educational counseling need not confine itself to being a relatively impersonal service-dispensing information. As Berdie (1949) has suggested, it can also spark the adolescent's intellectual curiosities through his interaction with a more experienced or mature person. An adolescent can enjoy a highly significant experience in talking with someone who can help him see the relationships between the particular studies he is pursuing and the particular role he is going to play in the world, occupationally and socially. When information is not enough, when the student's use of the information reveals distorted thinking and emotional conflict and the educational counselor begins to deal with the emotional factors that influence the use of information, then he begins to operate as a psychological counselor.

Marriage counseling

Marital and premarital counseling also is subject to the same range of emphasis, from giving instruction and information to handling emotional factors. Many marital counselors function chiefly as sources of information on what any young couple contemplating marriage should know. They are prepared to discuss some of the mechanics and physiology of adequate sexual relationships, conception, and birth spacing by contraception. They will discuss with couples the many practical problems they can expect to face as a family and will offer the benefit of experience and study which makes it possible to foresee the kinds of situations a particular young couple may encounter. Unquestionably, this is a very useful function. At the same time many couples, contemplating marriage but in conflict about it, will be reacting to dimly perceived ambivalences that might become the foci of marital discord and unhappiness. Marital counselors who talk to couples already in difficulty are more likely to find the roots of these difficulties in the relationship between the two personalities than in their ignorance of certain fundamental facts. Under these conditions, marital counseling and psychological counseling seem to become one and the same thing.

Religious counseling

Clarification of the relationship between religious and psychological counseling is difficult, for religious beliefs are so often an intimate part of a personality. One distinguishing characteristic of the relationship between the religious counselor and his client is the fact that the counselor is almost always chosen because he represents a particular religious faith. In a great many instances the counselor is the minister of the congregation to which the client belongs. The client has had contact with the counselor in this connection and chooses him because of this. The psychological counselor's client may have chosen him on the basis of some personal contact, but rarely in as distinct and as feeling-laden a role as is the case of the religious counselor. The religious counselor's relationship to his client centers around religion and the client's religious belief. He is usually trying to help the client come to terms with a particular set of religious beliefs. If the religious counselor attempts to understand the factors in the client's personality which make it difficult for him to come to terms with these religious beliefs, the religious counselor treads a common ground with the psychological counselor. If the religious counselor shifts his center of interest from the religious beliefs to the personality development of his clients, if he considers religious beliefs secondary to the personality development of his client, then he is engaged in what we call psychological counseling.[7]

Placement counseling

In industry, government, and education we have counselors who are middlemen between the employer and the employee (Alexander, 1946; Stead, Shartle, et al., 1940). In some instances, as in industry, they work for a firm that makes use of employees with a wide range of occupational specializations. In education

---

[7] In recent years there has been an increasing amount of interest in religious or pastoral counseling as psychological counseling. Many writers, for example, Dicks (1951) and Hiltner (1949), make no distinction between pastoral and personal (equivalent to psychological) counseling.

and government the placement counselor is likely to be independent of the prospective employer and the prospective employee. When the placement counselor confines himself to the
task of aiding his employer and the employee to match the
latter's training and work experience, his psychological resources,
and his emotional needs to the demands of a particular job, placement counseling is not psychological counseling. Sometimes, however, placement counselors interest themselves in clients who
seem to have difficulty in making job choices and who seem
unable to derive satisfaction from their jobs. When the placement
counselor concerns himself with these problems, he moves into
the area of vocational counseling and also into the area of psychological counseling.

Before leaving this topic, it might be well to call attention to
one potentially detrimental effect of an increasing preoccupation
with personality in our society. We have seen that each of these
other varieties of counseling has a distinct contribution to make
in aiding the individual to acquire some sort of skill, knowledge,
or intellectual understanding. Yet so great has been the pull toward
not only an awareness of personality factors but toward therapeutic
work, that many counselors in these other fields have begun to
abandon their unique functions for the seemingly more inviting
tasks of psychological counseling and psychotherapy. This trend
may reflect correct vocational decisions for the specific counselors,
but taken together, it represents a social loss. Each type of counselor performs unique tasks and makes a contribution that ought
not to be lost.

COUNSELING AND EDUCATION

Counseling has extremely close ties to education. They share
the common goal of contributing to personality growth and development. This includes the personality growth and development
of all people, not just those who represent the extreme of the
maladjustment continuum, with really incapacitating difficulties.
Counseling is tied to education not only through this common
goal, but also because the ages at which formal education occurs

are also those at which counseling can make its maximum contribution. It follows, then, that the educational setting will be one of the most important institutional locations for counseling. Counseling in the educational setting must be attuned to the entire range of difficulties in development, ranging from relatively specific informational deficits and faulty comprehension to massive and widespread emotional blocks.

The counselor must establish some division of responsibility with the teacher as to the roles they will play. This division of roles should not rest upon any artificial segmentation of the individual whereby the teacher deals with the acquisition of skills and knowledge and the counselor deals with emotions and motivation. The common goal of the teacher and the counselor is the most effective and most complete integration of skills, knowledge, and motivation. Both must be sensitive to all of these facets of the individual, but each should contribute to the individual's development according to his specialized training and experience. Both must deal with the person in his total context but always be aware of the other's role and the interrelationships between these roles. Many times it may be the teacher who contributes in the area of the emotions and the counselor who deals with information and skills. The teacher independently, or sometimes in consultation with the counselor, may contribute signally to the student's maturation by the nature of her relationship with him. Similarly, the counselor may operate as an educational "cleanup man." Our educational institutions are essentially the tools society uses in its efforts to acculturate its members. Any social system of acculturation will have weak spots; the individual may fail to acquire, or lack the opportunity of acquiring, particular kinds of information or skills necessary to his function as a member of his social group. The counselor, through his individualized contact with the student, is able to discern these blanks in understanding and should be in a position to help the student fill them. When he is transmitting enlightenment or know-how, the counselor is acting as a teacher. But the counselor also may discriminate instances when this information is appropriate from those when it is not, when this ignorance is motivated and is a reflection of the emotional conflicts and when it is not. He may make a judgment about the feelings that interfere with the use of this information and thus make it possible for the student to overcome these deep-rooted obstacles. Then, he is acting in his role as a psychological counselor.

RESPONSIBILITIES OF THE PSYCHOLOGICAL COUNSELOR

Although it has been given much less emphasis in his more recent papers and books, Rogers, in his early writings on nondirective counseling, emphasized that the counselor, in his method, takes no responsibility for the individual (1942: pp. 18, 96). His very goal is to enable the individual to take responsibility for himself. This attitude and this goal, he argued in earlier writings, mean that in nondirective counseling there is less or even no danger to the client compared to other therapeutic efforts. This point of view has led some enthusiasts to assume that no great body of training is necessary other than training in the basic nondirective methods. As Meehl and McCloskey (1947) so clearly pointed out, such arguments do not permit the psychological counselor to escape the fact that when he sets out to deal therapeutically with the emotional and motivational aspects of a person's behavior, no matter what goals and what methods he chooses, he assumes responsibility for the outcome. The very fact that he prefers one method over another, that he decides that one method leads to different outcomes than another, means that he has taken the responsibility for what happens to his clients.

At this particular time, when laymen have become increasingly aware of motivational and emotional factors in behavior problems and there is a wide dissemination of slight amounts of training, it is extremely important to emphasize that the manipulation of relationships for therapeutic purposes has potentialities for *hurting* people as well as for helping them. These responsibilities are not to be undertaken lightly. No person, no matter how fully trained and experienced, can undertake even relatively minor therapeutic responsibilities without a deep sense of the limitations of his own knowledge and skill and without an awareness that the person he is counseling may be risking his future happiness.

CHAPTER 2

Counseling and Interprofessional Relationships

OUR DISCUSSION of the goals of counseling has already shown that many other professional groups or persons with specialized training share the counselor's concern for the welfare of his clients. In this chapter we shall consider the counselor's place in this matrix of personnel services and how his objectives relate to those of other personnel workers. We shall discuss the organizational and interpretive problems that arise when we relate counseling to other services. Finally, we shall consider the rationale for the ethics of the counselor and its application.

A practicing counselor soon becomes aware of the other persons with specialized training who are interested in aiding his clients. If he is working in a college setting, there may be a Dean of Students or a Dean of Men and a Dean of Women, the staffs of a Placement Bureau, a Bureau of Loans and Scholarships, a Housing Bureau, and so on, in addition to faculty members, who as teachers, take a personal interest in the welfare of students. At the high-school level, he will find persons in similar roles, although so many different individuals may not be involved. If the counselor is working in a community, there will be public and private social agencies with their staffs of social workers, perhaps a state employment service with its job-placement facilities, and of course the community medical services, both psychiatric and other, either public or private. In an industrial or business setting, he may find a personnel manager, a combination practical nurse and social worker who acts as a home visitor, an educational director concerned with either induction training or leisure-time classes or both, and a health director or consultant. All these types of services, including counseling, are referred to as "personnel work." Most social units that have become aware of the need for differentiating between their methods of handling their human and non-human resources have personnel programs.

OBJECTIVES OF PERSONNEL WORK

We have already examined the goals of counseling. Let us now analyze the objectives of personnel work of which counseling is a part. Personnel work has been defined in part as a socially sponsored enterprise. By this we mean that some social unit, whether it is an educational, business, or community organization, takes the responsibility for setting up and operating the program. It follows that personnel work is expected to further the achievement of any objectives a particular social unit serves. If the sponsoring unit is an educational institution, it is assumed that personnel work will facilitate the process of learning. If the sponsoring unit is a manufacturing organization, it is assumed that personnel work will further maximum output at minimum unit cost. In the case of the total community, it would appear that the major objective is to provide its constituent members with opportunities for the maximum realization of their potentialities for a full life.[1] Personnel work in the community can be thought of as designed to further this general purpose, though in practice it takes on rather specific functions.

Statements about personnel work in educational institutions and in business and industry are widely available. Williamson and Darley (1937), Lloyd-Jones and Smith (1938), and Wrenn (1951) are among the many writers who have given the former topic full treatment. Tead and Metcalf (1939), Rothlisberger and Dickson (1953), and Cantor (1945) have written standard texts on the latter subject. However, the concept of personnel work in a community has had less explicit statement. It is also true that some

[1] In the statement of aspirations represented by his concept of "the great society," President Johnson has specified a similar goal for the nation.

community personnel services arise from individual rather than community initiative, for example, private medical practice or privately supported community services. Nevertheless, it is a concept which is capable of giving meaning to the varied community resources for dealing with individuals and their needs.

Only in the case of the community are we safe in assuming that the objectives of the social unit are similar to the objectives of the individual. Happiness, well-being, richness of living are the goals of individuals, whether acting as individuals or as parts of a social unit. However, even in this instance the goal of the individual is not identical with that of the group. The group aims to have all its members achieve happiness. An individual is concerned with achieving happiness for himself. The group sets up barriers against certain behaviors and facilitates others according to its assumptions of how it can achieve its goal. The individual's concept of how he can achieve his own goals may or may not coincide with the group's judgment as to what is best for it and all its members.

We must make it explicit that we are speaking of the assumptions held by a group operating within our American democratic culture. Groups within this culture tend to minimize the number of enforced behavior patterns or to enforce them less rigidly, with the result that there is much greater freedom of action for individuals in a group than would be true in some other political and social organizations. There is greater opportunity for the individual to vary from the group norm. It is this assumption, that within certain limits individuals should be given the opportunity to come to terms with society in their own way, which provides the rationale for personnel work. Practically all social units within our culture tend to be influenced by this basic assumption, whether they be private or public enterprises. The social unit vests in personnel workers the responsibility for helping the individual attain his goals within the framework of the social organization.

Sanford, while analyzing the factors influencing the demand for psychological service, points out very clearly the relationship to society's values and institutions. Discussing the hypothesis that "support for psychology will vary with the degree of individuation encouraged by a society," he says in part:

Societies differ from one another with respect to the amount of individuality forced upon the person. . . . Our own society puts a great emphasis on individuality, on individual initiative. The individual is taught that he is a free agent. He chooses his own friends, his own clothes, his own jobs, his own wives. . . . When individuals are no longer cogs in an industrial or educational or military machine, both the individuals and those responsible for them are prone to turn to specialists in human relations or "happiness." (1952: p. 84)

How much responsibility to society is implied in the aim, helping the individual to achieve his goals *within the framework of the social organization*? We take it that this means the personnel worker cannot permit his aid to result in behavior which is against public policy in the sense of being clearly prohibited, that is, unlawful. It is further assumed that as a personnel worker he is not responsible to society for resulting individual behavior which may be contrary to the preferred social norms implied by the sociological terms, *mores* and *folkways*. This delineation is often blurred by the fact that many kinds of personnel workers are simultaneously administrators of social policy. If it is desirable for all administrators of social policy to be imbued with the fundamental value accepted by the social unit, in this case, emphasis on the individual, then it is good to draw no hard and fast lines between personnel work and administration. Perhaps some concrete illustrations will clarify the point. The teacher is an administrator of social policy. In the earliest school years, he shares the parents' burden of inculcating social values. Later, he has responsibilities for transmitting knowledge, understanding, and skill. But we also assume that it is desirable for him to have the personnel point of view, to have some feeling of responsibility to each individual student, to understand their strivings toward realization of their individualized needs, and to be interested in helping them relate themselves to the things they are learning. Similarly, the personnel manager of a manufacturing organization may be expected to advise and influence company policy from the standpoint of the needs of the individuals who make up the personnel of the organization, but he also is usually given responsibilities for enforcement of company policies, for example, penalties for lateness, work spoilage, and so forth.

Should all personnel workers have some responsibility for the administration of social policy? Certain inescapable social responsibilities have been indicated. Note, however, that these may really be conceived as responsibilities of citizenship, insofar as all citizens have some obligation for the enforcement of laws, for example, aiding officers of the law. Since the social units in our culture are committed to the principle that it is desirable and necessary that individuals be permitted to follow their own bent within the broad framework laid down by society, it seems desirable that there be some personnel workers whose primary accountability is to the individual rather than to society.

Before we consider why the counselor should be responsible primarily to the individual, let us first relate the contributions of counseling to those of other personnel functions. The areas of action of the individual with which personnel work may be said to be concerned can be delineated as follows:

1. *Biological*—the individual's relation to his biological needs. The functions of college health services and hospitals, public and private community medical services and hospitals, are the sort designed to aid the individual in his efforts to achieve physical health.

2. *Sociological*—the individual's relations to his environment. Part of a person's physical as well as his psychological well-being derives from the success with which he copes with problems arising from his environment. Within the community setting, social workers, job-placement agencies, and the like represent efforts to aid the individual to manipulate some aspect of this environment. Similarly, in the educational setting there are several types of personnel workers whose function is to aid the individual manipulate his environment. Advisers on student social life try to help him relate himself to his fellows in terms of group identifications. Financial advisers attempt to help him meet the financial requirements of going to college. Educational advisers help him to plan his program of courses to conform to the requirements of the curriculum he has chosen. The housing bureau helps him find a place to live.

3. *Psychological*—the individual's relations to himself. Certain personnel workers are concerned with how the individual reacts to himself. Inevitably, all of us find that neither our physical nor our environmental conditions can be manipulated as freely as we would like. For some it may mean that they cannot attain normal physical health. For others it may mean that they face

greater financial obstacles than the average person, or that they differ from others in the degree of acceptance they can command in the social group; for example, this may be true of a member of a minority group. The foregoing implies some dissatisfaction of the individual with his biological or sociological state. The individual may also be dissatisfied with himself. By this we mean that he is not satisfied with his abilities, feelings, actions, and goals. Counselors, clinical psychologists, psychiatrists, and social workers are the chief groups of personnel workers whose function is to help the individual deal with himself.

Now we are ready to consider the question of why should society permit the counselor to perform his professional functions free of responsibilities for administration of social policy? The answer lies in our beliefs about the necessary conditions for psychological growth and increased reality in seeing oneself—which will be discussed more fully in Chapter 4.[2] As we shall see, part of the process of dealing with oneself involves differentiating oneself from others. As an administrator of social policy, the counselor would become identified with "the other" from whom the individual is seeking to differentiate himself. Thus, it seems probable that a counselor seen in that light by a client would lose some of his potentialities for aiding the client to delve deeply into his problem. A good illustration of this is the example of a college student whose consultation with the counselor was precipitated by a discussion with his dormitary adviser of his score on the Minnesota Multiphasic Personality Inventory. The adviser in question was experimenting with the test as part of his graduate training in psychology. His responsibilities as a dormitory adviser included aiding students to plan their curricular programs and approving these programs, as well as enforcing certain dormitory rules and establishing friendly supportive relationships with the students living in the dormitory. The client came to the counselor because he feared that he might have homosexual tendencies. During the first interviews he was moved to explain why he had not discussed this question with the dormitory adviser at the time that they were considering his personality test scores. His comment, "I couldn't talk to him about it; after all I have to live with him," revealed the need to examine himself free of the restriction placed

2 See review of Allen's concepts, pp. 124–129.

on him because of his group membership. Ivey (1962) found that clients were less willing to confide personal problems to a counselor who was also their teacher. The problem from the psychological point of view is not to force the individual into passive conformity with social requirements, but to enable the individual to accept, internalize, and act on whatever real pressures he is subject to. Society provides numerous mechanisms for enforcement of its standards through the medium of parents, teachers, law enforcement agents, and so on. It is in society's best interests to provide agents who can aid the individual in his process of internalization of society's standards. Thus, it is our conclusion that society's purposes are best furthered by permitting personnel workers who deal with an individual at the psychological level to treat this individual as their primary responsibility.[3]

ORGANIZATION AND INTERPRETATION OF COUNSELING AGENCIES

If psychological counseling is to reach its goal of providing positive mental health services and preventing maladjustment, its services must be described and organized so as to be maximally accessible. The bearing of physical and financial factors on accessibility is self-evident. How much of its total income society can afford to allocate to this kind of service and how costs are related to the optimal level of training for counseling are extremely complex questions, and no general formula is or can be available for settling them. However, one important and manageable factor in accessibility is the way in which the public perceives the counseling service.

In theory, one might suppose a law operating in such a way that an individual will come to an agency offering psychological help when the discomforts associated with his difficulties exceed the discomforts associated with what he perceives as the negative stimulus characteristics of that agency. What are the characteristics of a counseling agency which set up approach or avoidance responses in potential clients? The very nature of personality struc-

---

[3] See Correll (1962) for a discussion of the controlling aspect of student personnel work and how it leads to a split between faculty and personnel workers.

ture, the modes of defending himself against anxiety, may set up obstacles toward seeking help in a form which defines his problems as being within himself. People will, of course, come more freely to discuss problems that appear external, problems they perceive as resolvable through rational objective processes. They find it much easier to come to discuss the pros and cons of various occupational alternatives with someone in whom they have confidence because of his experience and training than to approach someone for the purpose of revealing intimate feelings of anxiety about themselves. The former action is completely consistent with the general social pressure that one should be independent and mature. The mature way to deal with any problem is to gather all of the information and advice available as a preliminary to the decision. But consulting with someone merely to pour out uncontrollable feelings is perceived as a regressive and childish action.

In the preceding chapter we referred to the hope that through educational efforts eventually the public's fears of emotional difficulties and their extreme manifestations will be removed. Undoubtedly much has been done and more can be done to remove superstitious and ill-informed attitudes toward emotional problems and reluctance to seek psychological help. If, however, our present conceptions of personality structure and dynamics are valid, it appears unlikely that those avoidance reactions which are intimately associated with the personality difficulty itself can be removed by education and example alone. The person who is capable of responding to these influences is probably the very person who least needs any psychological help.

Potential clients hold various views of counseling agencies before actually seeking help there. The name of the agency provides one kind of stimulus to the formation of their attitudes. Words like *welfare, psychiatric, psychological, treatment,* or *clinic* carry negative connotations. The act of approaching any agency identified with such words is likely to be viewed as an admission "there is something wrong with me." Among the most important sources of impressions of a counseling agency prior to visiting it are the various media of communication such as news stories or specially prepared pamphlets, radio or television interviews and public speeches.

In the light of the preceding discussion, it would appear that to achieve maximum accessibility, psychological counselors should emphasize their information-giving roles. Certain pitfalls emerge, however, when this emphasis is carried too far, and this is particularly true of vocational counseling where the information-giving facilities include the predictive interpretation of psychological tests. Exclusively test-oriented clients find it difficult, if not impossible, to give up this orientation and are likely to view as an affront any invitation to go beyond an impersonal question-and-answer relationship, or a "take-a-test-and-get-the-results" relationship. Therefore, it is well to prepare such clients for the fact that counseling is something more than a purely impersonal relationship. But on the other hand, many clients come to the counselor with the opposite attitude; while still perceiving a need for information and advice, they will be repelled by what seems an impersonal process. Therefore, while emphasizing a process of problem-solving that includes giving information, advance interpretations of counseling services should also try to make clear that an important aspect of the process is the personal relationship with the counselor.

Perhaps the most important medium through which clients learn about counseling services is through personnel workers in other agencies. Thus, clarification of the counseling agency's relationship to other personnel services is of prime importance. Since counseling is still in a relatively pioneering stage, we ought to take up the process of interpreting counseling services when they are offered by an agency newly introduced into a social unit.

It is important to keep in mind the human needs that lie behind the organizational chart of a university, an industrial corporation, or a government agency. One must take into account the satisfactions and needs of the persons within a social unit who man the various agencies that offer personnel services. We can assume that each subgroup within the organization arrives at a more or less comfortable state about its relationships to the other subgroups and their functions. The introduction of a new group upsets this equilibrium. Each subgroup becomes sensitive to the newcomer and asks, "Will it compete for budgetary allotments? Will it take away some of our functions and make us less important?" The subgroups whose functions are closest to the ones proposed for the new service and those that are most uncertain of their own status will be most sensitive. It behooves the new group to begin by making an insightful study of the organization of which it has recently become a part. Which groups or individuals are most likely to see the newcomer as a possible competitor? Such understandings make it possible for the members of the new group to reassure the rest of the organization and help to reestablish the organization's equilibrium as rapidly as possible. In the process, other personnel workers will acquire a clearer view of the functions of the new unit and be able to convey them clearly to potential clients.

Although we shall be concentrating on the counselor's direct and private relationship with his client, we want to call attention here to the importance of the psychological counselor's activities outside the privacy of his office. We have already discussed the importance of these activities in interpreting his services and creating an agency code of behavior which minimizes obstacles toward approach without inducing sets detrimental to the counseling process. His concern with individuals should not lead a counselor to lose sight of the fact that group norms and group attitudes are influential. Bixenstine (1959) has given us a graphic illustration of how such group atmospheric influences can interfere with the effectiveness of a service. In introducing a psychological counseling service in a small college, he discovered that the informal governing structure of the student group had established a subtly expressed boycott of the service because it had not been consulted or otherwise given the opportunity to form a judgment about it. He found that he had to interact with the student community in order to create a climate conducive to the seeking of his help by others than those whose extreme emotional difficulties had already cast them outside the group. Similarly, Warman (1960) has shown what gaps can develop between an agency's view of its functions and the views held by other personnel workers and by the faculty.

The shortage of trained personnel brought about by increased awareness of the value of personal consultation requires that the psychological counselor seek ways to multiply the numbers of persons whose development he can influence with his limited time. Via consultation the counselor may aid other personnel workers, e.g., teachers, physicians, educational administrators, or business executives, to help more effectively the children or adults with whom they work. As Bindman (1959) has so well described, the process of mental health consultation draws on the basic skills required for psychological counseling and, in addition, requires that the counselor know the language of the persons with whom he consults and understand the particular characteristics of the settings in which they work.

ETHICAL ISSUES IN COUNSELING[4]

The responsibilities of counselors to society and their relationships with other personnel workers are so intimately related to the ethics of counseling practice that we may well consider this topic now. The need for codes of ethics grows out of interactions among persons and the formation of social units. Part of the process by which interacting individuals form social units consists in agreeing on certain common ends and certain ways of acting consistent with those ends. This is true of a great variety of organizations, whether those of villages, cities, nations, or the United Nations. It is also true of the process of forming subgroups, for example, professional, commercial, or industrial organizations. Ultimately, the larger group exerts pressures on such subgroups to bring their ethics into line with its own ethics. This is not to imply that there is a unidirectional flow of influence from the largest unit to the smaller ones. On the contrary, it is also assumed that the subgroups act upon and modify the larger group. Thus our American democratic culture acts upon and influences the ethical concepts of all types of social units contained within it. At the same time, these social units may develop and express ethical concepts which are peculiar to that unit and which may in turn act upon and modify the American ideal.

Counselors, along with other psychological practitioners, have developed codes of practice in response to rapidly increasing public awareness of the applications of psychology and the consequent increased use of the services of psychologists (American Psychological Association, 1952). From a profession which before World War II was largely composed of teachers and consisted of about

[4] See Wrenn (1952) for a useful review of the sources of ethics for counselors.

twenty-five hundred members, the American Psychological Association has multiplied its membership almost nine-fold and has shifted to being a service-oriented group (Brayfield, 1965; Sanford, 1951: p. 74). With this increased responsibility for service to other people has come an increased awareness of group membership and group welfare. Thus, two main influences operate in the formulation of codes of ethics for psychological practice: the feeling of responsibility for the welfare of individuals seeking or needing psychological services, and the feeling of responsibility for the welfare of other members of the psychological profession. One of the characteristics of a practicing profession is that it is sensitive to public reaction. Committees on public relations come to the fore and professional consultants in public relations are sometimes employed. Controls will be placed on the conditions under which practitioners may criticize each other, especially in contacts with laymen. As long as concern for the profession's welfare is not incompatible with public interest, these developments are necessary and appropriate.

It is possible to identify four types of responsibilities that will govern the ethics of counseling practice: responsibility of the counselor (1) as a citizen, (2) as a member of the particular social enterprise that sponsors his services, (3) to the client who seeks his services, and (4) as a member of the psychological profession at large.

Ethics of Citizenship. Earlier the point was made that, like any other citizen, the counselor has a responsibility for the prevention of lawbreaking. No other responsibility of the counselor can cancel his responsibility for keeping the client from injuring himself or others. Yet this principle must be interpreted very carefully lest it be taken to include social definitions of injury which are not at the same time legal definitions. For example, the law prohibits suicide, but does not prohibit unwise marriages or unrealistic vocational choices or even bodily injury such as becoming undernourished in an attempt to slim down. Similarly, the law clearly prohibits any attempt at bodily injury to others or any attempt to steal their property, but does not prohibit shrewd dealing in the market place or injury to the psychological well-being of others through unfair criticism or other types of hostile behavior. One of the counselor's most trying moments comes when his client discloses past lawbreaking. Most counselors have interpreted this instance as one in which their responsibility as citizens is subordinate to their responsibility to their client.

Ethics of Membership in a Sponsoring Unit. Many times the particular unit sponsoring the services of the counselor may demand certain forms of behavior beyond those exacted by his other responsibilities. For example, a counselor may be expected to fit into a particular social pattern of dress which expresses the code of a particular unit. A counselor operating in one of the military services would be expected to meet minimum military standards of dress. Sometimes graduate students are not intially sensitive to the need to comply with the group's definition of the counselor's social role when they first undertake supervised practice. For example, it cannot be overlooked if a male counselor makes the mistake of not wearing a tie, except in the heat of summer. A woman may err either by underdressing or by overdressing. Since the counselor working in high schools and, most of the time, in colleges will deal for the most part with clients who are not yet either legally or economically independent of their parents, the administrators of these institutions consider themselves equally responsible to both students and parents.[5] Within such a framework, the counselor is likely to be held accountable for a wider range of his client's behavior. He must operate within the limitations implied by the institution and by the amount of freedom it is willing to give him, fitting his behavior to the ethics of the sponsoring unit; and whatever counselors might agree on as the ideal limitations on their responsibility to a client, the hard facts are that institutions and administrators will often differ from that ideal. Counselors may and can influence the position taken by the institution, but in the last analysis any code of ethics they develop must represent at least a minimum of agreement with the institution's code.[6]

Ethics Related to Client. The philosophy and practice of counseling demands that counselors emphasize their responsibilities to their clients. The major objectives of personnel work are to aid

---

[5] Currently college students are questioning the applicability of the *in loco parentis* principle to their age group.

[6] It is conceivable that the counselor may be faced with an administrative code which is in fundamental disagreement with his own code based on his responsibilities to the client. However, in most cases when counselors seem to act contrary to their responsibilities to clients, it is not because of irreconcilable administrative pressure but rather because of the absence of a clear enough conception of their responsibilities to be able to take a firm stand in the face of an administrative request.

the individual in using his opportunities for freedom of action and to help him settle his personal dilemmas. It follows that the counselor is primarily concerned with the individual's satisfactions in life. The client's needs and desires necessarily become the focus of the counselor's efforts which means, as was suggested in Chapter 1, that the client dictates the goals of the counseling process. It is the client who knows that he is unhappy and decides to do something about it. It is the counselor who decides how he can help the individual become a happier person. It is he who converts the consultation into a process that may result in a changed client. Ordinarily, the counselor does not have to consult with the client as to the methods he will use. On the contrary, he should insist that if the client is to use his service, the client must accept the counselor's judgment as to which methods will be effective. But, the nature of the counseling relationship is such that clients can call a halt at any time. Unlike a surgical operation, drug treatment, shock therapy, and perhaps, hypnosis, the client can stop or can continue according to his desires. This is a controversial position because some hold that, when an emotionally disturbed person enters an intense therapeutic relationship, he may be so caught up in it as to lose his power to extricate himself. Yet even though we assume that the client is a voluntary participant at all stages of the counseling process, we should guard against underestimating the obligation assumed by the counselor. In the preceding chapter this relationship was described as one that is controlled by the counselor with the expectation that it will result in increased happiness for the client. This means that counseling is not a process to be undertaken casually as an expression of an individual's curiosity about psychological processes or as the expression of a personal need to exercise this kind of power over individuals. As more and more is learned about its principles and the counseling process becomes increasingly rational, counselors become more and more aware of the responsibility that is placed in their hands and less willing to undertake it without adequate preparation.

Ethics Related to Profession. Sooner or later, individual members of a professional group learn that to a considerable extent they stand or fall together; that what each member of the profession does affects not only his own welfare but that of the group as a whole. When that time arrives, the situation is ripe for the development of an explicit ethics of the individual's accountability for the welfare of his profession. The professional group will become concerned with behaviors that might reflect unfavorably upon the name and reputation of the group, its practices, and the trustworthiness, competence, and standards of reward of its individual members. This concern for the welfare of the profession can and should be wholly compatible with its responsibilities for public welfare. If a profession has a social contribution to make, it can best make it when its name is held in high regard.

TYPICAL ETHICAL QUESTIONS IN COUNSELING PRACTICE

The practice of psychology and that particular phase of it included in counseling is maturing as a profession. Consequently, its code of ethics is still relatively new. The code identifies the four broad types of responsibilities discussed above and is expressed in general principles. Each person must then examine specific situations in the light of these principles. To aid him, some concrete illustrative cases have been taken up in the code adopted. We will here turn our attention to a set of typical ethical questions, and the writer will show how he would have resolved them in terms of the four general responsibilities of the counselor. We hope that this may aid the student counselor with his task of personally formulating his standards.

Should the Counselor Transmit Information About a Client to an Administrator? The counselor's dilemma which this question discloses is that he must balance his responsibilities to the client with those to the administrator who formally represents the social unit sponsoring the service. The counselor's decision will depend upon such a characteristic of the situation as whether the client came to him voluntarily or at the request of the administrator who expects the counselor to make a report or recommendation to him. Whether or not the request for a report was made with the knowledge and consent of the client is also relevant to the counselor's action. Where the information requested is of a general sort that might easily be obtained from many sources, and where the counselor feels he is in no position to press upon the

administrator the distinction between a counselor's responsibilities to an administrator and his responsibilities to a client, the
counselor would probably accede to the administrator's request,
even when it comes without the client's knowledge. Yet, it is
immediately clear that such incidents may call for clarification of
the counselor's divided responsibilities. When the counselor attempts to clarify for the administration the division of his responsibilities, it is usually wise for him to begin by choosing a clear-cut
case, for instance, when some intimate information about the
client has been requested. If the zealous counselor permits devotion
to principle to lead him to use a time when his administrative
superior requests some relatively innocuous information as the
occasion for clarifying his responsibilities, he is likely to risk
rejection of his ethics. The administrator may sense the compulsive
rigidity implied in the reaction of the counselor who tips over
backward in his desire to be fair to his client.

*What Should I Do When a Parent Asks Me for Information
or Advice About His Son Who Is a Client?* Counselors working in
schools and colleges are often faced with this question. Perhaps the
more clear-cut case of the child clinician would help to place the
problem in more perspective. Children rarely come to therapists
of their own accord. They are brought either by a parent, a
teacher, or some other adult. In these circumstances, therapists
customarily distinguish their responsibilities for changing the
child's behavior—in most cases his attitudes—from their responsibilities, perhaps, for altering the adult's behavior toward his child.
Each becomes a problem in clinical treatment. The parent is
either given direct recommendations or is aided to clarify his own
relevant attitudes, depending upon the nature of the situation.
Rarely is he given or is it necessary to give him an account of the
child's behavior in the therapeutic situation. Often, of course, it
is desirable to take a firm stand against parental requests for
information when doing so may help them to achieve a fuller
appreciation of their child's increasing need for independence
and for an opportunity to develop his sense of his own integrity.
On the other hand, this position must not represent a denial of the
palpable reality that the child is not yet independent in either
a legal, an economic, or even a psychological sense. Very rarely is

it appropriate for the counselor to answer a parent's request for information or guidance by saying only, "I do not think that I have any right to discuss this question with you." Where the counselor feels that he cannot or should not make any recommendations, perhaps because it is primarily a question of the child's attitude or because the major part of the difficulty is the parent's attitude which probably cannot be changed simply by recommending that it be changed, the counselor might respond, "Because a good deal of this situation can only be solved by your son's achievement of a deeper understanding of himself, I am afraid I cannot give you any concrete suggestions. Perhaps we would find it helpful if you can come in and talk it over." In any case the counselor will insist that the child be informed of the visit and may require his consent.

Should Interviews Be Recorded Without the Client's Knowledge? The increasing recognition of the importance of the recorded interview as a teaching and research device accounts for the universal interest in this question. It seems to involve a possible conflict between the counselor's responsibilities to the client and to his profession. However, if the issue is examined more closely, the conflict is more apparent than real. First, consider the fact that the client is turning over confidential information to the counselor. All clients assume that they are entrusting confidential information to the counselor, to be retained in some form, for instance, in memory, in brief summary notes, and so forth. In most cases the client does not like doing this. It usually has been one of the factors in his struggle with himself, as he foresees this will happen if he decides to approach the counselor. Therefore, it is already implicit in the relationship that the client has accepted as inevitable that he will leave confidential information in the possession of the counselor. The client's decision usually hinges on the use that he knows or supposes he knows is to be made of the information. He is most satisfied when he feels that the counselor will not reveal information without his consent or use it except for his own benefit. Barring the special significance often attached to a record of one's voice, asking permission to record may not be too different in principle from asking the client's permission to make notes from memory after the interview or even to retain the memory of what has happened. The basic question each counselor must ask himself is what purpose recording will serve. If, for example, he feels the need for consulation or supervision to verify his view of the client's needs, then it may be his responsibility to the client to insist on recording their interview. Often this is done with the simple statement that it is the counselor's practice to record or by setting up the recording machine without comment. This discussion does not imply that efforts to conceal the fact of recording or to mislead or delude the client are to be condoned. However, it does imply that making a big point of requesting the client's permission to record may stir up anew doubts and suspicions that the client has put to rest before deciding to consult the counselor.

In What Ways and to Whom Can I Legitimately Transmit Test Information? Often the counselor operates a psychological testing agency for the social unit. In schools and colleges, he may administer tests that are used for purposes of admission or placement; in industrial or commercial organizations, used in hiring and classification. Under those conditions he will routinely transmit test scores to other staff members.[7] Here, the question of whether he should also transmit test scores obtained as part of the counseling process may arise. A representative and often puzzling instance of this may be the request for this kind of information from a prospective employer. First of all, the counselor must make a distinction between the tests which have been taken at the request of the institution and those which have been taken by the client as part of his voluntary attempt to learn more about himself. In the first instance, the client has himself turned the information over to the institution. In the second instance, he has not. Therefore, it would appear that the counselor may not reveal test results derived from counseling without the consent of the client. A request for information from a prospective employer that involves use of the institution's test scores also presents an ethical issue. Usually, when a prospective employer asks for in-

---

[7] The increasing use of personality tests in selection has raised many outcries against invasion of privacy and led to re-examination of policies. Many now advocate destruction of test information after it has been used for selection or placement. (See *Amer. Psychol., 11,* 1965.)

formation, it is because the client has referred him to the counselor. In effect, this is the granting of a release from the responsibility of confidence, although the client may still expect the counselor to use the information solely for his benefit. Then, there is still another important obligation which requires the counselor to see to it that the information is transmitted in understandable form. This means that the counselor has a responsibility in furnishing test results to laymen to translate them into lay terms in such a way as to preclude any possibility of their misinterpretation. Every counselor who acts as a consultant to some administrative unit in the setting up of a testing program must ensure that the test results are not going to be interpreted by a person lacking proper training. Test scores look deceptively simple to laymen; all too many persons suppose they are equipped to interpret them, and actually try to do so when they are thoroughly unqualified to do anything of the sort.

When Is It Permissible for the Counselor to Discuss His Cases? A counselor has impulses to discuss his cases on several occasions. Sometimes he feels gratified because he has gained some particular insight into the counseling process and is bubbling over with it. At other times, he feels the need to impress others with his skills or successes. Or it may be that he is groping for interesting luncheon conversation and he has just been witness to the eternally interesting characteristics of a human in his self-struggles. At still other times he is puzzled and really needs to share his client's problem in the process of solving it. Sometimes, the counselor's use of his cases in situations such as these cannot be avoided any more than people can be kept from expressing their own inner needs in choosing an occupation or in some other activity. However, it must always be insisted that the counselor shall subordinate his need to that of keeping the client's confidence. Not only is this required by his responsibility to the client, but also by his responsibility to the profession. If many counselors made a practice of speaking of their clients' problems on almost any impulse, the public would soon lose confidence in them. Counselors would reveal that they were lacking in devotion to their clients' interests and in their willingness to respect clients' confidences. At the same time, it is perfectly understood that counselors may discuss their cases with other counselors in a professional situation for purposes of exchange of ideas or consultation, provided care is taken to preserve the anonymity of the client.

What Should I Do When the Client Criticizes Another Counselor? In some cases this question reflects an uncritical acceptance of the client's story. It is unlikely that a counselor who hears criticism can have sufficient information on which to form a judgment without hearing both sides of the story; there is little to be gained for the client by supporting his condemnation, and general harm to the profession can result from even tacitly accepting the censure. On the other hand, it is probably not useful for the counselor to defend the criticized counselor. The simplest and most direct response would seem to be to indicate as neutrally as possible that one understands the client was dissatisfied with the previous counselor.

CHAPTER 3

Introduction to Counseling Interactions

WHAT COUNSELORS are trying to accomplish and the types of settings in which they operate, we have discussed earlier. Now we can turn to the counseling process itself. In this chapter, we shall consider samples of the types of interpersonal relationships that develop in counseling interviews. Since we write for those who already possess a background in personality theory and psychopathology, we may assume that our readers are not entirely innocent of the general concepts of counseling and psychotherapy. We shall try to aid the reader as he analyzes these interviews to test the meaningfulness of his concepts against the realities of what actually occurs. Through our discussions of what is happening between the two participants in interviewing, we hope to establish a perceptual ground we can all share, and then use this to make perfectly clear and most comprehensible the subsequent treatments of theoretical and practical issues. Most important of all, perhaps, we will try to sensitize the reader to the complexities that lie beneath the surface of superficially simple behaviors. In all of our comments on the interviews, we shall try to point up the possible alternative actions the counselor could have taken and the kinds of theoretical issues that lie behind these alternatives.

We shall be engaged in this chapter in obtaining a closer view of how people arrive at new understandings of their situations, how they come to approach the problems they face with new attitudes and new sets of feelings and are thus enabled to arrive at clearer and more satisfying solutions. We shall examine *all* of the counselor's behavior in interviews for its influence on his client, not just that portion which reflects his planned efforts to be helpful. Let us now turn to some typescripts of interviews or parts of them. These have been drawn from many places and are intended to illustrate a variety of counselors, clients, and stages in the counseling process.

Case of Mr. Dut

Mr. Dut was in his first semester in college when he came to consult the counselor. We have here his first interview. The interview opens with the counselor getting certain information for his record:

C 1.[1] (*Asks for spelling of name*) And what is your home address?
S 1. _____
C 2. And are you in college now?
S 2. Yes, a freshman.
C 3. Uh-hum. Did you drive over this morning or did you take the streetcar?
S 3. Drove.
C 4. Oh. Was it slippery coming over?
S 4. Yes, it was.
C 5. Uh-hum. It's very slippery coming in from out of town. (*pause*) How old are you?

Notice that the counselor intersperses the questions he needs answered for his records with general get-acquainted talk. When we examine interviews, particularly beginning interviews, we find that counselors vary in how much small talk they attempt to introduce. Some counselors seem to act as though they saw the first interview as a replica of the usual social situation where strangers meet and try to get acquainted. They seek to find common ground with the other person by introducing many different topics, for example, where he comes from, who he knows, the weather, or some current events of general social interest. Other counselors are likely to turn directly to the question of the client's purpose in coming to the counselor. Perhaps they assume that the client's

[1] C and S will be used to identify respective responses of counselor and client.

reason for being there is the most definite and the clearest common ground for initiating their relationship, a relationship between two people who do not as yet know each other. In any event, one must keep in mind that in this first meeting between two people, each will be more or less aware of the fact that he knows very little about the other and will be looking for some answers to the question, What kind of person am I talking to? Their first impressions will undoubtedly be influenced by their respective purposes in this situation. The client will relate his unspoken questions about the counselor to the kinds of problems that have brought him to counseling. If he is feeling helpless, he may be looking to see whether the counselor is the kind of person he can lean on. If he has certain feelings that bother him but that he is also ashamed of, he may be interested in how this counselor is likely to react to his disclosing such feelings. The counselor, meanwhile, will be concerned about his own professional adequacy. Is he talking to someone he will be successful in helping? What does this person want of him? Will he be able to meet this need effectively?

But let us turn from the kinds of thoughts a counselor and a client may have on first meeting, to resume our particular counseling interview.

S   5.   I'll be 18 in January.
C   6.   And what high school did you graduate from?
S   6.   (*lost*)
C   7.   How did you happen to hear of the Bureau?
S   7.   Oh, a fellow I know in school. He is a graduate student and told me to come over here.
C   8.   Oh, uh-hum, and what was it that you wanted to know?
S   8.   Well, I've been kind of set on going into school teaching.
C   9.   Uh-hum.
S   9.   And I was just wondering if that is what I am best fitted for.
C 10.   Uh-hum. And how did you happen to think about going into school teaching?
S 10.   I was just kind of interested in it. I was going to be a veterinarian, but I kind of changed my mind.
C 11.   What changed your mind about the veterinarian work?
S 11.   Well, I just don't care to make animals my business.
C 12.   (*lost*)

S 12. Yes.

C 13. Uh-hum. Well, what kind of things did you feel you wanted to know from the Bureau?

Notice that in C 7 the counselor finally turns to the question of the client's purpose in coming to see him. Mr. Dut provides a relatively noncommunicative statement of why he is there. In S 8 and S 9 he makes statements which imply that he was once rather certain of going into teaching but now has doubts. The counselor gives no indication that he is aware of the client's doubts. In C 10, he seems to be turning to the question of validating to his own satisfaction Mr. Dut's choice of teaching and is simply drawn into a discussion of the different alternatives the client has been considering. Finally we come to C 13 where the counselor seems to feel some need for a definite orientation and so he asks what the client expects from him. One of the questions raised by this part of the interview is the wisdom of the counselor's choice of exploring the basis for the client's thinking about teaching instead of responding to Mr. Dut's doubts about it and attempting to draw him out on those feelings. Counselor response in that direction might have taken the form, "You had pointed toward teaching and now you have doubts." This would represent an invitation to talk about his doubts. If not accepted by Mr. Dut or if he only acquiesced but shed no further light on his doubts, it could have been followed up with a more direct invitation to tell the counselor more about his present feeling of uncertainty.

The choice between these two alternatives hinges on the relative desirability in the early stages of interviewing of securing information about the client in a systematic way as compared with permitting the client to proceed easily and unpushed by the counselor at his own present level of communication about his problems. Implicit in this issue is the important question whether the client has as yet really arrived at a meaningful statement of his problem. The counselor (in this interview), by his active questioning, seems to assume that the meaningful statement of the client's problem is the question whether teaching is a rational choice.

The interview proceeds:

S 13. Well, I'd like to know if that's where my abilities are—teaching school or if it should be in engineering or what.

C 14. Uh-hum. How did you happen to arrive at that in your own thinking?

S 14. Well, there's some doubt in my mind once in awhile if I should be a school teacher. I'd hate to go into a field like that if I wasn't best fitted for it.

C 15. Uh-hum. How do your parents feel?

S 15. Well, it's up to me.

C 16. Uh-hum, your problem.

S 16. Yes.

C 17. What are your friends here in school?

S 17. Well, my brother's in accounting, and a couple of kids I run around with are in mechanical engineering. There's one of them that's a school teacher. And then my friends, my real friends, are still going to high school.

C 18. Oh, are they coming over?

S 18. Yes.

C 19. What are they planning to go into?

S 19. Dentistry and engineering.

C 20. Well, I guess we'll have to start all over again.

S 20. Yes.

C 21. When you were in high school, what kind of grades were you getting generally?

S 21. Well, in my senior year I had about a B average. In my junior year, I didn't do too well in English but everything else was all right, I guess.

C 22. And how are you doing now that you're on the campus?

S 22. Trying my best. I'm not doing too bad yet, I don't think.

C 23. Are you expecting the worst?

S 23. Well, I don't know. I'll have to see after these finals.

C 24. How have you been doing on the midquarters?

S 24. Pretty sick, C's in all of them.

C 25. Uh-hum. Do you feel that your study habits and reading skills are pretty much up to par?

S 25. Yes, they are.

C 26. You're coping with that aspect of the situation?

The above sequence tells us that the counselor is in fact already intent on a systematic gathering of information from the client. In S 14 Mr. Dut comes to an even more direct statement of doubts about the choice of teaching, but the counselor chooses not to go into these doubts, how the client perceives them and what their sources might be. Rather he elects to question the client rather excessively on his parents' attitudes, the possible effects of his friends' attitudes on his own, his high-school record, study habits, and reading skills. Notice that the questioning is not directed toward ascertaining if the client considers that these are factors in his attitude, but rather toward getting information which would enable the counselor to do the deciding. We will not reproduce the next part of the interview which continues in the same vein, with the counselor exploring the client's attitude on various courses. Instead we will skip to the end of this phase of the interview:

C 34.   You're just about getting back into it.

S 34.   Yes.

C 35.   Well, perhaps I can tell you a little about counseling. Usually, following this preliminary interview, there are a series of tests which attempt to evaluate your aptitudes and your interests. As you probably know, it is equally important to be interested in a field and to have the ability to do it to be satisfied in that field. Also they check to give you some idea of how you stack up with other university students academically. Also some occupations are found to have rather generalized personality patterns associated with them, and if your personality falls with some of them, your chances for satisfaction are increased in the same fashion. Then usually following the series of tests, there is a counseling interview in which the results of the tests are discussed with you. We often find that the results are not terribly definite. You aren't told that you ought to take a specific job in the downtown area or anything of that sort. It tends more to point out general areas of your consideration. It will take some active thinking on your part to arrive at your decision, and to utilize the material.

S 35.   Yes. I took a Kuder test in high school.

C 36.   Oh, did you?

S 36.   It was an interest test. I was high in mechanical and social service.

C 37.   Uh-hum. And do you have that test?

S 37.   I've got the record of it.

C 38.   Uh-hum. You might bring that along for the next interview. Which were you highest on?

S 38.   Mechanical. But I've been working in a garage ever since I've been 15. Well, in that test there was no thinking. It was just picking out what I wanted to do.

C 39. You think that's changed.

S 39. It probably has.

C 40. Yes, that's possible. Now, our testing room is open from 8:30 until 12:00 and from 1:00 until 5:00—that's Monday through Friday—and Saturday 8:30 to 12:00.

It is quite evident from this interview that the counselor has perceived the client's problem as a relatively cut-and-dried, purely factual question of which should he choose: teaching, engineering, or veterinary medicine. The counselor has assumed also, one can judge, that he is going to help the client by a rather comprehensive assembling of test information which will enable him to give the client a great many pertinent judgments as an aid to making the decision.

Mr. Dut's behavior in the interview affords us relatively little opportunity to judge what kind of person he is and why he feels in need of help to reach a decision. We do not even know how his doubts happened to arise. S 17 gives us one clue. In that communication he tells us that his real friends are still going to high school, suggesting that he may be somewhat immature for his educational level. One wonders how important this is. We also notice in S 38 his depreciation of the possible meaningfulness of his mechanical score on the Kuder and wonder what this means. Thus we have only slight intimations of the important factors at issue for this client.

Case of Mr. Pol

This is another first interview, but between a different counselor-client pair. The interview begins:

C 1. Mr. ———

S 1. How do you do, sir? (*very hearty, "salesmanish" approach*)

C 2. How do you do. (*pause while student comes in door and seats himself*)

S 2. Well, sorry to be saying this—I—, nobody told me to come here, I just came on my own because I felt that—I need some help, because my marks have been going down.

C 3. Uh-hum.

S 3. And I think my IQ isn't the thing, my IQ is higher than what my marks show. Either (*short pause*) either I'm frustrated, which

I think I am in many cases or there is something else that's (*lower*) the trouble. I've, well, it's in many cases where when I start to get tests I get awful frustrated and my mind becomes a blank. And I'd like to have you, if you can, be very impersonal and objective and tell me, if you can, what is wrong. (*little laugh*) That's about all, I mean, whether you can or not.

C 4.   I'd like to be able to help you if you—perhaps you can tell me a little more about the situation.

S 4.   Well, there's plenty of situations like—take examples not of—not of just one type but of—of many where I show prejudice, frustration, and many times mal— (*lost*) of students—of doing things. On my tests for instance. (*short pause*) I saw a basketball game the other night of Bradley versus CCNY and for some reason I put all my hopes on Bradley, and they lost. I didn't—I felt frustrated and everything else, and I—I sort of had—. I wanted Bradley to win and there really isn't too much reason why I wanted Bradley to win. But I had all my—all my hopes on Bradley and when they lost I didn't feel good about it. I felt prejudiced towards people, especially who came from New York. Now that's common, I presume, but I want—I'm telling you the truth. I'm telling it without holding back too much you see. (*pause*) (C: yeah [*slow*]) (*pause*) Now whether I'm hostile towards people is another—is probably true. But could you—maybe you could ask me more questions and I could be more explicit in answering them.

C 5.   Uh-hum. You mentioned the ball game.

S 5.   Uh-hum. (*low*)

C 6.   When you say you have a prejudice towards people, does that imply any hostility of some sort?

S 6.   Well, is it geographical or whether it's whether it's got to do with race and religion. I doubt very much whether it's— (*pause*) somehow discrimination against any— (*lower*) any people but it's probably the main reason because Bradley was in the West—and CCNY was in the—in the East, but whether that's the main reason I'm not sure. And the main reason is I've been having trouble with my tests, and it's often, it's all based on this frustration (*pause*) and, well, I know one reason. I'll tell you right now that I'm epileptic, and that's, all of a sudden (C: uh-hum) tells you one thing. It's not—I don't have many spells, but I had one— oh—three or so a year. But just the same, it's important in the way I act, and possibly you can tell me some things.

Notice that Mr. Pol seems to be more ready than Mr. Dut to begin communicating his problems. In S 3 he voices the hypothesis that his difficulty has some emotional origin. He also expresses hope that the counselor will not be judgmental in his approach to him. In S 3 there also appear the first signs of a slight reluctance to go on, to which C 4 seems to be a kindly but firm response. In S 4 Mr. Pol confides still further but becomes aware of the fact that the counselor has not been saying anything. Notice that S 4 is not a consecutive communication but includes pauses where the counselor is not responding or has responded with his noncommital listening "yeah." We interpret the demand that the counselor ask more questions, which appears at the end of S 4, as an attempt to get some response from him. This is consistent with Mr. Pol's earlier concern about whether the counselor would be impersonal and objective. The counselor meets this demand by indicating interest in the client's feelings that he has a prejudice toward people. The client's response gives the impression that hostility may be more important than prejudice, since he seems unable to do anything with the idea of prejudice except to return to a more generalized statement of his problems. Here (end of S 6), after a pause, he feels the evident pressure to develop his problem further and confides about his epilepsy and his feeling that it is an important factor in his emotional life. Even at this point, we can see a very definite contrast between this counselor's behavior and the behavior of the counselor in the preceding interview. In the preceding interview, the counselor quite rapidly and actively defined the task for his client, namely, that of giving a great deal of information about those aspects of his life to be designated by the counselor. Thus far in this interview, the counselor has given the client little clue about the direction his communications should take. The interview proceeds:

C 7.   When you say you have a feeling of frustration, what—

S 7.   Well— (long pause) When I take a test I think, I study for it and I think I know it—I'm sure I know it. But when I—when I get up to take the test, I try to cram so many things in my mind, that I don't do good on it. (pause) Frequently my—my teachers—they say I know it. But I never seem to put it down. Therefore I'm not getting the marks that I think I ought to. I came for—I switched from another school, and I had close

to a B average there and then I came here and (*short pause*) I
didn't get a C average this year. (*pause*) Well, it's— (*little laugh*)
I know there's lots of people that come here and don't do well
the first semester, but this is one reason why I came here. It's
because I just started out the second semester, and I haven't
gotten bad marks. They haven't been D's, mainly C's. In fact
I haven't had a D yet.

C 8.   One of the things that leads to this feeling of frustration is this
inability to live up to your capacity. That is, you feel you can
do better, but something is interfering in one way or another.

S 8.   That is what I believe. In fact I've been told by my teachers that
they thought that I was very capable of doing better on the tests.
And I think so too. (*low*) But I get a bad mark on my tests and
then I, then I'll show hostility towards the teacher, in whom
I formerly, I— (*little laugh*) I'd had great faith. (*pause*)

C 9.   You get angry when (*short pause*) your grades suf—you get
angry when your grades— (*lost in student's next speech*)

S 9.   (*breaking in*) Well, I'm not used to that, you see. It's—

C 10.   Uh-hum.

S 10.   I got to—I want to stay in this place, you see, and I think I'm
smarter than what the grades—the grades I get. Generally I'm
not. I came from another school and although the competition
wasn't great I was getting A's and I was getting B's. (*low*) I was
getting C's too, but it sort of makes me mad—I mean in that
term to get marks like that. (*pause*)

C 11.   Perhaps you sort of feel that you're failing yourself, that is,
letting yourself down in your—

S 11.   Could be.

C 12.   Uh-hum. (*long pause*)

S 12.   (*low*) I mean, generally, most of the time, I'm—my actions towards people are normal but I show this hostility, (*still low*)
but this thing is—you see one of the main reasons I came here
is because I've been getting low marks in tests. (*pause*) And I,
as I said, I have this great faith, like in Professor ———,
I— (*pause*) He's a very good teacher, but I get a lousy mark in
the test and I—it sort of—show some hostile impulses. (*pause*)

C 13.   How do you feel about hostility like that?

S 13.   Well, I certainly don't—I certainly don't want it. I try to put
restraints on it, but this has been happening so many times now
that I'm getting sort of fed up with this situation. Not to the
extent that I'm having a mental breakdown, too— (*pause*) but
generally these things go away but (*lower*) I don't know (*clears*

throat). I'll get a poor mark on a test, and I'll perk up and say I'll do better next time, but this has been happening at the same—at the same level all the time, since I came here last June, it's a way of becoming discouraged. I mean I'm not pulling what I should do, really. (*pause*) I studied "British Government" and I had it down cold, or I thought I did and I got a C on the test. I thought I wrote a pretty good test, too. Well, (*pause*) I mean things like that, although I realize there is a lot of competition, I don't have too many excuses. And I don't want that to give you an excuse either (*pause*) but— (*pause*) So as I say, that's why I came to you, not by anybody's—nobody told me to come here. I'd taken psychology and the teacher said there was a psychological clinic. (*pause*)

C 14. Before you came, what sort of ideas did you have as to the method we might have to help you, how we could give help to you?

S 14. Well, (*pause*) I don't know. I really didn't, I came to you. (*little laugh*) Well, I had the thought you'd ask a few questions. The question whether I should be—whether the counselor should act fatherly to me—I don't want that. I thought that you might have some suggestions. (*low*) Certainly, you see, (*louder*) the way I act isn't the way I act in the dorm or most of the time, see. It's just at these frequent intervals. Generally it's based— it's this studying of mine which is—I got to bring it up, you see. I'm staying at the same level which is a C level, (*low*) and occasionally it dropped down. The last test I took dropped down. So I sort of— (*low*) I came in for some information or some advice, and I thought you might be (*little louder*) more concise and impersonal in your answers, than somebody else would be, than somebody else could tell me.

C 15. I think perhaps it breaks down into two problems or two possible problems. One would be the (*short pause*) objective question as to how much ability you have as compared to the other students—

S 15. Could be.

C 16. And the second question, assuming we could somehow establish that you have the ability, then we'd try to find out what the other factor would be, the problem you might have, why the hostility. Why you feel the way you do about having hostility. And the second problem would follow the first. And the method we have of trying to help people is mostly through interviews— through talking—and with the help we can give, we find people can puzzle things through and work them out. It takes time. It isn't done in one or two interviews. (*pause*) It would be difficult, let me put it this way, it would be impossible for me to give suggestions or to tell you how to handle this (*very low all through*) without my knowing very much about you.

S 16. Uh-hum. I realize that. I know I'm—to a certain extent I've been—from the very beginning, since I got this illness—there's only so far you can go, I know that. I've read a lot about it, and so I realize that it's, this illness has probably got (*lower*) quite a bit to do with it. It's not—I can control this pretty well.

In the first part of this interview sequence Mr. Pol abandons his efforts to get some definite response from the counselor and becomes more involved in communicating his feelings. At the same time, in C 8 and C 9 the counselor begins to clarify the implications of the client's communication. A picture of Mr. Pol's feelings begins to unfold. He confirms our earlier impression that hostility rather than prejudice is the main issue and tells us he is mainly concerned about his feelings of hostility toward teachers. He tells us that he also reveres these teachers and that somehow, in spite of this reverence and respect, these feelings of hostility seem to arise.

This gives us a further basis for attempting to understand his feeling. He has already told us that he is subject to epilepsy. Some feel that epilepsy, in addition to its physiologically determined mechanisms, is related to or becomes a form of expression of destructive impulses (Alexander, 1950: p. 161). The counselor's response in C 13 indicates that he sees the central importance of these hostility feelings. In the middle of S 13 Mr. Pol again begins to run down and after a pause talks once more about the fact that he has come on his own initiative. We now begin to guess why he is insistent on some kind of response from the counselor. If he is subject to hostile feelings which he is trying desperately to control, and which he knows from time to time will get out of control, then he needs some concrete signs from the counselor as to how the situation is going. He needs concrete evidence of the counselor's helpfulness in buttressing his struggle with these hostile impulses. His energies seem to be directed toward diverting these impulses away from expression aimed at another person.

His reiteration of the fact that no one told him to come to the counselor (see S 2) suggests a need for independence and hostility toward possible encroachment. This impression is reinforced also by his emphasis in S 3 on the counselor's being impersonal and objective and his effort in S 11 to reconcile his desire for some form of definite action from the counselor with his not wanting the counselor to be fatherly. This also raises the question whether his father is one of the main objects of the hostile feelings against which he is defending. This brings us back once more to the client's possible reaction to the counselor. He seems to approach the counselor as an adult of the same class as his father. He seems to show this by his expression of fear that the counselor will be fatherly, that he will not be just impersonal and objective. Again this suggests that his need to have a more structured and a more definite interaction with the counselor arises from the fear that he will develop hostile feelings toward him. If we were in the counselor's shoes, we would then be sensitized to possible feelings of hostility as they would appear.

This process of making inferences from client behavior in counseling, and of relating these inferences to information about his behavior in other situations on the basis of personality theory, is a subject of contention between rival points of view about psychotherapy. Some theoretical positions seem to prohibit this way of trying to understand the client on the ground that it turns attention away from the present, whereas others would contend that this way lies maximum sensitivity.

Let us return to our interview:

C 17. (low) When you mentioned illness, you meant the epilepsy?
S 17. Yeah.
C 18. How long have you had it?
S 18. Well, fifteen years or so. I've never had too many, just off and on. It's— (short pause), well, it's a mental disease. It isn't anything else but a mental disease. (pause)
C 19. And I suppose you had a pretty complete physical—medical check-ups.
S 19. Yes, physically I'm all right. Whether this has anything to do with the way I do in my work, I don't know. Maybe it doesn't. It shouldn't probably. But I don't want to blame it on this sickness and I doubt very much whether it is to blame at all. I notice that my reading isn't perfect. I have—just looking back— my reading isn't as fast as I think it should be. (pause) As far as

my study habits are concerned, I probably don't put as much time in as I should. On the other hand, I don't think I—I think I do put in plenty of time. I mean as much as I think I need to know the material. (*pause*)

C 20. Have any doctors told you—given you any ideas as to the cause of your epilepsy? Did you ever fall when you— (*lost*).

S 20. Well, I don't know about that. I mean whether it's a fall or whether it's my heredity. I don't know. I never did know. (*low*) I don't think they know. It's pretty hard to tell. (*pause*)

C 21. Do you get medication for it?

S 21. Yeah, (*lost*) and phenobarbitol. (*pause*)

C 22. Do you get that from Health Service?

S 22. No. My father's a doctor. I have that taken care of.

C 23. Uh-hum. (*short pause*) Perhaps you're wondering why I'm asking you about the epilepsy.

S 23. No. Not at all. That's—sort of glad you are. I don't see why the name. I mean, I know "epileptic" does get sort of a reaction toward it. In fact I (*little laugh*) don't like to be *called* it, but we got to face the facts. And you said the reason you wondered why I was asking, why you asked I was wondering—

C 24. You were wondering. Well, see the reason is, we're not physicians here, and I wanted to make sure that you had medical care for any possibilities that might come— (*lower at end*) (*pause*)

In the preceding excerpt, the counselor very clearly delimits the responsibility he is undertaking with this client as well as clarifying this issue for the client. The interview proceeds. They talk about Mr. Pol's feelings about epilepsy. He is sensitive about it and hates to mention it but also feels it is something he must face. He indicates that he had hoped to take personality tests, and the implication is that he thinks somehow his epilepsy is interrelated with certain personality factors that prevent his achieving a level of grades consistent with his capabilities and aspirations.

We look in again at C 30 after the client has finished reviewing how he stands in particular subjects and how he can discuss questions quite clearly in informal situations but seems to have difficulty when he is writing a test.

C 30. Uh-hum. (*pause*)

S 30. So (*low*) (*pause*) That—that's the way I think, see. (*pause*)

C 31. Things sort of get confused, mixed up? (*short pause*)

S 31. Yeah. I probably—if I have faith in the teacher and I have faith in myself, I'm bound to get a better mark. (*short pause*) It doesn't make any difference if I get—if I know these things cold and I get poor marks on them. By a poor mark, I don't mean E, but, well, by C. You see, I got to keep my average up to stay in this school. I don't consider a C a perfect mark. I got to get some B's. (*pause*) At the present time I've been getting (*lower*) C in just about practically all my courses. (*lower*) And not a terrifically high C. So (*pause*) (*whispering*) I think I have a better . . . (*lost*) (*pause*).

C 32. What course are you taking? What objective do you have in mind?

S 32. I'm—well, I did have law in mind, but I've given up law for the present time and I'm taking an Education course. I'm planning to get a—hope to get a teacher's certificate and then possibly go into law (*lower*) after I get my certificate. You see at the rate I'm going, I'd never get in Law School anyway so I decided to take teaching. A teacher's certificate I thought would be a pretty good insurance.

C 33. Uh-hum.

S 33. So I could always go and teach. Well, I think I'd like law too. (*pause*) Even when I came—when I came down here I was not acting sort of—sort of (*short pause*) too in a jolly mood. I came down here in a pretty good mood you know, but now I sit talking to you, and I—I think about these things and they bring back past remembrances which make—don't make me feel too happy. So the way I'm acting even now isn't the way I act to you—to people most of the time.

C 34. Uh-hum.

S 34. I mean I like talking to somebody, and get things down. Let people tell me what's wrong, and I try to follow a competent person's advice. I mean, not just everybody's advice. Because most of the time I got ideas of my own, and generally my ideas tick before somebody else's ideas unless the person is of competent caliber. That's probably another fault of mine. I don't have too much faith in people. I got to do things by myself. Whether that's a fault I don't know. I mean and—like some adviser or some doctor that I had faith in or some fellow that told me to take this, well, I would do it. (*pause*)

C 35. And perhaps you expected that I'd be doing more than what I'm doing.

S 35. Well, I don't know. I know—I know I gotta tell you the story first. I know you're sitting back there and sort of listening to me and I'm talking here and trying to ad lib as much as possible. I'm really not ad libbing but I gotta keep this conversation up to tell you what is wrong with me. I know very well you can't ask me too many questions because you don't know too many things about me. But—yeah, I'm a little surprised you didn't ask me more questions or keep the conversation up a little (*lost*), that is (*lost*).

C 36. Uh-hum. It's a little bit awkward to come into a situation and find that I lean back and listen. It's sort of hard for you.

S 36. Yeah. (*laughing*) (*pause*)

C 37. I might say that there isn't any special need to bring out anything. In other words, do not try and fit all the pieces together yourself or say anything that's especially important, that has all the answers to it or anything like that. You could just tell me a little bit more about yourself in general, what kind of person you are.

S 37. Myself in general. Well, (*pause*) well, do you want to ask me questions about myself and do you want me to answer them, or should I ask you what—what—or do you just want me to tell you about myself?

C 38. Why not try the latter method?

S 38. The latter method? (*both speak with little animation*) (*pause*) (*then with revived tone*) Well, I—I think I'm self-conscious to a certain extent. (*short pause*) I have a tendency to get red in the face. I find that sometimes I do—oh—for no particular reason. (*short pause*) Possibly I mean as far as friendships between boys and girls are concerned, I like to keep friendships very much. I'm pretty stable and I don't have a hard time making friends with boys or girls. That may—I mean that's just the opposite of my being self-conscious and making friends with people, but it's true. (*short pause*) (*low*) I don't know. (*short pause*) (*louder*) I'm, well, I'm considerably—sort of nervous (*short pause*) but I sort of control that by going in for athletics and so on and so forth. (*short pause*) Oh—some things aggravate me, like the noises when I'm studying. Of course that's not too uncommon. People talking too much. I probably got a superiority complex in one respect and I got an inferiority complex in another respect. But many people that have inferiority complexes, I think, have superiority complexes, so that might balance it up. In respect to manners and so on and so forth I have—I'm pretty well up on what things—how things go. (*short pause*) Sometimes I feel inferior. Those two things balance themselves up, generally, when I'm with—generally when I'm with people. I generally play quite a bit of cards (*little laugh*) you know when I'm not studying. And then I find I have pretty good control of myself. My sense of humor is pretty good and I can tell a joke and I can get very furious. (*pause*)

C 39. This is very difficult for you, isn't it?

S 39. No. (*almost vehemently*)

C 40. I mean to talk as you're talking now?

S 40. Well, I'm just thinking. As I'm going along I'm just thinking. It isn't too difficult. In what respect, as far as what I've just said it isn't difficult at all. I mean, I really want to tell you what is coming off. I mean I don't go out and tell everybody else this but it might be difficult. I'm not trying to—I know it's a common thing for other people to hide things. (*short pause*) It's psychology to realize that people have a tendency to hide things. Maybe I do hide things. I hide things like— (*long pause*). There's so many things to talk about probably (*lost*) wrong in thinking.

C 41. Uh-hum.

In this excerpt we see a relatively consistent picture unfolded. Mr. Pol is reacting to the counselor as we would expect. He tries to continue to talk to the counselor about his problem, but experiences considerable difficulty, becomes more and more aware of this difficulty and the kinds of feelings that go with it. There are certain specific questions that come to our mind as observers. We wonder whether the counselor in C 31 had lost sight of what seemed to be the main communication of the client in the preceding part, namely, that the only explanation he can think of for his difficulty is that there is some personality concomitant to the epilepsy. Our counselor's behavior certainly leads us to believe that he is reacting to the personality implications of the client's communication but we still cannot be sure whether it was a case of his not seeing this particular situation, or of choosing not to react to it in what he explicitly says. Mr. Pol in S 32, 33, and 34 explores his feelings and his situation to the point in S 34 where he is making certain comments about his relationships with people. This seems to be an important direction. One wonders whether when he talks about his fault of not having faith in people and goes on to say, "And like some adviser or some doctor that I had faith in," if again he isn't coming close to communicating his attitudes toward his father. At the same time, he may be indicating some of the possible hostilities he feels toward the counselor, to which the counselor reacts in C 35. The exchange around this and his awareness of the counselor's tolerance and understanding of his feelings seems to enable him to go ahead as he does in S 38. But of course he again experiences difficulty. So we see here that the client and counselor have operated quite differently from the pair in the preceding interview and we leave them at this point.

(Mr. Pol was seen for six more interviews. A Rorschach administered after the third interview supported many of the inferences we have made about his feelings of hostility, his need to divert these feelings inward, and his concern about controlling them. The counselor and his supervisor felt that intensive work with this boy would be sufficiently hazardous to exceed the responsibilities to be undertaken by a nonmedical agency. Consequently, the counselor adopted a supportive role which enabled Mr. Pol to get a little relief by discussing some of his feelings about domination by others including his father. His grades improved slightly, but the counselor did not feel that he had been helped a great deal.)

Case of Robert Winslow Smith

Our next illustration is a first interview in the case of Robert Winslow Smith, presented by Snyder (1947: pp. 21–31). A distant cousin of Mr. Smith had referred him to Dr. Snyder. The interview begins:

C 1.   I believe that Mr. Johnson said you had some things you would like to talk over with me.

S 1.   Yes, I thought maybe I could iron some of the wrinkles out. I'm always worrying about some things—not big things, just little things. I can't get over the feeling that people are watching me. Then I worry about personal things and other things. When I see an ad in the paper I worry about the things discussed in it although I know they aren't true. I always felt that other fellows could always do things, but I could never come up to the other group. No matter how much people said otherwise, I didn't believe them. I'll worry about exams that I've got even though there's no possibility of not making out well on them. Things just cram up inside of my head—little things. They just keep coming back. I keep worrying about them and thinking about them. Like in ads, ads like Lifebuoy ads. When I'm going out on a date I'll take a bath and then maybe I won't feel clean enough so I'll use a cold shower and then after that I'll use a half dozen deodorants. But I still worry about it on the date. And sometimes I worry about—when Jack and I get together—that's my friend. He's a swell guy. It's the same way with him. There's nothing we can do about it. We have just got to let it go on and try to live it out. It just seems like the world is crowding in on us. There's a feeling of frustration and nothing you can do about it.

C 2. You feel pretty much upset about the thing, and that keeps you worrying about it.

S 2. Yes, I know I shouldn't worry about it, but I do. Lots of things —money, people, clothes. In classes I feel that everyone's just waiting for a chance to find something wrong. At school there were fellows like that waiting for me. I can't stand ridicule. That's why I'm afraid of kids. When I meet somebody I wonder what he's actually thinking of me. Then later on I wonder how I match up to what he's come to think of me.

C 3. You feel that you're pretty responsive to the opinions of other people.

S 3. Yes, but it's things that shouldn't worry me.

C 4. You feel that it's the sort of thing that shouldn't be upsetting, but they do get you pretty much worried anyway.

S 4. Just some of them. Most of those things do worry me because they're true. The ones I told you, that is. But there are lots of little things that aren't true. And time bothers me, too. That is, when I haven't anything to do. Things just seem to be piling up, piling up inside of me. When I haven't anything to do I roam around. I feel like—at home when I was at the theater and nobody would come in, I used to wear it off by socking the doors. It's a feeling that things were crowding up and they were going to burst.

C 5. You feel that it's a sort of oppression with some frustration and that things are just unmanageable.

S 5. In a way, but some things just seem illogical. I'm afraid I'm not very clear here but that's just the way it comes.

C 6. That's all right. You say just what you think.

S 6. That's another thing. When I speak I know what I want to say but I don't seem to be able to say it. The wrong words come out and I can't express what I want to say even though I have the idea. Sometimes I'll have to go back and recover the thread of it. I'll find I'm not on the subject. Sometimes I can't find words to express what I mean.

C 7. It's pretty upsetting when you find you can't express yourself.

S 7. Yes, words are just piling up. I've got something to let out but I can't find words to let it out. Sometimes I worry about just where the line between sanity and insanity really is. That's why things I shouldn't worry about worry me. I worry about trivial things that are all illogical.

C 8. You worry for fear that these things may be an indication that you are not in control of yourself.

S 8. I feel maybe it's not insanity the way most people think of it. I'm not violent but in a certain sense it's unbalanced. Maybe there is a wheel off the track. I had a toy train that if the wheel came off the track, the whole thing slowed down.

C 9. You feel you aren't violent like insanity is pictured by most people, but you feel that you're abnormal and it worries you.

S 9. Yes, I feel some part may be deranged some place. Some minor part—very small thing, but it upsets everything. Sometimes I want to do something and get the energy out. We used to do things to try to forget. Some things, my parents and my brother didn't know. Sometimes we'd go to Tony's Tavern. Personally, I can't stand the stuff. It's just the feeling you forget and everything seems to adjust itself.

C 10. You feel a tension which you have to release so sometimes you go away from things and try to get rid of it.

It is quite evident here that Mr. Smith is readier to communicate to the counselor than either of our preceding clients. At the outset he conveys the impression that he has lots of feelings, some of them potentially explosive ones, bottled up. One infers that he sees his suspiciousness and his compulsive actions as efforts to control those feelings. We notice that this interview proceeds at quite a different tempo and in quite a different style from either of the preceding ones. This counselor reacts more frequently and does not seem to permit any long pauses to occur as compared to the counselor in the preceding interview. At the same time, his activity is of quite a different sort from that of Mr. Dut's counselor.

That counselor immediately began to set up rather specific conditions for the conversation, namely, that Mr. Dut transmit information in designated areas. In the immediately preceding interview the counselor did not necessarily respond after a client paused. The counselor in this interview tends to do that, so that the interaction becomes one where the client completes a thought and then expects the counselor to make some kind of comment upon it, either to accept it, or clarify it in some way before proceeding to speak of a succeeding thought.

Analyzing the process in more detail, we notice that in S 2 Mr. Smith seems to be emphasizing his suspiciousness of people. We wonder whether he is indicating his sensitivity to the counselor's opinion. The counselor's response is a relatively mild statement of the implication of these remarks and perhaps S 3 represents an effort by Mr. Smith to suggest that in being responsive he is reacting to fancied rather than real characteristics of the behavior of others. In S 4 he emphasizes still more his tendency to distort things, and at the same time stresses how unmanageable he thinks his feelings are. In the original report the counselor himself called attention to the uncommunicability of C 5, which leads to the expressions in S 5 and S 6.

The interview proceeds:

S 10. I try to get away from the feeling that things inside of me are going to pull myself apart. I'd do anything to get away from it. We used to go swimming in the quarry when we felt like that. We used to swim and swim until our arms were falling off. That relieved the tension. We used to fight each other just to get rid of the feeling that things were there.

C 11. You had a sort of inexpressible anxiety about a good many pressures.

S 11. Yes, internal ones. I can't express it. It's like a balloon swelling up inside and some day it's going to burst. It's like an appendix. It swells up and eventually it bursts and gets rid of infection.

C 12. You get to the point where you're pretty much worried and you feel you can't do much.

S 12. Yes, I want—I worry whenever I'm alone. If I'm alone and I think about it, then I know it's going to come. If I keep busy, I don't worry too much.

C 13. You have sort of an anxiety that something's going to happen to you.

S 13. Something from inside. I'm afraid even to be a failure. I haven't got anything to hang onto. I'm afraid that when college is done I can't find what I want. And maybe I won't be able to do anything.

C 14. Some of the anxiety ties up with the future and what's going to happen to you.

S 14. Yes, not anything past but what's coming ahead. (*pause*)

C 15. You don't feel sure enough of yourself that you can meet the issues that you have to face.

During most of this portion, particularly in S 10, 11, and 12, the client expresses more fully his fear of his own impulses and to what their uncontrolled expression might lead. In S 13 he seems to turn away from this. After making clear that the threat is from inside, he turns to the problem of what external support he can hope to gain by accomplishment. C 14 seems to lose the implications of the sequence of responses and assumes that the client's anxiety is primarily about what his accomplishment will be. The client agrees with C 14, emphasizing that his anxieties do not have reference to the past, which sounds like a denial. Then the first pause in the interview occurs. C 15 seems to come closer to capturing the client's fear that his impulses are going to run away with him.

At this point we might also call attention to another therapeutic issue. When the client shows this kind of anxiety, some counselors might be inclined to offer some form of reassurance. Others would be inclined to take the categorical position that reassurance is never therapeutic. As our reader will see in the future discussions, we think the problem of reassurance has been oversimplified. At this point, let us simply rephrase the issue as being that of when and what kind of reassurance is really reassuring. S 16 (in the succeeding excerpt) suggests to us that the client might not find reassuring efforts to tell him that he is better off than he thinks he is. He would probably see this as another case of people "building me up and I am going to fall short of the mark."

The interview proceeds:

S 15. Yes, I don't feel I can do what people think I can do.

C 16. You worry because people think you're pretty good and they're expecting more of you than you can do.

S 16. They're building me up and I'm going to fall short of the mark. And sometimes the feeling that's inside sort of wells up and the only way to let it out is to listen to the music we fellows like to listen to. It seems to express our emotions—Tschaikowsky's "1812 Overture" or Wagner's "Introduction to the Third Act of *Lohengrin*." You have the feeling that it builds up to a huge climax and it gets bigger and bigger—then bang, it hits and falls. There's a feeling of dejection. It's almost grief.

C 17. You have the feeling that classical music tends to express your frustrating experiences and it gives you release.

S 17. Sometimes we listen to it and it helps. Sometimes it makes it worse. You listen to it and you feel you're a part of the music. And your whole being depends on it. You actually think you can see the music. You feel it.

C 18. It's an experience which seems to become a part of you.

S 18. Why, your whole surroundings fit into it and everything.

C 19. And it gives you a certain amount of release from this tension.

S 19. A certain amount. It doesn't release completely but it helps. (*pause*) Sometimes I'd start for a date and I'd walk three-quarters of the way to the date—that's about a half mile—and I'd suddenly decide to go back and change my socks or my handkerchief. I felt maybe the colors were wrong. And yet they seemed all right at the time I put them on. So I'd go back and change them.

C 20. After you'd made the decision then later you wouldn't be too sure of it. Is that right?

S 20. The first decision, I wasn't. But after I'd made the second one everything was all right. (*pause*)

C 21. You feel that most things are little things that shouldn't make a difference.

S 21. Some of them *are*—queer little things that shouldn't bother me.

C 22. There's a certain amount of personal inadequacy tied into it?

S 22. Yes, I'm not up to the other fellows. I can't make the grade. The other fellows are heavier, they're taller, better looking, they wear better clothes. They know what to do—they're completely adequate to every situation.

C 23. Most of the inferiority you feel is in regard to other fellows.

S 23. Yes, they've got everything over me. I've got two strikes against me when I begin the game. I just can't win, that's all.

C 24. You feel things are pretty hopeless because of your inferior abilities.

S 24. Yes, people say I have abilities but I don't believe 'em. It's just flattery. They're just trying to build you up.

C 25. When you feel these inadequacies people don't recognize them, but they tell you you're all wrong, is that it?

S 25. Yes. (*pause*)

C 26. They're always trying to make you believe it isn't true.

S 26. Yes, they're always trying to make me believe I can do things I know I can't. And little quirks bother me, too. Some colors offend me more. Violet and blue depress me and yellow makes me feel self-conscious. Green makes me feel swell and red makes me mad, anything with red in it. All the colors have some effect. Red makes me feel depressed, then it's that feeling of wanting to let off steam and just blow up.

C 27. Even colors tend to symbolize these various frustrations and annoyances.

S 27. Not symbolize, but just different colors have various effects. That's just like music. (*pause*) I hate to be in the forefront. I hate to be where people can see me. Yet, I like people to like me. I never have the courage to go up in the front where people will notice me. In classes I always start in the last row.

C 28. Most of your feelings of inferiority come up in relation to what other people are thinking.

S 28. Uh-hum. In comparing myself with other people.

C 29. Uh-hum. (*pause*) Well, perhaps I can tell you something of what we can do here. We can talk these things over together somewhat the way we're doing now and give you a chance to express your ideas and your feelings and maybe we can work out together what the cause of them is and what you can do about them. It probably isn't the sort of thing where I can just give you a short answer and say, "Well, here's what your problem is," but it's the kind of thing where we have to give you a chance to come to a realization by working it out together. You'd find that you would be free to talk about most anything you wanted to, and that I'd scarcely ever even ask you questions. By working it out that way probably we could come to some understanding of what is wrong. And because you'd be making your own conclusions they'd have a lot more meaning for you than if I tried to do it. Now if you'd like to try that sort of thing, I believe we could arrange for regular meetings at this hour on Wednesdays and Fridays. The whole thing would be entirely voluntary and if you came to feel that we weren't getting anywhere then you could stop coming in whenever you felt that way. And if I felt we weren't accomplishing anything, I'd tell you so. I'd go on writing down notes just the way I'm doing here. They're private notes and just for me to read. I keep 'em in my room and they don't have your name on them. But when I take these notes, then I can go over them between interviews. Also if you want to, they'd be here for you to look at. You may find you'd want to read them and you'd be welcome to do that. Now if you think you'd like to do that sort of thing, that's what we can arrange.

S 29. Well, I tried to tell you everything I thought of. It seems as if I don't think I could make decisions. I'll try though.

C 30. Well, I feel perhaps that going over it this way would tend to build up your confidence in your own decisions. As I suggested, we would be both working together, but you would be the one who would be arriving at conclusions. Do you think you would like to carry it on?

In S 19 and S 20 we get a little bit of repetition of the previous material. Perhaps the counselor's failure to react to the more direct implication of the client's communications contributes to lack of movement. C 22, which the counselor in a footnote apologizes for because of its interpretive character, seems to stimulate the client to further confiding. The fact that these inferiorities relate particularly to masculinity is not picked out by the counselor in his reaction. Nor does his summary of the interview suggest that he thought this was the case. In any event, the interview proceeds with relative inaction. Finally in C 29, whether in reaction to the preceding reaction on the part of the client or because it is his definite practice, the counselor attempts to orient the client to the therapeutic task and perhaps the client's response in S 29 is flavored with the feeling that the counselor is instructing him at this time because the interview hasn't been progressing the way the counselor feels it should and that it is the client's fault.

We turn now to the closing phases of this interview.

S 30. Yes, I would. Let's see, I'd just talk about anything. Well, I'll talk about my senior year. I'll give you my impressions. (pause) Everybody let loose what was inside of them. All of the fellows just went to the dogs and me with them. There were certain kids I idolized—kids I would like to be like. Then there were some freshmen I tried to help over the bumps and keep them from getting the same knocks I got. They hurt, and I tried to save them from that. I tried to take these freshmen kids and show them where they were heading. I tried to keep them from dropping off where I did. I even helped people with their homework. But they got the grades for it and never thanked me even. I tried to warn them about "wolves"—about certain boys, but they went ahead anyway. They took the consequences. I wanted to help them ease over the knocks they'd get, but they didn't want my help. Jack and I went to this one home. Everything was nice. We had a great deal of fun and cooked up games and played records and things like that. I tried to keep it off the rocks, but then all of a sudden someone else came in and broke up the bunch and the kids didn't bother to wave a fist at you. There was this one little girl in particular. We'd had hard knocks and we told her to stay clear of them and she didn't do it. That's all about that so we just quit going around. Then there were three teachers that will always stand out. One teacher in particular. There was a good friend of mine. A swell fellow —he was president of the Hi-Y. This teacher hounded him and belittled him and picked on him until his grades came down. The same thing happened to Jack. He tried it on me but I didn't let him bother me. Then he went on to Spike. We got tired of being kicked around. Nobody wanted us. We had to be careful where we went uptown because we were the kind of boys that mothers told their little girls, "Now there's a nice boy. Why don't you go with him?" We tried to make 'em different, but we didn't belong because people thought we were goody-goody boys. They didn't give you a chance. We went to football games but never yelled very loud because we were afraid of attracting attention. We never wanted people to look at us. We went to basketball games and did the same thing. If we did things, we went out of town. We used to go uptown to a little soda fountain. We were accepted by one group—the better group—but whenever they did things that were shady, we were left out. Then Jack found the solution. When the other fellows came around, he went out and got tight while I worked. We had a standing date after twelve o'clock each night. The rest of the fellows would bring him as far as Fifth Street and I'd take him home. I was the motherly type. Then we'd take care of him and if he was too tight, we'd take him to the reservoir and duck his head in it. Then we'd feed him black coffee and greasy doughnuts to make him bring it up. If he was too bad, we would take him to Spike's house, or else over to his garage and put him in his car. Then we'd let him sleep it off there. But I was on the outside. The fellows never thought I'd get drunk because they never tried me. I never got the chance. I don't know—I never went places with them. I don't know whether they thought I'd be a wet blanket or what. That was up until the last month of school. Then the last month of school I kicked loose. I guess that's all.

C 31. Uh-hum. You feel that covers pretty much what you'd like to talk about today.

S 31. Uh-hum. And it looks like our time's up, too.

C 32. Yes, I guess it is. Would you like to talk some more about this on Wednesday?

S 32. Yes, I would like to talk about it and get it out this way. I like to get these things off.

C 33. Well, we'll plan it then for Wednesday at the same time. Shall we plan it then?

S 33. Well, this isn't too much trouble for you, is it?

C 34. No, I feel I can arrange the periods we've planned, and I'm interested in helping you with this just as long as you feel you want to come in.

S 34. Well, I'd like to come.

C 35. All right. We'll go on Wednesday then.

S 35. Yes. Thank you for doing this.

We see that in S 30 the client has reacted quite seriously to the instruction. First rehearsing what his instructions are and quite obviously picking out a specific topic and after a pause, perhaps to organize what he is going to say, he begins to talk about his senior year in high school. Although he may have tried to organize his comments, one gets the impression that they flowed rather freely and had considerable meaning for him. He conveys, in discussing his relationship with the freshmen and with Jack, his emphasis on helping others and his disappointment at not getting something in return. Here again he also brings out feelings that seem to be related to masculinity when he talks about the efforts of his group of friends not to be such "nice boys." Yet throughout this discussion there is an underlying theme of defeat and failure that his friend and he, particularly he, were not able to achieve this masculinity nor able to convince others of it. He brings the interview to a close himself, perhaps partly because there has not been a really strong acceptance of the therapeutic task; perhaps also as a very realistic recognition that time was up.

The issue of defining the therapeutic task is a very important one, particularly in counseling. Even when a patient comes to a psychotherapist and when there has been considerable preparation for the therapeutic situation through reading or referral, there is a need to clarify what aspects of the person's difficulties are the objects of attention and what is expected of him in the relationship. This is even more true in counseling where clients are not as likely to be oriented toward a therapeutic goal and are more likely to start with the preconception that the counselor will serve as an informational resource. Mr. Dut's expectation that he will get information seems very clear in our first example, and in fact his counselor reinforces it both by his behavior and by some of his definitions. In the case of Mr. Pol, the definitional process proceeded more gradually and at some points more subtly than in the last one. It was not so much a matter of the counselor providing a miniature lecture on the therapeutic situation as of conveying to the client, through the way the counselor reacted at relatively nonverbal levels, what is expected of him at various stages in their interaction. (This case went on for twenty-one interviews. Dr. Snyder reports that when interviewed four years later Mr. Smith expressed satisfaction with his own adjustment.)

Case of Mr. Bav [1]

The next interview we turn to is a third meeting between counselor and client. Mr. Bav is a senior student in a premedical curriculum who has expressed uncertainty about continuing in medicine. In the first two interviews, attention moved quickly to his dependent relationship with his parents and others.

C 1. One thing and another coming up, it's kind of hard to get together, isn't it?

S 1. I guess it really is. How long has it been now, about three weeks?

C 2. I guess it's been about that time. I've been away once, and you've been away once and that's the way it works.

S 2. I guess so. (*little laugh*)

C 3. How are things going?

[1] The first interview with Mr. Bav is discussed in Ch. 10.

S 3. Well, things are okay, I guess.

C 4. Sounds like you're not too sure though.

S 4. Well, I would say I have a pessimistic attitude.

C 5. Uh-huh. (*pause*)

S 5. I wonder if I—I guess I could have really come in last week, but at the time I didn't think I should, because I had a—I had a physics test on Monday, and I—my fraternity was having a (*lost*) over the week-end, and I wanted to study.

C 6. Uh-huh.

S 6. But from the way it looks right now I should have come in, (*little laugh*) because it didn't make any difference.

C 7. Uh-huh.

S 7. But I was working on the physics test.

C 8. Yeah. You're not sure which way you're expending—if you would have expended your time more satisfactorily.

S 8. Yeah. That's very true.

C 9. Uh-hum.

S 9. Do you think maybe I was—I was—suppose I was putting up resistance or anything? By not coming in? Maybe I didn't feel that I had anything to say. I don't know.

C 10. Sounds like you might have some feelings concerning— What I mean is you're not really very sure of just what you're supposed to be doing or how you feel about these things.

S 10. Maybe that's it. You know what I—I think—I certainly remember the last time I came in here, I—after I left—I had feelings that I was—well, that everything I said was going to be found out by other people, and I think it sort of—I don't know—it sort of made me feel funny. I mean—I was sort of resisting coming in here, because I was afraid other people would find out (*little lower*) those things.

C 11. Did you have anything particular in mind that sort of contributed to that feeling?

S 11. Well, what do you mean, did I have anything particular—

C 12. Well, anything that kind of—

S 12. Well, yeah, because of the recording of the conversation sort of, (C: uh-huh) I mean it seems that everything is so public.

C 13. Yeah. You were uncertain about really how personal—how intimate you can be in the situation.

S 13. Yeah

C 14. Uh-hum. I might point out first of all that the recordings are never identified with a personality. The only one who knows that it's you talking is me. You see?

S 14. Uh-huh.

C 15. So that might offer you perhaps a little support. On the other hand if you felt you'd rather we didn't have the recordings—

S 15. No. It doesn't matter, I guess maybe that was the thing, and I thought possibly everybody would be able to identify me, including—

C 16. No. Nobody would know who it is at all. Because what happens to this recording is that a number is given to it, and I'm the only one who knows what it is. You see? So there is definitely that assurance that it's not going to be public information.

S 16. Uh-hum. I was just wondering. (*little laugh*) I guess it's natural that I'm wondering how much this is getting anything—I mean how far we're getting. If we're getting anywhere at all. (*short pause*) (*slightly lower*) I really don't know if I am or not.

C 17. Yeah. Maybe in a way you're kind of saying something else. Maybe you're kind of saying that perhaps there's a little reluctance to go into this situation at all.

The opening exchanges illustrate several interesting points. Mr. Bav starts by giving relatively direct voice to certain negative attitudes about coming in. He is sufficiently sophisticated, or perhaps the counselor has already introduced him to the concept, to try to pass off his negative feeling with the glib labeling of resistance in S 9. In C 10 the counselor does not let him stay at this glib level and he turns to the issue of being recorded. Frequently a client makes the fact that he is being recorded a basis for negative and resistive feelings about the process. Some counselors are led by such experiences to argue against recording. The answer usually given to this argument is that if the client were resisting and there was no recording he would make use of something else. The counselor deals realistically with the subject of recording, attempting to point out that there is no rational basis for the client's concern. In S 16 Mr. Bav gets more directly to the basis for his resistance in the feeling that they were not progressing fast enough, but the counselor suggests that the client is really afraid that they may be going farther into feelings than he wishes.

The interview proceeds in this direction.

S 17. I don't know. Possibly.

C 18. These things have been kind of hidden underneath and sort of bringing them out can be a little frightening sometimes.

(*little lower*) And so when you did bring them out a little bit you sort of feel "Is that in me?" And you sort of draw back.

S 18. Yeah, that's—I don't know (*C gives little laugh*) whether that's it or not. (*pause*)

C 19. In that sense you might kind of want to perhaps deny to yourself that there are any of these feelings that are real.

S 19. None of these feelings are. I—I don't know. I know that, lately, these past few weeks I haven't felt like doing anything. I—

C 20. Uh-huh.

S 20. I don't know. Ever since I came back from vacation, I really haven't felt (C: uh-hum) in the mood of doing ever—anything. But I've noticed that well, I haven't had too much work this semester, and I planned to do a lot of other things, and yet I haven't done them. And I—instead (*little laugh*) I'm just—I just waste my time. I'm always afraid that I'll have too much excess time, and it seems that I don't have the excess time that I—that (C: uh-hum) I just have enough time, you know, for what I do.

C 21. Uh-huh.

S 21. But I'll just sit and not do anything at all. And I can't understand it, because I had planned these few weeks to go out and play tennis and play golf, and I haven't even done that. And I just sit—I have no classes usually from 11 to 3 and I just—I don't know where those hours go. They just seem to go away without getting anything done. I can't understand what it is. I just have—when I pick up a book even to study, I have—I feel like that—that if I get done with this then—then I won't have anything to do, so I don't do it. I don't know what it is exactly, and even when I went into the physics test, I told myself that I—that I won't pass the test if I don't think. And yet, when I reached the problems, I just didn't think. I just looked at them, and I tried to remember formulas, but I didn't try and reason them out. And I don't even—I wasn't even too concerned. Oh, I still didn't get the test back, but I know I didn't do good on it. I wasn't too concerned after I walked out of the test. I just laughed at it. But then I, (*little laugh*) I had feelings of wanting to quit school. And, I mean, just leaving school, because it wouldn't be any use if I flunked physics, because I gotta stay in the first ten. And I don't know.

C 22. You kind of have a sense of falling apart a little bit.

S 22. Yeah. I don't know what it is. It seems that—even—oh, I know all last year and the year before I enjoyed staying up at school on week-ends. I always wanted to stay up here, I didn't want to go home. It seems like I'm sort of regressing. That's one reason I go home.

C 23. Uh-huh. (*short pause*) Are you saying you felt a little more comfortable at home over the vacation than you had here? (*rather softly*)

S 23. Yeah. I, sort of, I guess. (*pause*) I thought at one time that I was just interested in getting into Med School, but it doesn't seem that—when I think of it—it doesn't seem that that would solve the situation either. I don't know how—whether that would mean anything or not. I was wondering—I found out that when I was young, I used to be afraid of men. My dad told me that when I was about 10 months old, I had my tonsils taken out, and I was—I was really afraid of the doctor, and I put up terrific resistance to have him give me gas and after that I was always afraid of men until I was about 5 or 6 years old. And also he said that whenever I'd hear a fire-engine, I used to run inside crying. I was so afraid of it.

C 24. Uh-hum.

C 24. And I wonder if that—if that is anything. I mean, if that ties in in any way at all.

C 25. Kind of sounds as if you've been doing a lot of thinking about yourself here. And what sort of person you are.

S 25. Yeah. I'd like to know. (*short pause*) I was just wondering, if that could've been—if that could've been a traumatic experience that I sort of— (*pause*)

C 26. Maybe you can talk a little bit about the sorts of conditions that you had in your home this vacation. How you felt toward your mother and your father and so forth.

Mr. Bav rather passively resists the counselor's interpretation of his negative feelings toward further progress, but the counselor continues to press this interpretation until in S 20 the client turns it into a question of why he seems to be subject to a rather general apathy. In S 22 the client introduces the additional note that not only is he feeling apathetic but that he has a feeling of wanting to withdraw and operate at a less mature level. Mr. Bav seems to be utilizing a method of rational search for reasons for his problems as, for example, when he labeled himself as resisting and when he brought up his fear of the doctor in S 23. At the same time one cannot help wondering whether, embodied in S 23, there is not some possible expression of fear of the counselor who presses on him dissatisfying and perhaps fear-provoking interpretations. This part of the interview is punctuated by a number of pauses, and finally in C 26 the counselor attempts to assign him a definite topic and the interview proceeds.

S 26. (*little laugh*) It—I didn't even think of that.

C 27. Uh-huh (*pause*)

S 27. The vacation was so long ago—I can't—I can't remember that— I think—I guess it was just really the same as ever. I (*pause*) well, I didn't spend too much time at home. I know I felt guilty because I didn't stay home as much as I should have. Because I know that—I tried to go one night, or sort of stay home when there was nothing else. (C: uh-huh) Because I know they felt— they felt badly that I didn't stay home a couple of nights. (*little laugh*) And yet I couldn't find any time to stay home.

C 28. Uh-hum. (*pause*)

S 28. And I don't know—I felt—I think—. Well, let me see, I—when I did come home, I felt sort of queer, I guess, towards—towards my mother. Because at that time, my dad's best friend's daughter was getting married at the University of Washington and well— these people put up a terrific resistance to have their daughter get married. (C: uh-huh) And finally they consented and they went to Seattle and my dad went with them, and he asked my mother to go. My mother didn't go because she planned to go the next week. But I felt that she should have gone as she was going next week-end. She said she was going to get a suit, but as it was, I believe there's somebody that she meets there, and I— I did feel sort of strange and bitter to her (C: uh-hum) at that time, and yet, I mean, I didn't do anything about it, because I—I guess I was thinking of myself too, and I wanted to get as much as I—I was selfish I think, and I wanted to get as much as I can out of being at home. And I know if I—that everything would be real nice and that she'll do what I want if—if I act— I mean, if I don't do anything that she wouldn't like.

C 29. Uh-hum. Sounds like you're still pretty much involved in your mother's feelings concerning you.

S 29. Well, I know that. I mean I—she does—she does cater to me because it means a lot to her when—to say that she has a son that's going to college. When I come home she—she likes to do everything she can for a while and I know if I do anything *to* embitter her she won't do this and then she'll make me do more work. I may have to go shopping or something. Also she'll tell my dad not to give me the car. So I used to—I used to try and argue with her, but she's very dogmatic and she believes that she's right all of the time. So that I found it's even silly to argue, because you don't prove anything. And she won't listen to me, (C: uh-huh) more than one side and she always tries and if you argue with her she projects on to you and tells you to—that you can't listen to reason. And so I guess I just—well—I try to protect myself and do (*low*) the best for myself.

C 30.   Sounds like there are really two different sides of her. Aren't there? One is sort of a warm, emotional side that you can cater to, and the other is a side that involves a disciplinarian or a punishing person.

S 30.   I guess so.

C 31.   You—kind of like one, but don't like the other. Huh?

S 31.   I don't know how true the other side is. I—I really don't know. Because it sort of interferes with me (*quickly*) when, I mean, I don't like to be catered to. I like to be catered to, but I don't like to see—somebody else—I don't like to see my brother or my father neglected on account of me.

C 32.   Uh-hum.

S 32.   And yet I really don't know. (*little laugh*) It isn't that I— (*unclear*).

C 33.   You're not really sure of what your feelings toward her are.

S 33.   No, I guess not.

C 34.   Uh-huh. On the one hand it's perhaps some sort of feelings of attraction, and on the other hand there's some sort of rejection of those feelings.

S 34.   I know. It's just that every time Mother's Day used to come along, every mother used to be idealized so much and I never could look on my mother as being the same type of person as idealized over the radio and school and everyplace. And so I just don't know how to look on her. I know I can't confide in her. (*lower*) But I said that before.

C 35.   Uh-hum. You can't trust her though you'd like to.

S 35.   Yeah. It— (*pause*).

C 36.   So you really want your mother, but you don't feel you have her, because she's off flitting about with someone else.

In S 27, 28, and 29 we have rather long confiding statements followed by the counselor's interpretations which start with C 29 and culminate in C 33. In S 30, which is a more direct statement of the client's feeling of ambivalence towards his mother, there is also an implication that she is pushing him into a position of rivalry for her affections with his father and brother.

In S 33 Mr. Bav may be responding to the implications of this rivalry by talking as though he could not react to his mother in the same way that others react to their mothers. The counselor picks out his remarks about not being able to confide in her and then in C 35 makes an interpretation which would seem to be at least a partial offshoot of the rivalry theme but might be quite a jump for the client.

Let us now return to the interview.

S 36. Possibly. Well, I think—I mean before last time I came here, I thought I did say that. I was striving for some sort of love, and I think that's—that's very true. *(lower)* But I think basically I'm very insecure and I just want to have something I can be sure of. (C: uh-hum) It doesn't matter what.

C 37. At least mother is there and you've kind of always had a relationship with mother, so it's kind of hard to think that maybe she isn't the person that—. In that sense I wonder if there aren't a lot of feelings involving sort of reaching out toward her, kind of wanting to have her— *(short pause)*.

S 37. In what way do you mean?

C 38. Kind of wanting to possess her warmth, and her support, her love and so forth.

S 38. Well, now, I don't know if it is exactly or not. I don't know if it's—if it's again just for my own self. Well, I guess I mean, for getting as much as I can out of being at home.

C 39. Uh-hum.

S 39. Because I know if I—I mean, if I do a piece of it, I'll get whatever I want.

C 40. Uh-hum.

S 40. For instance, if I wanted a suit and it was, well, during the summer vacation, and if I shopped—I wanted to shop with her because I knew I'd always get something pretty good. I mean, more good than my dad, because my dad is more economical than her. (C: uh-huh) And I think consciously I acted very nice that day, because I knew that if I did, I would get—she was either to go with me or I wouldn't get exactly what I wanted.

C 41. Uh-huh.

S 41. So I don't know—I don't know exactly what it is.

C 42. You kind of reach out for her a good deal, but you can't quite have it the way you want to. She sort of has her own feelings. A sort of independence.

S 42. I suppose so, but I don't know. It's just—now—it's—I don't know —what sort of relationship you're supposed to have with your mother anyway. (C: uh-hum) I know she doesn't—as far as her mother is concerned, her mother is nothing. She doesn't like to even invite her parents over to dinner. She'd rather invite her girl friend over to dinner than her parents.

C 43. Uh-hum.

S 43. It's just a task to her. Just a lot of work and her mother is really—well, she's sort of neurotic, and she's an invalid. She has rheumatism and arthritis and everything else and she's always sick and I don't think she has too much use for her, even when she calls up on the 'phone. She doesn't like to talk to her. She figures it's just a waste of time and it's so boring. Another thing, my grandmother is getting older now, and she can't—you tell her something, but she doesn't quite grasp what we tell her, and you have to repeat it a lot. So I don't know. Maybe I'm supposed to act the same way. I don't know.

C 44. You're not sure really of what type of relationship you are supposed to have with your mother.

S 44. I don't think so. I know we've never been actually close. She never let my brother or I even to—well, even kiss her on the lips because she felt that this spread germs.

C 45. Uh-hum. Uh-hum. (*very short pause*)

S 45. I know I—I even feel strange, oh, kissing her. When I say goodbye to her, we kiss goodbye because it's a formality. I suppose I thought it's supposed to mean anything. (*low*)

C 46. Uh-hum. (*short pause*) In other words, sometimes you tend to think in terms of a much closer and more emotional relationship, and she seems to reject that, and yet in other ways she doesn't.

S 46. Well, like—yeah. I don't try for (*clears throat*) a closer relationship. I—I—I don't want that. (*low*)

C 47. You don't think so, but you're not sure.

S 47. No. I'm not sure. (*short pause*) I did actually think that if I got into Med School that I'd be able to spend all my time studying and I wouldn't have to devote my time to worry. I mean I wouldn't have time to worry about her.

C 48. Uh-hum. That might be a—

S 48. (*breaking in*) I'm afraid, I'm afraid that maybe I wouldn't be able to study then.

C 49. Uh-hum.

S 49. I don't know.

C 50. In other words, these are sort of things that live inside of you and you sort of carry them with you wherever you go.

S 50. Uh-hum.

C 51. Sounds like you're not very sure at all about—both about how you feel towards your mother and about how she feels towards you, what sort of person she is. The both sides of it.

S 51. Well, I—just—even I don't know what the—what the (*little laugh*) relationship is.

Through C 41 the counselor is trying to push the rivalry and insecurity themes and the client is in passive ways not accepting the interpretation. Somehow this process leads to S 41 where the client returns spontaneously to a more direct statement not knowing whether he has a normal relationship with his mother. The counselor now abandons his interpretive push and responds with more passive attention until his verbalization in C 43 seems to lead to further active consideration by the client of his feelings about his mother and of the fact that they are a source of anxiety to him.

C 52. Uh-hum.

S 52. I know my brother just feels the same way. He says that he just listens to the guys and he doesn't—doesn't pay any attention to her. The story—he used to be bothered every time he'd get yelled at, but he just doesn't care any more. He takes her—it doesn't faze him one way or another.

C 53. Uh-hum. He doesn't seem to be as much involved perhaps as you are.

S 53. (*very low*) I don't know. Maybe—

C 54. In a way, perhaps you don't know, and perhaps in another way you're afraid to say. Sort of a—

S 54. (*breaking in*) I don't know.

C 55. And sort of really down to an understanding of how you do feel. (*pause*)

S 55. (*low*) I don't know if that's—if that's it or not. (*pause*)

C 56. Uh-hum.

S 56. I know another thing. The girl I'm going with now isn't too sure about herself, because I have a lot more school—about five or six years, and her parents have been bothering her, and I know my dad had her over, because once a few weeks ago—I don't know if I told you or not—I went home, and saw my dad, and told him that I didn't think I wanted to go to Med School, even if I got in. I thought I'd like to quit school. I don't know whether I said that or not. (C: uh-huh) But he was very worried and he had her over to the house. Well, she wants to start going out with other people again. In fact, she said she doesn't want to go out with me. She wants to get some other dates just to see how she actually feels. And I know I've been very bothered about that. I think again, it's just the same thing though. I think that it's just—I'm just trying to get somebody—I don't think it exactly matters who—to—to actually love or to have love, or— (C: uh-huh) just some sort of secure relationship.

C 57. You might say you're actually working out another situation that you've been trying to work out with your mother.

S 57. And I think that possibly that is it.

C 58. Uh-hum.

S 58. I know even when this boy and I were very close up in school, and he had gotten into Med School, I didn't care especially, I mean, I was sort of jealous I didn't get into Med School, but it meant a lot more to me that our friendship was broken up, because we were very close. (C: uh-hum) And still we're very close, but we're breaking apart now. We didn't want to— although he's going to live in a separate house now—I guess that was another thing that's—

C 59. Uh-hum. (*low*)

S 59. —sort of bothering me. (*pause*)

C 60. These sorts of relationships which kind of provided you with security and love are kind of breaking up.

S 60. Yeah. That's another reason why—why I didn't want to—I didn't know if I wanted to get into Med School or not, because if I got into Med School, I was sure that I'd have to study a lot more than I am now, and I wouldn't have time to—to go home, or to have my girl come up here—to—to be sure of anything, and I'd probably lose her then, because I know the first year or the first two years, you really don't have much time at all to do anything but study.

C 61. It sounds like maybe what you have to do before you acquire a sort of stable situation is to clarify how you feel about these different things and sort of get settled about what your mother means to you, for instance. You have to see your relationship clearly.

In S 46, 47, and 48 the client had continued to express his ambivalence and his anxiety about his feelings about his mother. Finally in S 52 he attempts to get some relief from the problem by talking about his brother's attitudes toward his mother. However, as the counselor presses him, he seems to be thinking hard about it, emphasizing his need for security and its ramification in other relationships, which culminates in C 61 where the counselor attempts to establish more firmly the rational goal of understanding his relationship with his mother.

The counselor in this interview illustrates still another facet of counselor style in relating to clients. This counselor reacts frequently and in that sense is like the counselors in the cases of Mr. Dut and Mr. Smith, but he attempts to push interpretations and concepts at the client at a relatively rapid rate, much more rapidly than Mr. Smith's counselor. This epitomizes one of the big therapeutic issues, namely, how much effort the counselor should give to establishing the rationale of client behavior and feeling and when this should be done. Mr. Dut's counselor appears to emphasize rationale almost to the exclusion of feeling. In contrast, Mr. Smith's counselor seemed to emphasize and encourage expression of feeling. The counselor in this interview, while giving considerable emphasis to rationale, did not appear to exclude the presence of feeling in its expression. After eleven interviews, Mr. Bav withdrew from counseling "because of the pressure of final examinations." At this point he seemed less anxious and a little more realistic. However, the counselor was dissatisfied with the help he had given, feeling that his pressing interpretations so hard had caused the early withdrawal.

Case of Miss Tir [2]

Thus far we have been observing interviews which occurred in early phases of the relationship. Our next example comes from the sixteenth meeting between counselor and client. Miss Tir is a twenty-year-old girl with a problem of fear of being dominated by her mother and of not being able to face up to her in regard to her marital plans. The interview opens.

[2] Other interviews with Miss Tir are discussed in Chs. 10 and 13.

C 1. Match?

S 1. I swear I have them! I just can't find them! (*pause*) Thank you. I realize I went off on a tangent in that story last time. But the whole idea behind my feelings toward my roommate—well, this seems to have brought it to a head, and it seems to me if I could overcome in some way the fear I have of them, it stands to reason I could overcome it with my mother. Not exactly overcome the fear. The feeling might remain, but that my—my sort of intellectual realization of it would help me say the thing I'm afraid to say even though I'm afraid to say it.

C 2. Uh-hum.

S 2. And I tried—something happened since Thursday that gave me a little opportunity on the same old issue of my roommate's smoking, and I didn't do it. I honestly don't know how her mind works! I can't talk to her about it and find out! I don't know what she thinks about watching me clean up, pick up her mess, and never—it isn't like her to take advantage that way, but that's just what she's doing. And she called up early the other morning, doing me a favor. She was waking me up in time to go to class, and the room was really very bad. And it was all hers. One of the girls that entered said it looks as if a hurricane had entered. Well, I didn't say anything about it, but she said, usually, "Don't look at the room. I know it's a mess and I'm sorry. I'll clean it up this afternoon." And I usually said, "Oh, that's all right." Which is the last thing in the world I feel, but the only thing—I always naturally calm down when she apologizes. I came home in the afternoon. She had been home. The room was still in its original state. I began to get angry but I said nothing again. She was home in the evening, and you can make time if you want. That doesn't take more than fifteen minutes to hang away your clothes and put your books in the bookcase. So it isn't a question of her not being able to. She just doesn't! And I didn't say anything about it. I did unburden my soul to Vi, and in saying it I felt that somehow I ought to force myself to do it, and she said she didn't see why I should *force* myself— (*spoken rapidly and unintelligibly*). Anyway, the next morning, I cleaned up and there was a time when I would hang her stuff up. I'm beyond that stage. It makes me too mad! I simply take everything up and fling it on her bed (*much feeling*) in the biggest mess I can create myself, but all on her bed, or on the dresser, and the things—the bed and dresser that is mine, and the things we share, I cleaned. I did it. And I had planned—it was sort of a coward's way out—to put a note on it with something about "I heard somebody say the road to hell is paved with good intentions." And I realized that she had had the intention to do it. But before I (*sigh*) got through and got out, I—I—in order to leave a note, I'd have to guarantee my being out when she came home and read it. Then it was silly to leave a note when you're there to say it. Well, it just didn't work out. She came home sooner than I expected, and she began to put her things away, while I was so angry, I hardly said, "Hello," that's about all. I didn't say any-thing to her. She didn't say anything to me. Silence occurs when one or the other or both of us is in a bad mood. You know it's miserable. I didn't know whether the silence was in response to mine or whether she was depressed for some reason. But she cleaned up halfway. She had worn a skirt of mine and had gotten it dirty, and she told me when she took it off a couple of days, last Sunday this was, that she would wash it for me as she had made it dirty. She hadn't and I wanted the skirt so I would wash it myself. The thing was it happened before. She'll use my stuff and mess it up and then I have to wash it in spite of all her promises. And she saw it hanging up in the bathroom and she left. Finally when she came back later on in the day, I had come home. And she walked in and said, "Hello." I had been very mad at *myself* and at her all day. I don't know at who more, me or Betty. And I said, "Hello" and I didn't hear the answer, so I decided, well, if she was mad I would be mad too! And I got out one word in a very aggressive tone of voice, and said, "What's the matter with you?" So she said, "Nothing's the matter with me. Nobody's been saying anything to me all day so I'm not saying anything." And she said it very softly, so I said, "I said hello." She said, "I didn't hear you." And she was—she had something to tell me, and she was feeling good, and she began to tell it to me, and we were very friendly, and forgot about the whole thing, and I flopped again. And I'm *very* annoyed! I can't do it when she's happy and I can't do it when she's mad at me. And when she is in a good mood, and we talk sort of intimately, I enjoy it so much, I don't want to ruin it. It's again—it shows my insecurity. It means that I'm afraid. It certainly wouldn't ruin it for all time. It would upset her, but let her be upset. She's wrong, and she's got it coming to her (*sigh*) but I (*low*) can't fish it out. (*short pause*) It would almost be easier to do it to Sylvia, only . . . (*lost*). . . .The whole thing is very discouraging. (*low*)

C 3. Rather than being a tangent, you really feel that this is very close to you.

S 3. Yes. I also discovered that Vi has the same behavior toward Sylvia and probably toward Betty because she comes in conflict with Sylvia more often. Well, Vi and I were sitting in the room. We had just been talking about how unhappy we both are, and Sylvia walked in wearing Vi's raincoat. And Vi said, "Where are you going with that? It's going to rain. I'm going to need it." And Sylvia said, "Oh. I didn't think you were going out. If you are, I'll take it off." And Vi said, "No. Never mind." She was very annoyed but she said "Go ahead and wear it." Then later on, Sylvia came home, took off the raincoat, and shoved it down on my bed. They leave their stuff in my room, and— (*slight laugh*) (*short pause*). When Vi came in later in the evening, the raincoat was all wrinkled as if somebody slept in it. And Vi is very very neat. The things she wears—she is sloppy too, but some-how she never looks like it. Nothing is ever wrinkled or anything like that. But a thing like a raincoat which one doesn't iron she would hang up. She was very annoyed about it. And when she came in to get it, I said, "Are you going to say anything?" She said, "No. I won't say anything to her." And I asked her later on and she said she doesn't say anything just like I don't say anything. The both of us have a legitimate grudge. And she began to explain to me that I was looking for the reason for my not being able to tell Betty and for not having the same feelings for Sylvia. And I said, "It seems to me it must be something in them that affects me that way, combined with something in me that makes me react that way." She said that there's a time—she thinks it's a kind of selfishness in both of them, that their be-havior is not to be questioned. They won't be questioned, or criticized. (*short pause*) It's true of Betty, that she can't—in one way she can't take the criticism because she's so immature her-self. When you tell her she's doing something wrong, that you don't like what she's doing, she thinks that you don't like Betty. And she's a very touchy person. Less so now than she was before, but she still is. And that is a kind of weakness in a person that I would be willing to cater to. Because I realize how very insecure she is, how unhappy, how inadequate she usually feels about everything. But this particular kind of behavior isn't a scared kind of behavior. Here it is selfish. It's—well, it's aggressive to her. She is stepping on me. (*short pause*) And well I know that strength is the wrong word to apply to it, but if this insecurity, this afraidness of her own inability to add up in a lot of situations, this sort of weakness, you might say. But the way she treats me and situations like that is not weakness, it's acting more or less—

C 4. She's the stronger in the—when you let her be the stronger. (*very low*)

S 4. Yes. (*pause*) It's funny that in spite of all that insecurity, and the weak kind of person she is, in some ways people are afraid of her. I think her mother, of whom she's told me, is afraid of her. And she doesn't—I've tried to explain that to her. It might be a projection, my thinking her mother is afraid to face up to her, afraid to object when she doesn't want her to do the things that Betty does.

C 5. Uh-hum.

Miss Tir is evidently in a very communicative mood as the interview starts. Apparently she has carried the topic over from the preceding interview and is quite preoccupied with it. Notice also that she is communicating more of the flavor of a series of events, rather than introspecting so completely into her own feelings. There is a great deal of pure release involved in her communication as contrasted to an association of thoughts and feelings. Nevertheless, even though she starts the interview describing this topic as if it were a tangent, the additional comments on the typescript as well as her choice of words and general nature of her expression tell us she is putting a great deal of feeling into this communication. One notices also the flexibility with which she gives expression to her feelings. After S 1, in which she indicates both that she felt she had gone off on a tangent in talking about her feelings toward her roommate and that it really was related to her problem with her mother, she plunges fully into talking about the most recent incident involving her roommate. At the same time, there is an implicit goal of showing through this incident how incapable she is of expressing negative feelings. Note that this cannot be a very deeply repressed prohibition, because in her communications to the counselor about the incident she is expressing her negative feelings quite freely and quite vividly. The counselor's only comment (C 3) following this deluge of communication is simply to reaffirm her feeling that what she is talking about is important, and she continues somewhat in the same vein in S 3.

But toward the end of S 3 she is beginning to be a little more analytical and less expressive. She is beginning to look at the reasons for her roommate's behavior and to compare herself with her. The counselor reacts to this by picking out the issue of the relative strength of the two girls and the client responds by turning still more from her dependence on pure expression.

Now let us proceed with the interview.

S 5. And when I try to tell her something like that, she'd say "No." Because she thinks that her mother tries to domineer her. *(lower)* I don't know how right she is. I don't think she knows— only *she* can know all the answers. *(very low)* It might be just a streak of that same power in her that my mother has. Well, Sylvia certainly has it, because she doesn't exhibit any kind of weakness, of giving you—of giving in to any of her men or to her people. Maybe that is it. *(pause)* Still I despise myself for being the kind of person that's victimized by that. Vi is too.

C 6. For being so weak. *(low)*

S 6. I don't like it. I don't like being able to be stepped on. I'm not in a lot of places. A lot of people can't step on me. But in certain cases they can.

C 7. It seems to be a kind of a localized weakness. That is, you're not necessarily generally weak.

S 7. Yes.

C 8. Uh-huh.

S 8. Just with regard to— There was a time when—uh—that same thing occurred between me and Jane *(referring to a friend back home)* when I first knew her, when we were about thirteen or fourteen. I was afraid of her. And I used to have some difficult times on specific issues. She was pulling me in one direction and my mother pulled in the other direction, because she saw Jane was managing me, so to speak. But Jane herself grew out of that. She recognized it in herself, and disliked the idea, and she doesn't do that to me any more. Otherwise, something disastrous would have happened. I couldn't be friends with her as I am, because after a few years I would have discovered the position I was in. When I got a little older and was able to see— and I don't like it. Although maybe I would have stayed with her, much as I do stick to Betty in spite of it.

C 9. The difference in your relationship with Jane is not because you were able to overcome it with her, but more that she changed.

S 9.   Yeah. (*pause*) I sort of am a modified version of the sort of
person Vi used to be. She's changed since. When I first met her
two years ago, she had been rooming with this girl, Dee, a
spoiled neurotic brat! Well, she runs everybody that she can
run. She ran Vi completely. And when we first met her, she was
rooming with Sylvia, and Dee was living in the same house,
and it was so obvious that she was her lackey. She was her
servant. Anything Dee wanted, Vi would do, and if Dee
wouldn't want it, Vi would not. She was very frightened of her.
It was a terrible thing to watch. And—uh—Sylvia set about
actively pulling Vi away from her, and in the end it came to a
choice between Vi being friends with her roommate—with Betty
and me, or being friends with Dee. None of us got along with
Dee. We had no use for her at all. And she couldn't—well, she
could have—she could have if she was strong enough, been the
friend of both parties so to speak. But Sylvia forced the decision on her, and she chose Sylvia and I. And since then she
dislikes the idea thoroughly as she claims—and it's true—that
Sylvia and the rest of us—well, Betty and I were not less active
(*lower*) in that Sylvia was the one who did it—that Sylvia had
no right to make her have a choice. She could have whomever
she wanted for a friend, and if Sylvia didn't like her other
friends it's too damn bad. Well, Vi realizes that now and, as a
result, has gone back to Dee, and is friends now with both. And
it so happens that Sylvia is also friends with Dee, friends with
her, she goes with her; she still doesn't like her. But (*short
pause*) there but for the grace of God go I. If—I don't know
if they could have done that much to me. Nobody ever has.
Maybe because the situation never arose where I had to choose.

C 10.   Uh-hum.

S 10.   But I wonder if they could do—Vi was weaker than I am, but
it's the same kind of weakness in both.

C 11.   You wonder just how weak you really are.

S 11.   I sort of haven't been under the test. Unless this situation is
a test. (*pause*) And I build up such arguments for myself. I
have such a case to present to my roommate. One of the things—
whenever she talks about somebody she likes, one of the first
adjectives she uses—it's very noticeable, she does it all the time—
is describing how considerate they are.

C 12.   Uh-hum.

S 12.   And what could be more inconsiderate than this particular way
she treats me. She apparently doesn't see it. Maybe she does.

And I've also—I'd like to know how every once in a while she apologizes for that room. And there was a week where she began to clean it up just out of the clear blue sky. And, well, she goes to the Psychiatric Clinic. I got the idea—I know she talks about me there. That maybe it had occurred to her that she was walking all over me, and didn't want to, and so set out not to. But she's a very undisciplined person. She can't make herself do something that she doesn't want to do. Like in studying, well, we all waste time, but not the way Betty wastes time. She'll have a test and start studying for it two o'clock and stay up all night to two A.M. This is after having wasted a day. (*short pause*) You see she always has a lot of good intentions, but is too lazy or too something else to carry them out. But it always seems to me that no matter how lazy you are, if you are really bent on doing something, you get it done.

C 13. Uh-hum.

S 13. And it's only when you're not too anxious to do it, or you have some doubts about whether you really want to do it, rather than this that or the other thing, you don't get it done. So it seems to me her determination, if there is any determination, to get rid of this particular point of inconsideration for me. It doesn't go very well; if she ever does think about it, it's in fits and starts and she forgets about it as soon as it's convenient for her. (*pause*) I don't know how I'm going to do it. I've had so many opportunities. (*low*) She even took me aside once and began to tell me that she felt something was wrong, between us. (*this is low*) (*then louder*) She is now a great believer in having the whole thing out, and sitting down and talking sensibly about everything that's bothering you. Because she comes from a family who don't tell each other anything. When they're offended they retire into a room in silence and wild horses can't drag the cause out. She recognizes how bad it is. So she makes a point when any little thing is bothering her to sit down and tell me about it. And at least on one occasion we've gone for a special cup of coffee in order to have this—special conversation. And she always said, "Whatever you feel against me, I want you to tell me." And I never do. I say, "Oh—nothing." (*short pause*) But I haven't taken it before. I don't know how I can take it now, except now I realize the importance of taking the opportunity. (*short pause*) And I always let it slip by. Purposely (*low*) accidentally on purpose, it doesn't work out.

C 14. Uh-hum.

In this section of the interview we see that the counselor's selection of the issue of her strength or weakness strikes an answering chord in Miss Tir as she proceeds to struggle with this characteristic of herself and her dislike of it. In S 6 and C 7 we get the working out that this weakness is not a general characteristic and there follows a further analysis of her behavior in this respect; and this leads to the emphasis on her being at the mercy of different people who are close to her and who might try to control her. Her discussion of Vi's behavior in S 9 seems to give still further expression to her feelings of dissatisfaction at being a person who can be controlled by others, who can be the passive object in the struggle between two people rather than be in a position to be a determiner of her own fate. Notice that the counselor continues to be relatively inactive; he does not attempt to set forth any rationale of her behavior as our preceding counselor did and is perhaps even more confining in his responses than Robert Winslow Smith's counselor. In S 11 Miss Tir seems to be seeing this situation with her roommates as a test of how weak and strong she really is. In S 12 she starts trying to analyze the roommate and how she sees things, trying to see if her roommate's behavior is justifiable.

Now let us see how the interview continues:

S 14. I don't know what I can do. (*short pause*)

C 15. It just seems to be something pretty strong pulling you back from doing anything like that. (*low*)

S 15. And—and it seems quite necessary that I do.

C 16. Uh-hum.

S 16. It seems to me once I do it—even once to her, I could do it with my mother.

C 17. Uh-hum. There's quite a lot at stake. (*low*) From the point of view of you as a person.

S 17. Yes. (*long pause*) One of the excuses I use is that— Well, she really has troubles with herself much more than I do. And I want very badly to help. I've tried to in many conscious ways to— well, whatever sort of behavior I know is true of her family, I will do just the opposite. I think we all do.

C 18. Except one thing.

S 18. What would that be?

C 19. You talk about her being very conscious of her family in terms of their not being able to— (*pause*).

S 19. Well—that I do in that I listen to her and I answer her.

C 20. Uh-hum.

S 20. She can't get—first of all its hard enough for her to get hold of her parents to have a little talk. They're *fear*fully afraid.

C 21. Uh-hum.

S 21. They avoid it and when she's been writing to her mother, she hasn't gotten any response.

C 22. This kind of even makes the parallel even closer to the relationship to your mother (*low*) because one of the things you've done when you started talking about your antagonisms towards your mother, you started talking about her problems and how you would like to try to help her.

S 22. Uh-hum. (*pause*) Her whole problem seems very different. It's much worse. (*pause*) I know I've been sort of advising her and when I give the advice and she certainly doesn't have to take it. I say, "Well, you might try this," to do the same thing I did and I got a response. She doesn't.

C 23. Uh-hum.

S 23. She just emphasizes how worse it is—

C 24. You mean Betty's mother—uh—Betty's problems are much worse.

S 24. Yeah.

C 25. I was thinking of another parallel between you and Betty— between your attitudes toward Betty and your attitude toward your mother. When you start thinking about your antagonism towards your mother, you also begin to think about your mother's problems and how you can help her. (*low*)

S 25. Oh—

C 26. Her problems— (*pause*)

S 26. (*low*) Yeah, (*short pause*) (*low*) and then it seems wrong for me (C: uh-hum) to begin to attack them when they're so bad off. (*short pause*)

C 27. It seems as though those separate feelings aren't really completely the way you're presenting them. That is, it's not so much that—that you really feel—you *do* intellectually—are very much aware of their problems, your mother's and Betty's. But you use your awareness as a way of kind of holding back the expressions of your own antagonisms.

S 27. Uh-hum. (*pause*) I don't suppose that would be good for *me* anyway. I wonder how good that is for them. (*low*) (*long pause*) It would seem as if they both rely on me for something. Betty for (*unclear*) for love and friendship than before. And I'll be denying it to them or making it less—I mean taking a part of that by attacking them. And yet, on the other hand, at least for my own benefit and maybe for theirs partly I ought to (*low*) express myself. It's an excuse.

We note in this excerpt that she continues the analysis of her roommate with considerably more sympathy for her. She points out that her roommate invites her to express her feelings toward her but she seems unable to do so. The counselor remains relatively noncommittal but still concentrates his responses on the major theme of the ability to assert herself. This helps Miss Tir to keep on the major issue as she does in S 15 and S 16. In S 17 we see that she has apparently stopped to think, as indicated by the long pause followed by a response explaining her inability to express her feelings about her roommate. The counselor seems to have been expecting this, and then he begins to interpret. His interpretations are so subtle that she does not quite get the drift and still stays within the framework of her roommate in both S 19 and S 20 as well as S 21. In C 22 the counselor is now ready to make his interpretation more pointed, but Miss Tir continues to look at it from the framework of her roommate, although she is being very thoughtful as indicated by the pauses. In C 25 the counselor restates his interpretation, and in S 25 and S 26 we see now that the interpretation has struck home. In contrast to her highly expressive communication earlier, the client is now being quite thoughtful. In C 27 the counselor has brought out more clearly the defensive value of the client's use of pity and empathy. In S 27 we see Miss Tir still continues to be thoughtful. We notice also that the slowing up of her expression does not seem to be evidence that she is resisting. Rather, where before her expression of feeling served solely the function of release, she is now seeing her feelings in new perspective and being made thoughtful by it.

Let us now see how the interview continues after her long pause.

C 28. This that you presented now also has potentialities of being an excuse. That is, (*low*) you're saying that they lean on you. And how you have to take away from them the support you've been giving (*very very low*). But we've also seen quite a bit of it in your feeling of fear of losing them. (*pause*)

S 28. It seems to me the feeling of fear of losing them only comes from their feelings towards me not being strong enough. (*low*)

C 29.   No. When you feel—uh—you connect that with your feelings of antagonism. (*pause*)

S 29.   (*low*) I don't understand.

C 30.   Well, it's—if you express your antagonism then possibly you will change their feelings towards you.

S 30.   The feeling seems to me to be in me and not—

C 31.   Oh! Yes!

S 31.   Wouldn't be true, really—

C 32.   Oh, I see. You're saying that that's an unrealistic feeling that you have. Yes. But what I was suggesting was that you're saying that if you were to be antagonistic, you'd be taking away their support from you, instead of your support (*little laugh*) —their use of *you* as a support. (*S: yes*) And it seems to be an emphasis on something different from what you really feel about it, when you think about being antagonistic.

S 32.   Yes. I see what you mean. (*long pause*) Doesn't it—it seems right that I ought to express my own feelings and nothing would *really* be lost (*lower*) in spite of it.

C 33.   If you can't give yourself permission to do it, maybe I can give you permission. (*he smiles, she laughs*)

S 33.   Yeah. (*laugh*) That's what it comes down to—I sort of feel as if I'm looking for the right thing to do. I don't know (*low and unclear*) just what the right thing is.

We notice that in C 28 the counselor has taken quite a jump. If we look back at the client's full expression in S 27 we see that her long pause, apparently in deep thought, started around the question of whether she was really doing her roommate and her mother any good by holding back the expression of her antagonism. The second half of S 27 seems to be the answer to this question, namely, that she is increasing their dependence upon her by not expressing her feelings. The counselor is unwilling to let the interaction rest at this point and attempts to push the explanation of her behavior still further in C 28. In his series of responses through C 32 he calls attention to the more subtle aspects of her defenses. We notice that Miss Tir resists these interpretations, as indicated most clearly in S 29, but in S 32 she acts as though she has seen and accepted them. Thus we see again illustrated the problem of how much and how quickly rational considerations can be introduced into the interaction by the counselor. We notice also that this counselor followed a pattern of not introducing rationale until the client's expression had reached a particular level. For the first part of the interview he was quite passive, operating solely as a kind of reinforcing agent to facilitate more direct affective expression and the analytic reactions which follow. It is only when the client's reactions reach a particular point which the counselor seems to have been anticipating that he more actively calls her attention to the possible meaning of her behavior.

Case of Mr. Wis

Let us look at still one more interview. This also is a sixteenth interview; with Mr. Wis, a young veteran, who in his third year of college is not achieving at a level appropriate to his ability. The interview begins.

C 1. Do you mind if I record this conversation? It's just for research purposes, and it (S: no, *little laugh*) won't have anything to do with identifying you or anything of that sort.

S 1. Do I have to sit up front?

C 2. No. (*little laugh*) We'll probably both forget about it.

S 2. (*low*) It's gonna rain. (*louder*) I was a little scared about this afternoon—after last week—after missing a week. I sort of got ... (*too low*). (*louder*) Well, something has been bothering me a lot. I guess it started— (*pause*) I guess it started last week. It carried over right up until yesterday morning anyway. But (*louder*) the whole feeling that everything is too much for me is coming back and (*lower*) I don't know why, I just—. From time to time, I felt like I'd just like to throw everything over again. And (*little laugh*) e-e-even death has come to my mind. Something which is—in a way scared me, and yet something which hasn't affected me at all. I—I don't feel anything when I think about it, and yet at other times, I know that it's not too pleasant a thought. (*fairly low, but matter-of-fact tone*) Of course I react against it. I mean, (*short pause*) I mean just (*sigh*) the idea flies through my head that maybe it would be a good thing to get out of it. And it would be an out ... (*too low*). And I—I've tried more or less to dig to the bottom of it and find out why I never get anywhere with it. It seems to be connected with this general lack of ambition, which has settled on me now. (*sadly*) Like this—I had a test yesterday and I had to put in three or four days on it before I could get to the stage where I thought I could go in and take it.

There was a lot of material but I could have covered it in less time. I know that. But I just had to force myself to sit down and work and concentrate and do it over and over and over again just to try to at least go into the thing feeling half way secure. And I don't know—just everything is—some days seems too big.

C 3. You seem to be describing a feeling of being sort of burdened down. (*short pause*)

That Mr. Wis starts this interview with indications of possible underlying negative feelings toward the process is suggested by the fact that he has missed the preceding appointment, always a potential indicator of some form of resistance, and also by his discouraged feeling. He wants to throw everything over, and even the thought of suicide has come to mind. Notice that he quickly reassures the counselor that this is not a permanent thought, or something he would act on, but in general he is saying that he isn't making too much progress and his problem seems to him too big to handle. The counselor avoids reacting to these specific implications and responds in more general terms.

The interview proceeds.

S 3. Yeah. It's a combination of burden and fear of the future.

C 4. You're a little bit scared (S: yeah) of how it's all going to come out. (*short pause*)

S 4. I— (*short pause*) I can't connect it with anything except just this feeling that it seems familiar. It seems to me maybe I've had it before. Or something like it. There's a certain similarity there but I— (*clears throat*) I haven't been able to puzzle anything out of it. (*pause*)

C 5. You seem to have also mentioned that something came to an end? That is you went through a period of feeling overwhelmed and scared in this way and you seem to be indicating that it isn't all there right now. (*short pause*)

S 5. Well, I guess it does come and go.

C 6. Uh-hum.

S 6. It fluctuates but I don't—it's never been exactly this way before. It never bothered me just this way. I—I—I've—I felt overwhelmed before, and my reaction to that was, well, to quit and go someplace else and try over again. But this seems rather extreme. And it's the extreme to which these thoughts are running which is scaring me. (C: uh-huh) And I don't know, it's—. It gives me a funny feeling. It's depressing. I can't shake it off. I try to dismiss it from my mind, but it doesn't (*lower*) work too good.

C 7. You seem to be making an effort to get rid of it, but it doesn't seem to be going.

S 7. Well, I try. Yeah. Just to see if I can do it. (*sad*) And more or less expect that it'll come back. (*very low*) This is California weather. (*little laugh*)

C 8. Yes. That's right. (*low*) In bringing up this recurrence of your feeling of being sort of threatened by the whole situation, I'm wondering if you'd admit that you were now going to try to hustle out something of what it is that brought it on, of what it all means?

During this section Mr. Wis responds as clients often do by starting on a rational search for the causes of certain reactions. But even this he seems to be doing reluctantly, as indicated by his sudden shifting to the weather in S 7. Perhaps he is being threatened by his inability to produce anything. This seems to be the counselor's assumption in C 8.

The interview continues.

S 8. That's the only way I know how to handle the thing (C: uh-hum). I mean (*pause*) it all meant—it does mean something. But what it does mean, though, I don't know. And in the past anyway, when once I could get to the root of these things, I could cope with them. Things like that. I mean that's the way—that's the way I've gone into these things. (*faster*) I don't know whether that's right or not. Once I—once I know my enemy more or less, I (*lower*) can take my precautions against him. The—this—I—I—I've—I just haven't been able to hit anything. (C: uh-hum) There's nothing that even comes into my mind except that it's too much, and I'd like to get away from it. (*pause*)

C 9. You're indicating that *it* is too much. I wonder if you've arrived at any conclusions as to what that is? You did mention that there was a test that bothered you quite a bit.

S 9. Well, the test is something that bothered me. Except that I had to prepare for it. (C: uh-huh) And the subject was a little trite and oh, a lot of time was spent on things which weren't too important. (*lower*) And people would agree with me on that. But (*pause*) it just seems like I—I have to put so much more into things like that—than I feel I should have to put into to have it make sense. (*very low at end*) I spent too much time, way too much time on this thing. And everything else. It seems like I just put everything I have more or less, everything I can give it at the time, anyway, I put everything I have into everything I do. And it doesn't seem to be productive. Even—I try hard and nothing happens.

C 10. You're wearing yourself out and not getting any results that you'd expect.

S 10. Yeah. And then that—this feeling today, just in any situation in the present time gives me (*sigh*) fears for the future, because then again I'll be trying for something, and if I just keep trying and trying, and never get any place (*little laugh*) what's the use of trying? That's just the general feeling I get. (*pause*) And you can just knock yourself out so long and then you stop trying.

C 11. You start asking yourself if it's worth it.

S 11. Yeah and if it squares up with just exactly what you're getting out of it, and it's not (*louder*) school work either because (*clears throat*) I—I think I've more or less passed that stage, where school work is getting me down.

C 12. Uh-hum.

S 12. I'm learning something. I've learned a lot, and I'm enjoying it again. I'm back to that stage. (*short pause*) But I don't know— I seem to differentiate learning and tests. I can go in, and a person lectures, and enjoy it and feel I'm getting something out of it and reading the text too. And when it comes on the test and I—I don't (*pause*) (*low*) feel I've done anything.

C 13. You have sort of a kind of special reaction to the testing.

S 13. It seems that lately I have. I don't remember that I'm at ... (*lost*) but generally I have— (*pause*). Even looking over tests, I even go and do such stupid things as saying, "These questions are ambiguous," and making all sorts of rationalizations about it, but I know that even if they had been any other way, I would have come out the same way. As you said, dead feeling. I can't say any more about it. (*long pause*) And I had the idea that if I could just stop worrying about what's going to happen and take care of today that it might ease up—ease up a little bit.

C 14. Maybe that would be the place for us to *start*, to talk more about your worries about what might happen. That seems to ˙ be the thing that's got you going around.

Mr. Wis responds to the counselor's interpretation of his efforts by trying to justify them in S 8, but ends up by reiterating his feeling of being overwhelmed by his problems. The counselor tries to deflect him into responding to his present feeling, but for some reason does not stop at leaving it as a relatively open question and points more specifically to the topic of tests. This precipitates considerable discussion of the client's feelings about his tests. One could not help wondering a little bit about the reactions indicated in S 13. To what extent are they directed at the counselor? There is the possibility that indirectly he is also saying that he has been blaming the counselor for the types of questions he asks and at the same time blaming himself. Again in C 14 the counselor attempts to give him a new task based on his last comment and the interview continues.

S 14. (*sigh*) Well, I know what I want as far as that goes. The idea that I mightn't be able to get exactly what I want distresses me. (*pause*) Grad school and some sort of a future. And you know the general picture for grad school now doesn't look very good. And my grades aren't too good, and this special thing right now isn't making them any better. That should—it seems to be adding more coal to the whole thing. And I thought about having to go out and look for work next June. That I don't mind working but—I sat down and I tried to figure out just exactly what I could do to go out in a job situation. About the only thing I—the only thing I could see is pick and shovel work or some manual work, because I don't have enough psychology to do anything with—perhaps some counseling job or something like that. (*clears throat*) And liberal arts training isn't too much help from what I've seen and from what I've heard, and I have no experience in anything but more or less manual labor flunky job. I had that in the summertime. So that again is depressing. Because I can't see any future in it. I'm just—I know I'm making it more than it should be, I mean I'm just painting a blacker picture than what I ordinarily should but this is the way things stack up right now and (*lower*) I can't do anything to change it. (*pause*)

C 15. You seem to have almost an all or none conception of the job possibilities—that you get something real fine or you are left at the ditch-digging level.

S 15. Yeah, (*clears throat*) but maybe the jobs which I could get may be office work and routine and monotony, oh, file clerk I think is the best example of something like that. And I'd go batty with something like that. (*pause*) And I don't—just don't see how in four years I'm going to use anything I've learned in school. This is the way I feel now. I don't know. It's a whole picture of a messed-up situation. I can't even get it out.

C 16.   You seem to get pretty anxious about everything that isn't settled, everything that isn't decided. (*short pause*)

S 16.   That's something I've noticed more and more. I don't say I'm doing it more and more but I'm more and more aware of it. I can go into a new situation without everything planned out for me, but there are a lot of things which I like to have down pat, and to know when (*lower*) the next step is going to be. (*pause*) I thought that maybe my early days could explain that— would be some partial explanation for that. I didn't know what was going to happen the next day. It was just an extreme in that way. Now I have to know, otherwise I just don't feel I can go on. And maybe it doesn't apply but it doesn't mean anything. (*lower*) It doesn't hit home. (*pause*) It's depressing. I don't know what else I can say.

C 17.   Looks as though something is kind of missing here, that we have this picture of the way you've been feeling the last week or so, and yet it doesn't seem to have, well, any really meaningful connection with anything that you're really concerned about, more a vague kind of thing.

S 17.   Just the future, that's about all. (*pause*) Are you suggesting that there is something else that—this could—just couldn't come up by itself?

C 18.   Well, I guess that what I'm implying is that this must have some connection with many other things that you and I have talked about. It simply isn't an isolated feeling. But there must be some relationship to the whole rest of our discussion of what it is that's been worrying you this year. (*short pause*)

S 18.   I've thought along those lines and just aside from the fact that I had insecurity before and don't want anything like that now, that's the only tie I can make between them. (*pause*) What do I do? (*little laugh*) (*pause*)

C 19.   Well, of course, one thing that we do in a spot like this is that I can make a guess as to what the connection might be and we could scrap over that awhile, and see if that (S: yeah) has a bearing on it.

S 19.   We've got to do something here.

C 20.   (*laugh*) You're thinking that we'll have to react to this situation somehow

S 20. Well, (*clears throat*) it is just like something standing out in the middle of nowhere. You have to fill in some of the details around it and even if you just make a stab it may not be the right principles. I guess something like a black mark in a big wide open space.

C 21. Uh-hum.

S 21. That's the way I picture it. W-w-what was the guess?

The new tack offered by the counselor leads to a new burst of expression and communication from the client but again primarily to reiterate and underline his lost condition. Everywhere he turns it looks black. In C 16 the counselor tries to give more point to his remarks by suggesting that things look black to the client when he faces questions that haven't been settled yet. Mr. Wis admits this is true and goes on to say that it is something he has become more and more aware of, but turns again into the purely rational isolating kind of tying to some vaguely unspecified earlier experience and himself admits that it doesn't mean anything and again grinds to a halt. The counselor suggests there must be some answer to this inability to perceive something more specific than the client has been mentioning; Mr. Wis infers that the counselor perhaps sees something and there ensues one of those familiar little situations where the client tries to draw out the counselor, trying to get him to communicate his perceptions. In C 19 the counselor expresses ambivalence about communicating his idea, suggesting that he really is not very certain of it and that anyway revealing his hunch would only bring about resistance on the part of the client. But the client persists, assuring the counselor that this is better than leaving him in his present state. Counselors vary in what they would do in this situation. Some would not even have hinted that they had any perception and in any event would have refused to introduce their perception into the situation, whereas others would not hesitate to do so.

Let us see what our present counselor does.

C 22. Well, it's merely a matter of my attempting to think of this in relation to all the rest of the process of talking things through that you and I have gone about the past several months and it seemed to me that last time you were centering quite a lot on the whole general issue of your reaching the place where you felt that you needed to become a little more independent from your relatives, particularly your mother, that it was time for you to kind of be more on your own. And now today you come in and start talking about feeling pretty anxious about the future. Now I was wondering if maybe there is a connection between this—these efforts on your part to become more independent and at the same time becoming more concerned about, well, where is this going to lead me? Where is my life taking me? That kind of problem?

S 22.   I've just realized the other times I've had this feeling and one was when I was just about to graduate from high school, and the other time was after I'd gotten out of the navy and I was applying to various schools and my—nothing was settled.

C 23.   Uh-hum. (*pause*) It's sort of a reaction to being pushed out on your own.

S 23.   Yeah. (*clears throat*) There again I had the same reaction that everything was too much or that I either was going to get a good job or I was going to be a ditch-digger. That's the same thing again. I didn't realize that. (*pause*) Would that be—it almost seems to me as though I don't want to go out on my own. I liked the school—mother, navy—mother, whatever mother I had.

C 24.   You're kind of facing the fact that there are satisfactions in staying within these more limited situations, that is, where you can be a little more dependent.

S 24.   That's something I've been aware of. I—it's nothing new to me, and when I was faced with my discharge I—I—I felt a little jittery because now I'm going out into the world and I won't have anyone to tell me when to get up and go to bed. Although I resented those things, but still that amount of security which I wanted, I guess I needed it too. (*pause*) Well, it's just like a kid. You give him a pair of skates and tell him to go out skating. Just like that, and (*clears throat*) (*lower*) he'll have a rough time. He may hurt himself so bad he won't want to try again. My old pessimism comes back where I always expect the worst. (*little laugh*) (*short pause*)

C 25.   You have a lot of pretty strong feelings about *not* venturing out on your own. That is, you get pretty scared as to what possibilities might come up.

S 25.   Yeah, the possibilities and how I'd react to them and how people would react to me. (*pause*) I've had so many experiences where—. Like last summer, I had tried a few different jobs. My inexperience and my complete lack of knowledge for what was

going on. I just couldn't fit myself into those pieces of equipment. So I ran into ditches and I scraped up the highway and
ripped up pieces of highway (*lower*) and one thing and another.
And (*louder*) well, then they gave me the shovel detail and I
spent most of the summer with a shovel in my hand. And
there again I tried and despite all my efforts I would end up
back there with the box cover and shovel. It's just something
which seems to have repeated over and over again. It seems
to be—seems to give me reason to worry about the future. I say,
"Look, now see what happened there? Now see what happens
here. You try your best and you still don't get any place. What
can you expect?" It's the same thing over and over again.
(*pause*)

We see that the counselor has chosen to communicate his perception, and this leads to a burst of activity on the part of the
client. He now begins to specify events in the past which illustrate
the same kind of reaction as he is having at the present and to
amplify and pull together various aspects of his feelings. He has
become more aware of his negative feelings toward independence.

(In the rest of this interview and the remaining ones—there
were twenty altogether—Mr. Wis continued to move toward a
fuller understanding of the complexity of his feelings about dependence and independence and their connection to his inability
to work up to his capacity.)

In this chapter we have tried to establish some foundation of
common experience in actual interviews which can serve as the
basis for our future discussions. The heart of the therapeutic
process is the ability to be sensitive in the fullest possible way to
the reactions of clients and to one's own reactions to them. In
addition to serving as a basis for future discussions, this introduction to the interpersonal process of counseling focuses on the
type of sensitivity the student must strive for as part of translating
intellectual understanding into the concrete execution of counseling functions.

Part II

THEORETICAL FOUNDATIONS

PSYCHOLOGICAL COUNSELING is herein treated as the application of a general theory of psychotherapy to the special conditions and purposes which surround this particular enterprise. Therefore, a general review of psychotherapeutic theories and their applications to counseling is undertaken. Then our own integration of these different positions is defined and elaborated in terms of the aspects of interpersonal relationships which make them therapeutic.

CHAPTER 4

An Analysis of Theories

In the preceding chapter we had an opportunity to compare several counselors and their ways of contributing to a client's efforts to grapple with his problems. We were able to note many differences. We not only found that one counselor will differ from other counselors, but that the same counselor will often vary in his modes of interaction from one client to another. Counselors also vary in the effectiveness of their help from one client to another. The extent to which variations in counselors and in their effectiveness is a function of their particular theoretical orientation is still a moot question. There is not yet available any compelling evidence that makes possible an estimate of the relative importance to his therapeutic effectiveness of a counselor's theories on the one hand and of his personality on the other. This is one underlying issue in counseling; and the other is how closely counseling behavior corresponds to theory and whether it is possible to produce consistency of the two through either group or individual didactic experiences.

An ingenious series of studies by Fiedler (1950a, 1950b, 1951) has often been taken to support the hypothesis that the therapist's attitude toward the patient, not his theory or technique, makes the relationship therapeutic. In this series of studies Fiedler asked therapists to sort a series of statements into piles indicating degree of correspondence to their concept of an ideal relationship. He demonstrated that experienced therapists with different orientations—Adlerian, orthodox analytic, and nondirective—had concepts of the ideal therapeutic relationship which resembled each other more closely than they resembled those of inexperienced therapists with the same therapeutic orientation. Further, it was found that when observers were asked to sort the statements into piles indicating degree of correspondence to therapists' behavior, after listening to recorded interviews, again experienced therapists of different orientations resembled each other more than they resembled inexperienced therapists within their own orientation. Unfortunately, this question cannot be tested in this way, except as an artifact of the method of measurement. Whether one gets great or small differences between the therapeutic orientations depends on the number and kinds of statements selected. If one were to select only those statements about which theories are in disagreement, then there would be little or no agreement between expert therapists who represent the theories and, conversely, almost perfect agreement could also be obtained. On the other hand, if one made no particular effort to identify in advance items which therapists of different theoretical orientations agreed or disagreed with, and simply tried to think of as many items as possible which were descriptive of therapeutic behavior, it seems likely that the easiest statements to write and therefore the greatest number judged would refer to those issues about which theorists do not disagree and are likely to be present in the behavior of the naive, inexperienced therapist. Perhaps this is the set Fiedler chose and accounts for his results. In any event, the number of statements over which there is disagreement cannot be taken as an index of the importance of the disagreement, which is the way Fiedler's results have been interpreted. A disagreement over one statement may refer to an aspect of therapy which is important to its outcome. Therefore, we must conclude that Fiedler has not supplied an answer to the question of the importance to be attached to differences among theories of psychotherapy.

Whether or not a valid psychotherapeutic theory could in itself make counselors more effective, analysis of therapeutic theories is necessary for understanding therapeutic phenomena, the variation among counselors, and their variable effectiveness with clients. In this chapter we shall confine ourselves to reviewing theories of counseling or psychotherapy as they apply to the counseling task. There are many nuances of Freudian theory and of neo-Freudian theory which will not be referred to. This does not mean that it is not worth the student's while to cover the therapeutic literature comprehensively. On the contrary, we believe that the therapist's need for intellectual stimulation, for the opportunity to look at his basic data from as many vantage points as possible, is insatiable. On the other hand, when it comes to dealing with the emotions and their complexities, analysis and discussion cannot proceed effectively in advance of building up stores of experience in therapeutic situations, out of which analysis obtains fuller meaning. All too frequently students of therapy, when they rush ahead into its formal and intellectual aspects, are limited to acquiring a rote understanding and acquaintance with different points of view and subtheories. Their understanding is so superficial they cannot even recognize concrete referrents of theoretical concepts when they come face to face with them in actual situations. Therefore, we shall be temperate in our introduction of theory and in this way try to avoid the Scylla of over-intellectualized understanding and the Charybdis of shapeless conviction.

THEORIES EMPHASIZING INSTRUMENTAL BEHAVIOR

As we suggested in Chapter 1, there seem to be two rather broadly oriented ways of looking at human behavior. One of these is to adopt a relatively uncomplicated conception of human motivations and goals and to assume that the big problem in living happier lives is to learn the best ways of achieving this goal. As we look at people in problem situations from this point of view, we assume that things are as they seem. People are motivated either to avoid some form of punishment, such as academic failure or public censure, or to achieve some reward, such as being in the top ten of the class or getting the girl. A student fails to achieve his goal because he lacks certain information or skill. His lack of information has led him to choose a particular curiculum which is not in accord with his own abilities. He either has misjudged his abilities or he has misjudged the demands of the curriculum. In some cases he just has not seen the logical connections between certain information and the types of goals he is setting for himself.

This is a very easy and natural point of view to take when one is dealing with relatively well-adjusted people trying to decide about some very specific aspects of their lives. Decisions about education, vocation, and marriage do involve securing information if one alternative or another is to be chosen. The information may be about prerequisite skills or abilities or answers to questions about the influence of personality or other factors on eventual outcomes. Thus, some counselors who deal with people faced with these decisions have tended to become immersed in the informational aspects of the decisions. Williamson has often been seen as the main advocate of this conception of people's difficulties and the functions counselors can perform in helping people.

In Williamson's treatments of counseling (1939, 1947, 1950) we find a very definite emphasis on the counselor's information-giving functions. For Williamson, diagnosis is the effort to decide whether or not a person is operating on misinformation as he proceeds in his decision-making. Thus he is likely to speak of "diagnosing a client's aptitudes," which means finding out whether his level of abilities is consonant with some contemplated choice of curricular training or vocation.

Although he approaches counseling with much more eclecticism, Thorne (1950) is another who gives considerable attention to aiding clients to acquire the information or skills necessary to the mastery of problem situations or in the process of decision-making. He gives considerable attention to a variety of methods of maximizing the intellectual resources of clients. He calls attention to the potential usefulness to the layman of psychological facts and principles, and discusses techniques of teaching reality-testing methods, of improving voluntary control, and of improving thinking through applications of semantic analysis.

An even stricter emphasis on the instrumental act is found in efforts to apply learning theory and methods derived from experimental psychology to counseling and psychotherapy which have received increasing attention in the last decade. Most of these applications have been taken from either Hull (1943) or Skinner (1953, 1957) and of course, originally from Pavlov. One of the most clinically active proponents of the applications of learning theory has been Wolpe (1958), who championed a set of methods which he groups under the "principle of reciprocal inhibition." The clinical applications of Skinner's ideas regarding the shaping of behavior tend to be concentrated in work on language development and mutism in children and adults (Lovass, 1965; Salzinger, Portnay, & Feldman, 1966), usually involving very regressed states. These competing theories of learning are bound together by their common rejection of the kinds of inner determinants of behavior that characterize dynamic positions. Each act, or series of acts forming a unit, is treated as independently determined and subject to external control by manipulating the external conditions of reinforcement. The concepts of centrally organized networks of behaviors and motives and the associated notions of core conflicts and derivative symptoms are denied.

Therapeutic Implications. The inevitable truncation of concern with affective factors which characterizes an instrumentally oriented view is balanced by a searching attention to the specificities of behavior (Krumboltz, 1966). Specific situations in which the individual experiences difficulty and which frequently make up the content of his orientation toward change are examined minutely. Information or skills needed for a more effective response are identified and actions taken to transmit them.

As represented by earlier proponents, such as Williamson, this view does concern itself with the methods of keeping the client motivated to learn, of keeping him from becoming discouraged, and with showing him that he is irrational when he evinces any rejection of the information or skills he needs. The clinically sophisticated form of this position does not deny, for the most part, the reality of the client's emotional and motivational forces toward irrationality. On the contrary, it advocates employing those means by which people can be aided to be realistic and rational. In many cases the methods used apply principles of learning derived from the acquisition of cognitive materials (Darley, 1950). It could be argued that an increased emphasis upon intellectual and discriminative capacities is a necessary antidote to overpreoccupation with the impulsive side of behavior, a trend which has come in the wake of the ascendance of Freudian and neo-Freudian theories of personality. On the other hand, the very development of ego psychology (e.g., Hartman, 1964) suggests that the balance is being redressed within the Freudian point of view.

Among the proponents of a more self-conscious application of learning theories, who have taken to referring to themselves as "behavior therapists," Wolpe proceeds in a manner resembling earlier representatives. The main difference is that his remedies for establishing more effective responses concentrate on inhibiting the response of anxiety which he accomplishes by suggesting or inducing responses contradictory to anxiety, e.g., relaxation. There are two important features of this method, only one of which is stressed by Wolpe. That is the method of desensitization whereby the substitution process gradually arises within a hierarchy of situations involving the particular class of anxious responses. The unstressed part of Wolpe's method is the patient's active collaboration after what is being done and why is explained to him.

The methods stemming largely from Skinner's views usually involve a passive collaboration by the patient. In their most extreme statement (Krasner, 1962), the therapist is seen as a dispenser of reinforcements via his verbal responses, "a reinforcing machine," and his client or patient as an unthinking, unreflecting organism to be acted upon. More typically, however, as illustrated by the work of Lovass (1965) with severely regressed children, the therapist is seen as the inheritor, via generalization and the development of social reinforcement, of the reinforcing power inherent in the parent-child relationship. Within the counseling framework, applications of these methods have as yet been largely limited to experimental demonstrations, using mass recruited subjects (e.g., Ryan, & Krumboltz, 1964; Krumboltz, & Thoresen, 1964).

THEORIES EMPHASIZING THE DYNAMIC ASPECTS OF BEHAVIOR

The word *dynamic* has been used so freely and so frequently for hortatory rather than descriptive purposes that it has begun to lose some of its specific meaning. We use it to refer to those views of behavior which consider behavior a product of an inter-woven pattern of forces, a pattern that undergoes continual modi-fication. The dynamic view of behavior emphasizes that successive experiences have the effect not only of accumulating information and other instrumental behavior potentials, but also of modifying and reorganizing the emotional life and the motivational demands of the individual. In comparison with the emphasis on the instru-mental aspects of behavior, the dynamic view treats goals as more complex phenomena. People's goals are not always what they appear to be on the surface. At the simplest level, a person may appear to be in a situation from which he would be motivated to withdraw. This person may tell us that the only feeling he is aware of is that of wanting to avoid some kind of experience, and to a certain extent he may seem to give the impression that he is exerting himself to avoid the situation. Yet the dynamic view, taking into account his life history and certain assumptions about the ways in which various goals affect each other, can discover reasons for asserting that he is subject to a more domi-nant and stronger need to come in contact with the very experi-ence he says he wants to avoid. Many cases of repeated failure in certain enterprises or of repeated rejection by other persons may reflect motivations to experience exactly those ordinarily avoided outcomes.

This brief reference is, of course, a simplified statement of Freud's tremendous contribution to behavior theory and more particularly to personality theory, a contribution with an influ-ence so widespread that no area of psychological theory is immune to its effects. Even those who consider themselves non-Freudians or anti-Freudians adopt some of his fundamental concepts. On the other hand, there is enough variability among those whose basic assumptions might be classed as dynamic to warrant considering some of these variations and their relationships to counseling.

Orthodox analytic views

Freudian personality theory is so complex that we cannot hope to present it here. We shall assume that the reader is already acquainted with it or recommend that he become so if he has a serious interest in psychological counseling or psychotherapy. Our discussion will summarize those aspects of Freudian personality theory which are most directly related to Freudian therapeutic theory. We shall neither attempt a detailed outline of the schematic concept of personality structure represented by the concepts of ego, superego, and id (Freud, 1949), nor shall we discuss the intricacies of the theories of the stages of psychosexual development and their relation to psychopathology (Fenichel, 1945).

The representative Freudian view is that the personality structure of the individual, the types of goals that he consciously sets for himself, and the methods by which he deals with the interpersonal aspects of achieving these goals are a systematic outgrowth of two factors. One is that each person learns early in life that the unbridled expression of his impulses[1] leads to disintegrating experiences, so that he then must learn ways to protect himself against these disintegrating experiences and against fear of them. The second principle is that insofar as impulse represents energy, the expression of impulse cannot be completely blocked, but only modified. The ego refers to the organization of cognitive processes which develop in response to the individual's efforts to discriminate those conditions under which it is safe to express his impulses and those conditions under which his impulse expression must be modified. Self-protection becomes to a considerable extent a process of protecting against the destructive and disintegrative forces of fear involved in the expression of impulses. This, according to the theory, results in the development of various ways of reducing anxiety which are called defense mechanisms.[2] Defense against anxiety may take many forms. Where the impulse is relatively weak, it may be possible to block expression by behavior designed to distract attention from stimuli likely to tempt expression of the impulse. When the impulse is strong, blocking expression becomes impossible and defensive behavior is designed to effect a compromise by reducing awareness of the true meaning

[1] Psychoanalytic theory uses the term *impulse* in a special sense to refer only to native, presumably biologically linked, sources of motivation. These are the motives which can release energy at its source; all other motives, those associated with preparing for expression of impulse or with retarding or forestalling expression, make use of energy derived from the impulse. Thus, the psychoanalyst speaks of "confluctual impulses" rather than "conflicting impulses" when he is referring to an impulse which is surrounded by many motives to retard or forestall its expression.

[2] See Anna Freud (1946) for a more extended discussion of defense mechanisms.

of the impulse through disguising the aim of the behavior or through distorting one's perception or both. Thus it can be seen that the concept of defense is intimately connected with the concept of the unconscious.

The individual first experiences the negative effects of unbridled impulse expression in interaction with his parents or parental surrogates. Therefore, his anxieties and modes of defending himself against anxiety will be manifest in interpersonal relationships, particularly with his parents or other persons who share any of their distinguishing characteristics. This potentially satisfying or threatening relationship with parents is present at various developmental stages of potential impulse satisfaction. The mother plays an important role in the infant's successive concentration on its nourishment-taking and waste-eliminating satisfactions. Later, she is a factor in the child's attitude toward continence. Parents are factors in the development of the infant's capacity to experience mature love relationships. In essence, parents serve as the original sources of external environmental stimulation which permit a satisfactory culmination of impulse expression, or they behave toward the child in such a way as to create anxiety. Often, as in the case of internalized standards or prohibitions, the stimuli are no longer the parents themselves but are their intrapsychic equivalents. However, in this case, as in most others, they still have their interpersonal referents as well, since it is assumed that internalized standards result from introjection and identification with parental figures. Throughout, the defenses the individual develops are organized around his relationships with people.

Therapeutic Implications. From the Freudian point of view, a therapeutic process is one in which the individual gives up his efforts to keep his impulses from awareness and begins to react to situations, principally people, in terms of their present demands rather than as though they were repeating demands made upon him in his infancy. The Freudian hypothesis is that if these defenses developed when most of the individual's behavior was on a nonverbal level, and when these impulses are surrounded by the greatest anxiety, provoking the most rigid defensive reactions, giving up the defenses can proceed only under conditions of transference. By transference Freud means that the patient must react to the therapist as if he represented some important figure in the patient's early life, and not in terms of the therapist's own characteristics. The psychoanalytic therapist uses transference as an important form of support which enables the patient to proceed with his impulse expression, to face feelings he has been avoiding, and, more importantly, to become aware of them as they are being expressed toward the therapist in this unrealistic fashion. Thus the psychoanalytic therapist assumes that the unconscious cannot be made conscious except through the medium of transference.

Classical psychoanalytic therapy assumes that the patient's problem, his needs to distort his world and to keep his impulses from awareness, will become evident when he attempts to communicate with the therapist. Therefore, the psychoanalyst defines the patient's task as communicating any and all thoughts which come to his mind during the course of the therapeutic hour. He makes it clear that all the usual social taboos applied to thoughts are not supposed to apply during the session. "Free association" is the basic rule for the patient in psychonalysis: "Tell me whatever comes to your mind."

The psychoanalyst does not assume that free association will in fact be free. He assumes that the patient's desire to get well will motivate him to strive to talk freely but that as the patient's thoughts begin to approach strongly defended impulses, defensive behavior patterns will appear to block or distort communication. This is what the psychoanalyst means by resistance. *Resistance is the reflection of the patient's inability to deal directly, realistically, and constructively with his impulses as they appear during the process of therapy.* Resistance is the appearance of the defensive ego barring progress in the therapeutic task.

Inevitably, as a function of their extended personal relationship, the patient's unconsummated impulses, whether aggressive or loving, will center on the therapist. They center on him not because he is lovable or anger-provoking, but because the patient has so much pent-up need to express anger or love. The reader will recall that the theory presupposes that temptation or partial expression of forbidden impulses will be accompanied by anxiety and the need to defend against it. Consequently, it follows that the patient directs toward the therapist not only his pent-up anger or love impulses but also the defensive reactions to the anxiety associated with these impulses. So transference, which refers to these intrapsychic determined reactions to the therapist, inevitably becomes a part of the resistance process.

When the analyst uses the term *interpretation,* he refers to his own communications to the patient designed to call attention to unconscious aspects and determinants of the patient's behavior. The primary referent of the analyst's interpretation is the patient's resistance to the therapeutic task. He reveals the patient's inability to comply with the basic rule. He points to the feelings that are associated with this noncompliance and to what the patient is gaining in the way of reduced anxiety through noncompliance. He calls attention to the incompatibility of resistance with the patient's ultimate purpose in seeking therapy. He counts upon the patient's decision that the ultimate goal of therapy is more important than the momentary reduction in anxiety which resistance can provide. This decision will lead the patient to seek ways to overcome his own resistance.

One of the common misconceptions of psychoanalytic theory centers around the appropriate depth of the analyst's interpretations. Depth of interpretation refers to the gap between the patient's awareness of some aspects of his feelings or behavior and the therapist's communication of his view of these feelings or behavior. If the therapist's description corresponds exactly with the patient's awareness, then it is the shallowest interpretation. When the therapist's interpretation corresponds least to the patient's awareness, it is the deepest interpretation. It is often assumed that because his goals are to bring to awareness the patient's deeply repressed impulses, the analyst proceeds through a process of deep interpretation. Contrast this misconception with what Fenichel says of interpretation: "We interpret, as is well known, what is already in the preconscious—and just a *little bit more*— which thereby becomes capable of entering consciousness" (Fenichel, 1941: p. 53). Deep material is brought to consciousness not by deep interpretation, but by more shallow interpretations of derivatives of repressed impulses which are already nearly conscious. As these less deeply repressed derivatives are brought to awareness, other distorted derivatives of the repressed impulse come closer to consciousness and are in turn the object of interpretation. This process continues until the undistorted experience of the impulse is brought to light. If the psychoanalytic therapist behaves in accordance with this theory, his interpretations will not become deeper as therapy progresses. Instead, they will tend to remain on a relatively constant level—at the surface "and slightly more."

In the eyes of the psychoanalytically oriented therapist, psychological counseling is a much more limited form of therapeutic treatment than psychoanalysis. It does not aim to bring unconscious infantile conflicts to the surface and resolve them. It is concerned rather with the ways in which these conflicts appear in conscious or preconscious actions. Psychological counseling attempts to bring to awareness those aspects of infantile conflicts which are already close to awareness and are not deeply threatening to the ego. In counseling, increased insight into ego defenses is won through the counselor's interpretation of omissions, contradictions, denials, forgetfulness, and so on, as these occur in the client's story. In such a process the client is able to approach his situation more realistically, to abate some of his tendencies toward self-defense, and to become more effective in controlling the distorting effects of his infantile conflicts. Although the counselor makes use of transference elements in his client's reactions, unlike the analyst he does not encourage an intense, consuming, transference reaction. He may make use of positive transference, but does relatively little interpreting of it.

As Blos (1946) has pointed out, the psychoanalytically-oriented counselor does not consider this kind of treatment appropriate for all clients. He holds that this treatment is appropriate for those persons who are experiencing relatively fluid reactions to the emergence of a specific infantile conflict and that it is inappropriate for the person who has already established a relatively rigid neurotic pattern. This seems quite comparable to the conceptions of psychological counseling discussed in Chapter 1, where we stated that it is most appropriate for those persons who have attained a fairly high degree of emotional maturity and integration.

Client-centered theory

The central theme of client-centered theory is the individual's need for self-maintenance and self-actualization, or self-enhancement. Rogers, in his most complete statement of his personality theory (1951: Ch. 11; 1959), speaks of the tendency of organisms to maintain themselves physiologically and psychologically. He calls this the single "directional force in organic life." However, this is not a negative force directed solely at survival. Rogers takes the view that each organism exhibits the directional tendency to actualize itself by greater differentiation of organs and function. This self-actualization takes the form of increasing self-government, self-regulation, and autonomy.

In his postulation of a directional force and of response systems organized around that directional force, Rogers stamps his theory as dynamic. The individual's phenomenal field is defined as including all that is being experienced whether or not consciously perceived. The self is a portion of this phenomenal field which the organism perceives as its locus and to which values become attached. The self-structure is seen as:

. . . an organized configuration of perceptions of the self which are admissible to awareness. It is composed of such elements as the perceptions of one's characteristics and abilities; the percepts and concepts of the self in relation to others and to the environment; the value qualities which are perceived as associated with experiences and objects; and the goals and ideals which are perceived as having positive or negative valence. (Rogers, 1951: p. 501)

Like the Freudians, Rogers stresses a process by which experiences are denied to awareness. Very early, he points out, the child discovers that many satisfying experiences are disapproved by his parents with an accompanied threat of withdrawal of love. This leads to distortions in his perceptions of parents and denials to awareness of the satisfactions experienced. When parental disapproval of a specific act does not entail a basic lack of acceptance of the child, it is possible for him to deal with the experience in a realistic and undistorted way. The "self" is an organized, fluid, but consistent pattern of perceptions of characteristics and relationship of the "I" or the "me." This organized set of perceptions of self, in addition to realistic ones, may include twisted images of parents and misrepresented awareness of one's own behavior or experience.

Rogers uses the terms *psychological adjustment* and *maladjustment* to refer to the degree to which significant behavior and experience have been assimilated in distorted form into the system of self-perception or denied to awareness. Every person feels pressure to maintain his self-consistency. The more experience is denied to awareness, the greater the difficulty in maintaining a consistent self-concept, with the result that eventually functional illness or other neurotic symptoms may develop as ways of satisfying needs which must be denied to awareness in order to maintain self-consistency. Experiences which are inconsistent with the self-structure are seen as threats and are responded to with increased rigidity of the self-concept. Under conditions of freedom from threat, the self-structure becomes more permeable and more modifiable. Where there is no threat, inconsistent experiences are more likely to be perceived for what they are, and after examination the structure of self may be revised to assimilate and include such experiences.

Perhaps an illustration will help to make Rogers' reasoning more concrete. An athletically inept son of parents who set great store by athletic prowess may cling with pathetic intensity to an image of himself as a potentially accomplished sportsman when he feels, either realistically or unrealistically, that his parents' affection is at stake. However, if he finds that he can retain his desired relationship with his parents even after disappointing them in this way, he may more readily accept the evidence of his poor athletic ability.

Therapeutic Implications. Unlike psychoanalytic theory, client-centered therapeutic formulations seem to assume that the process and goals are the same for all patients or clients. Whether the client-centered therapist is dealing with an essentially normal youngster whose symptom is vocational indecision, a person with a psychosomatic complaint, or an early schizophrenic, he proceeds in the same general fashion.

Since he holds that a permissive, nonthreatening relationship will enable the client to begin to examine repressed experiences, this therapist strives to attain such a relationship. In early client-centered writings and research we find emphasis placed on procedures specifically designed to permit the client to assume responsibility for the direction taken by his communications and for his life decisions. Porter (1943), for example, distinguishes between nondirective leads which force the client to choose the topic for discussion, for example, "How would you like to use your time today?" or "Would you like to tell me more about it?" from directive leads which probe for specific information, for example, "How did you and your brother get along?" As communication with the patient proceeds, the therapist tends to confine his responses to restating or clarifying attitudes directly and immediately expressed. Any interpretive effort which tries to go beyond what is the client's present awareness (compare Fenichel's "what is preconscious and a little bit more") represents to this therapist an effort to impose upon the patient an alien view of himself. According to nondirective theory, such a move represents a threat which will be met with rigidity and therefore resistance. Thus we see that unlike psychoanalytic theory, which views resistance as not only inevitable but also necessarily part of the therapeutic process, nondirective theory sees resistance in the counseling situation as the consequence of misdirected therapeutic effort. If the therapist will but avoid trying to guide the patient, to evaluate his feelings and behavior, and instead concentrate on accepting him, resistance can be avoided. True, the patient cannot so quickly be certain that he can rely upon the therapist not to force experiences upon him. He will have to test the therapist's acceptance many times in many different ways. As therapy progresses, the need to test diminishes and the patient becomes freer to examine previously repressed experiences and to struggle with the painful process of assimilating them.

Rogers' current writings place less stress upon specific behavior of the therapist and more upon the therapist's attitudes. More and more stress is placed upon "understanding," which means getting inside the client's frame of reference, seeing his phenomenal world as he sees and experiences it. The more fully the therapist can concentrate his efforts on understanding him, the more certain the patient can be of his accepting attitude.[3]

When he discusses transference, which plays such a central part in psychoanalytic conceptions of therapy, Rogers takes the position that it is not necessary for therapeutic progress. He admits that transference reactions are sometimes exhibited by patients of nondirective therapists, but he claims that they are less frequent and generally not as intense in cases handled by the methods he advocates. Rogers' position is that when transference

[3] For the most comprehensive discussion of this topic see Rogers, 1951: Ch. 2.

attitudes are accepted like any other attitude, they are not likely to present any special problem. He argues that the interpretive and evaluative behavior which he attributes to psychoanalytic therapists facilitates a "dependent transference." At this point Rogers seems to be equating transference with a positive transference and with dependence. Psychoanalysts would probably deny the accuracy of this equation.[4]

The Rankian view

The contributions of Otto Rank are of particular interest to us here because of their influence on Rogers and because they have led to a widely held point of view among social case workers. Taft and Allen, two of Rank's major American interpreters, have contributed a much more detailed conception than Rogers of the psychological growth process and the pressures on the individual for self-actualization. However, it is important to note that a pressure toward regression is also stressed in this theory. Rank's basic insight was his realization of the influence of the biological events of birth and subsequent biological development on psychological development. Allen traces the full implication of these in the opening chapters of his book *Psychotherapy with Children* (1942). As he points out, the organism, in the biological act of birth, is ejected from its all-need-satisfying environment. This ends the time when the organism will be in such a relationship to another person that its needs are automatically satisfied, if necessary even at the expense of the other person. In pregnancy the mother has relatively little choice between her own needs and the needs of the child.

With the event of birth, the physiological conditions necessary for the child's perception of himself as different from the mother are attained. When, as is inevitable, he experiences frustration of some need which hitherto had been followed by need-satisfying action on the part of the mother, the child must also internalize that his mother is not simply an extension of himself. At the same time the infant also internalizes his own ability to

---

[4] We believe Rogers has reached a correct conclusion but for the wrong reasons. We shall see in Chapter 6 that there is a sound theoretical basis for expecting less transference in client-centered therapy.

do things, to suck in his food, to manipulate objects, to control his eliminative processes, to talk, and to walk. These are the two aspects of the growth process: first, the increasing awareness of one's capacities and their organization to meet one's needs; second, the recognition that one exists as an independent entity possessing common characteristics and common needs with other people and at the same time is different from them and has different needs. These two ideas are epitomized in the twin concepts of integration and differentiation.

The will to be healthy or more generally the will to self-actualization now becomes a much more specific concept. The infant's experience after leaving the uterus makes his own independence and the ability to satisfy his own needs attractive. However, there is another side to the picture. When the organism feels overwhelmed by the demands being made upon it, one of its natural reactions is to attempt to recapture the lost security of its earlier dependent relationship. Then, the will to regress, the desire to remain dependent, even to the extent of wishing for ill health all arise.

Allen believes that people's neurotic difficulties arise from demands made upon them before they have the capacity to meet them adequately. And this threatening state of affairs is made worse for the infant because, correlated with these premature demands, is usually the implication that the other person's love and support will be withheld unless he meets the demand. This fixates the infant on the goal of retaining as much of the other person's love and support as possible, rather than on the positive goal of becoming able to assert and satisfy himself as much as possible. Thus the necessary conditions for the psychological growth process of increasing integration and differentiation are met when parents manage to limit the need-satisfaction of their children at just the time when the children acquire the capacity to satisfy a need themselves—without seeming to put at stake other needs which they still must satisfy for the child. Thus, when the child is ready to leave the breast or the bottle, or to regulate eliminative processes, or walk, or talk, or later goes to school, chooses a vocation, and marries, critical points in the growth process are reached.

The effectiveness with which the individual and his parents

meet these successive challenges has cumulative effects in either a desirable or undesirable direction. The drama of the child's first day in nursery school is re-enacted at each critical point in his development. The child going to nursery school is to some degree facing a rather distinctive separating experience from his mother. As mother and child approach the school, the child, to a degree, fears giving up what he knows—the support and love that his mother gives him. To a degree, he exhibits reluctance and fear, and clings to his mother. The mother's confidence in herself and her child's capacity to deal with the situation are communicated to the child by the gentle firmness with which she carries out her part in taking leave of him, and this enables him to face alone a situation which possibly holds feared frustrating experiences as well as the thrill of realizing that he is not quite as helpless as he thought. At the end of the day as the child's fears have proved unfounded, as he has experienced a new and thrilling experience without his mother's presence and protective hovering, a new relationship is evident when mother and child walk out of school. Perhaps the mother reaches for the child's hand; but momentarily he is so impressed with his ability to get along without her that he must tell her so by withdrawing his hand and insisting that he walk alone. Perhaps he even puts a greater distance between them than has been usual when they were walking together. Soon, however, other situations will arise which he is not yet ready to face up to, and he will creep back into his mother's arms; but also he will retain the effects of this experience in that he will now be looking forward eagerly to the next experience that will show him he has now acquired a new way of becoming independent.

Therapeutic Implications. For Allen, the therapeutic implications of this conceptual scheme are similar to but not identical with those of Rogers. Again the emphasis is upon the immediate relationship to the therapist, upon the individual's feeling in the relationship. It is assumed that the individual will recapitulate the conflict between his drive for independence and his drive for dependence. At specific points he will experience the therapist as not meeting some specific need he feels while still remaining willing to meet many of his other needs. He will realize that he can oppose his own wishes and his own will to that of the therapist and not lose the therapist as a supporting person. It is this very emphasis which leads to a Rankian insistence on the setting of limits as the heart of the therapeutic process. Around the individual's efforts to extend the hour or the child's angry attempt to assault him, it is possible for the therapist to demonstrate to the child or the adult that having limits imposed does not mean a loss of the supporting relationship. The client finds that he can accept certain conditions and still not be overwhelmed, not lose his identity as a person. By being able to accept limitations in his relationship with the therapist, by discovering again and again that, no matter how supporting it may be, a relationship does have limitations, he becomes ready to accept responsibility for himself and all the impulses that are part of him. By being able to accept limitations from others, he becomes capable of imposing limitations upon himself.

Allen's conception of transference and resistance is closer to the orthodox Freudian than to the nondirective position. Like the Freudians, he sees these two phenomena in an intrinsic relationship to therapeutic process. Resistance is the reaction of the child (it is mostly about children that Allen speaks) to the expectation that the therapist is going to do something to him. He reacts to the threat by projecting great power onto the therapist. For some children, the therapist becomes the all-powerful protector who can satisfy all needs, obviating the necessity for growth. For others, the projected power in the therapist becomes a testing ground for the child. "If I can defeat this powerful antagonist, if his efforts to change me can be blocked, then it demonstrates my own power." Both of these reactions are evidences of the child's capacity for growth. They demonstrate that the child has the capacity to oppose his will to that of the therapist. The therapist needs only to understand this need for autonomy and be able to react to it in such a way that this drive can be used positively.

Allen discusses the child's projections of unacceptable aspects of himself upon the therapist in essentially the same terms that Freudians use in discussing transference. Through projection, disowned parts of oneself (the Freudian would say disowned impulses) are objectified in another. When they are placed on him, the therapist is in the strategic position of allowing the projection without becoming "in actuality what the child tries to create in him" (1942: p. 68). This process of projection goes hand in hand with an identification with the therapist which the child must acquire if therapy is to occur. Whatever these unacceptable aspects of himself may be, such as ambitiousness or the feeling of being small and weak, they will color his relationship to the therapist. He may try to make the therapist a critical and demanding person as a way of making him assume responsibility for his own ambition. This process of experiencing oneself through another, after skillful help, leads to differentiating the therapist's real characteristics from those projected on him, stimulates the development of the child's ability either to take back into his self-percept those feelings he can use constructively or to discard the useless ones.

On the other hand, Allen places little emphasis on interpretation. Verbal communication is one of the child's modes of expressing his feelings. Allen warns against being caught up in the content of these communications and losing sight of what the child is actually doing or feeling. He emphasizes the benefits to be derived from the living experience itself, whether through a play relationship or through direct interaction with the therapist. Perhaps the fact that Allen is talking about therapeutic work with children whereas, for the most part, psychoanalysts are talking about work with adults makes the differences over interpretation appear greater than they are. In our earlier discussion of the psychoanalytic concept of the appropriate depth for interpretation, we called attention to the importance attached to staying close to the patient's level of awareness. So much of adult life is embodied in language behavior and so little of the young child's language behavior has been established at this level that it would not be expected to play as important a part in therapy with children. There are also cognitive aspects of interpretation (to be discussed more fully in Chapter 7) which can account for appropriate difference in the role of interpretation between therapy with children and adults. It suffices to say that the differences in cognitive resources cannot help but be important.

Finally, in examining Allen's concepts of the therapeutic process we should note his stress on the positive role of the therapist. The therapist's contribution is not simply a negative one of avoiding the imposition of his will upon the patient and of not becoming what the patient's projections try to make him. He also understands the patient's feelings of weakness, his desires to recapture lost security, and undertakes to serve as support while the patient gathers the courage to strike out for himself. Allen puts it this way:

An extremely neurotic girl of ten, after a two year stalemate with a psychiatrist, made her new therapist, in her first hour, the perfect person, able to do everything that had not been accomplished previously. To the other psychiatrist she ascribed all the danger and all the bad. On to the new therapist she projected the perfection craved for herself. Her need led her to make him an unreal person who would carry all her hopes of the present and future. Through this projection she was trying to get a sense of achievement of perfection in herself and to be rid of her sense of inadequacy without, however, doing much in herself to bring the changes about. *This was necessary, however, as a beginning* (1942: p. 69). (Italics are ours.)

Again, in talking about play activity, he says:

Occasionally there is a place for such games as checkers. This may offer a child a familiar activity which he can carry on with the therapist. It may offer a timid child with few resources an opportunity to do something with the therapist, as in the case of a twelve-year-old girl who found initiating anything almost impossible (1942: p. 133).

Allen does not himself give much attention to the application of his concepts to counseling. However, the functional approach of the Pennsylvania School of Social Work stems from Rankian theory through the influence of Allen and Taft.[5] The issue of taking responsibility for oneself is likely to loom large in the many problem situations and decisions that are brought to the counselor. For the adolescent and adult, the ambivalence about taking help will loom especially large in our society, which emphasizes independence and autonomy.

The Adlerian view

Even though the number of explicitly self-identified Adlerian therapists is relatively small, Adler has considerably enriched the vocabulary we use in describing personality. When we examine the therapeutic implications of his views, we shall see that, in contrast with Rank, he goes to the other extreme of seeming to attach

[5] In addition to Allen, see Taft (1944) and Kasius (1950).

great therapeutic power to therapist-constructed and therapist-induced cognitions.

Adler was not a systematist.[6] Therefore, it is difficult to discern his beliefs clearly. It is clear that he rejected Freud's attachment of central significance to the motive power of sexual impulses. Instead, Adler saw a lifelong and inevitable feeling of inferiority as a major driving force in personality development. Although he gave significance to specific physical defects (organ inferiority), the ubiquity of feelings of inferiority was attributed to the helplessness of the infant and young child in coping with his environment and in his relations with adults. Adler saw a universal tendency to respond to feelings of inferiority by striving for superiority. This becomes a "striving for success," a "seeking for perfection," which is positively expressed as a creative and achieving force. When the child is spoiled and pampered, or neglected by his parents, the negative side of the striving for superiority is exhibited in the form of "fictions" and "arrangements" erected to create and preserve a self-perceived image. Here, Adler uses his other native force, "social interest," through which the ideal of perfection is pursued without pathology and the departures from common sense that are entailed in fictions and arrangements.

Adler introduced the term, "style of life" to give a special thrust to the idea of the unity of personality. "Style of life" refers to persistent patterns of thinking, feeling, and acting, through which an individual seeks security and the feeling of superiority. It is manifested in various situations and in relations with all kinds of persons. Whether or not this "style of life" develops abnormally is attributed principally to the degree to which parents foster the development of social interest. Pampering or neglect are seen as retarding the child's readiness to empathize with others and, eventually, to direct his achievement toward society.

Therapeutic Implications. Since the individual's "style of life" is pervasive, Adler expects it to be manifest in his responses in psychotherapy. Undoubtedly, Adler's ideas contributed to the development within psychoanalysis of ego psychology and its accompanying concepts of character. The diagnostic insights stem-

---

[6] Two carefully selected and annotated selections from his writings by the Ansbachers (1956) and Adler (1964) are very helpful.

ming from Adler's point of view seem to have had a great impact on Adlerian psychotherapy. Very quickly and astutely, out of observations of the patient's initial behavior in psychotherapy, out of many details of family experience, for example, the number of siblings and the patient's position in the birth order, out of the patient's productions in response to such questions as that of his earliest memory, the Adlerian arrives at a formulation regarding the individual's "style of life" and the fictions and arrangements which play a prominent part in it. With this understanding, change is brought about by a gradual process of disclosure of the style to the patient. Although the process is gradual, in the time dimensions of psychoanalysis it would be seen as compressed; the range is in weeks and months instead of years. Along with disclosure, the Adlerian therapist plays the role of a parental surrogate in supporting and encouraging the development and strengthening of the force of social interest in the individual's life style.

As is implied in the above, repression and the unconscious do not figure prominently in this process. How the individual construes situations and his relation to them, as Ford and Urban (1963) point out, are the important determiners and change is brought about by bringing about change in these constructions. Dreikurs, an Adlerian, gives us a particularly clear statement of this position, "He needs our help to see what he is doing and to free himself from his false assumptions. In other words, our treatment is not directed toward a change in emotions, but a clarification of cognitive processes, of concepts. We do not attempt primarily to change behavior patterns or remove symptoms. If a patient improves his behavior because he finds it profitable at the time, without changing his basic premises, then we do not consider that as a therapeutic success" (1961: p. 79). In this position we find the roots of all those current therapeutic conceptions which place their emphasis on seeing, thinking, and reasoning as the root sources of behavior and behavior change (Kelley, 1955; Ellis, 1962). Adler warns the therapist that he must treat his patient as an equal and as a collaborator in order to avoid stimulating feelings of inferiority which will make change difficult. Yet the glimpses of Adler's methods that come through his writings and the opportunities to observe Adlerian therapists in action belie this specification. The Adlerian therapist comes through as an authoritative, firm but kindly person who knows what is wrong and intends, with all good will and consideration to show it to his patient. In this sense the relationship borders on that of teacher to student rather than one of equals. When one contrasts the Adlerian working relationship with that demanded by the specifications surrounding free association in psychoanalysis, Adler's description of the working relationship takes on more meaning. Unlike psychoanalysis, in which for the purposes of regression in free association the patient relaxes from the active reality-oriented stance of everyday life, Adlerian therapy proceeds from the everyday position in which the goals and the methods are more familiar and more clearly understood. In this sense the patient feels like an equal and active collaborator.

Adler's emphasis on disclosure and the changing of cognitions does not mean that he abandoned completely the Freudian emphasis on learning in the relationship and on the dynamics of resistance. We find Adler saying,

The means at the disposal of individual psychology suffice amply for eradicating the patient's mistrust against people in general. Patience, prevision, warnings make progress fairly certain for the physician. The progress consists in disclosing to the patient the pathogenic infantile situation in which his or her masculine protest is rooted. The friendly relation . . . permits both patient and physician to get complete insight into the neurotic activity, to realize the falsity of his neurotic promptings . . . (1924: pp. 151–152).

Again (the therapist continues)

. . . trying to discover and explain until the patient completely upset gives them (his particular arrangements and constructions) up *in order to place new and better hidden ones in their place* (1924: p. 44). [Italics are mine.]

ECLECTICISM-PSYCHOBIOLOGY

A great many counselors have attempted to straddle alternative camps, one emphasizing the problems of persons in need of counseling as problems of cognition (understanding matters of fact), another emphasizing, modifying or substituting specific instrumental acts, and, finally, the various views of the person's troubles as stemming from problems of motivations and emotions. Thorne has probably made the most complete effort to reconcile these positions through applying the psychobiological approach of Adolph Meyer (Lief, 1948) to counseling. His point of view tends to reject as doctrinaire too great a reliance on theory in any method of analyzing human beings in therapeutic practice. The eclectic refuses to identify himself with any one theory and consequently in his own eyes becomes invulnerable to attack from any side and, perhaps, from the standpoint of others, opens himself to attack from all points of view.

In many ways the psychobiological point of view is an extension of medical practice, in that it involves empirical, nontheoretical sizing up of the individual as a whole and the application of some common-sense hypothesis to him and his needs. It calls our attention to the fact that man is a biological, social, and psychological creature. In order to understand a person's problems, all three of his aspects should be examined. Only through a comprehensive case study can we hope to understand him and the problems he faces with any completeness. Adherents of this position would argue that overemphasis on any one aspect and neglect of the others may lead to seriously inadequate understanding of the individual's needs. What may appear like psychologically determined apathy may turn out to be a biologically determined low energy level. What may appear as brusqueness or combativeness may be typical friendly behavior for this fellow's social class. The psychobiologist would argue that he aims to understand people just as much as the psychoanalyst or the nondirectivist. Perhaps he understands them better, he thinks, because he sees them in all three of their dimensions.

Therapeutic Implications. Since the basis for this threefold approach to understanding persons is nontheoretical, it follows that treatment will not fall into a fixed pattern. The therapist has his large armamentarium of techniques upon which he draws according to the strategy of the moment. Great stress is placed upon an elaborate process of examining the client in which social, psychological, and biological data are accumulated. The client's assets and liabilities are weighed. This is likely to force the client into a relatively passive role. The part of the process which is designed to aid the client to gain command of his emotions is likewise seen as the selection, as the therapist sees fit, of the appropriate technique. At one moment he is nondirective, the next moment he encourages free association or interprets, and so on. Considerable effort is expended in making the client aware of his assets and liabilities and in encouraging him to test various courses of action.

Naturally, in this orientation there is less concern or emphasis on some systematic use of a relationship. Where the relationship is utilized it is for more specific purposes such as for pressure, suggestion, or persuasion. It seems likely that the psychobiologist's thoroughness, his evident desire to leave no stone unturned in his analysis of a client, will often engender confidence, identification, and positive transference. Where the issues are primarily matters of knowledge or understanding or are biological, this relationship may help the patient acquire the knowledge he needs or carry out the required physiological treatments. Where motivational or emotional factors are paramount, the profitable effects of this relationship are debatable. With some kinds of persons for certain purposes, it may be helpful, whereas for others it may block progress.

As had been suggested above in connection with our discussion of theories emphasizing instrumental aspects of behavior, psychobiologists like Thorne are likely to give greater emphasis than dynamicists to the cognitive aspects of behavior. In terms of dynamic personality theory, they give great attention to the integrative, as differentiated from the defensive, aspects of the ego. They would tend to make positive use of the adaptive resources of the ego.

Having reviewed in limited space a variety of theoretical positions with respect to counseling and psychotherapy, we are ready to lay a theoretical foundation for a discussion of the counseling process. In the four chapters which follow we shall present our own integrations of these different theories, discuss the pivotal aspects of therapeutic relationships and their applications in counseling.

CHAPTER 5

The Dimensions of Therapeutic
Relationships: A Point of View

IN THIS CHAPTER we shall introduce the idea that to a considerable extent the various positions with respect to psychotherapy
and counseling discussed previously can be reconciled and integrated, although parts of particular theories must be rejected or
modified. This chapter will develop the thesis that the therapeutic
character of interpersonal relationships is multiply determined.
The succeeding three chapters will elaborate this thesis further by
taking up in turn three significant aspects of therapeutic interactions and their application to counseling goals.

PERSONALITY THEORY AND THERAPEUTIC
HYPOTHESES

We believe that our review of various theories of the therapeutic process has made clear the intimate relationship between
therapeutic and personality theory. In fact, we tried to demonstrate that therapeutic theory is best conceived as one application
of personality theory. As we come to learn more and more about
personality development, we become able to specify more precisely
the conditions under which the controlled modification of personality, that is, therapy, will occur. However, this conception of the
relationship between theories of personality and of therapy does

not mean that progress in therapeutic theory will be dependent solely on progress in personality theory, but rather that the two will proceed in an interacting relationship. As a matter of fact, the development of personality theory did not receive its greatest impetus from experimental research in personality or research in the development of personality. Instead, the greatest contributions came from Freud's experiences with persons undergoing therapy and the assumptions about personality that he found he had to make in order to understand what he had observed in the therapeutic situation. Thus we should think of therapeutic experience and therapeutic theory as leading to the development of theories of personality, and vice versa.

Personality theory

In order that the reader may understand and evaluate our treatment of counseling he should understand what kinds of general assumptions about personality theory we have made. These we state as follows:

1. *Centralism.* We shall be committed to a centralist conception of the determinants of behavior, though not to a simon-pure version. As our historical review disclosed (Chapter 1, pp. 12–18), counselors have become increasingly aware of how organized their clients' motivations are. Daily experience with individuals struggling to change their behavior has taught us to look beyond the specific purposes this behavior seems to serve at a particular moment. Too often to be ignored, the search for the sources of a particular client's reactions and for the way by which his reactions could be modified led to some more general and more enduring characteristic of his motivations that emerged after an integrative analysis. Most of the bigger problems we face tap far-reaching systems of motives and emotions. This, however, does not preclude the existence of behavior which touches only the periphery of the personal system and thus is less tightly bound to it. A youngster may have a well-organized set of motivations around situations calling for closer, more personal relationships with men. When his mathematics teacher makes friendly gestures to him, he is uncertain and timid. He yearns for a close relation-

ship but fears it also, with the result that he is immobilized. Yet he is not at all hampered by this conflict when it comes to making a vocational decision. His work relationships with men are free of such entanglements, even though some aspects of his feelings about such personal relationships may influence his choice of work. Stating our centralist principle—it is that in an individual we expect to find systems of motives which are relevant to a wide range of his behavior, along with other systems, either independent of the more comprehensive ones or loosely related to them, which are relevant only to a narrow segment of behavior. It follows that when a larger system is modified, then a more sweeping change in behavior is effected. It follows also from the assumption that there is at most a loose relationship between two systems, that a change in a smaller one can be effected without necessitating a basic modification of the larger.

Our orientation to larger units of behavior and the systems of motives underlying them, should not deter us from being able to examine human behavior in detail in the manner of the behavior therapist. Our search for the larger integrating aspects of behavior must rest on observations at the microscopic as well as macroscopic level. Our concern with inner determinants must be balanced by a complete awareness of the degree of control exercised by situational stimuli external to a person. At the same time, we know that we shall have to turn elsewhere when we seek a point of view which tells us where to look in searching for the specific experiences which have led to particular behavior patterns and have shaped certain persistent motivational patterns.

2. *Psychoanalysis.* Our view of the development and form of these systems of motives—that is to say, of personality development and structure—will draw heavily on psychoanalytic theory because it seems to offer a basis for explaining more of human behavior. Unlike other theories which emphasize personality dynamics and the centralist hypothesis, psychoanalytic theory goes beyond broad propositions about the effect of interpersonal relations on personality. Where Rogers stops at attributing repression and distorted perception to the effect of parental threats of withdrawal of love, Freudian theory formulates hypotheses about the differential effects of these threats depending upon the stage of

development at which they occur. If these threats occur in the earliest years when orality is seen as the child's primary mode of contact, different effects on the individual's love-hate impulses and his way of expressing or defending himself against them are expected than if they occur later when eliminative systems come under voluntary control. Freud not only introduces a time factor, but in addition he considers the purpose of parental pressure. Was the mother trying to hurry the child into giving up the breast, or did she show excessive disgust of smeared faces? Further, where client-centered theory talks in generalities about the process of repression or distortion as a defense against threat, psychoanalytic theory spells out different forms of defense and relates them, albeit rather loosely, to the genetic process. Most decidedly we do not hold that all psychoanalytic hypotheses have been fully and generally confirmed. But as we see it, accumulating evidence supports more and more aspects of this conceptual system which encourages us to believe that it has distinct value as a preliminary to the more tightly reasoned and more thoroughly validated system of some future day (Blum, 1953). Pragmatically, right now its breadth and depth provide a perspective adapted to the subtlety and complexity of human behavioral phenomena.

3. *A Rankian Trend.* We find no great difficulty in incorporating some of the basic Rankian concepts in an essentially orthodox psychoanalytic view. With our conception that counseling is oriented toward helping people at crucial stages in their growth, it is not surprising that we find something useful and illuminating in Allen's concept of integration and differentiation as he derives it from the Rankian position. Independence is highly valued in the United States. Whether it originated in a recent frontier society or arises from more complex sources, our ideal for each child seems to be for him to stand alone, to surpass his parents, and to set up an independent family unit (Mead, 1943: pp. 80–98). But in practice parents and children are often caught up in a snarl of contradictions while trying to live up to this ideal. Personal conflicts which result in lack of self-differentiation can be traced back to experiences in the first six years, and even persons who passed successfully through this crucial period may later exhibit such conflicts.

As we look at the efforts of clients to surmount their problems, we must be sensitive to their pressures to realize their potential. We can safely assume that all persons are motivated in some degree to establish themselves as distinct individuals. However, we must also expect them to exhibit contradictory motivations toward regression, that is, toward retreat from opportunities to differentiate themselves. One of the goals of the therapeutic process is to make possible the ascendancy of motivations to grow and achieve further differentiation.

4. *A Developmental Emphasis*. Rooted as it is in experience with persons presenting distinct emotional problems of a long-standing nature, psychoanalysis has tended to center attention on the formative influences of the earliest years. Basic personality patterns are laid down in the first six years; the later periods of life are merely the occasions for exhibiting the established potential. Erikson (1959) has modified this view by concentrating on the psychosocial as opposed to the psychosexual aspects of development. In doing this, attention is turned from the first six years to the entire life cycle. In Erikson's view each phase of the life cycle is characterized by a specific developmental task which must be mastered in it. Yet each phase is not independent because the solution of each developmental task is prepared and influenced by previous phases and is worked out further in subsequent ones. Each phase is described in terms of the extremes of successful and unsuccessful solutions which can be arrived at in it, though in reality the outcome is usually somewhere between the extremes: (1) basic trust vs. mistrust; (2) autonomy vs. shame and doubt; (3) initiative vs. guilt; (4) industry vs. inferiority; (5) identity vs. identity diffusion; (6) intimacy vs. isolation; (7) generativity vs. stagnation; (8) integrity vs. despair.

We have here the scaffolding for the fuller conception of personality development which is particularly germane to psychological counseling and its goal of furthering personal development rather than only undoing maldevelopment. We have already suggested that counseling will need to be lodged in the social institutions (parental care, schools, teachers, occupations, etc.) which are created to meet each developmental phase. Counselors concentrating on a particular phase will need to elaborate their conceptions of the developmental principles involved as they have begun to do in connection with vocational choice (Bordin, Nachmann, & Segal, 1963; Roe, 1957; Super, 1963).

Resistance and transference in psychotherapy

Our readers will want to know where we stand on two broad issues, resistance and transference, about which various theories of psychotherapy disagree. First our position with respect to these points will be outlined, then later in this chapter we shall try to summarize our stand in the form of an answer to what makes relationships therapeutic.

We deal with these therapeutic concepts in the following manner:

1. In our view *defense* and *resistance,* as defined by Freudian theory, are important aspects of the therapeutic process and of counseling. Although we can accept Rogers' view of resistance as a patient's reaction to inappropriate interpretation or to lack of acceptance by the therapist and Adler's closely related view of it as an effort to perpetuate some fiction of superiority, we must agree with the psychoanalysts who view it as arising *also* in response to internally determined anxiety. The client's need for autonomy or his sensitivity about asking for help may make him reject a counselor's efforts to press help upon him either in the form of premature interpretation or premature information. When, however, the psychoanalyst speaks of resistance, he does not refer to the patient's willingness to accept his interpretations, but instead refers to the patient's unwillingness or inability to proceed with free association. When the patient's associations and his perceptions of the therapist provoke impulses of which he is afraid, then he is likely to try to prevent the possibility of these forbidden impulses escaping his control by substituting other activities for the therapeutic task. The form of these substitute activities will probably reflect the patient's preferred mode of defense. If he is an "intellectualizer," under the guise of having just had a great insight, he will launch into a long exposition of some aspect of his feelings. The therapist will recoginze that even when this exposition is an accurate description, it will have so completely drained off its affective components as to have little value as a

medium of potential change. In effect, the patient will be practicing his usual habits of distorting or repressing his feelings instead of learning to face up to them.

Recapitulating, we see two types of reactions of clients to which the term *resistance* has been applied. One refers to the patient's seeming unwillingness to give up his autonomy or to fail to live up to the social standard of acting independently. The other refers to the expression of the patient's defenses against his inner conflicts when the nature of the therapeutic situation tempts him to express conflicting impulses. Both types of resistance are the concern of the therapist. The therapist must learn to avoid the first through avoiding encroachment upon his patient's feeling of independence. He must learn to see his patient's desire to differentiate himself as evidence of the constructive forces in himself instead of as an obstacle to the therapeutic task. The therapist must learn also that the second type of resistance is an unavoidable part of successful therapy. Whenever the theraptist hopes that his efforts will effect a reduction in the self-defeating behavior of his patient, he must expect to deal with this self-defeating behavior as it appears in the form of this second type of resistance. If this second type of resistance does not appear, the therapist must examine his own behavior to see whether he has unconsciously allied himself with his patient to prevent expression of the impulses which underlie the difficulty.

2. In the preceding chapter we called attention to the differences in attitudes toward the role of transference in therapy among psychoanalytic, Rankian, Adlerian, and client-centered points of view. The client-centered and psychoanalytic attitudes are the most directly opposed to each other. Transference in the psychoanalytic view is a crucial part of psychotherapy. In contrast, Rogers, while acknowledging the phenomenon of transference, sees it as relatively immaterial to the therapeutic process. In Adler's position that life style will be expressed toward the therapist, as elsewhere, we see little contradiction with the characterological aspects of ego psychology. On the whole, Allen's position on transference is not too different except in complexity from that of the psychoanalytic view. The more complex psychoanalytic utilization of transference can be attributed to differences that arise between therapy with children and therapy with adults.

Transference appears when a person's relationships at the infant stage have been such that he has never moved beyond them. All new relationships take on the essential characteristics of these prototypes, with the result that the development of new or modified types of relationships becomes either difficult or impossible. In the child, especially the younger child, these basic relationships are not yet completely formed and therefore are more fluid. In this sense, unlike the neurotic adult who is reacting to present relationships with obsolete infantile reactions, the young child may still be in a semi-infantile stage and his present relationships are realistically those basic ones upon which the neurotic adult is unrealistically fixated. This current status of the basic relationships which trouble the child makes it possible for the effect of a constructive experience in therapy to be transferred to the home relationship. Thus, in therapy with children, it is the basic relationship itself which is modified to provide the groundwork for fuller growth. In contrast, psychotherapy with adults must go through a more difficult process of extricating those adults from the binding effects of relationships which are already far in the past and therefore not readily accessible to change. This state of affairs often necessitates the lengthy development and resolution of transference stressed in psychoanalytic theory. The analyst so conducts the therapeutic meetings that the patient to an ever increasing degree recapitulates childhood relationships. The therapist carries out the long, measured task of gradually calling the patient's attention to more and more of the relationships that the patient has tried to force on him until the release of dammed-up impulses and the accompanying increased insight enable the patient to develop new kinds of relationships. This interpretive process usually reaches levels of intellectual complexity beyond the cognitive resources of the young child, even were this kind of process necessary for successful therapy.

While accepting the analytic position on transference in general, we lean toward the client-centered view, also implied in Adlerian methods, to the extent of assuming it is possible for people to hurdle the barrier of repression without an intense use of transference. When one deals with an essentially mature person, one who has achieved considerable creativity in expressing his feelings and forming new relationships, it can be expected that the therapeutic relationship will have rapid effects and that the defensive process will be a relatively flexible one which gives way readily. There is still a great deal about ego processes, particularly defense mechanisms, which is not well understood. It is only the negative or self-defeating ego processes which we find elaborated in the form of defense mechanisms.

When it comes to the positive or constructive ego processes, no correspondingly extensive scheme has been developed. It appears self-evident that systems which permit successful and satisfying expressions of impulses require equally complex processes and organizations of subsidiary motives, resources for action, and reasoning as are necessary for impulse-defense systems. Hartman and his collaborators have dominated the recent trend to fill this gap in psychoanalytic theory. Hartman (1964: pp. 37–68) thought of the roots of ego development as independent of conflict. The ego apparatuses (motility, perception, memory, etc.) provide coordination to external reality as well as coordination between impulses and their objects. Kris (1952) supplied us with the concept of regression in the service of the ego as a basis for understanding creativity. Somewhat independently, but not necessarily incompatible with psychoanalytic theory (Rapaport, 1959: p. 138), Piaget (1952, 1954) has been studying the development of reasoning. These developments promise to give greater depth to the offering of information or training of the kinds advocated by Williamson, Thorne, and many of the behavior therapists.

DIAGNOSIS AND UNDERSTANDING

Our review of theories having hitherto touched only lightly on attitudes toward diagnosis, we propose to consider the topic more fully at this time. There are a number of possible attitudes toward and definitions of the role of diagnosis in psychotherapy or counseling. Psychoanalytic theory calls for the therapist to use his theory of personality to understand his patient and to intervene therapeutically, for example, to interpret. Although the theory assumes that the therapist will draw on his observations during the associative process, the development of special psychological diagnostic tests and procedures has led to an increased emphasis

on a specific diagnostic process apart from, but of course not independent of, the therapeutic hour. Rogers finds diagnosis inimical to his theory of psychotherapy because he sees it as evaluation
and therefore a threat which will make impossible the permissive
accepting atmosphere upon which, in his view, therapeutic progress depends. Allen's attitudes are very similar to Rogers' insofar as he links special diagnostic procedures with too great an
emphasis on past relationships. Allen, however, more than Rogers,
accepts the therapist's need to be aware of the client's present
resources and to lend himself as a supplement to these resources
when the situation demands it. Adler, as do Williamson and
Thorne, places great emphasis on a distinct diagnostic process from
which, in effect, all therapeutic effort derives. Though they do
not, of course, use the term, behavior therapists engage in the
equivalent of diagnosis during their searchingly minute examination of behavior sequences and their efforts to specify the conditions fostering the emission of the responses which define the
problem.

The development of concepts of diagnosis in counseling has
followed a course parallel to the changes in counseling goals discussed in Chapter 1. The early emphases in counseling were upon
the content of the client's difficulty or the area of his life in which
the problem situation arose. For example, Williamson and Darley
(1937) suggested five categories for describing problems encountered in counseling college students. Williamson (1939) developed
a more complete description of them. A summary follows:

Personality Problems. Difficulties in adjusting in social groups,
speech difficulties, family conflicts, and infractions of discipline.

Educational Problems. Unwise choice of courses of study, differential scholastic achievement, insufficient general scholastic aptitude,
ineffective study habits, reading disabilities, insufficient scholastic motivation, overachievement, underachievement, adjustment of superior
students.

Vocational Problems. Uncertain vocational choice, no vocational
choice, discrepancy between interests and aptitudes, unwise vocational
choice.

Financial Problems. Difficulties arising from need for self-support
in school and college and correlated questions of student placement.

Health Problems. The individual's acceptance of his state of health
or physical disabilities or both.

These kinds of categories are roughly parallel in function to psychiatric diagnoses in that they represent crude, more additive rather than integrative, groupings of symptoms. Also writing from his experience with college students, the author (1946) pointed to evidence of overlap between the above categories and proposed an alternative set which would be closer to the basic psychological issues and therefore more related to differential treatment. He suggested that an even more basic question than the *kind* of difficulty experienced by the client is to ask what is the *source* (especially the psychological source) of the difficulty. He suggested five sources of problems:

Dependence. Conflict in this area immobilizes the client and blocks active efforts to resolve the problem or reach a decision.

Lack of Information. Sheer restriction in range or appropriateness of experience or in special opportunities to acquire necessary skills.

Self-Conflict. Conflicts between self-concepts or between a self-concept and some other stimulus function.

Choice Anxiety. The need to decide among alternative plans all of which upset present life.

Lack of Assurance.[1] The decision is made, but the client wishes to play safe by checking with others.

The question of an appropriate set of diagnostic categories seems of less importance than it once did to the writer. Systems of categories like those described above are useful as a general framework for examining the problems of students, but one must go much deeper to achieve fuller understanding of a particular student. As Rogers (1951: pp. 219–221) has suggested, this search for diagnostic categories and specific therapies may be illusory. The disease concept of psychopathology may not apply in any way. In any event, it seems more fruitful to rely on a well-differentiated theory of personality as a basis for trying to understand a particular person. When we talk to people about their problems, we are interested in how their basic impulses and satisfactions enter into the problem. Does this boy's choice of medicine represent his way

---

[1] A modification by Pepinsky (1948) of the original term *no problem*. Pepinsky also added a lack of skill category and further subdivided self-conflict into cultural, interpersonal and intrapersonal. Robinson (1950: Ch. 8) suggested a compression of categories into three: adjustment problems, skill learning, and immaturity. That the issue of diagnostic categories continues to be a lively one is attested by Robinson's more recent article (1963) in which he reviews a number of later versions.

of becoming an admired figure in the eyes of his mother or his way of identifying with his admired, and perhaps feared, father? Does another's seemingly unrealistic plan to go to college involve seeking the satisfaction of independence, or does it involve a form of retaliation against his mother who seems lately to be favoring his younger brother? We try to understand the ways in which the individual attempts to reconcile the pressures of his impulses on the one hand and of reality on the other. We are sensitive to the degree to which he tries to have his cake and eat it through some destroying process, such as one that leads him to act as though he were independent while he is actually dependent.

Further experience has moderated the view that diagnostic classification is lacking in utility. The developmental orientation of the psychological counselor and the lowered psychological barrier toward approaching him which accompanies his efforts to define his services in that direction, mean that an extremely heterogeneous clientele are attracted to his agency. Without selection and referral, a psychological counseling agency with limited staff might easily become an intensive treatment center with long waiting lists. Another need for careful diagnosis arises from the fact that it is not always in the client's best interests to encourage his desires for an ambitious therapeutic effort. For one client such an effort will mean several years of work while he will be leaving the city within a year. Another client's turmoil makes him desperate enough to try anything, but his inner resources are sufficiently limited so that the major effort would best be expended in helping him to get into a more stabilized living arrangement to cope better with daily living and to build up the resources for coping with his inner conflicts in a constructive, more enduring manner. These varied goals require varied therapeutic methods which we will be discussing in more detail in the succeeding three chapters. Although our present diagnostic categories in psychiatry and counseling are not fully adequate, we must continue to make judgments when facing choice points in the therapeutic process.

All of the above refers to diagnostic categorization and concerns itself solely with the question of whether the number of categories must equal the number of persons, which defeats the intent of categorization. We cannot agree with Rogers' view of diagnosis as inimical to therapeutic relationships. Although current client-centered theory accepts the principle of repression, its goal of understanding through the internal frame of reference seems to work out as a self-imposed rule to try to understand only that part of the client's experience of which he is aware.[2]

In speaking of understanding it is important to make certain distinctions. First, we must separate understanding and communication. Second, we must discriminate between understanding current feelings and understanding the history of those feelings or knowing what feelings to expect under other circumstances. By interaction with a client or by diagnostic testing, I can arrive at the judgment that when he is with his parents or parental figures he feels angry but acts meekly. To infer that this is true does not necessarily mean that he feels this way toward me. However, if I have inferred correctly, I will be more sensitive to covert signs of anger when he begins to treat me as one would treat a parent and to manifest exaggerated meekness. My perception of his feelings does not mean that I must attempt to communicate this awareness to him. I may decide that he does not yet have a sufficiently strong commitment to the therapeutic process to make constructive use of such a disclosure at this time. The main point is that I can have a deeper understanding of what he is feeling by taking into account everything I know about him while observing his present actions. Often interest in understanding a client's history and his potential feelings leads to a neglect of the present significance of current behavior. It is this kind of error that Rogers and Allen seem to be trying to prevent in their attitude toward diagnosis. Rogers also assumes that inherent in the diagnostic attitude is a lack of acceptance of the client. This is equivalent to saying that understanding is the same as trying to force that understanding on the client.

THE MULTI-DIMENSIONALITY OF THERAPEUTIC RELATIONSHIPS

Having identified the sources and nature of our personality theory, commented on, reconciled, or selected from therapeutic concepts which are subject to dispute, we now can state a con-

[2] For example, see Porter (1950: p. 63).

viction that will profoundly influence our further analysis of the process of counseling. The counselor's relationship to his client will serve therapeutic ends not as a function of one aspect of that relationship, whether it be permissiveness, interpretation, or support, but as a function of many aspects of that relationship. We are convinced that multiple factors, rather than just one factor influence the therapeutic value of the relationship.

As we have seen, our preferred concept of personality development visualizes the individual's growth as a function of and intimately reflected in his interpersonal relationships. This tells us that the major medium for contribution to this psychological growth will also be interpersonal relationships. Therefore, when the psychological counselor applies his understanding of personality development to the problem of helping a particular individual remove obstacles which block his development, he looks toward the relationship between himself and the client as the major instrument with which that contribution can be made. As yet, no one can speak with the authority derived from scientific demonstration about the ways in which relationships do become therapeutic. However, the varied ramifications and implications of interpersonal relationships for personality development make us certain that the therapeutic effect of interpersonal relationships cannot be traced to any single feature of those relationships. The needs of men and women in interpersonal relationships will be as complex as their development and as their personality structures. Therefore, it seems axiomatic that the answer to the problem of meeting the needs of people who come for therapy must arise out of the fullness of our understanding of each individual's requirements and the flexibility of our capacity to interact with him.

In the next three chapters we shall discuss three broad aspects of relationships which we believe to have relevance to their therapeutic value. With respect to each aspect we shall analyze its place in personality and psychotherapeutic theory, what research evidence is available to support each, its general therapeutic applications, and finally its application to the specialized goals of psychological counseling.

CHAPTER 6

The Ambiguity Dimension of
Therapeutic Relationships[1]

In the last chapter, we pointed out that the central question in counseling and psychotherapy is, What characteristics of interpersonal relationships make them therapeutic? In this chapter we shall confine ourselves to just one characteristic of therapists and their behavior which, in our opinion, makes their relationship to clients or patients therapeutic, namely, their ambiguity and the ambiguity of their definitions of the counseling task. First, we shall describe this concept. Then we shall attempt to show the degree to which ambiguity already plays either an explicit or implicit role in both personality and therapeutic theory. Finally, we shall discuss further conceptions of its relationship to therapeutic processes.

WHAT IS AMBIGUITY?

Ambiguity can best be understood as an attribute of stimulus situations. Some stimulus situations do not elicit any single response or demand the same response from everybody. If, for example, someone hands us a poorly developed, clouded-up photograph and asks us, "What is it?" there is no ready-made

[1] This chapter is adapted from a paper which was prepared at about the same time (Bordin, 1955a).

specific response tied to that photograph as a stimulus object. One person might look at it and say, "Well, I can't be sure, but it looks to me as if this is a photograph of three men standing together having a conversation." Another person looking at it may say, "I see three trees in the foreground, and way in the distance there seem to be some animals milling around." When the stimulus configuration to which we are exposed is incomplete and vague, in that no clear-cut response is predetermined, we say that the stimulus configuration is ambiguous. We say to ourselves in effect, "I can't really be sure what it is," and then try to judge what it is. Under these conditions a decision is made from among the types of objects in our previous experience, which seems to be the best possible explanation for this particular stimulus configuration. Ambiguity, then, is that attribute of a stimulus situation whose demand character on different persons is different, that is, its demand character is variable.

The degree of ambiguity that exists in therapeutic interpersonal relationships is controlled by the therapist. As two people interact, each by virtue of what he does defines himself as a stimulus object to some degree. While interacting with a client, a counselor defines himself and the situation either directly, that is, by direct statements or, most frequently, indirectly by the total import of his actions. It is possible to conceive of three relevant areas in which definition can take place: (a) the topic he considers appropriate for the client to discuss; (b) the closeness and other characteristics of the relationship expected; and (c) the counselor's values in terms of the goal he sets up toward which he and the client should work as well as his values in general.

The therapist may define with different degrees of clarity these three aspects of himself or the therapeutic task. He may define two of them quite clearly and leave one of them vague or in various other combinations and degrees. He may make clear to the patient that he is supposed to talk about his dreams, or his job, or his sexual relationships. The choice of topic may be more restrictively defined, for example, the patient's relationships with his boss, or the courses he will be taking next year. The area may be more ambiguously defined, for example, anything that is of personal concern to him. The analytic rule, "Tell me anything that comes to your mind," represents one of the least restrictive, and therefore the most ambiguous, definitions of the appropriate topics for discussion. The psychoanalyst's definition of the close-ness of the relationship is undoubtedly reflected by his choice of topics. By making clear that he expects the client to talk about very personal topics such as his sexual experiences, his emotional relationships with his family, and so on, he is saying that this will be a close, confidential relationship. He may, following custom, introduce the analytic rule by talking about the difference be-tween the therapeutic situation with its freedom from the usual inhibitions and ordinary social intercourse. However, even if he does this, many other aspects of the therapist's behavior are prob-ably more important in defining the characteristics of the rela-tionship. For example, the counselor who addresses his clients by first name on first meeting them is suggesting an adult-child or fatherly relationship. Again, a counselor who is overly solicitous and over-gallant about helping his female client get herself settled in the room emphasizes that this is a relationship between two people of opposite sex. Whether the counselor permits himself to exchange emotionally tinged feelings with the client or preserves his emotional distance is influential in conveying his definition of the counselor-client relationship. Similarly, the counselor may be openly communicative in his values or leave them relatively undefined.

The client reacts to all these aspects of the situation simul-taneously. All three aspects (topic, closeness of relationship, and values) are dynamically interrelated parts of an organic whole. Therefore, the effect is to create situations which vary in the degree to which the stimulus field determines the response. In more ambiguous situations, there will be greater variability in client reactions. Some will see the counselor as demanding and critical and others will see him as aloof and disinterested, and so forth. In less ambiguous situations, clients will tend to agree more in their perceptions.[2]

In sum, we are talking about the degree to which the therapist either advertently or inadvertently gives structure to the stimulus field for the patient. The analyst who appears to be a blank screen to his patient represents one extreme of the ambiguity-

[2] Townsend (1956) illustrated this when he asked undergraduate students to rate four therapists for personal characteristics after listening to a recorded inter-view conducted by each one, which had previously been rated for therapist ambiguity. The raters agreed most in their judgments about the least ambiguous therapist and their order of agreement corresponded exactly to rated ambiguity.

structured dimension. By long periods of only listening, the analyst minimizes the amount of structure the situation presents to the patient. His admonition, "Tell me whatever comes to your mind," gives the patient no clue as to what he is to talk about. The analyst's customary position behind the patient eliminates or minimizes the possibility of the patient's obtaining structuring cues from facial expressions, gestures, or other movements, however fragmentary. Information-bound counseling relationships are good examples of extremely structured situations where the purposes of the meeting and the goals are usually both explicitly and implicitly defined in relatively definite terms and where the topic is often restricted by a series of very limited questions which can be answered "Yes" and "No."

How does the counselor structure the counseling task? Osburn's studies of the problems of measuring this characteristic of counselor behavior give us a basis for answering this question (Osburn, 1952). After establishing that even relatively untrained observers can consistently, both within themselves and from observer to observer, discriminate different counseling situations in terms of structure, Osburn proceeded to study the relationship between this characteristic of counseling interviews and a number of specific aspects of the counselor's behavior. He was able to identify a number of facets of counselor behavior which would seem to be highly correlated with ambiguity. Osburn classified counselors' communications in several different ways. One of these was whether the counselor was giving or seeking information. He found that information-giving was less structuring and therefore more ambiguous than information-seeking. He also classified all of the counselor's responses on a scale ranging from specific to general. Where, for example, an information-seeking response was very restrictive, for example, "How old are you?" it would be considered among the most specific responses. On the other hand, an information-seeking response which asks the client to "Tell me about yourself" would be considered very general because it leaves open what aspect of himself the client can choose to describe. Similarly, a counselor's information-giving response was rated between specific to general depending upon how restrictive and focused the information was. Osburn correlated his judges' summary rating of the ambiguity of a counselor's behavior over an entire interview with various combinations of his categories for rating specific responses. He found that when he took all of the counselor's information-giving responses, selected from these the responses that represented giving information about the client, and then classified this residual group of responses with respect to the scale of specificity-generality described above, the obtained distribution on this scale differed markedly according to the interview's rating for ambiguity. In those interviews that had been rated most ambiguous, more of the counselor's information-giving responses, referring to the client, were rated toward the general end of the scale. Naturally, one of the most frequently recurring examples of information-giving client referent responses would be where the counselor imparts to him his view of the client or of what he says. Osburn differentiated *generality* for this group of responses in such terms as these: the most general response was just listening, the second most general kind consisted of the counselor exactly reflecting the thought or concept expressed by the client. Coming down the scale of generality, the next response was the type where the counselor summarized the previous responses of the client in such a way as to change or enlarge the ideas expressed, or the counselor responded with some idea selected from a number of ideas that the client had brought up. The most *specific* category would be where the counselor responded to the client's statements with an entirely new idea or new interpretation of the client's remarks. The combination of the mean of the ratings described above with the counselor's responsiveness, the number of words he spoke during the interview, yielded the index which correlated highest with the judgment of the ambiguity of the interview as a whole. Turning to another aspect of counselor behavior, Osburn found a close relationship between the number of topics initiated by the counselor and the over-all judgment of ambiguity. In other words, when a counselor changes the subject of conversation, it tends to define more clearly himself and the counseling task.

RELATIONSHIP OF AMBIGUITY TO PERSONALITY THEORY AND MEASUREMENTS

Our interest in ambiguity as a factor in the therapeutic relationship derives rather directly from the theory of personality we are drawing upon. In previous chapters we have already indicated our assumption that motives and their effects upon behavior and its changes must be viewed as parts of a dynamically organized developing system. When we attempt to understand human behavior we must attempt to trace back any particular goal, inferrable from a specific behavioral unit, to this system of motives. We assume that the individual's reaction to any situation represents an interaction between the goals that are inherent in that particular stimulus situation and certain pressures growing out of the larger, more enduring aspects of his motivational organization. We can obtain the clearest evidence about this motivational organization when the demand of the particular stimulus situation is restricted as much as possible. To put it another way, we can highlight the inner determinants of a person's actions by weakening external demands. In therapeutic situations, when a client reacts to the counselor as someone who is critical of him when most other people would agree that the counselor was not so acting, it is usually safe to conclude that the distorted perception of the counselor as critical has not been determined so much by the external aspects of the situation as by the needs of the client. The latter's behavior is one reflection of, or becomes a basis for inferring something about, his personality. Out of many such reflections it is possible to understand his personality.

Ambiguity as a factor in personality analysis is fully exploited in the basic theory of projective techniques (Abt, & Bellak, 1950: pp. 12–16). Projective tests have two characteristics. First, they require that the subject react to stimuli which do not have demanding structural determinants for perception. Second, most projective tests make possible the identification of the dimension of the stimulus to which the individual has responded as well as the content of his response. By analysis of both determinants and contents of perception, it is possible to make inferences about the motivational and emotional structure of the individual. In personality measurement there has been a tendency to look at the stimulus situation and its ambiguity from a more restricted point of view than we have been applying in our consideration of the therapeutic situation. In the former there has been a tendency to concentrate only on the stimulus which is being presented to the subject. However, studies by Miller and his students have demonstrated that a projective test must be studied not only in terms of the test stimuli but as a total situation. They found that such factors as the personality of the examiner and the types of tasks given the subject, for example, "This is a test of intelligence," or "This is a test of imagination," influenced Rorschach results (Miller, 1953).

In addition to its association with personality measurement, ambiguity has demonstrable relationships to the individual's comfort or anxiety. According to psychoanalytic personality theory, the ego represents the organized efforts of the individual to establish harmony between his own impulses and the stimuli impinging upon him from the outside world. The term includes the resources, the skills, and other instrumental behaviors which a person develops as a means of achieving this goal. Where the ego is relatively weak in the sense of not having developed an effective supply of resources for dealing with the potential dangers attendant upon expression of his impulses, and where the impulses and the conflicts surrounding them are so strong as to tax the ego's resources, the individual becomes fearful of his ability to deal with reality in such a way as to preserve himself from harm. Therefore, situations in which it is more difficult to utilize knowledge, skills, and other resources will be more anxiety-producing. Frenkel-Brunswik (1949) and her collaborators, whose immediate interest was not therapy, studied the susceptibility of people to anxiety or other responses to ambiguity and found interrelationships among intolerance of cognitive ambiguity, emotional ambivalence, and rigidity.

In his formulations regarding ego autonomy, Rapaport (1958) enriches our ideas regarding the influence of personality organization for response to ambiguous situations. In essence he underlines the fact that psychic structures useful for memory storage, inhibition and delay, and reasoning, evolving out of native sensory-motor-cortico-neural equipment, are interposed between the individual and the pressures from drives and external stimuli. Since complete independence of either drives or external reality is inconceivable, Rapaport speaks of the relative autonomy of the ego. A necessary condition to effective functioning is the organism's capacity to maintain this relative autonomy and thus escape slavery either to drives or external stimulation. He points out that sudden intensification of drives (e.g., in puberty) or conditions of curtailed stimulation and information (e.g., in sensory deprivation), especially when coupled with humiliating, degrading, and guilt-arousing information (e.g., in brainwashing), all diminish ego autonomy. Rapaport seems to argue that personalities tend to be organized to maintain one side of the autonomy at the expense of the other. Using obsessive-compulsive personalities as an example, he emphasizes the increased elaboration of the secondary process in this condition which makes for the substitution of intensified observation and logical analysis for affective and ideational signals. "Obsessive-compulsive defense thus maximizes the ego's autonomy from the id, but it does so at the cost of ever-increasing impairment of the ego's autonomy from the environment: the suppression of affective and ideational cues of drive origin renders the ego's judgments and decisions increasingly dependent upon external cues" (p. 23). Conversely, borderline and psychotic patients are seen as instances where reduction in the ego's autonomy of drives results in vulnerability to losing touch with external reality. Thus, we can arrive at the general formulation that the balance of personality organization between autonomy of drives versus external stimulation will predict how an individual will respond to ambiguous situations and tasks. Recent research has contributed to the empirical basis for this principle (Bordin, 1966; Mann, 1965).

RELATIONSHIP OF AMBIGUITY TO THERAPEUTIC THEORY

Of all therapeutic theories, Freudian theory makes the most complete and explicit use of ambiguity. Freudian emphasis on the therapist as a blank screen is a way of describing him in the role of an ambiguous stimulus object. In his discussions of therapeutic technique, Fenichel (1941) has dealt rather directly with the relationship between ambiguity and the effectiveness of transference-interpretation. Although he does not use the term *ambiguity*, he does point out that the therapist's interpretation of transference will fail to make the patient aware of distortion in his perception of the therapist when the latter has acted in a manner consistent with the patient's transference-determined perceptions of him. He suggests further that a therapist cannot be certain that he is dealing with transference unless he guards against offering realistic foundation for the patient's reaction to him. Only thus can he demonstrate to himself, as well as to the patient, that the patient's reactions to him are controlled by irrational, infantile feelings.

When we turn to client-centered theory, we find that being "nondirective" means in part not defining or imposing one's own values on the client. Also, by definition, a client-centered counselor is supposed to avoid "directive" leads. A directive lead seems to be a demand for the client to talk about a very specific topic in restricted terms as contrasted with a nondirective lead, which is a more general invitation to communicate, sometimes including a relatively unrestricted designation of a topic. Despite these two emphases on ambiguity, one gets the impression that nondirective therapists are much less ambiguous than orthodox psychoanalytic therapists. This impression is based on the fact that the former seem to talk more, particularly in the early stages of therapeutic relationship, and both our concept of ambiguity and Osburn's study suggest that mere talking decreases ambiguity. It is relatively rare for the client-centered therapist to respond to a patient's response with silence. It seems as though the Rogerian goal of understanding the client becomes a command to attempt to put into words what the client is trying to communicate whenever he has completed expressing some thought. Perhaps client-centered therapists do this as a consequence of their tendency to minimize the importance of unconscious material as a source of understanding. At any rate, Seeman's comparison of nondirective therapy ten years earlier with more recent interviews appears to demonstrate that there has been a trend in nondirective therapy towards more rather than less responsiveness by the therapist (1949). One of his findings was that a greater proportion of current client-centered therapists' responses could be characterized as clarification and a smaller proportion as simple acceptance. According to the meaning of these categories, it would seem that nondirective therapists have tended to increase the amount of effort expended in verbalizing clients' feelings and to decrease the frequency with which they respond with simple listening. This might lead to the

possible conclusion that client-centered therapists are less ambiguous now than they were ten years ago, as contrasted with the
nondirective interpretation that they are understanding their
clients better.

FURTHER APPLICATION TO
THERAPEUTIC THEORY

Having sketched the relationship of ambiguity to personality
theory and measurement, and to therapeutic theory, we can proceed to take up various aspects of the relationship of ambiguity
to the therapeutic process.

The functions of ambiguity

Our hypothesis is that ambiguity in a therapeutic relationship
serves three major functions. First, it capitalizes on the principle
that people invest ambiguous stimuli with those responses which
are most heavily laden with the unique aspects of their life history.
In other words, they find in ambiguous stimuli something that
touches their own motivational and emotional life. This makes
it possible for the client or patient, no matter how well-oriented
to reality, to bring into the therapeutic relationship his major
conflicted feelings, no matter how unaware he may be of them.
This we assume is identical with the Freudian concept of transference phenomena and with Allen's concept of the projection
onto the therapist of the unaccepted aspects of oneself. So we
see that ambiguity facilitates the appearance of transference phenomena in therapeutic relationships. Since we have cited evidence
that suggests that nondirective therapists may be less ambiguous
than therapists in a classical psychoanalytic process, it follows that
we can agree with Rogers (1951: pp. 199–201) when he suggests
that transference phenomena do not appear as often or in as
intense form in nondirective therapy as compared to psychoanalysis. Second, we assume that this investment of the client's
motivational and emotional structure in the relationship enables
the therapist to understand more fully and more deeply the main-
springs of the client's actions. The conscious use of ambiguity in

therapeutic relationships becomes a medium for finding out important things about a personality similar to a projective situation. From the client's reactions to the ambiguity of the situation we can draw inferences about the general nature of his defenses, and from the content and sequence of his responses we can obtain some understanding of his conflicts and the types of relationships with people which embody them. Third, by being ambiguous, the therapist provides a background against which the client's irrational feelings will be more clearly etched and therefore more readily brought to awareness. Ambiguity helps to insure the effectiveness of the well-timed interpretation.

There is some indirect empirical support for these assumed functions. The degree of starvation for cues induced by the experience of an ambiguous interpersonal relationship is demonstrated by laboratory studies of verbal reinforcement, of which Greenspoon's (1955) was the first. Greenspoon gave his subjects the open-ended task of talking about themselves and demonstrated that he could influence the content of their talk by offering "uh-huh" responses in response to verbalization of selected content. Many other investigators have followed up on this paradigm, exploring facets and extensions of this behavior. From our vantage point, these results show that in an ambiguous interpersonal situation, initiated by the other person, a person is likely to be searching so hard for cues which will structure his task and his relation to the other that even subtle, partial cues may influence him. A person's need for structure may be so great that he may unrealistically extend incomplete cues or cues inadvertently given. Just such a process is presumed to underlie transference phenomena—a person already unable to establish satisfying relationships and faced with an ambiguous relationship will fashion it to fit his recurring and unsatisfactory pattern. The further assumption is, of course, that this pattern will be based on early ones drawn from infancy and childhood.

Recently reported research by Heller (1966) and Matarazzo and his collaborators (Matarazzo, Wiens, Matarazzo, & Saslow, 1966) has offered indirect support for the latter two functions of ambiguity. Heller, pitting negatively and positively reinforcing verbal responses against ambiguous ones, demonstrated that, while subjects talked more under the conditions of clear reinforcement, there were a greater number of self-references and greater self-disclosure under the ambiguous condition. That one form of ambiguity, silence, acts as a pressure to communicate is indicated by Matarazzo's finding that rate of subject-initiated talk increased markedly when interviewers increased the latency (silence period) for offering remarks beyond five seconds.

Considerations influencing control of ambiguity

It is important to note that our emphasis on ambiguity as an important ingredient of the therapeutic relationship does not mean we are assuming or suggesting that the therapist should strive for maximum ambiguity in his relationship with all patients or clients. The complexity of therapy and the large gaps in our own understanding make such reductionistic solutions tempting. We must resist our own intolerances of uncertainty and maintain clearly before us the realization that, while eventually we may be able to specify all of the important variables which characterize therapeutic relationships, we shall not be able to reduce these variables to constants. The personality and the current need of each client will determine which stress on each of the relevant therapeutic variables will lead to the therapeutic solution. Specifically, what we try to do by using ambiguity in therapeutic relationships must be balanced against our conceptions of the role of anxiety. In general, all schools of psychotherapy seem to agree that people must have some anxiety about their problems—must be concerned about themselves—in order for therapeutic progress to be possible. However, while anxiety is considered a necessary ingredient of effective therapy, our present knowledge also leads us to believe that there is an optimal level of anxiety for each person. When the level of anxiety exceeds that point, a person is so overwhelmed by his anxiety that all of his energies are consumed in self-preservative efforts, leaving no energy for therapeutic movement. To the degree that ambiguous stimuli strain discriminative and defensive capacities, they arouse anxiety. We cited general experiments by Frenkel-Brunswik which confirm the assumption that ambiguity may arouse anxiety. Dibner (1958) gives us still further confirmatory evidence from studies of ambiguity as a characteristic of interpersonal relationships very similar to those in psychotherapy. He applied Osburn's (1952) methods of measuring ambiguity to admission interviews with patients referred to the psychiatric service of a general hospital. His interviewers, clinical psychologists, carried out half of their interviews with a strong set to be ambiguous and the other half with an equally strong set toward structuring the interview. Their compliance with the instructions was confirmed by measures of ambiguity applied to typewritten transcriptions of their recorded interviews. According to expectation, patients experiencing the more ambiguous interpersonal relationship were found to be more anxious during the interview. Since we may assume that people vary in the flexibility and effectiveness of their ego processes, and therefore in their susceptibility to anxiety in ambiguous situations, it becomes necessary for the counselor to relate the degree of ambiguity to the level of anxiety that will be optimal for the particular client.

Ambiguity may be one of the critical factors distinguishing effective therapeutic work with psychotic as compared to neurotic patients. Freud doubted the applicability of psychoanalysis to psychotic patients because he doubted they were capable of establishing a transference relationship. At present, therapists do hold that schizophrenic or psychotic patients are amenable to psychotherapy but they differ on the methods that should be used (Brody, & Redlich, 1952). Since it is assumed that schizophrenic personalities are characterized by inadequate and weak ego resources and therefore need help and encouragement to increase contact with reality,[3] one can infer that therapeutic relationships with schizophrenic patients, at least for a long part of the first stage, will be characterized by less ambiguity than relationships with neurotic patients. Even when presented with a relatively unambiguous stimulus situation, a schizophrenic is likely to react in purely idiosyncratic terms. Fromm-Reichmann, on the basis of considerable experience with psychotic patients, writes:

At the present state of psychoanalytic knowledge about repressive and dissociative processes, it proves to be unnecessarily time consuming, in my experience, to make the patient's free associations a central part

[3] See Eissler (in Brody & Redlich, 1952: pp. 130–167).

of intensive psychotherapy. In borderline patients and with outright psychotics this procedure carries with it the possible danger of inducing and increasing disintegrated thinking. For this reason encouraging psychotic patients to freely associate is strictly contraindicated (1950: p. 72).

This principle can be applied to counseling. For example, a counselor talking to a person of rather marked schizoid personality about his vocational plans must be sensitive to this person's need to try to be realistic—to validate and to revalidate his perception of the outside world. Such a person who is sufficiently in contact with reality to be aware of his tendency to distort is likely to be fighting a grim battle to maintain his contact with reality. Counselors who too readily interpret early requests for help and direction from the client as evidence of simple dependence are likely to overlook the occasions when these efforts represent desperate attempts on the part of the other person to get assistance as he gropingly tests the reality of his perceptions of the world. In such situations, not meeting the person's needs may discourage him in his efforts to be a healthy person and force him to choose the defeated approach of the psychotic. We cite this rather extreme example—a schizoid person—to underline the fact that the therapeutic needs of a particular person may call for less ambiguity and more structure, rather than the reverse.

Another limiting influence on the ambiguity of the therapeutic situation, which applies particularly to counseling, is the orientation to therapy of the person who comes to the counselor. The latter, because he interprets his services as being appropriate to all people and not necessarily limited to those who are being seriously incapacitated by their emotional problems, is often consulted by persons who do not by any means see their act of consultation as an admission that their problems have become too great for them and that they must come to someone else in order to unsnarl the situation. Many clients will, in fact, be reasonably adequate individuals who are faced with rather specific problems and decisions which they can and will be able to deal with, at least with a fair degree of adequacy. With or without the counselor's help, they can take care of their problem and can be expected to live satisfying lives, on the whole. In these instances, the act of coming to the counselor is more a symptom of adequacy than of inadequacy. They come to the counselor not out of desperation but as a positive and constructive act of using all resources in the solution of a particular problem. Their emphasis is upon what specific information or insights the counselor can contribute by his view of the problem they face or the decision they must make. An ambiguous therapeutic relationship calls for a relatively extended and intimate relationship with the counselor or therapist and the client must expect this in advance. It also presupposes a certain amount of giving up one's responsibility for oneself. In the free associative process one gives up, momentarily and to some degree, the responsibility for being rational, and depends upon the other person to ensure that the consequences of not being rational will not be unpleasant or destructive. The relatively adequate person whose coming to the counselor is more of a positive and constructive act usually has not made the decision to place his welfare in someone else's hands. He is not willing to assume an almost childlike role in his relationship with the therapist. Consequently, the amount of ambiguity that the counselor can introduce into the relationship is extremely limited unless these initial interviews do in fact uncover conflicts and release sufficient anxiety to lead to a modification of the person's perceptions of his goals for the relationship. The counselor must be ready to relate to people in ways that are appropriate to the kind of use they want to make of him. The counselor cannot interact with a person as though his needs were for intensive analysis of his own feelings when that person is only ready to use him for the purpose of testing external reality— the public or shared world about him.

Our emphasis on the fact that the client's needs influence the ambiguity characteristic of the therapeutic relationship should not divert us from noticing that the counselor is also subject to the anxiety-provoking effect of ambiguity. In an ambiguous counseling relationship there is less certainty and less control of the client's reaction. In this sense, ambiguity gives a certain freedom to the relationship, leading either to greater anxiety or greater expression of feeling by the client. One possible consequence is the more direct expression of feelings toward the counselor. This can be very threatening to the counselor if he is not both personally and professionally secure. Especially where negative feelings are elicited from the client, the inexperienced counselor (or one who is undertaking counseling without competent supervision) will be particularly prone to become fearful and attempt to escape through more structured manipulation of the relationship (see Bandura, Lipsher, and Miller, 1960, and Munson, 1960).

On the other hand, the counselor who is being ambiguous can be serving his own rather than the client's needs. As Benedek (1953) has pointed out, a counselor may react ambiguously, not because an effective therapeutic relationship demands such response, but rather as the expression of a need to avoid revealing himself as a person to the client, or, in the case of inexperienced therapists, as expression of his uncertainty and fear of making a wrong move. It was the failure to consider this function of ambiguity that probably led to negative results in part of Rigler's (1957) study of countertransference. Rigler expected that therapists, when anxious because of their own conflicts, would attempt to structure as a way of gaining control over the range of their patient's behavior. He found no special tendency in this direction, probably because in many instances his therapists reacted in the opposite manner, becoming more passive.

Because the counselor deals with relatively well-integrated individuals who are reasonably free from intense conflicts, his clients are not likely to exhibit many transference phenomena and will not readily develop intense transference relationships unless subjected to quite ambiguous relationships over a relatively long period of time. Since most clients will not come with a profound therapeutic orientation, deep transference can take place in only a minority of instances. However, this fact cannot conceal the other side of the picture, that all counselors are likely to work with an appreciable number of clients who come to them therapeutically oriented and are therefore ready to accept an ambiguously defined therapeutic relationship. In some settings, perhaps even a majority of the counselor's clients will come with this orientation. Among these clients there will be those whose conflicts are massive enough to constitute pronounced neurosis.

It is our conviction that ambiguity is a powerful tool in therapeutic relationships. To the degree to which this conviction is a valid one, its use is weighted with responsibility. The counselor who undertakes its use without adequate training, without a sufficiently deep knowledge of human behavior and personality, is irresponsibly playing with other people's lives. To do this is equivalent to prescribing powerful antibiotic drugs without knowledge of the conditions under which they will be harmful or helpful.

This is no imaginary danger. It has been attested too many times by our experience with relatively untrained counselors who have attempted to be "nondirective" with their clients. On such occasions, the effort to be nondirective often results in a counselor's being relatively ambiguous. We have seen the inexperienced counselor becoming involved in a very intense relationship in which the client exhibits feelings with which neither he nor the counselor is prepared to cope, and the result may be considerable emotional disturbance, sometimes even actual psychotic breaks.

We assert, therefore, that relatively untrained personnel workers, such as teachers, counselors, financial aid advisers, and so on, should establish definite limitations on the amount of ambiguity which they permit to arise in their advising relationships. Under these circumstances it is potentially much less harmful and much more appropriate to encourage rational, factual discussions of problems and decisions that must be faced, in the form that these are brought to the counselor, than to set as the goal of counseling the relatively free exploration of feelings, motivations, and emotions.

CHAPTER 7

The Cognitive and Conative Dimensions
of Therapeutic Relationships

ONE OF THE prime characteristics of purposive action is that it demands that attention be given to methods of achieving goals. Purposes involve the use of knowledge, motor skills, conceptual tools, or whatever resources the organism has available to employ in the attainment of a desired goal. Any analysis of a person's efforts to deal with his strivings inevitably includes the instrumental and cognitive aspects of what he is doing. In this chapter we shall consider the ways in which cognitive or instrumental behavior becomes a part of the therapeutic relationship and the purpose it serves.

The issue of the role of cognition in therapeutic processes becomes very specific when we compare the attitudes of Fenichel, Rogers, Allen, and Adler toward interpretation. Fenichel sees interpretation as the *sine qua non* of therapeutic progress. He assumes that the major goal in therapy is to permit the patient to become aware of his feelings, particularly conflicting ones, and to deal with them openly and realistically so that fuller integration of feeling and action is achieved. Our discussion on pp. 115–117 pointed out that Freudian theory assumes that in the neurotic process the individual develops elaborate systems of defense against awareness of conflicting feelings. These systems of defense are more or less intensely activated in the therapeutic process and appear as resistance to therapy and the therapeutic task. Therapy,

166

then, can not progress unless this resistance is removed, and, according to psychoanalytic theory, this removal is brought about through interpretation. The therapist points out to the patient that he is acting in certain ways toward therapy and the therapist, not because therapy and the therapist are the normal stimuli for eliciting these actions, but to protect himself against conflict. When the patient has consciously and rationally committed himself to the goal of therapy, this type of interpretation appeals to those motivations which are driving him toward positive effort and hence it enables him gradually to become more aware of his own efforts to defeat these positive goals. With more and more interpretive work he becomes increasingly aware of what lies behind his self-defeating efforts.

Rogers, on the other hand, considers interpretation inimical to therapeutic progress and emphasizes responses designed either to communicate the counselor's acceptance or to clarify whatever attitudes the client explicitly communicates. Rogers' position on interpretation follows logically from his assumption that the client's emotional difficulties arise when he internalizes the nonaccepting and threatening attitudes of other people toward him. Rogers argues that interpretation is a form of nonacceptance of the client, since when he is interpreting the counselor is assuming that the client is incapable of learning something about himself through his own efforts. This, Rogers says, is the equivalent of adopting a nonaccepting attitude toward the client and will simply reinforce the client's own internalized nonaccepting attitude toward himself, thus perpetuating the neurotic circle.

Allen also minimizes interpretation, but does not rule it out. His main concern is that the interpretive process be aimed not at the historical antecedents of the patient's present behavior but rather at the full meaning of the present behavior itself. This flows naturally from Allen's conception that it is the present relationship which is therapeutically important, that it is not necessary for the person to look backward to see that in this present relationship he is attempting to act in terms of past relationships rather than in terms of the reality of the present. He feels that it is sufficient for the person to learn to act in a new way in the present relationship and that this will transfer to his behavior in other situations. Thus Allen believes that too much importance can be attached to interpretation and that the real vehicle of therapy is not so much what the therapist says but how he acts in his relationship with the patient.

Adler goes to the opposite extreme in his view of interpretation. As we have seen, he is unimpressed by the Freudian's involvement with repression. Seemingly, he relies on the vividness with which he can portray the patient's life style to him by constructing the portrait out of the patient's words and actions which were displayed in the relationship. He seems less concerned about the separation of ideas from feelings, and the power of anxiety and impulses to block self-awareness and self-understanding.

THE COGNITIVE AND CONATIVE ASPECTS OF BEHAVIOR

Before we can resolve the issue of the use of interpretation, we must consider the functions of cognitive processes in behavior. We believe it is useful to look at behavior as possessing two aspects. One of these is affective, which refers to people's strivings, feelings, and emotions. We use the general term *conation* to include all these. The other aspect is instrumental, which refers to the conceptual, perceptual, and motor processes involved in response to the pressures inherent in the affective aspects of behavior. The general assumption is that the affective aspects of behavior are associated with the release of energy demanding some form of discharge. In the infant this release takes the form of disorganized, unintegrated motor discharge. When the infant is hungry, cold, wet, or otherwise uncomfortable, he thrashes about with arms and legs, cries, and so on. As he develops perceptual and motor integrations, he releases energy in organized action designed to provide the fullest possible expression of his need-dictated behavior. As needs and emotions become increasingly complex, conceptual aspects play an increasing role. This is why cognitive processes, particularly those derived from our use of language in communication, are probably the most critical ones in the modification and control of our most complex and most meaningful behavior.[1]

[1] Shaffer (1947) presents an analysis of psychotherapy as "a learning process through which a person acquires an ability to speak to himself in appropriate ways so as to control his own conduct."

In many ways our differentiation between the conative and cognitive aspects of behavior parallels the psychoanalytic concept of the relationship of id and ego. The id is, of course, the primary source of energy. As Hartmann has pointed out, a person, partly through biologically determined growth and partly through learning, acquires the apparatus which becomes a part of the ego and serves either the instrumental or defensive purposes of the ego.[2] He speaks of the relation between them in these words: "However, we also speak of collaboration of ego and id and in doing so seem to point to a variety of processes: The ego may serve the aims of the id; or the energy of the id is available for the aims of the ego; there may be substitution of ego aims for id aims or neutralization of instinctual energy" (1952: p. 16).

What we have sketched in brief thus far is a course of development whereby a person is able to achieve that perceptual and motor organization which leads to fullest expression and realization of the conative aspects of his life. However, processes of development are not characterized solely by this type of organization. When a person experiences the outside world as unusually punishing in response to his disorganized expression of affect, the perceptual and motor organization becomes designed to minimize the expression of impulse (Hartmann's "ego aims"). The cognitive and motor processes divide up the affect in order to keep a considerable portion of it from expression except as tension or else to drain off excess amounts of it in a number of different directions rather than in the direction naturally called for by the affect. These different means of indirectly draining off energy, of diverting it into a number of different small channels or controlling it and keeping it from expression, are defense mechanisms.

Thus we are suggesting that the cognitive aspects of behavior can serve two possible functions in their relationship to the conative or affective aspects of behavior. The cognitive aspects may either serve the purpose of controlling affect in the sense of leading to less or no expression, or may serve a truly instrumental function through the fullest possible successful expression of the affect.

Perhaps one meaningful way to describe neurosis is to say that the neurotic is one whose major efforts in the cognitive sphere are directed toward control and repression of impulse. The thera-

[2] See also Hartmann, Kris and Loewenstein (1946).

peutic process is intended to help him temporarily give up his efforts at control by investing the responsibility for control in the therapist, and finally to establish a new means of channeling his energies in a way which will be truly instrumental. Notice that in one sense both functions of the cognitive processes serve to control and organize energy. Uncontrolled and disorganized expressions of energy cannot be the goal of therapy. That this is frequently misunderstood as the goal of psychoanalytic therapy is probably because the analyst's initial aim is to enable his patient to give up his efforts at controlling his affects and to rely upon him, the therapist, to keep the affect within bounds. But later, by interruption of the cycle of self-defeating control, the therapist hopes to enable the patient to re-establish control in a more positive satisfying form.

Before discussing how these concepts apply to interpretation, let us also examine the concept of ego strength. In general, this term has been used in reference to the number and quality of the resources available to the ego in carrying out its defensive or instrumental functions. Those biological and environmental factors that contribute to the development of intellectual capacity also contribute to the development of a strong ego. Intellectual capacity refers to the ability to perform certain kinds of functions which are included in the term *ego*. However, ego also refers to specific information and skills, to modes of thought, and to modes and techniques of interpersonal action. All of these contribute to ego strength. Thus, a counselor who makes relevant educational or vocational information available or who explains certain aspects of marital relations to a client is contributing to his ego strength. As we have suggested, the ego's resources may be used either for defensive or for instrumental purposes. Thus, ego strength is not in itself identical with freedom from neurotic conflict.

APPLICATIONS TO INTERPRETATION

Let us now apply our conception of the role of cognition to the questions that arise about interpretation in the therapeutic process. Because the person in conflict is using all available means to keep his affect from awareness and expression, any strong emphasis on cognition in early interactions with him will be used by him in the service of these defenses through the mechanisms of intellectualization and isolation. This suggests two principles for the use of interpretation in therapists' communication. The first of these is that prior to the loosening of the tight grip of these defensive processes on expression and experiencing of affect, interpretation whether accepted or rejected will be relatively ineffectual. Too often inexperienced counselors attempt to judge the appropriateness or accuracy of their communication by whether the client accepts or rejects it. This is a wholly fallacious criterion. In some cases, the too-ready acceptance of an interpretation may mean that the client has succeeded in momentarily achieving an objective view of himself by divorcing this view from the affect with which it is usually associated. Momentarily, he is being rational. However, he has not learned to utilize these resources of rationality on occasions when he experiences the affect. On the contrary, when he is in the affective state he will revert to anxiety and to the associated need to defend himself against impulse expression. One way of doing this may be to use the counselor's communication as reassurance that this affect cannot threaten him. A counselor need only have a short interview with a psychologically sophisticated client who makes use of a great deal of intellectualization and isolation to see this phenomenon in action. Such a client may talk about his deepest and most intense feelings with the objectivity and detachment he might feel in talking about some hypothetical man on Mars. On the other hand, a rejection of an interpretation may be expressed with a kind of affect which indicates the client's awareness of the accuracy of the communication and, if the interpretation is not withdrawn, this can lead to further therapeutic progress.

A second principle in the use of interpretation is that the amount of emphasis on the cognitive aspects of the interactions between the therapist and the client should be related to the intensity of affect which the client expresses. The more intense the affect, the more cognitive can be the communication by the therapist without causing the client to revert to cognitive processes as a means of repression. On the other hand, where the client's resources for channeling his affect are relatively limited, it may be necessary for the therapist to encourage cognitively dominated intercommunication either to give the patient a momentary respite from the tension involved in the expression of affect which threatens to run away with him, or to enable him to develop the cognitive resources necessary for successful channeling.

It follows from the foregoing two principles that interpretation is not necessarily of therapeutic value. It can only be of use to the client when he is ready for it, when he can achieve through it some more effective integration between the affective and the instrumental aspects of his behavior, a new integration which will lead to fuller and more successful expression of affect and the satisfying release of energy.[3]

Cognition and ambiguity

The encouragement of cognitive processes and the maintenance of ambiguity are closely linked in an inverse relationship. Intensive psychoanalytic therapy with neurotic patients seems to be characterized by a great deal of ambiguity in the prolonged initial phase of the process and an increased cognitive emphasis in the latter stages, at a time when the client is better able to release his rigid controls on expression of his feelings. However, whether the increased cognitive emphasis results in decreased ambiguity will depend upon the timing and appropriateness of these communications. Inappropriate complexity of interpretation has a way of being exierenced by the client as "This is what he thinks about me." But when the interpretation is accurately stated, appropriately timed, and directed toward the client's level of thought, it will be experienced by him as "This is how I feel," accompanied by a more vivid awareness of those feelings. Such interpretations will contribute not so much to the client's perception of the counselor but rather toward an increased awareness of himself and will not change the essential ambiguity of the counselor and the counseling situation.

Cognition and play therapy

As we suggested in Chapter 5, cognitive processes will not play such an important role in play therapy. The young child is

---

[3] Speisman (1959) provided one kind of empirical support for these assertions by demonstrating that interpretations that are directed slightly beyond the patient's level of awareness are more likely to be followed by increased effectiveness of therapeutic work than either shallower or deeper ones.

still relatively dependent upon motor and nonverbal perceptual resources for the expression and control of his feelings. He has not yet developed the resources of conceptualization and language which he will have at a later stage of his development. Consequently, helping him to establish new types of cognitive-conative relationships will depend less upon the language aspect of interactions with him. It is natural, then, that one, like Allen, who is speaking primarily of therapeutic work with children, should place less emphasis on interpretive processes, particularly the more complex ones that must be used to link feelings immersed in the past with present feelings.

Cognition and respect for the individual

One of our chief aims in this book, as is reflected in a reappearing theme, is to free the counselor of the burden of unnecessary guilt he might feel, for example, on being told that his methods implied lack of respect for his client. We have already said we do not believe that assuming a person will not discover something for himself is in any way an expression of lack of respect for either his integrity or his capacity to learn. Perhaps our position can best be clarified by an analogy: We neither expect our children to rediscover for themselves euclidian geometry or calculus or the principles of atomic physics, least of all in the same way that they were originally discovered, nor do we think anyone would claim that such a process is necessary for the fullest development of the individual. Even the "learning by doing" enthusiasts do not expect the learner to have conceived on his own the idea for an experiment which he repeats. To require this would in effect mitigate against progress in the accumulation of human knowledge, since each generation would in the extreme case have to repeat the same mistakes, the same trial-and-error processes as the preceding generation, only finally to break down at the same point as they did. Progress demands that we start with the discoveries of others and proceed beyond them. For the development of our children this means that we must guide them to certain cognitions and teach them certain skills so they can more quickly discover the modes of action which are likely to lead onward to their fullest self-realization.

UNDERSTANDING THE CLIENT

Counseling as compared with psychotherapy is likely to be more dominated by cognition. The client most typically comes to the counselor because of some very specific situation, some very specific decision, with which he feels unable to deal. Typically, also, these external problems are not as much of his own making as are those that require psychotherapy. His difficulties are certainly less severe, with, therefore, less distortion of reality. Less frequently than the person who needs psychotherapy, he comes to the counselor with the vaguer and more ill-defined feeling of being generally unhappy and dissatisfied with himself. Consequently, the usual client's initial orientation is toward dealing with some specific problem that faces him. Only partially does he acknowledge that he, rather than the outside world, is the critical factor to be understood. His attention is focused on what manipulations of his external environment will produce a solution of the specific problem. Thus, his communications will be heavily dominated by the instrumental aspects of his situation.

Either through inexperience or through a theoretical orientation to counseling which plays down the affective aspects of behavior, a counselor may be disproportionately sensitive and responsive to the cognitive aspects of the client's communication. He may get involved in such relatively objective questions as whether one university or another offers the best training for particular occupations, or whether the client's job prospects are sufficiently stabilized to warrant the responsibilities of marriage and a family. In concentrating on these judgments of matters of fact, the counselor may lose sight of the strivings that are being communicated to him. In his communications, from one point of view, the client seems to be trying to decide which school offers the best training for his occupational choice. When looked at from another point of view, it is evident that the client's discussion of these choices is more oriented toward the question of how near or far from home certain schools are. If one follows this thread further, one begins to see evidence of a conflict about whether to get farther away from his parents or stay near them.

Undoubtedly, emphasis on the affective and personality goals of counseling has often led counselors and psychotherapists to the opposite mistake, namely, to neglect the realistic and cognitive aspects of the person's life. In fact, psychoanalytically oriented psychotherapists frequently set up the condition that the patient not make any definite decision or change his life in any drastic way during the period of intensive psychotherapy. This prohibition seems defensible from the point of view that patients who are prone to use motor defenses, or, as it is termed, "acting out,"[4] might make decisions and take actions in their lives which are designed to defeat the aims of therapy and which are expressions of resistance to the therapeutic process. However, it is unrealistic to assume that patient and therapist can and should exclude from consideration or preclude action on the many realistic problems that can beset a patient during therapy. It is rarely possible for a patient to suspend all changes in his life for the two- or three-year period required in intensive psychotherapy. People change jobs, their fiancés demand definite decisions now, the army calls. The very fact that one cannot stop the movement of the world around him means that he cannot completely neglect major relationships to it. Therefore the psychotherapist as well as the counselor must balance concern for the patient's emotions and motivation with consideration of the specific decisions that the person faces in his life, decisions that must be made now and cannot be postponed.

In the school setting, even though the counselor may be convinced that the eventual resolution of conflict about a vocational choice lies in the unraveling of certain emotional problems, he may still have to recognize that a student has reached the end of one semester and is forced by circumstances to make certain immediate choices. Such a student cannot postpone decision until he has resolved his conflicts. Therefore the counselor must be prepared to interrupt intensive analysis of feelings to consider with the client the best decision he can make at that point. If the final directions he will take are not yet clear, the counselor will help him accept the necessity of straddling the issue for the present.

Agreement with what we have been recommending does not preclude the possibility that with a particular client it may prove more appropriate for the counselor to minimize the part he plays in helping the client make this particular rational decision and to

[4] See Greenacre (1952: Ch. 11) for a more thorough discussion of acting out.

encourage his client to go to another—an academic—counselor for
the actual review of the pros and cons he must weigh. Such an
arrangement might be particularly suitable if the time for the
decision came when the client was experiencing considerable negative feelings toward his counselor. Under these circumstances,
these negative feelings toward the counselor, which will pass only
after some time, may interfere with cooperative work on a specific
decision. In other instances, it may be important for the psychological counselor to send the client to the academic counselor with
a decision virtually made.

Thus, we can say that to understand the client most completely, it is necessary for the counselor to understand as fully as
possible both the cognitive and conative aspects of the client's
communications. Focusing attention on one aspect to the exclusion
of the other is likely to give the counselor a distorted picture of
the client. Talk that may seem a distorted message or an effort to
resist therapy may turn out on further examination to be a realistic attempt to deal wihh some very specific phase of his external
situation. The conative aspects of the client's communication are
the ones which will tax to the utmost the counselor's sensitivities
and understanding of human behavior. Here we hold that a
correct theoretical orientation to personality and personality development is important. We believe that the counselor will be
most sensitive to the subtlest nuances of the client's communications when he has begun to develop an understanding of the
client's major conflicts and his ways of dealing with them. Without
such understanding, the counselor may achieve only a superficial
sensitivity to his client's feelings and needs. He may become aware
that his client is reacting to him in a hostile and aggressive manner, yet he may be insensitive to the further cues that the client
is using this hostile and aggressive manner to fight off feelings of
affection, feelings of being drawn to the counselor, which make
him feel anxious.

Although we have emphasized personality theory as an aid to
understanding, we should also call attention to the part played by
empathy. A number of writers, like Reik (1949), have argued that
understanding is almost a process of free associating to the patient's associations. In this sense, the therapist gains his understanding through the chords struck on his emotions by those the

patient is experiencing. In effect, Fenichel argues that some balance between "free floating" and compulsive intellectualism is necessary to provide a desirable "oscillation from intuition to understanding and knowledge" (1941: pp. 3–14). What this amounts to is that the counselor cannot hope to understand his client deeply unless he can apply his own cognitive and conative capacities to the task.

Whether one assumes that the processes of therapy are solely those of understanding and acceptance of the client or one assumes that therapy involves understanding plus some form of appropriate interaction with the client, achieving the deepest possible understanding will remain as one of the prerequisites of effective counseling or psychotherapeutic processes.

COGNITIVE-CONATIVE BALANCE IN THE RELATIONSHIP

We turn now to consider how both cognitive and conative aspects of understanding are manifest in the interactions between counselor and client. By his actions and by his communications to the client, the counselor can encourage greater or less dominance of the cognitive or conative aspects of the client's communications. He may ask questions about the relationship of one set of feelings to another or the relationship of a set of feelings to certain past events or by similar means focus the client's attention on the rationale of his behavior.

When the structural psychologists were studying emotion through the method of introspection, they discovered that the process of introspecting a feeling leads to its disappearance and only the emotional idea or subject is left (1919: pp. 22–23). This phenomenon must be at least somewhat related to what accounts for the effectiveness of intellectualization and isolation as defenses The intellectualizer is one who removes the anxiety associated with his impulses by the process of examining and analyzing them.

The counselor must gauge the amount of encouragement to cognition he offers by his understanding of the client. A client who represses his motivations and emotions by an over-rational and over-intellectual examination of them needs to be encouraged to pay less attention to his feelings, to express his feelings more freely, and to relax these efforts at controlling them. On the other hand, a client who seems to freely express his feelings but to repress the ideational connections with them needs to be encouraged to introduce more conceptual aspects into his communications.

One feature of the cognitive aspects of the interaction between counselor and client which may be more characteristic of counseling than of psychotherapy is the rather specific role that cognitions, either in the form of information or a particular rationale, can play in helping the client reorient himself. If we accept the view that integrated behavior is the ability to apply our information, our motor skills, and our reasoning resources to the process of satisfying our needs, then the more resources the individual has when he is free of conflicting goals, the more adequately he can attain this integration and the more completely he can attain his goals. People who are relatively well-integrated emotionally are able to make fuller use of these resources. Thus, in a counseling situation, and more particularly in the frequent case where one is dealing with a normally maturing personality, one can afford to expend more effort in aiding the person with the acquisition of these instrumental resources.

Giving information and calling attention to general understandings of human behavior will be of use when they are introduced during a period of relatively low resistance. The therapeutic process is characterized by an undulating curve of resistance. There are periods when the client rushes ahead eagerly to new insights, or, if he doesn't rush, at least progresses with ease and with comfortable feelings toward what he will learn. At other stages he is fearful and defensive. The introduction of new cognitions would seem to be most appropriate at times when the client is neither rushing ahead, stimulated by his discoveries and relieved by finding that his feelings do not lead to the anticipated punishment, nor when he is caught up in feelings of fear and discomfort at what the process might bring, when he is trying to avoid the pressures of the process. In the first instance, attempts on the part of the counselor to introduce cognition could appear as either annoying, distracting evidences of the counselor's lack of understanding the client, or, where they are perceived as relevant to the feelings and ideas being discovered, as efforts to rob him of initiative and the feeling of having accomplished something by his own efforts. This is a period where it is likely to be neither necessary nor therapeutic for the counselor to provide the significant interpretation. This is the period when the counselor can react so as to prepare the ground for the client's leap in awareness of some important aspect of himself. It is the client who makes the final interpretation. The counselor's role is that of making partial interpretations which lead up to, but do not themselves state the important ones. On the other hand, when the client is defensive and fearful and motivated to avoid therapy, any effort to introduce cognitions that are not specifically related to the avoidance will be seen and distorted in the light of the defense. The counselor will appear to the client as trying to lecture or force certain ideas and certain conclusions upon him. It is probable that in most cases the most effective approach to the interpretive process, when it is aimed at the resistance itself, is likely to be a period of relatively little cognitive emphasis on the part of the counselor. In some cases, it may be best preceded by a period of relatively little activity of any kind by the counselor. In this way, an opportunity is afforded for feelings to build up more strongly in the client with a consequent increased pressure for some form of expression which should be responded to in relatively descriptive rather than interpretive terms. Finally, when the feelings are built up and their implications of avoidance are close to awareness, the significant interpretation of resistance is made.

INTERPRETIVE TECHNIQUE

There is also the question of how one interprets. Preceding discussions have applied mostly to the timing of interpretation. The counselor will wish to think also of the form in which he will deliver his interpretation. This is less a matter of theory than of art. Though each counselor will want to observe the modes of expression used by others, he will also want to discover which modes are most natural for him.

In various places, therapists have discussed these problems of technique.[5] Colby has provided useful definitions of three types of interpretations: (a) clarifications; (b) comparisons; and (c) wish-

[5] The reader who wishes to pursue this further is referred to Fromm-Reichmann (1950: Ch. 8) and to Colby (1951: pp. 82–106).

defense. This classification refers both to content and technique. *Clarification* interpretations are defined as statements designed to crystallize the client's "thoughts and feelings around a particular subject, to focus his attention on something requiring further investigation and interpretation, to sort out a theme from apparently diversified material, or to summarize the understanding thus far achieved. They make take the form of questions, mild imperatives or simplified restatements" (1951: p. 83). This formulation corresponds closely to the nondirective conceptions of reflection and clarification. *Comparison* interpretations are those in which "the therapist places two (or more) sets of events, thoughts or feelings side by side for comparison. They may parallel one another or show contrast. They may be concurrent or separated in time. Common typical subject compared are present with past behavior, fantasy with reality, the patient's self with others, childhood with adulthood and attitude toward parent with attitude toward friend, spouse or therapist. Comparisons may be used to emphasize patterns of repetitive similarities or to indicate recurring contradictions. They may be phrased in any form, the most frequent being the everyday ways of matching things" (1951: pp. 84–85). Finally, *wish-defense* interpretations are defined as those which point directly to the wish-defense components of a neurotic conflict. Following psychoanalytic theory, he suggests that, as far as possible, the defense components be interpreted first.

Working through

Although the client may become aware that his highly negative attitudes toward his instructors reflect his fear that he will give in to impulses to become highly dependent upon them, this does not necessarily mean there will be any significant change in his general reactions around wishes for dependence. He may not even change his behavior toward his instructors. This phenomenon reflects the highly organized character of impulse-defense conflicts. Major modifications are achieved when a significant portion of the contexts for the conflict and the kinds of defenses against it are successively brought to awareness. As the client begins to see in context after context, one method of defense after another in which the aim is to protect against the wish, he achieves the generalized awareness which can lead to more positively purposed, less distorted action on his impulses. Fromm-Reichmann writes, in explaining why she prefers to use the word *insight* to refer to something beyond the referents of the terms *understanding* and *awareness:* "I wished to convey, by this very choice of terminology, that the intellectual and rational grasp of one interpretation of a single experience, as a rule, will be changed only by the process of 'working through' into the type of integrated creative understanding which deserves to be termed 'insight'" (1950: pp. 141–142).

It is this phrase "working through" which has been used to refer to the repetitive process of rediscovery where the client finds that "there, too!" his needs to defend against his dependent impulses are the primary determiners of that interpersonal relationship. In intensive psychotherapy, working through is an extended process. Where counseling is carried on with an already well-integrated client, the need for working through may be considerably diminished, to the point where awareness of one or two experiences will serve to activate "creative understanding." From experience with such clients, one becomes convinced that it is the defensive attitude toward the impulse that must be changed. Extensive working through becomes necessary only when the individual is so beset with conflicts that these defensive attitudes will not give way easily.

COUNSELOR NEEDS

It has been generally assumed that the interpretive work of counselors and psychotherapists will be influenced by the distorting effects of countertransference. Cutler (1958) has demonstrated the validity of this assumption in a study of therapists' recall of events in therapy and their behavior in response to client reactions which reflect their own areas of conflict. With two therapists as subjects, he identified areas of defensive behavior in interpersonal relations (as developed by Freedman, *et al.* [1951]) which revealed evidence of conflict. When he compared therapist recall of his own or his client's interpersonal behavior with actual events as shown by typescript, he found that the therapists had distorted recall for those areas in which they had shown conflict. Cutler also related the frequency of defensive behavior of any type by the therapist to the area of defensive behavior manifested by the client. As expected, he found that the therapists manifested much more frequent defensive behavior in response to client behavior which impinged on their own conflicts than in response to behavior toward which they were neutral.

When the client reveals conflicting feelings that bear on his own conflicts, the counselor may press upon the client certain interpretations and cognitions which are not necessarily relevant to the client's problems or to his present stage in the counseling process but which are imperative to the counselor's defense against his own conflicts. This will be true where the counselor's preferred defenses are intellectualization and isolation. On the other hand, the counselor may be unaware of the conflicts expressed by the client because his own defenses involve keeping the conflicts out of awareness.

Many times it is less the content of a conflict than the intensity of a close emotional relationship which the counselor is defending against. To avoid the latter, the counselor may be impelled to encourage considerable cognitive interchange between himself and the client. In several ways he seems to be saying to the client, "Don't let your feelings run away with you, be rational, be a sensible, emotionally controlled person." According to his own dynamics, the client may respond to this anxiety on the part of the counselor with fearful compliance on his part. Or, again, he may feel it necessary to torment the counselor into making it possible for him to withdraw from the therapeutic situation.

It seems as though a natural selective process operates to attract as counselors and psychotherapists persons who make a great deal of use of intellectualization. Consequently, counselors will be particularly prone to overencourage dependence upon verbalization and the use of reasoning. Therefore, we cannot close this chapter without re-emphasizing the point that interpretation can advance the therapeutic process only at those times when it is relevant to a client's needs.

In this chapter we have, for the most part, directed our discussion to the general considerations influencing the introduction of information, skills, or concepts by the counselor. In Part III we shall take up some of the more specific problems of process that are associated with the use of interpretation or information.

CHAPTER 8

Personal Dimensions in Therapeutic Relationships[1]

IN THE TWO preceding chapters, we discussed those phases of therapeutic relationships which are more nearly under the conscious control of therapists. Even there we pointed out personal factors of which the counselor is largely unaware that may introduce therapeutic elements into these relationships. Now we want to say more directly that the knowledge of how relationships become therapeutic is not to be applied mechanically. The counselor or therapist who mechanically applies the formulas of therapy probably will not be of much help to his patients. His reactions must be relatively spontaneous manifestations of his understanding of the client and his current needs, both overt and latent. His knowledge of psychotherapeutic theory may, of course, enable him to spot, in retrospect, occasions where his response may not have been therapeutic and to seek the personal reasons for his inadequacy. But that is another matter and does not alter the general recommendation of spontaneity.

In this chapter we shall consider the contribution of emotional tones to therapeutic relationships. We shall discuss those aspects of the therapist's interaction with his patient which are probably least subject to conscious control. The emotional tone of the counselor's relationship to the client probably reflects most

[1] This chapter is largely drawn from two papers (Raush & Bordin, 1957; Bordin, 1965).

fully his natural ways of interacting with others, his personality conflicts and integrations—his life style. How various emotionally-toned relationships may contribute to the client's therapeutic progress is our topic.

The psychoanalytic and client-centered theoretical orientations, which have most influenced therapeutic style, started by driving underground the positive role of personal factors in the therapist. In its own way, each theory saw a departure from ideal therapist behavior in any intrusion of the therapist's personality. The principle of the "blank screen" as a cornerstone of the psychoanalytic method seemed to dictate the blurring of the therapist's real characteristics. Departures from this specification were part of the condemned "countertransference." The prohibitions for the client-centered therapist centered on the imposition of values and goals. This theory's concern with respect for individuality and its faith in a person's inner resources, which only need release which can be brought about by an experience of this faith in another, confined the therapist to understanding and reflection. To depart from these specifications was to be "directive," as condemning in this framework as "countertransference" is in psychoanalysis.

With the passing of time both positions have had to be modified. Psychoanalysts had to recognize that the ideal of the blank screen was just that—a human relationship cannot proceed meaningfully without some degree of expressed mutuality, even within the confines of a technical situation (Stone, 1961). Papers on countertransference (Flescher, 1953; Racker, 1953; Spitz, 1956) began to pull and stretch the term to include positive uses of the therapist's personal conflicts and it was often used to refer to any expression of the therapist's personality occurring during the therapeutic hour, whether or not it reflected inner conflict. In the case of client-centered theory the transition was easier. Attention simply shifted from the therapist's behavior in psychotherapy to his general attitudes and understanding of his patient. Current concerns are with the therapist's genuineness (Rogers, 1957) and transparency (Truax & Carkhuff, 1965).

This new emphasis on the kind of person the therapist is, as contrasted with principles of therapeutic change and training to apply them, may seem to take psychotherapy out of the realm of science. If we look below the surface, however, we can see that the same processes of acquiring and verifying knowledge underlie these features of the enterprise. In order to understand why certain ways of responding, now seen as more spontaneous than calculated, play a part in personality change we must search for their connections to personality development and personality differences. This means that a person cannot learn to be, or function as a therapist without being wholly involved. He cannot approach psychotherapy as he would a purely intellectual exercise—antiseptically free of any contact with his personal reactions. On the contrary, he will need to come to grips with the whole range of his own impulses, their derivatives and offshoots in the forms of fantasy, feelings, ideas, and defensive reactions. He must be sufficiently at home with himself to be able to contribute the humanness of personal encounter which is a vital part of psychotherapy.

Before proceeding further, some comments on the confusing issue of the role of the therapist's values in psychotherapy are in order. Freud's insistence on muting the therapist's impact as a means of opening up the patient's inner life and Rogers' devotion to the role of acceptance and respect seemed to rule out active expression of the therapist's values, either as judgments or determiners of the directions in which behavior is to be molded. Yet, if psychotherapy requires involvement, can this involvement occur without bringing the therapist's values into the relationship? One source of the confusion lies in the referents of the term *value*. In some contexts, the term refers to a general view of man. Most theories of personality and psychotherapy have been accompanied by an implicit commitment to the goal of fostering maximum self-fulfillment, usually with the assumption that it cannot be achieved at the expense of others, not only because societies impose sanctions against some forms of self-centeredness, but because self-centeredness is in itself an obstacle to fulfillment. In the above we can see a view of how man functions, which is empirically verifiable and which happens to coincide with the sets of values that have been espoused by societies. This is to be expected. Just as man seeks to come to terms with his natural environment, so he seeks to come to terms with his own nature. It is not surprising, therefore, that man's social organization and the rules and commitments which underlie it will be reflections of his state of understanding human behavior and the motives which are part of it.

In the above discussion of *values*, psychotherapists' conceptions of human behavior and the goals of their therapeutic work are in an intimate and interacting relationship with the values of the societies of which they are a part. But this term is also used to apply to the particularization of the general formula of fulfillment which a specific person evolves. Within our social fabric and natural environment it is possible to pursue alternate paths of fulfillment which reflect the unique biosocial resources of the individual and the special experiences which condition his interests. In this context, the individual's values become his unique response to the choices available to him. One chooses the artistic rather than the scientific, the active materialistic life rather than the passive contemplative life, etc. There are many ways in which the general formula for self-fulfillment can be particularized and specific psychotherapy represents only one particularization. It is consistent with the theoretical positions to stipulate that an effort to impose one's own pattern is likely to interfere with the general aims of therapy.

We must acknowledge that in an intense relationship of some duration, where one of the participants feels bereft of resources, there is going to be considerable stimulus to use the other as a model. In some instances the therapist's pattern will be compatible with the patient, making this modeling process useful. Therefore, some therapists come to emphasize this feature of therapeutic effort. One cannot, however, count on such compatibility. Too great a reliance on modeling will provide ineffective therapy for many patients. The kinds of technical specifications discussed in the preceding chapters will introduce the means by which the patient achieves change other than by modeling himself after the therapist. Further, the personal reactions of the therapist can contribute to the therapeutic process in other ways than as a model so that the patient may realize his unique possibilities.

One more issue beckons us, namely, that of the role of disliking a patient. Some therapists speak as though all patients are likable if only they are approached in the proper frame of mind. Others recommend that if the therapist dislikes a patient he should refer him. Surely, there are dislikable persons, persons who cannot be honest with themselves or others, who are sly, hating, and craven. The therapist is unlikely to be helpful to his client when he must defend himself against feelings of dislike by denying or distorting them. Yet he must be able to achieve enough distance from them to give his attention to what part the dislike-provoking behavior plays in the balance of forces within the patient and how the patient is defeating himself by this behavior. When he finds that his dislike for a particular person is so great as to preclude this step, then his ethical commitments require him to suggest another therapist. One of the most insidious defenses against one's dislike of and irritation with a particular client is to tell him "for his own good" how dislikable he is. There are times when it furthers therapy to acknowledge the reactions the patient provokes, but we must also be sensitive to the countertransference potentialities in such a maneuver.

WARMTH AS A THERAPEUTIC INGREDIENT

Discussion of the personal qualities of psychotherapists which facilitate therapy has usually dealt with subtle qualities touching on liking and caring, expressing and giving, and being genuine and human. Usually, this conception has incorporated both the objectivity and the closeness that idealize the parent. "Warmth" is the term most frequently used to refer to this complex of qualities, as when Braatøy says: "Psychoanalytic and related personal psychotherapy are based on the changes which occur in a person when he is given the chance to unburden himself in the presence of another healthier, more independent individual. This process will never start unless the therapist from the beginning has a surplus of warmth" (1954: pp. 1–2). Warmth has had so many referents and has been used ambiguously so often that it has lost some of its communicative value. Therefore, we shall concentrate on three specific components of warmth—commitment, effort to understand, and spontaneity. After a brief description of each, we will consider, in turn, the relevance of each component to personality development and differences, and its role in psychotherapy and counseling.

Commitment—The therapist demonstrates some degree of willingness to be of assistance to the patient. This assistance may vary in degree of activity and concreteness. For example, the therapist may offer help in the form of setting limits, breaking limits, or actively collaborating with the patient in the solution of an external problem, or he may offer help only by giving his time. At any given moment, the therapist occupies some point along a continuum representing degree of commitment. Commitment as a therapeutic variable is a measure of the therapist's willingness to substitute his own resources for those the patient lacks or is momentarily unable to use.

Effort to Understand—The therapist shows his effort to understand by asking questions designed to elicit the patient's view of himself and the world, by testing with the patient the impressions that he, the therapist, has gained of these views, and by indicating, by comments or other actions, his interest in understanding the patient's view. At the other extreme, in addition to the absence of the kind of behavior just described, the therapist tends to act as though he had a preconceived view of the patient, his actions and his feelings.

Spontaneity—The least spontaneous therapist is guarded, either consciously or unconsciously masking all of his feelings. These masked feelings may be intimately related to the underlying needs and feelings of the patient, or they may be those which occur as part of the natural interaction between any two people. Such a therapist maintains an impassive mien and is likely to be inhibited in all of his motor expressions, i.e. gestures. His verbal communications are marked by stereotypy, formalism, and stiffness. The least spontaneous therapist, may, however, seem to act impulsively. Such impulsivity will have a compelled and unnatural quality.

Commitment and dependency

The relevance of commitment to psychotherapy is obvious because it is characterized by one person, the patient, turning to another, the therapist, for help. Understanding what degree of commitment by the therapist will be beneficial necessarily turns attention to the issue of dependency—patients' dispositional states which influence their seeking or avoiding the aid of others. Therapists must concern themselves with how and to what degree the behavior of their patients is influenced by the necessity of having to reply on another person.

For descriptive purposes it is convenient to group dependency reactions into three types. The pattern of reaction most easily identified is overt dependency. The patient exhibiting this pattern never seems to get enough help from the therapist. He tends to react in a hostile demanding manner. He complains of others' coldness, distance, and unconcern for his welfare. When he criticizes himself it is for his inability to appeal effectively to others for help. He wants to be led through therapy, to comply with the directions of the therapist and to acquiesce to the therapist's wishes. An alternative defensive reaction to the necessity of relying on another is more subtle because it entails denial. Following Thelen and Stock (1958), we will call it counter-dependency. The counter-dependent patient reacts to the therapist's offer of help as though it were excessive, inappropriate, debilitating or, in fact, unhelpful. He is likely to emphasize his ability to solve his own problems outside of therapy. He refers to others as oversolicitous and interfering. This patient criticizes himself in terms of his inability to achieve. He speaks of the need to overcome his deficiencies, master situations, take himself in hand, and control himself. He will often take an active, leading, and even competitive, role in therapy. He tries to achieve and retain control of the situation. In the third pattern of response, true independence, or freedom from dependency problems, the person exhibits his readiness to rely on his own resources and to increase them where possible, while not being made uncomfortable when he must rely on others. Even more, he is able to establish close mutual dependencies with others that involve merging into a larger unit.

Dependency is treated in a variety of ways in clinical and theoretical discussions. It usually includes patient maneuvers designed to shift responsibility to the therapist or others for problem-solving, choice of content for communication, etc. In many instances the term is applied to efforts to achieve gratification through eliciting expressions of interest, affection, and love. Customarily the contrasting state of a patient is explicitly or implicitly defined as that of independence, when he no longer turns to others for assistance or emotional support. Apart from other complications, it is as though there were a single continuum from behavioral dependence to independence, with psychological maturity to be found at the latter end. The idea that the evolution of personality is characterized by a persistent push toward independence and self-reliance has been featured by most of the neo-Freudian points of view, especially by Rank ("will") and Rogers ("self-actualization"). As the above described patient behavior illustrates, a single continuum does not seem adequate. One difficulty is that psychological maturity hardly seems to require that a person be sufficient unto himself either instrumentally or in terms of gratification. Mutuality of dependence rather than independence seems a more exact description of mature interpersonal relationships. In fact, the image of an exaggeratedly independent person, seeking to live as though he needed no one was associated by Alexander (1934) with certain gastro-intestinal disorders. Others, such as Cairns (1961), have described the same behavior in terms of dependency inhibition.

One of the ways of dealing with this complexity is to posit two opposing forces, one that pushes the person toward separation and self-reliance, and another that pushes toward intimacy and mutuality. One might have chosen Allen's terms, "differentiation" and "integration," but I prefer to designate the opposing sources of this ambivalence around dependence and independence as a drive toward mastery and anxiety surrounding its exercise. Man can be described as responding to the long period following birth, when he must rely almost fully on others, by developing a drive toward mastery[2] which exerts a lifelong pressure to accumulate the resources, knowledge, strength, and skills upon which self-reliance can rest. The opposing pressure is seen as anxiety arising from the fact that total self-reliance is an impossibility and that even mutual reliance inescapably leads to some delay and frustration. The forces opposing the urge to mastery are augmented by those created by the circumstances that our deepest gratifications are to be gained in interpersonal rela-

---

[2] White (1963) has suggested a somewhat similar concept which he calls "effectance," and which he describes as "inherently an urge away from the necessity of being mothered" (p. 77).

tionships in which we give up our autonomy in connection with friendship, love, and marriage. One of the important tasks of maturation is the resolution of this timeless dilemma of reconcil-ing the competing motivations toward mastery and intimacy.

To recapitulate, in order to understand better why and how the degree of therapist commitment can be adapted to the nature of the patient's dependency problems, a conflict has been suggested between the urge toward mastery and the inescapable anxiety associated with limitations of self-reliance. Before moving directly to the applications of these concepts to psychotherapy, we shall consider their application in the context of the child's develop-ment as he evolves in his relationship with his parents.

Development of mastery drive and anxiety about its exercise

The infant's inability to cope with his own needs means he must rely almost completely upon his parents for need-satisfaction, producing a one-sided relationship. Commitment is almost exclu-sively infant-directed. This condition has given rise to the concept of the infantile illusion of omnipotence in Freudian theory. It is assumed that for the infant no boundaries exist between himself and his environment. His wishes are followed by gratifying ac-tions on the part of his caretaker with the result that he develops the illusion of being in complete control of his world. Unfortu-nately this idea rests on a wholly improbable conception of a parent. It seems self-evident that from the very beginning the infant will experience delay between the onset of a need and its gratification. The length of these delays will vary at least as a function of the distance between mother and child when the child begins to emit signals of need. The period of delay will also vary as a function of the interposition of those needs of the mother that are contrary to the act required to gratify her child. Even the most dedicated of mothers will not always drop what she is doing at the first cry. Thus, the infant experiences variations in the time intervening between the first part of the sequence, feel need, and the second part, someone else satisfies, and after a while forms an ideal of a minimum period of delay. The infant learns also that other persons, principally his mother, do not always act to satisfy that ideal.

While all this is happening, presumably over a period of weeks and months, the infant is maturing to the point where sufficient eye-hand coordination is attained to reach, grasp, and convey to the mouth. Now under certain circumstances which are very limited at this stage, the infant can by his own actions shorten one of these less than ideal intervals of delay. The very early formation of a generalized concept of self-reliance is demonstrated to anyone who has observed the intense delight expressed by infants at early stages of mastery of grasping, crawling or walking. Hendrick (1942), who has also proposed a mastery drive, suggests that there is satisfaction inherent in the very use of any apparatus and, therefore, looks to the infant's exercise of the suckling function as one of the earliest experiences of mastery. No doubt, whether it is inherent in the exercise of one's capacities or arises from the reduction of delay, the pleasure in any of these acts is enhanced by the rewarding reactions of parents to these initial achievements. Very early these reactions of parents serve to augment the push behind the drive toward mastery and play a part in the formation of the set of standards which will guide the direction of later achievement aspiration. The main point, however, is that we are assuming that there is a universal phenomenon of development of an ideal minimum interval of delay in being gratified, or in feeling relief from discomfort, and from the experience of developing one's own resources as a preferred means of reaching that ideal. The resulting universal push toward action deserves to be called a drive even though it does not depend upon a specific physiological mechanism as is involved in the hunger drive.

Now we turn to the problem of anxiety. We do not attempt to relate this type of anxiety to any conception of a prime source of anxiety, e.g., the flooding of excitation experienced at birth. Instead we trace the connections between initial feelings of discomfort and impotence to secondary feelings associated with failure to reduce discomfort by one's own efforts, and finally to its more generalized form of failure to live up to a set of standards of what is to be accomplished by one's own efforts. We visualize wide individual differences in susceptibility to this kind of anxiety. One mother achieves an incomplete commitment to her child and consequently that child's early experiences are marked by wide variations in the intensity and duration of intervals of discomfort. Absence of resources for coping, whether those of others or his own, is a matter of greater moment to this infant than it is to one whose mother is more completely dedicated to his welfare. For this infant, discomfort, and, later, challenging situations stimulate more vivid images of failure and the re-arousal of all of the old feelings. The sequence of development of anxiety, then, is as follows: first, the more primitive experience of intense unsatisfied needs; second, the re-arousal of these primitive feelings in situations where the individual faces the challenge of using or developing his own resources and fears failure; finally, the more complex set of discomforts associated with the incorporation of parental standards about which kinds of achievements are to be most highly valued, and when failure is to be associated with the withdrawal of love.[3]

Psychoanalytic thinking alerts us to look for reactions which represent a diversion from the primary purpose of satisfying the drive to the secondary purpose of reducing anxiety. Our clues to the different ways anxiety might be dealt with come from an analysis of the direction in which this anxiety may be focused. One direction is a function of early repeated devastating experiences of being overwhelmed by feelings of frustration and helplessness. These experiences arise out of the relationship among three factors: (1) the extent of the individual's resources; (2) the willingness of parents to substitute their own resources for those the child lacks, and their patience in waiting for maturation; (3) the severity of environmental press. Some families live in circumstances which diminish the difficulties experienced while others live in circumstances which are harsh and beyond their capacities for coping. Where parents are niggardly with their own resources and the child is repeatedly overwhelmed, his anxiety will become focused on how much help will be withheld, and his efforts will be directed toward wangling more.[4] Such a child

---

[3] The work of McClelland, Atkinson and their associates on need achievement and fear of failure is relevant. See, for example, Atkinson (1958).

[4] For purposes of this discussion, the modes of dealing with dependence anxiety have been simplified. For example, another reaction at this early stage may be withdrawal from object relations. Presumably there is a failure to develop basic trust (Erikson, 1959). I suspect that those who survive anaclitic depression (Spitz, & Wolf, 1946) become fixated on a schizoid defense. Guntrip (1962) supports this position in arguing the schizoid's noncommittal in and out of psychotherapy is his rejecting response to his infantile feelings of helplessness.

will not appear to have a mastery drive, and in fact, its expression can only be elicited if the child's fear of being overwhelmed in any difficult situation is decreased by another's willingness to intervene whenever such a possibility is imminent.

The more the individual is supported by the nurturing actions of others during his early stages of extreme helplessness and the more he is encouraged to make use of his developing resources, the more he will turn to his own achievements as a possible escape from helplessness. It would seem that high parental commitment during the first year or two is crucial to the avoidance of an overtly dependent reaction to dependancy anxiety. Parents who accelerate the pace of withdrawal of commitment after the first two years, breaking its cadence with the developing resources of the child, are likely to contribute to the development of the counter-dependent pattern of behavior. We assume that minimum anxiety and therefore minimum need to defend against this anxiety is created when parents are consistently able to synchronize the rate of withdrawal of commitment with the rate of development of their child's resources.

Townsend's (1958) study offers support for the belief that the time of giving and withdrawal of parental support is a critical factor in the development of anxiety around dependency and achievement. By means of a projective measure, he divided a sample of 9–12 year old boys into overtly dependent, counter-dependent, and independent. Although mothers of these three groups did not differ in their response to standard questionnaires on child-rearing practices, they did differ in attitudes expressed during open-ended interviews. Mothers of counter-dependents gave them more freedom and demanded independence and achievement; mothers of overtly dependents emphasized compliance with their standards of morality and exerted constant control; mothers of independents took middle positions. When Townsend asked what percentage of a mother's time a child requires at different ages, the differences obtained were according to our expectations. Naturally, the mothers of all types of children were alike in suggesting a descending curve of time commitment as the child grows older, but at about one year of age there was an interesting change in the ordering of time commitment among the three groups of mothers. Prior to the first year (three month intervals were used in this segment of time) it is the mothers of the independent children who stipulate the highest percentage of time needed by the child. The other two groups were essentially similar in their lower estimates. After the age of one, the mothers of overtly dependent children reported the most time commitment at each subsequent year level, the mothers of counter-dependents reported the least time commitment, and the mothers of independents fell in between.

Psychotherapy, like other human relationships, may occupy any of a number of positions along the range of mutuality of commitment. Intensive psychotherapy is usually characterized by deep mutual commitments. The therapist, in addition to committing certain portions of his time, energies, and skills, dedicates himself to protecting his patient and to furthering change. He cares about the patient and places the patient's needs and interest in the foreground, minimizing his own personal demands. The patient makes his own commitments: to honor appointments, if fees are involved, to pay them regularly, to comply with whatever task the therapist sets, in short to exert his utmost efforts toward the mutually agreed-upon goal. Yet the nature and depth of commitment must be adapted not only to the kind of relationship, but to the characteristics of the patient. Even in an intensive relationship, the therapist may need to mute his expressions of commitment to correspond with a counter-dependent patient's anxiety about such relationships and his need to emphasize his own resources. In contrast to the overtly dependent patient, with whom he will take pains to spell out clearly his willingness to step in with aid of all varieties, the therapist pushes such communications into the background while emphasizing his recognition of the resources the patient possesses and his readiness to allow their fullest use.

Ultimately, of course, the therapist's aim is to facilitate the maximum use by every patient of his own resources. But, how the therapist reacts in particular situations will be conditioned by his understanding of the patient's dependency anxiety. For one severely disturbed patient, overtly dependent, a clearly expressed "take charge" attitude in which the therapist encourages him to call any time between meetings when his feelings seem to be getting out of hand will often reduce his anxiety sufficiently to make operative some of his own hitherto blocked capacities for self-control. For another equally disturbed patient who is counter-dependent, the fact that the therapist does not rush in with offers of help, but calmly asks about his capacities to control himself often reassures the patient that he is not succumbing to dependence, which, much as he longs for it, he fears so deeply. He feels that he can exert some control over his dependent desires and may then even be able to accept help.

As should be clear from earlier discussions of the conditions under which counseling takes place, clients are likely to approach it with much more limited commitments than patients in psychotherapy. Because they think their problems are rooted in the externals of situations and can be remedied through the acquisition of certain sometimes superficial knowledge and skills, clients are likely to enter counseling expecting certain positive action on the part of the counselor without anticipating that they will have to offer or receive any personal commitment. Again, there is no single response that is therapeutic in all instances. Should the counselor deem it appropriate, the overtly dependent person will have no difficulty in accepting a deeper commitment, especially if it places emphasis on the therapist. When the counter-dependent or independent person's commitment is inappropriately limited, the counselor may have to accept it as a beginning. The counselor should, of course, in the interest of candor, make clear his doubts as to the usefulness of such a limited venture.

One way of stating the significance of anxiety about dependence for psychotherapeutic effort is to assert that a counter-dependent person finds offers of help distracting when he works on a problem and that an overtly dependent person must have assurance of outside help before he can tackle one. These factors ought to enter into the usefulness of interpretation for reducing resistance to therapeutic work. Typically, the therapist's interpretation is experienced as a helping contribution to the patient's struggles with the task of communicating his self-experience. For the counter-dependent person, the cognitive elements in the interpretation (depth) will take secondary place to his sensitivity to this helping act. When his anxiety is activated and not worked through, he can be expected to respond by defensive efforts directed toward this aid and its stimulus toward dependency rather than be able to respond to its disclosing qualities which could serve to free him of his need to resist. At the same time, the effectiveness of an interpretation, even when appropriate, depends upon the use of the patient's capacities. An overtly dependent person must have experienced the steady reliability of the therapist's willingness to help before he can trust himself enough to make the effort. All this suggests that some degree of temporary or permanent resolution of the issue of trust of himself for the counter-dependent person and trust of the therapist for the overtly dependent person is necessary as a condition for the usefulness of interpretation, regardless of its depth or other characteristics.

Partial support for this picture of the relationships between usefulness of interpretive activity, commitment, and dependency anxiety was given by Williams' (1959) study. Judging on the basis of first interviews, she selected three overtly dependent and three counter-dependent patients and analyzed five interviews drawn from the early stages of therapy with each one. Six different therapists were represented. She found that for this sample the relationship between depth of interpretation and resistance, found by Speisman (1959) and replicated at least once, did not hold for this population of patients and interviews. Unfortunately, it was not possible to ascertain whether in later stages, presumably when dependency problems had been dealt with, the expected relationships did hold. Williams did find that counter-dependent patients were more willing to proceed with the therapeutic work of self-exploration when the therapist offered less commitment.

It would be useful to examine two kinds of committing acts and their theoretical and practical significance.

Acts in the Service of Gratifying Need States—One cannot talk about psychological problems with a man who is undergoing intense hunger or thirst, or whose consciousness is dominated by physical pain. Need-gratifying responses are called for, and there is no distinction as to what is somatically or psychically satisfying. The relationship between such a person and another whose role is to help him—that is, the response and the appropriate action—corresponds to the relationship between the infant who is hungry or in pain and the parent. All this is obvious, but it must be recognized that the same situation holds for any affective state that is momentarily so strong as to capture all the individual's attention and effort. Thus, states of panic, intense mourning, overwhelming elation, or violent passion require of the therapist such interventions as are required of the parent when the child has not yet developed the elements of a rational coping ego or when this aspect of the ego is momentarily overwhelmed.

Such interventions may involve direct help, such as drugs for the relief of anxiety; they may involve protective responses ranging from holding a panicked or uncontrollably aggressive child, or preventing a schizophrenic from self-injury; to setting prohibitions on a patient's neurotic acting out of transference. In such instances, when the patient is momentarily or generally incapable of foreseeing the consequences of his actions, the therapist, like the parent, must institute the necessary controls. Even though less extreme, the student whose ambivalence has driven him to the brink of academic failure or whose paralysis of decision has carried him to the eleventh hour, requires the counselor's attention and effort as a preliminary to dealing with the sources of such predicaments.

We must emphasize that active commitments in the service of need-gratification have the purpose—in our discussion thus far —of solving an immediate need-problem. For the ego-disturbed child, the schizophrenic, and perhaps also for the chronically severely anxious patient, the need-problem may be continuous and recurring. In these cases an extended period of aid may be required before the person can tackle other problems. The therapist faces the problem that such necessary and humane actions often also have transference implications. A direct aid or comforting response may be interpreted as a seduction; control or prohibition may be interpreted as rejection. As Jacobson points out in connection with work with depressives, ". . . we are always between the devil and the deep blue sea; this cannot be avoided" (Jacobson, 1954: p. 604). Recognition of the necessity for need-gratifying interventions must be joined with recognition of their cost and with considerations of timing.

The necessity for need-gratifying commitments must be distinguished from the naive assumption that all psychological problems can be solved via the gratification or the discharge of impulses in the therapy situation. There is sometimes the impression that if the therapist were "giving" enough, or if the patient "got out" enough hostility, or "satisfied his dependency needs" sufficiently in therapy, a cure would be achieved. The belief that gratification or impulse discharge will by themselves solve psychological problems results from a failure to recognize that psychotherapy is not a substitute for need-satisfaction, but deals rather with the derivatives of conflicts over need-satisfaction.

Acts in the Service of Establishing a Relationship—Giving and taking are primitive forms of communication. For the young child, to be given to, if it is without ambivalence, is to be loved, and to give without ambivalence, is to love. More advanced forms of communication develop from this. The child's first words perhaps develop less as demands for direct need-satisfaction, and more as gifts which mutually gratify parent and child. Commitments, then, are a way of communicating and of establishing a relationship. For the schizophrenic, for the affect-hungry child, and for any severely regressed patient, an act of giving by the therapist may be the only way of communicating and the only way of establishing a relationship. Bettelheim describes this aptly in connection with treatment at his Orthogenic School:

> Giving things when no mutual relation exists often satisfies little or nothing; now I shall add that the younger, the more emotionally immature a child is, the less he is able to establish personal attachments without being given generously, by an adult, time, concern, positive emotions, tender care and objects. The infant's utter dependency makes it impossible for him to relate unless he feels assured that he will always receive tender care from this one person, usually his mother. And because of the primitive organization of his personality, this security can be conveyed to him most easily when the appropriate emotions are accompanied by tangible evidence of their existence.
>
> Thus, in all our work, success depends on whether we can offer tender care to the child so that it is acceptable to him, and can persuade him to avail himself of our offerings—be they of time, concern, services, or presents—not as things in themselves, but as appropriate expressions of our genuine emotions. The child who comes to us has been severely disappointed over such a long period that he is not ready to believe in our good intentions. (Bettelheim, 1955: p. 434.)

The individual's immaturity or amount of regression influences how concrete and how directly gratifying the therapist's acts of commitment must be to communicate. In a college counseling agency, meeting the client's immediate demand for occupational or educational information may be sufficient evidence of concern to allow him to discuss his difficulties in more personal terms. Or, in a child guidance agency, the clinician's willingness to provide the parent with an assessment of his child's intellectual capacities will communicate enough to permit the discussion of the anxieties which underlie the request.

Once more we must emphasize the element of mutuality that surrounds the question of commitment and determines its usefulness. A therapist's offers of commitment have little power to activate change unless they are met by his patient's giving the corresponding commitment of which he is capable. In the next chapter we shall discuss this further when we take up the forging of therapeutic contracts in the process of initiating relationships.

The parent's and therapist's effort to understand

In infancy, effort to understand, like commitment, is a one-sided affair. The direction is from the parent, who tries to understand the infant's needs so as to engage in appropriate commitments toward him. The infant, apart from emitting cues as to the parent's success or failure, is a passive recipient. When the child becomes capable of meeting some of his own needs and responding to the parent's requests or demands—that is, of making some return commitment—effort to understand undergoes a corresponding shift. Now the mutual efforts at understanding become a significant part of the process by which the individual forms stable self-perceptions which serve to fit him into meaningful relations with others in which rules and obligations are understood and accepted. The child learns that revealing oneself and being understood can further satisfy intimacy without a loss of essential individuality.

As in the case of commitment, parental behavior can have an adverse effect on development in two ways. If parental commitments are unaccompanied by efforts to understand the child, he has little basis for developing individuality. Under these circumstances the parent-child situation becomes primarily a battle of wills involving who superimposes what on whom. On the other hand, parental efforts to understand may be so intrusive that the child becomes involved in a struggle to set up barriers to communication between himself and his parents in order to preserve a sense of integrity. Failures to resolve either of these two problems of parent-child relationships will force the child to transfer these modes of dealing with parents to his relationships with others, and will lead to a failure to differentiate more adult roles. For example, all relationships may be perceived solely in terms of commitments to be obtained. Further, the effort to understand others, instead of becoming a way of achieving a relationship, may become a technique for defending oneself against relationships. Thus, thinking becomes separated from doing and feeling. It is possible that the excessive need to defend his inner feelings from the scrutiny of others which characterizes the paranoid's defense, has its roots in just such malfunctions of effort to understand in parent-child relationships.

All psychotherapy involves an effort for the therapist to understand another person. This is one of the recurrent themes of this book. However, here we speak not of the acuteness of the therapist's understanding, but of the genuineness and dedication of his efforts. To some extent our comments here must overlap with those in the section on commitment, since in some ways the line we have drawn between them is tenuous and perhaps artificial.

Certainly, it is the therapist's effort to understand which produces the first major emotional tie between patient and therapist in most forms of psychotherapy. The "give-and-take" of this effort on the part of the therapist will be a major determinant of "rapport" and communication between them. Such an effort is communicated in many ways: by intent and unintrusive listening, by questions indicative of interest and reflecting awareness of subtle underlying themes, by checking one's understanding ("Is this how you feel?"), by any of the verbal and nonverbal cues which say in effect, "I am interested in what you are saying and feeling—go on." Whatever the manner of communication, the effort to understand on the part of the therapist, even though the comprehension achieved is incomplete or not fully accurate, is a communication of warmth, and represents a relatively unique experience of an actual characteristic of the therapist, although it may set the stage for the formation of transference. But as experienced at the outset, these efforts are the natural responses to warmth, in the sense that both children and adults feel gratified when their communications are listened to seriously.

It is clear that this aspect of understanding does not refer to the therapist's efforts to create a theoretical formulation nor to fit the patient into one, nor to his intellectual interest in one aspect of the patient's communications—whether behavior, fantasies, or feelings. It involves rather the poorly understood process of entering another person's contextual world. Effort to understand refers to the therapist's attitude of seeking to perceive how the patient is experiencing his world. Though receiving some discussion (e.g., Fenichel, 1941; Fliess, 1953; Reik, 1949; Rogers, 1955; Snyder, 1946) relating the process to splits in the ego or to temporary introjections or identifications, or to other phenomena, the problem of how it occurs, both in therapy and in other relationships, remains important and unsolved.

As we have seen, the Rogerians' concern with acceptance led them to react against the overintrusiveness of the therapist's theories and values, and to emphasize the effort to understand their client's contextual world. Our view agrees with their contention that this way of relating contributes an ingredient necessary to effective therapy, though we cannot agree that it is the sole ingredient. Nor can we share the view that a dedication to understanding how a person experiences events somehow precludes directing one's sensitivities to the forces at work in determining the nature of that person's experience. On the contrary, we contend that deeper, more subtle levels of understanding are reached by being able to sense what features of a situation are threatening and therefore subject to denial or distortion. Without such aids understanding is likely to be fixated on the banal, as exemplified by the therapist who can merely echo the patient's last words.

We have stressed that when we speak of effort to understand in relation to warmth we refer to the effort directed toward the patient rather than toward theory. There are also problems involving the quantitative aspects of the therapist's efforts. For example, patients of some character types will interpret silent listening by the therapist as an indication of lack of interest or rejection. While this problem can be handled once a relationship is established, failure in the beginning to give positive indications of effort to understand may interfere with the formation of a working relationship. On the other hand, obsessive patients will tend to use their own efforts at understanding as a defense, and here the therapist's positive expression of effort to understand may serve to support intellectualizing defenses, with consequent failures in therapeutic movement. With paranoid types the issue of intrusion will be great—the patient may interpret active seeking of understanding as an attempt to ferret out his secret thoughts, while he may take passivity as the cue to the formation of massive projections. Children, too, as a result of their experiences, may often feel that the adult's seeking of understanding is a mask that carries no true feeling. They must have other more concrete experiences of that feeling before they can be assured of the genuineness of the concern. The balance between activity and passivity in effort to understand thus becomes a delicate matter. In all of these problems it must be remembered, however, that the therapist's efforts at understanding will not exist in isolation, but that the patient will interpret them in the context of the therapist's active commitments and spontaneity. Variations in these latter two aspects of the relationship serve to correct or further distort interpretations by the patient of the therapist's efforts.

Spontaneity in parental and therapeutic relations

Spontaneity as an attribute of behavior is difficult to define. One may take several approaches toward the definition of the concept. Our suggestions here are tentative and have recognizable limitations. One may start with tension or inhibition as a clue to lack of spontaneity, but this requires awareness of the fact that some state of muscular tension is a biomechanical necessity for the performance of a directed complex act, and some state of inhibition is necessary for a thought or action in accord with the demands of a specific task or situation. Thus, one must focus on tension which cannot be attributed either to the requirements of a specific task or to the structure of the situation.

What is the source of the latter type of tension and inhibition? The familiar psychoanalytic theory of conflict gives the answer. When an unconscious conflict is involved, energy is required to institute a defensive operation against the arousal of anxiety. This is the process of countercathexis. The impulse aspect of the conflict will appear in a distorted form, producing a derivative. Even when an act appears to be directly impulsive, certain approximate criteria will indicate when excess tension or inhibition are involved because of the energy consumed in the defensive process (Dittmann & Raush, 1954). There will appear to be a "compelled" and stereotyped quality about the act. On the other hand, behavior will be spontaneous to the extent that inhibition and tension as a function of anxiety are absent.

Spontaneity may easily become confused with unorganized and undirected behavior. Thus, the observer might be tempted to look for behavior in which there is no element of tension due to efforts to control—in effect, for impulse expression free of all restraints. Only at those simple and primitive levels of expression characteristic of the infant is there impulse expression which can be satisfactorily consummated without organization and direction. Indeed it is because the most significant processes of impulse expression depend upon planning and organization that the development of ego becomes a necessity. According to our analysis, however, spontaneity is coordinated with, rather than contradictory to, planning and organization. That is, it is only to the degree that the ego is free of the energy consuming burden of anxiety, that conscious goals and situational realities can be recognized and met, and impulse expression can be maximized *within* rather than *against* other aims and situational requirements. Thus, spontaneity, as we see it, is freedom of impulse expression, where countercathexis is not involved. Such freedom is not inconsistent with cognitive organization.

By itself spontaneity does not communicate warmth. It communicates simply freedom of expression unless it is combined with commitment and effort to understand. On the other hand, it is a necessary component of warmth. Commitment and effort to understand will appear cold, impersonal, and stereotyped when not accompanied by spontaneity.

The course of spontaneity seems to be somewhat different from and less clear than those of commitment and effort to understand. For the child, the stages discussed above seem to require learning to limit impulsivity. Yet warmth in all three of its aspects on the part of the parents continues to evoke in the child the relaxation and freedom of expression that characterize spontaneity in any relationship. If spontaneity is lacking in parental behavior, the tension underlying the behavior will be perceived by the child, and this will tend to induce a complementary tension in him. Such tensions, depending on the parents' conflicts, may come to characterize the entire relationship, or they may be confined to specific content areas, such as eating, toilet training, mobility, sex, and aggression. The achievement of spontaneity in a relationship seems to presuppose that problems of commitment and effort to understand have been at least partially worked out. This would seem necessary if spontaneity is to be part of a relationship rather than an autistic expression. Perhaps spontaneity, as something not merely evoked but mutually given, cannot truly occur until preadolescence. At that time, unlike commitment and effort to understand, spontaneity seems to be worked out with peers first and then gradually transferred back to the parental milieu (Sullivan, 1953). Perhaps it is only with the passing of adolescence, at which time all three aspects of warmth must be worked out, a completely spontaneous relationship can exist between parent and child. Needless to say, such an achievement is rare and perhaps only an ideal, not only in the child-parent relationship but in any human relationship.

Although spontaneity as an aspect of psychotherapy has not been explicitly conceptualized in theoretical formulation,[5] it has occupied an important place in the lexicon of supervision and practice. "Simply going through the motions of psychotherapy is not enough," is a maxim which must be emphasized by supervisors of students of this process. The therapist must be capable of expressing something of himself. Earlier, we distinguished tension whose origin lies in the biomechanics of an act from tension deriving from the defensive process of countercathexis. When we turn to the question of how spontaneity manifests itself in the therapist's actions and what influence it may be expected to exert on therapeutic progress, it is clear that a difficult task faces an observer who must distinguish spontaneity from impulsiveness.

A tempting alternative is to try to simplify the attribute of spontaneity by reducing it to the level of affect being expressed, for it is certainly to be expected that a more spontaneous therapist will, on the average, interact with more expression of affect

[5] Moreno (1953) has used the term but in a less restricted sense.

than will a less spontaneous one. Unfortunately an impulsive emotionally disturbed therapist will also react with more affect. Thus, the clearest visual attribute of spontaneity must be accepted with reserve. In any case the purpose of understanding the role of spontaneity in therapy will necessitate taking into account the role of parental spontaneity, or lack of it, in the difficulties which patients have.

The gross observation of different therapists indicates considerable variability in the amount of affect expressed. Some therapists seem to always have a tight rein on themselves; they are, or seem to be, emotionless. Others seem to feel much freer to express themselves; they seem more "natural." One important source of this variability is countertransference. With closer observation, one can note that some therapist's self-expression is not in the service of the therapist's main purpose, namely, to help the patient learn to adjust his modes of behavior to the realities of his own needs and of the needs of others. To the extent that the therapist has needs for self-expression which are contrary to the therapeutic goal and acts without check on them, he acts impulsively. Naturally, countertransference may take the opposite form. Because he defends against inappropriate impulse expresssion which is tempted by the therapeutic situation, the therapist's behavior is more affectless and tension-laden than would be natural. Fenichel calls attention to this when he says, "There is another danger connected with countertransference: fear of the countertransference may lead an analyst to the suppression of all human freedom in his reactions to patients. . . . They (some patients) had believed that an analyst is a special creation and is not permitted to be human! The patient should always be able to rely on the humanness of the analyst" (Fenichel, 1941: p. 74). Adherence to therapeutic theories often imposes restrictions whose effects are very similar to those brought about by the therapist's need to defend himself against inappropriate impulse expression. The client-centered therapist's taboo against imposing his own values on the patient or the psychoanalyst's devotion to the requirement of the "blank screen" may limit their spontaneity. We think that there is still another source of variability which results from empathy with the patient. The therapist who has the acuteness to sense that his patient is shrinking away from even the slightest contact with feeling will automatically feel less moved by any set of events than he would under other circumstances, perhaps with a different sort of patient. Can this variability be called variability in spontaneity? Since the therapist is being responsive to his patient's mood, he naturally does not feel as strongly. There is no need for repression and countercathexis or its conscious equivalent, suppression. We, therefore, are forced to conclude that there is no difference in spontaneity.

The assumption that expressiveness might vary according to the patient would seem to be contradicted by the work of Butler, Rice, and Wagstaff (1962). Their studies, conducted within a client-centered framework, revealed a positive relationship between therapist expressiveness and patient progress in therapy. There need not, however, be any contradiction. They were collecting data covering the entire process. We would assume that the above described patient would eventually be aided by his therapist's expressive capacity exhibited at the proper time, just as dampened expressiveness arising from his sensitivity and tact were helpful at other times. It is also posssible that the large majority of patients in this study were not of the kind illustrated above.

There does appear to be little basis in current theories of the origins of various psychopathological states for assuming that lack of spontaneity in the parent's relationship to the child has a specific effect which selectively determines the type of pathology. It seems that spontaneity is a generally hygienic element in parent-child relationships and, correspondingly, in therapist-patient relationships. However, there are certain types of patients with whom it is of special importance. Jacobson (1954) in her discussion of the treatment of depressives has stressed the intensely ambivalent transference which these highly demanding persons exhibit. She emphasizes that in the face of these demands, the tie between the analyst and his patient is crucial. He must never give too little or too much. She also clarifies what this giving is to consist of: "In any case, what those patients need is not so much frequency and length of sessions as a sufficient amount of spontaneity and flexible adjustment to their mood level, of warm understanding and especially of unwavering respect; attitudes which must not be confused with overkindness, sympathy, reassurance, etc." (1954: p. 604).

Another group of patients who would seem to need a therapist capable of considerable spontaneity may cut across the common nosological categories, namely, those who can be said to suffer from affect-hunger. These persons are marked by their certainty that others only suffer their presence. They are likely to be sensitive to any signs that the interest or affection being shown them is a forced display. Only a therapist who is genuinely interested and is capable of direct expression of that interest is capable of establishing the kind of relationship which will provide the foundation for a less overweening narcissism.

There is one kind of person with whom the therapist does well to check his own freedom of expression—the person who is already made extremely anxious by impulses which are alien to the ego and which he is just barely able to contain. He is so vexed that an indication of free expression of feeling in another seems to attack his own resolution to keep control and creates the possibility of a panic reaction.

SUPPORT AND REASSURANCE

With the groundwork laid by the foregoing general discussion of the therapeutic role of emotional tones in the relationship, we can turn to the more specific question of the usefulness of support and reassurance in counseling. There is considerable difference of opinion about the value and appropriateness of efforts on the part of the counselor to reassure or support the client. Rogers, among others, argues that support and reassurance reflect disrespect for the client and discount his ability to solve problems himself. Rogers takes it for granted that a client's appeals for support or reassurance are subtle tests of the counselor's respect for him and therefore should be met with reflective and clarifying responses. He states it this way: "It [the nondirective relationship] is experienced as basically supporting, but it is in no way supportive. The client does not feel that someone is behind him, that someone approves of him. He does experience the fact that here is someone who respects him *as he is,* and is willing for him to take any direction which he chooses" (1951: p. 209).

On the other hand, Thorne, for example, contends that, under certain circumstances with particular clients, support and reassurance are warranted. Though he acknowledges that their effects are purely palliative, he defends their use on the basis that such palliative measures are sometimes necessary where more basic changes are not possible or in order to move the client toward a more fundamental attack upon the sources of his difficulties.

Thorne has outlined eight types of reassurance:

1. *Reassurance that not unusual case.* Many clients have had no experience with personality disorders and are bewildered and fearful. They fear that they are unique, rare cases unlike anything ever seen before. The counselor may reassure the client that the disorder is very common and not unusual.

2. *Reassurance that nature of condition is known.* People are fearful of the unknown, perhaps more so than of the known. It is reassuring to know that the disorder has a known cause and that therefore something can presumably be done about it.

3. *Reassurance that symptoms are annoying but not dangerous.* Anxious people tend to fear the worst. Their imaginations about disease are frequently worse than the real thing. Explanations of the nature and prognosis of symptoms may be very reassuring.

4. *Reassurance that something can be done.* It is not enough to know that the nature of the disorder is known. The client is also interested in whether anything can be done. Traditionally, the field of mental disorders has been very alarming and productive of anxiety because of the implications of such statements as, "He lost his mind," implying that what is gone can't be recovered. The client needs to know that specific methods of treatment are available.

5. *Reassurance that cure is possible.* The client's principal interest is to get well. He can usually tolerate symptoms if he knows they are temporary.

6. *Reassurance that not going crazy.* Most clients have conscious or subconscious fears that their condition may lead to insanity. He may not admit such anxieties but they are usually there. He wants to be told that this will not happen.

7. *Reassurance about getting worse.* Any temporary relapse or setback may be interpreted as a sign that the condition is getting worse. The client should be warned of the inevitability of relapses and reassured when they occur.

8. *Reassurance that client is not sinful or blameful.* The popular identification of mental disorder as a result of sinful actions stimulates guilt reactions and attempts to fix blame or secure revenge. Reassurance that this is not a moral problem, but can only be understood with impersonal objective scientific attitudes, may relieve some clients (1950: pp. 201–202).

It does not seem possible to take a definite stand on either the pro or con side of the controversy over reassurance as it has been stated. The utility of support and reassurance varies according to the specific type of interpersonal relationship in which it occurs. This requires us to make our own recommendations in terms of these more specific instances.

1. The client complains about various discomforts or dissatisfying situations in which he finds himself or tells how difficult it is for him to master certain problems. It will probably be annoying and frustrating to this person, intent on trying to convey how bad things are for him, to be told that this is not unusual, that many people experience this kind of difficulty or state their problem in the same way. Too often such a response gives the impression that an unsympathetic person is making light of one's troubles. Where such complaints or feelings of inadequacy represent rather complex emotional responses to some inner conflict, a counselor's attempt to dismiss or minimize their importance will be seen as a failure to grasp how much is at stake for the client. Under such circumstances, efforts to reassure or comfort may prove quite frustrating and only inspire lack of confidence in the counselor's ability to understand. On the other hand, when a counselor plainly shows an interest in his client's dissatisfaction just as he does in all other communications of the client and responds with appropriate affect, this demonstrates that he may be able to help him get out of his difficulties. At the same time, the counselor must be able to spot those situations where anxiety over shortcomings arises more from ignorance than from efforts to deal with emotional conflicts. Here correct information may be genuinely reassuring.

2. The next instance is that of a client who has specific relationship needs. As suggested earlier, he is one of those clients whose demand for reassurance or comfort from the counselor represents an effort to obtain a commitment that he will stand by him in the stormy period that lies ahead. For some of these clients it would be equivalent to expecting them to run before they can walk to suppose they have the emotional maturity to proceed without reassuring signs from the counselor. When a child is learning to walk, the fact that his mother stands nearby with arms outstretched is a clear sign that she will help him up if he falls and will prevent him from really harming himself. This encourages the child to try further to delight himself as well as please his mother. We must also realize that the same child, who is at first encouraged to walk farther by his mother's presence and her implied promise to keep him from harm, would become angry, resentful, and perhaps unwilling to try further, if later on in the learning process she still continued to hover protectively over him. In the same way, a counselor's efforts and attitudes, the degree to which he is protective or to which he leaves responsibility in the hands of the client, must be attuned to the client's level of development and emotional maturity.

3. In the third instance a client is having difficulty in controlling his impulses. We have already said something that bears on this case in our discussion of ambiguity as a factor in the therapeutic relationship. We pointed out that a certain amount of anxiety is necessary for therapeutic progress and that too much anxiety may swamp the client. Many times a counselor or therapist must function in a supportive or reassuring role as part of the process of aiding the client to control his anxiety lest he be too free in expressing his impulses. One of the ways in which the counselor can convince the client that his impulses and feelings are not out of control is by encouraging him to talk about them in a rational way. At times like this, encouraging the client to look for reasons, suggesting explanations, and the like should help the client see that he can dare to come to grips with these feelings without fear they will run away with him. Another important means for supporting a client who is fearful about his ability to control and guide his impulses is for the counselor to demonstrate his willingness to take part of the responsibility for this control.

An overzealous and misguided enthusiasm for permissiveness may often be a source of anxiety in the client. Where impulse control is important from the client's point of view, his realization that there are firmly though not punitively imposed limits on what he does can increase his confidence in himself and in his freedom to explore his feelings.[6] Most adolescent clients are already having difficulties in controlling turbulent emotions. At the same time, they are at a critical stage in their growth toward independence. The counselor must yield to their immaturity enough to establish clearly defined limits and thereby demonstrate that he is not just another person who is rushing them onward to adulthood. At the same time, he must allow the adolescent enough freedom so that it is not necessary for him to revolt in defense of his need to be independent or to hide his regressive need to avoid independence.

In the section that follows we shall examine further the influence of emotional tone on a therapeutic relationship. There we will be able to look at many more specific situations as they arise in the context of initiating a counseling relationship, utilizing psychological tests, or in the middle or ending stages of counseling.

[6] For a good discussion and for illustrations of the role of limits in psychotherapy see Bixler (1949).

Part III

THE PROCESS OF
PSYCHOLOGICAL COUNSELING

THIS FINAL DIVISION aims to show the answers to practical problems of counseling which derive from the theories and concepts set forth in the foregoing part. It includes examples of the many events in which the counselor has a part to play that furthers his client's progress toward emotional maturity and well-being. Where the issues fall beyond the circle illuminated by theory, we depend on accumulated experience and the use of concrete illustration to clarify the many questions about procedure which arise in getting a counseling relationship under way and carrying it through to a successful conclusion.

CHAPTER 9

Initiating the Counseling Relationship[1]

IN THIS CHAPTER and the following one, our attention turns to what happens after a person acts upon his decision, whether blithely or reluctantly made, to discuss a personal problem with a counselor. The process of establishing a counseling relationship has many subtle characteristics. We shall see that a number of attributes which distinguish counseling from psychotherapy have a bearing on this process. Menninger (1958: Chapter 2) has chosen apt terminology when he speaks of the "therapeutic contract." In order to work effectively together, counselor and client must reach a common understanding of their mutual goals and commitments. This process entails gathering information bearing on their expectations and clarification of their respective tasks.

VARIATIONS IN INTAKE PATTERNS AMONG AGENCIES

Counselors and counseling agencies vary in the amount of information they demand prior to making counseling decisions. At one extreme are those who would approximate the procedures followed in child guidance clinics and medically administered mental hygiene clinics. The commonest procedure in these clinics is to subject prospective clients or patients to a relatively elaborate

1 For other discussions of this topic the reader is referred to Colby (1951: Ch. 6), Fromm-Reichmann (1950: Ch. 5), Porter (1950: Ch. 5), Powdermaker (1948), and Voiland *et al.* (1947).

intake procedure. Typically, this entails an interview with a social worker, a series of diagnostic sessions with a psychologist, which might include some rapport-establishing discussions in addition to appropriate psychological tests and, then, when a psychiatrist is available, a brief diagnostic interview. This team then pools its findings during a therapeutic planning session in which the anticipated needs of the patient are analyzed, a therapeutic plan is discussed, and a therapist assigned.

Relatively few counseling agencies, however, employ representatives of all three professions. Consequently, even though still insisting upon thorough diagnostic analysis prior to initial counseling, they adapt their intake procedures to the facilities available. As an example of this, many counseling services arrange for an intake interview by a staff member who specializes in this task. Usually this staff member will lack graduate training in any of the mental health disciplines. Under the most fortunate circumstances, he will have earned an undergraduate degree in one of these fields. During the intake interview the client will discuss his problem, that is, his reason for coming and will give a considerable amount of information about himself and his life history by means of oral or written questionnaires. On the basis of this information, psychological testing will be arranged and, when this is completed, the client will then have an interview with his counselor. The latter has in the meantime reviewed all of the materials available, and, under the best circumstances, discussed with a supervisor what he foresees in the way of problems and indicated decisions.

At the other extreme of the information-collecting continuum are the counselors and counseling agencies who arrange that the client's first contact after seeing the receptionist will be with his counselor. Under these circumstances, the counselor starts with minimal information about the client. He will certainly know the sex of the client, perhaps the client's age and his home address, which may give him some clue to his socioeconomic level. In educational settings, as in school or college, he may know the school year of the client and in some instances have available the results of tests derived from the testing program of the school or college.

There are advantages and disadvantages in either of these

plans of operation. It seems to the writer that the balance tips in the direction of the second method. The most important factor is that it simplifies the process of seeking counseling. Under the latter arrangement, applying for counseling can be more casual and this in itself furthers the goal of providing a constructive influence on the mental health of a relatively undisturbed person. Consistent with this purpose, it is necessary to enable people to see the act of seeking counseling as a noncommitting, uninvolving, and non-time-consuming action. In schools and colleges, it is desirable that students be able to drop in and talk to the counselor on the spur of the moment in the same way they might talk to an instructor, an academic adviser, or a dormitory house mother. To be caught up in interviewing and testing, in telling and re-telling one's reasons for seeking these services, a procedure which can stretch out for several days and even a week, is to experience a feeling of being engulfed which is incompatible with the tentative character of many clients' initial approach.

Another reason for choosing the second procedure might apply also to both child guidance and mental hygiene clinics. Even when his intense feelings of discomfort emphasize his need for help and when the client has acknowledged that he is an important source of his own difficulties, elaborate intake pro-cedures may be too overpowering or otherwise incompatible with meeting his needs as he sees them and thus makes it unappealing for him to go on to use the help available. Although systematic data warranting confident generalization are lacking, our famil-iarity with several counseling and mental hygiene clinic programs which utilize extended intake procedures suggests that such pro-cedures are likely to be accompanied by a high rate of broken contact. In some organizations, between a third and a half of the clients who started through these intake procedures either did not complete them, did not return for their first real counseling (therapeutic) interview, or stayed for only one such interview. Although for some of the clients who were seen for single inter-views this brief contact can be assumed to have met their needs, in the case of a number of them it seemed more likely that some other factor had accounted for interruption of the contact. To a client or patient who is considerably troubled, elaborate intake procedure may appear as obstructive red tape and as evidence that the counseling staff is more interested in technical devices than in him as a person.

On the other hand, since mental hygiene clinics and also, to some extent, counseling agencies, are sought out by sorely tried people requiring discerning and painstaking treatment, therapists and counselors may be appalled by the apparent necessity of proceeding solely on the basis of the information obtained in the first contact. They will fear, and rightly so, that with disturbed people, where controls may be tenuous and mistakes disastrous, more information must be obtained. The truth of the matter is that the therapist's need for information about his client or patient is quite properly insatiable, and in some cases must not be postponed too long.

The therapist must adapt his procedures to the range of commitments he and the agency he represents are prepared to undertake. A service which seeks to offer preventive and developmental aid must guard against having all of its energies absorbed by a few persons with chronic and severe difficulties, each of whom requires an herculean effort, or of subjecting these vulnerable persons to the unnecessary and often damaging trauma of being cut off from a relationship which had promised so much. When he senses that his client is ready to throw himself into a very close dependent relationship, the counselor should take pains to make clear the limitations of his own initial commitment. It is certainly proper to show interest and concern, and to commit oneself to seeing that the client will be apprized of what facilities there might be for giving the kind of help he proves to need. It should be made clear, that it is unsettled whether this counselor or even this agency will prove to be the appropriate source of aid. Making such matters plain will aid the deeply disturbed client to check his natural tendency to build great hopes in a person who seems so interested and understanding, and will prevent the surge of distrust and hopelessness he might otherwise feel if the necessity of going elsewhere was communicated without prior warning.

In effect there are a series of potential counseling contracts to be negotiated, many of them successively with the same client. A universal contract, once it is known what prompted the client to seek counseling, is for a mutual closer examination of his difficulties and what doing something about them might entail. When a counseling service has been properly interpreted to its community, perhaps a third of its clients will neither need nor be motivated toward any greater effort than is contained in this commitment. It will permit a self-survey and self-confrontation which will be sufficient for moderately well-integrated persons to respond constructively and with personal growth to dilemmas arising from an age-specific transition which provides the stimulus to further development. For the client, who more typically seeks the aid of an intensive treatment service, this commitment must be slightly modified to emphasize the extensiveness of the process of examination of the problem, including testing and interviewing. In the case of those clients who will need more than three or four interviews, it is probable that the initial contract will not suffice. When the mutual survey—and with nontherapeutically oriented clients we must emphasize the theme of mutuality—has disclosed personal obstacles toward effective functioning which are not dissipated in the initial confrontation, the client faces the decision of whether he wishes to put out an additional effort of less circumscribed duration. The mutual commitments in this contract may differ only slightly from the kind of contract the therapist and patient agree to in a long-term intensive effort.

THE CLIENT'S EXPECTATIONS

Having explained why we favor minimal intake procedures, we go on to take up the initial contact as it occurs within this kind of framework. The client approaches the counselor's office. How does he feel? What anticipatory images of the counselor does he have? How does he expect him to act and what kinds of relief does he expect? Unfortunately, there is relatively little factual basis for answering these questions. We rely mainly on our accumulated impression of clients' anticipations, subject as these are to errors arising from our own anticipations and hopes, our natural wishes to protect ourselves, and the sheer superficiality of the relationship between our observations and whatever inferences we make.

One impression is that clients are likely to be looking for help and for reassuring signs that this help will be forthcoming. Usually they are looking for some such sign from the counselor, some token that he has met their act of self-committal with some committing response in return. These needs and expectations find their expression in such remarks as, "I don't know if I have the right to expect this of you," "I don't know whether I am expecting too much," or, after a counselor seems to rebuff some attempt to obtain commitment, "Maybe I came to the wrong place."

Almost all clients consider coming to the counselor a reflection upon their adequacy as individuals. Particularly characteristic of the client of a counseling organization is his sensitivity and defensiveness about how adequate he may be. If the counselor's behavior implies that he thinks the client cannot get along without his help, it will probably elicit strong denial. The client will go out of his way to show the counselor that whatever his troubles may be, he is "absolutely" a rational, responsible person. He exhibits how competently he has gone about solving his problems and bridles at a too-ready implication that he has in some way been irrational.

Different persons come for counseling with very different perceptions of themselves as factors in their problems. Often they are little aware that conflicting feelings are sources of difficulty. This usually shows in their initial definition of the problem and in their expectations of how counseling will help them. On this matter we have some information. In a brief study of clients' expectations about counseling, a tendency was found for clients to anticipate (1) a personal relationship between client and counselor, or (2) an impersonal process primarily devoted to receiving information and advice (Bordin, 1955[b]). Sample clients were asked to accept or reject a series of statements about either the counselor or the counseling process as descriptive of their own expectations. They were also asked to indicate the three statements which most nearly coincided with their expectations. Two groups of clients were identified as having chosen the same two statements and as differing on the third one. The two statements chosen by both groups referred to the information-securing and testing uses of counseling. They differed in that one group's third choice was a statement about a counselor's helpfulness with educational and vocational problems, whereas the other chose a statement about a counselor's helpfulness with personal problems. It was noted that the first group tended to reject statements about the personal characteristics of a good counselor. This was true

even in some cases when the descriptive statements were contradictory, that the counselor is good when he is "impersonal and
objective" and is good when "fatherly, someone you can lean on."
On the other hand, the second group, which wanted a counselor
who was helpful with personal problems, tended to accept personal characteristics of the counselor as being important. Again,
this was a relatively undiscriminating reaction in that contradictory personal characteristics were often accepted. In effect, the
first group were saying, "As far as I'm concerned, this is an impersonal relationship. I don't want any personal characteristics
of the counselor to enter, no matter what." The second group
seemed to be saying, "This is going to be a personal relationship.
I am concerned about the personal characteristics of the counselor,
even though I'm not sure which characteristics will be important."
Clients in the first group are likely to prefer an initial definition
of their problem in abstract, rational terms, leaving themselves out
of the equation to be solved; whereas those in the second group
are more likely to define their problem in personal terms with
an emphasis on understanding themselves rather than on obtaining better manipulative control over their external environment.
Naturally, these two categories do not have clear-cut, mutually
exclusive boundaries and do not encompass all clients. In fact, in
the particular study cited less than half of the total group could
be classified into these two subgroups, so that those remaining
probably came with variations or combinations of these two sets
of attitudes. Another facet of expectations of clients and patients
has been examined—how much faith in therapy and the therapist
they contain (Frank, 1961; Goldstein, 1962). Frank has presented
evidence to support his contention that it is the patient's and
therapist's mutual faith in the efficacy of treatment which is the
specific therapeutic agent. There are few who would disagree that
it is *a* therapeutic agent.

THE COUNSELOR'S INITIAL ORIENTATION

As the counselor sits down to talk with a new client one of
his most definite feelings is the need to begin to understand this
client. He wants to be able to see the client's needs so he can meet
them in a helpful way. The inexperienced counselor is often

impatient with the necessarily slow process of accumulating understanding by constantly attentive listening and observing. Sometimes he foolishly rushes ahead, assuming he can more efficiently
extract the information he wants through direct questioning or
by indirectly (or "subtly" as he hopes) guiding the conversation.
The inexperienced counselor may overvalue the neatly concise
outline of the client's past history and be relatively insensitive to
the cues the client communicates by his tone of voice, his pace
and his interruptions of the level on which talk is proceeding, his
changes in bodily position and facial expression, and all the other
signs not found in the mere words.

Too often, in reviewing therapeutic situations the student
concentrates on only one person—the client. The counselor seems
to be merely an impersonal equation; he may act according to one
formula or another which will have the expected effect upon the
client. But of course the fact is that the counselor is also a person,
and human. He has other goals than simply being an effective
mechanism at the service of the client, even though that role may
be consistent with his other goals. The counselor wants to be an
adequate person, but his adequacy is only partially defined in terms
of his counseling role. He wants clients to have confidence in him
and he wants to feel likeable and respected. As we have reiterated,
the counseling situation is so very frequently one in which a client
presents his problems as pretty much outside of himself. To the
degree that the counselor sees himself as providing mental health
service, he is likely to experience considerable pressure to have his
client move from this impersonal to a more personal plane of
discussion. Adequacy or inadequacy in the counselor, professionally judged, often becomes closely tied to this criterion. For the
beginning counselor the issue of adequacy is likely to be even
more intense, since he has less experience and less competence in
meeting such interpersonal responsibilities.

CLARIFYING THE GOAL

In our earlier discussions of the interpretive process we
mentioned briefly the importance of the client's strong conviction
that he needs therapy. Let us now consider this a little more fully,

particularly as it bears upon initiating therapeutic relationships. Before the counselor's interpretations can help the client deal more freely and more fully with his own feelings, the client must have reached an understanding that the complicated maze of his own feelings has been an important factor in bringing about whatever dissatisfying situation he finds himself in. He must have been presented with a reasonably clear statement of what the therapeutic task is and must have accepted his share of the commitment to it. Counselors' interpretations are likely to call attention to ways in which a client seems to be now either attempting to deny his initial acceptance of the fact of his own involvement in his difficulties or trying to avoid the therapeutic task of communicating his feelings. It is the client's clear recognition that he needs help and that he is a prime source of his own difficulties which helps him to use the counselor's interpretation as a means of re-examining himself from a new point of view. Without these initial commitments the interpretive process is relatively meaningless.

In their eagerness to have the client move from looking outside to looking inside himself, counselors will knowingly or unknowingly make efforts to entice the client into a more personal relationship. They will encourage the client to become more personal by showing an interest in his feelings and by taking advantage of whatever specific signs he shows of needing to express his feelings. Thus, the client may have shifted from matter-of-fact and relatively uninvolved talking about his problem and the possible conclusions or decisions he might make, into a much more personal and direct outpouring of his own feelings without at the same time having arrived at any particular acknowledgment, either explicitly or implicitly, that these feelings are a critical part of the problem he faces.

Discussions at this more affective level may continue beyond the first interview, with the counselor already congratulating himself on having been so successful in involving the client in a therapeutic process. However, the counselor is often astonished at the consequences of his failure to help the client arrive at a redefinition of his goal and task. Suddenly the client will pull up short and say something like, "Well, this has been very interesting, now I guess we'd better get down to business and talk about my specific decision." Then he proceeds to return to a very matter-of-fact, externally oriented discussion of his problem in which the feelings discussed earlier are pretty much disregarded. At other times, the client may suddenly terminate the interviews with a remark like, "Well, I guess this is as much of your time as I ought to take. It has been very worth while talking to you and I would be tempted to continue but I don't think I have any right to."

What has appeared to the counselor as a revision in the client's conception of his problem and of the uses to which counseling can be put has all the while seemed to the client an irrelevant interlude. Where the shift to a more personal relationship has been induced by efforts to seek gratification for some deep-lying impulses through the relationship with the counselor, it may even be associated with considerable guilt. Often these guilt feelings are used by the client in partial defense against getting more deeply involved in the therapeutic process. Many times the break will occur at some point where his discussions with the counselor were approaching especially sensitive and firmly defended areas of his emotional life.

CLARIFYING THE TASK

All therapists, whether they strive for comprehensive personality change, as is the case in psychotherapy, or for relatively restricted change, such as characterizes counseling, plan to draw the client into a relationship which they can then use as the vehicle for achieving therapeutic goals. To establish this relationship, the therapist must give the client a task which will facilitate its forward movement. That task is, naturally, revealing himself to the therapist. Since counseling has been initiated by the client, it is natural for him to start by telling why he came. And since he is usually unknown to the counselor, he begins by telling the counselor something about himself and his general situation. The early phases of the task of communicating are accomplished with relatively little defining from the counselor. Many times he need only pause expectantly after he and the client are seated and the client will take the cue to explain why he is there. A certain proportion of fearful and passive clients will want the counselor to take the initiative and set even this first task more overtly. This the counselor can accomplish with some simple direct question like, "Would you like to tell me what brings you to see me?"

It is beyond the point where the client tells why he wants counseling and has reached the boundary of his initial free communications about himself that some of the important clarifying problems appear. First of all, the counselor must decide how close to free association he wants to come in the task he imposes. Since our earlier discussions of ambiguity have already dealt with this problem in detail, we can here confine ourselves to a relatively brief summary of the issues. We must emphasize the fact that the definition of the task is communicated only partially by explicit statements such as these:

1. This is a situation which is different from the usual social situation. In the usual social situation you have certain thoughts or feelings which it would be considered a social mistake to express. They may be critical thoughts about the other person. They may be certain kinds of admiring thoughts. They may be thoughts which are far away from the particular people and the particular topics being discussed. In this situation you are expected to give expression to all thoughts, no matter how inappropriate or how irrelevant they seem to be.

2. Almost anything you think of to tell me about this problem will probably be useful to talk about.

3. Whatever you want to tell me will probably be useful.

4. We find that when people try to think through these questions out loud with us it can help them to see their problems in a new light.

The definition of the task is conveyed not only by such statements, but also by indirect verbal and nonverbal cues. For example, as the counselor responds to the client's recital of his problem or his general circumstances either by questioning him or by indicating that he understands, the counselor inevitably, through the selective character of his responses, lets the client see in part what aspects of his communications he considers most important. The fact that the counselor asks questions about or otherwise responds to the client's attitudes indicates his special interest in them. If, for example, he responds to the client's attitudes toward and relationships with parents, he is signifying his special interest in that set of feelings and relationships. But of course he can do this in other ways than by direct reference to them. He can show it by his posture, whether relaxed or leaning forward as though to catch every word, or by cues to the amount of his involvement and interest in what is being communicated. He can show by the loudness and tone of voice that he is reacting differently to different things the client is taking about. The client, who feels uncomfortable in this situation and feels unfamiliar with its demands, and who is consequently looking for any sign that he is meeting the demands of the situation positively and constructively, seizes upon and reacts to every cue the counselor gives him.

As we suggested in Chapter 6, in most of the short-term contacts that arise in counseling, the client comes to the counselor without feeling any need to admit a pronounced inability to handle his problems and certainly with no salient expectation of becoming personal or giving up responsibility for himself, even momentarily. Thus, the typical counseling client is not prepared to accept a task which is pure free association. This client will be given simply the task of telling about feelings which seem to have a bearing on his problem. He will naturally be expected to go beyond reporting on mere matters of fact. He must be willing to come out with his feelings. It is not unusual for a counseling relationship to proceed stepwise from the client's initial task of describing his problems to the free communication of his thoughts and feelings without taking any responsibility for their relevance.

MEETING THE CLIENT'S INITIAL NEEDS

This topic, already touched upon in the discussion of variation in intake procedures and of the types of tasks defined for the client, must be treated more directly.

We go back again to the very beginning of the counseling relationship. At this point many counselors are moved to establish rapport by such devices as talking about the weather, trying to find something out about his client's antecedents or whom he knows. All this is in order to get on common ground with him. In most instances this turns out to be a relatively artificial process. We note that the client is so preoccupied with an explanation for soliciting counsel that he is unresponsive to the counselor's chattiness. Since he has thought enough about his difficulties to come to someone for help, he is anxious to begin "really" talking. Time and again in these cases it is apparent that he is wondering why the counselor is wasting all this time with small talk. Fortunately, the counselor has a ready-made relationship to the client, established by his purpose in coming, so he can get going quickly. However, we do not want to suggest that the counselor should be a lifeless machine or a cold fish. If the weather does in fact seem to be extraordinary, a remark about it certainly would not be out of place, since most people who meet casually mention it to each other. But this should come as a spontaneous reaction—this day the weather *is* something to remark about—rather than out of a false heartiness of the Babbitt variety.

As the client begins to describe his problem, he may convey a sense of particular urgency about one aspect of it. Perhaps he is a student who must complete registration that week and feels helpless in the face of the big or little decisions this involves, or the father of a family who must meet an immediate financial obligation, or an unmarried pregnant girl who must make some kind of arrangements for the period immediately before and after delivery. The urgency of these needs will vary. If they exceed the client's present capacity to meet them, the counselor cannot remain detached, doggedly adhering to the role of an uninvolved sounding board for the client's feelings. It is out of the question for him to ask the client to postpone facing such needs until perchance he has somehow acquired the capacity for meeting them without aid. The client must be freed of the relatively disorganizing pressures and helped to avoid the panic that comes from facing overwhelming tasks without prospect of succor. At the same time, the counselor must beware of underestimating the client's resources so that he helps the client beyond what is necessary. The more the client is able to contribute to the solution of his own problem, the less he will suffer from having had to be dependent upon someone else. The fact that the solution is not all the counselor's doing, but the client's also, can be a source of encouragement to the client that he can take over full responsibility for himself in the near future.

Many times meeting the client's immediate needs is not so

much a matter of helping the client take care of some pressing demand as it is the much more subtle and prolonged process of adapting one's relationship with the client to his present capacity for interacting, all for the purpose of ultimately closing in on the client's difficulties. In addition to gauging the client's readiness for a relatively ambiguous task, the counselor must be able to recognize when he is going to be threatened by any appreciable decrease in distance between him and the counselor. A counselor's efforts to establish the kind of friendly atmosphere that prevails among social associates may foster unnecessary defensive reactions. Conversely, the counselor who maintains his impersonal remoteness may repel many clients, particularly those who are very dependent. Similarly, the time when and the degree to which a counselor encourages objective analysis will be related to the particular client and his state. With some clients the counselor may have to interpret early, to foster their recognition that helping them control their feelings will also be part of the process.

THE DIAGNOSTIC POTENTIALITIES OF INITIAL INTERVIEWS

Since we advocate that counseling start with the very first interview rather than allotting time in first contacts to diagnostic testing, we must underline the need for exploring the diagnostic potentialities of the early meetings. The unusual diagnostic possibilities offered by the first contact have been emphasized by Voiland, who writes of them:

To view the client's reaction as he presents his problem for the first time has a diagnostic advantage which is invaluable and which seldom presents itself at a later time in the same dynamic way, for as the contact develops the material becomes more detailed and consequently more difficult to sift in terms of significant trends. For this reason it is highly important that the worker develop real sensitivity to the client's problem which can be utilized to the fullest at the first points of contact (Voiland et al., 1947: pp. 6–7).

Many other students of counseling and psychotherapy have written in the same vein, stressing the usefulness of going back to the first interview as a means of regaining perspective on the client's problems. They believe the first interview frequently contains the clearest representation of the core problem. The client's first efforts to verbalize his problem and the feelings he experiences as he sets about sharing it with another person are likely to lead him to express his major conflicts unconsciously, thus providing a basis for understanding all of his other ambivalent feelings. It seems probable that if the initial interview or interviews is to have this potential significance, certain requisite conditions must be met. In the kind of first interview that has the characteristics mentioned above, a client, approaching the therapeutic situation for the first time, has already reached the stage of feeling that his difficulties are to some extent of his own making. He has already decided that he needs to understand himself, his emotions, impulses, and feelings. Because he has reached this decision, he will be predisposed to reveal his inner life as fully as he can comfortably. In these circumstances there is an opportunity to observe in what terms he chooses to begin talking about these issues, how he tries to describe himself and his feelings, and at what point and in what ways he has to defend himself against too-free expression of affect.

A certain number of clients will come to the counseling situation with this kind of readiness. In such instances it should be possible to obtain considerable understanding of each of them and their present ways of operating. Many clients will not have reached this stage of thinking. Their first interview will reflect how they are defining their problem and how they define their relationship to the counselor, but may not reveal a great deal about their personality structure. This is not surprising. Virtually the same phenomenon is encountered in diagnostic projective testing when the subject has not been adequately prepared for the confidential relationship. He is likely to give only a barren, rigidly controlled record, reflecting his condition with his defenses up. Very perceptive observation can sometimes enable one to make use of the slight variability in behavior which appears in even this type of interview; for example, attention to points where the client seems to approach the threshold of involvement and how he tries to withdraw from such involvement may provide important cues.

The function of ambiguous characteristics in the therapist and the therapeutic task in understanding the patient has already been discussed. The freedom with which the client responds to this ambiguous situation can be an index of his over-all flexibility and spontaneity. The particular aspects of his problem which he chooses to take up and their order of appearance, along with the accompanying affect, can all be meaningful. One of the important diagnostic sets of the counselor will be the amount of attention he gives to understanding the sequence of the client's communications and his surmises concerning what has accounted for this sequence. He must be able to pick out what parts of the continuity have been fostered by his own defining behavior and what parts of the continuity reflect the motivational sets of the client. To take an example, the client starts talking about his inability to control his anger. He would like to be able to keep his temper better. He is afraid that he will do something that he will regret. Under the influence of anger he fears he might actually do serious harm to someone else. Then he begins to talk about how his father seems to be able to control his own anger and how his father has given him suggestions for improving his self-control. He speaks of his admiration for his father and how much he desires to be like him. Then he begins to talk about teachers he has admired and how often he has become disappointed with them and how many times his admiration has turned to dislike. He talks about how he often loses his temper with teachers and how guilty he feels afterward.

Already the emerging pattern and continuity are easy to see. This client's communications and his feelings are flowing quite freely. It is true that he has defenses against his feelings. He is not expressing them in their most direct form. At the same time, he is moving toward direct expression with relatively little anxiety and relatively little holding back. Other clients might be evolving the same pattern but with greater anxiety and therefore with a more subtle continuity, a continuity which taxes the sensitivity of the counselor. Each time the client introduces a new topic the counselor must ask himself, "How did he get from the previous topic to this one? What is the connection between them?" In some instances the counselor will become aware that the client, in going to the new topic, was reacting to something that he, the counselor, had said earlier. Or he may note that one thing the two topics have in common is that they deal with the same affect, whatever it is. The counselor will need to seek connections between the persons the client mentions under each succeeding topic. He must try to understand their functional psychological relationship. In this example, the first topic deals with the client's father, the topic which follows deals with teachers. In some ways, teachers are a lot like fathers. They are older. They have authority. They are also looked up to and emulated.

If we examine the above communication with the assumption that fathers and teachers are in some respects equivalent, still further impressions emerge. Father was talked about directly when his helpful and admirable qualities were being emphasized. But when the client discusses feelings of disappointment, anger, and dislike, teachers are cited as the objects. When we examine the beginning of the client's message, its total import is revealed. It seems reasonable to say the client started with concern about his anger and feared that he would yield to aggressive impulses. His association to hurting someone is to talk about his father. Can his father be the object of his anger and does he fear for his father's safety? The tenor of his remarks seems to deny this. Can this be their purpose? The shift to teachers, the implication that they may be the objects of his aggressive impulses, and his concern that this is so seems to give affirmative answers to our questions. We may want to test our impressions with data obtained from his subsequent communications before we give them more than hypothetical status, but we will have made an important start toward understanding the conflicting feelings which beset this young man. Continued alert listening to the sequences of his verbal behavior will insure the richness of the diagnostic yield.

In most cases, initial contacts will offer the counselor similar opportunities to acquire important diagnostic insights that help him make the decisions necessary at this point. He will be able to judge the level of disclosure on which the client is approaching his problem, the salient features of his motivation and his conflicts, and his methods of defending against the latter. In a small proportion of cases, the counselor will feel he has not been able to establish contact with the client. He may observe enough to feel sure the client's difficulties are profound. When such problems face the counselor in the initial meeting, he will need to proceed with caution, avoiding any definite therapeutic move until there has been an opportunity for more thorough diagnostic analysis, including the administration of psychological tests.

CHAPTER 10

Analysis of Initial Interviews

IN THE last chapter we analyzed the problems and situations found in first interviews and discussed proposals for meeting them. Here our aim is to give the reader an opportunity to observe initial interviews and to analyze them for him. After completing this chapter, the reader may want to return to Chapter 3 and review the examples of first interviews included in it.

Case of Miss Tir [1]

This client is a twenty-year-old senior woman student.

C 1.   I guess now we're ready to start. Would you like to tell me what brings you in?

S 1.   Well, (clears throat) I don't know how exactly to get started, but at home my brother-in-law is a sociologist, and I have been— he gave me a Rorschach Test and I have been going to him, but well—I suppose he—uh—it's not a good idea for a member of the family to do. And my particular problem would be with my mother, and I—well—I'd like to be able to do something about it before I go home. I don't know how I can explain it, so maybe if you can—

C 2.   Uh-huh—

S 2.   —question me, or—

C 3.   Uh-huh—

S 3.   —something—I could start— (end low)

---

[1] The sixteenth interview with Miss Tir appeared in Ch. 3.

C 4. Uh-huh. Kind of hard to—is it kind of—so hard to talk about that it's hard to start anywhere?

S 4. I don't know where to start. I mean—

C 5. Uh-huh.

S 5. I don't know *what it is* that—the immediate thing that brings me here was I called up home the other night—

C 6. (*low*) Uh-hum.

S 6. We had a discussion on the phone. I talked to my mother—but very nice. But once I got off, I—my whole feeling toward her changed.

C 7. Uh-hum.

S 7. I can't explain any of the reasons for it, but it isn't even a kind of love anymore.

C 8. Uh-hum. (*low*)

S 8. It's fear and kind of hate, I think. (*softly, with tears*) I don't know why it is. I don't like having it. I'd like to get rid of it.

C 9. (*low*) Uh-hum. I see. (*little louder*) So in other words, as you see the problem now it's a case of having feelings about your mother that are pretty distasteful to you, feelings that you feel you want to get rid of.

S 9. Uh-hum.

C 10. Feelings about her that make you unhappy.

S 10. (*low*) That's right.

C 11. I see. Well, one way to start might be to just tell me about yourself more generally.

S 11. (*low, after slight pause*) Well, I don't—with relation to her, that would be, wouldn't it? (*ends in louder tone of voice*)

C 12. Well, whatever you think fits in any way. I don't know very much about you. (*friendly tone*)

In this excerpt we see evidence that Miss Tir comes in with considerable amount of pent-up feeling which she expresses immediately but with a certain amount of reluctance. We notice in S 1, 2, and 3 that she begins by talking about certain general circumstances, namely, that she has been talking to her brother-in-law about a problem of her relationship to her mother. She seems unable or unwilling to talk about this problem in any spontaneous way, indicating she rather wants to elicit some kind of reaction from the counselor. In C 4 the counselor reacts to her apparent difficulty in starting, which in turn leads to the confiding that culminates in the statement in S 8 of unwanted hostile feelings toward the mother. In C 9 and 10 the counselor tries to be helpful by verbalizing the feelings that upset her and then suggests a broader therapeutic task, namely, to talk about herself in more general terms, not necessarily only about this specific set of feelings. This was carried over in C 12. Apparently the counselor felt she was having such intense feelings about this particular situation that communication was blocked. Consequently, through broadening the therapeutic task he gives her a choice between talking about her mother and her feelings toward her or about another topic. The interview proceeds:

S 12. (*low*) No. I know that. (*little laugh*) (*whispered*) Yes. (*now louder*) Well, as far as that was when I first came out here three years ago everything was—well, a little too fine, I suppose. I—my relationship with her had been good (*slight hesitancy*) so far as I could see. It was not too strong an attachment, not an unnaturally strong one, but a—a love between us, and I found very little fault with her as a mother and much to admire. (*slight pause*) The main thing I felt that did it, I felt, was when I—I have an older sister who got married two years ago and when she met her husband, and the point finally arrived where she announced that—well she didn't announce that it— one can see that it—

C 13. Uh-hum.

S 13. They were in love. Wanted to marry. My mother was very violently opposed to it. (C: uh-huh) Well, she had reason from the face of it. He was still studying. He had many years to go. Neither she nor my father knew anything about this fad, sociology—

C 14. Uh-hum.

S 14. —which he was studying.

C 15. Uh-hum.

S 15. They didn't feel he could make a living, and they thought she could do better. And well, I came back to school. I was in school through most of this. (*sighs*) But when I was home I saw what had been going on. My sister told me. She made life sort of impossible for her. She took every chance she could get to try— it was breaking her heart, and she tried in every mean way she knew how to stop the thing—only in the family—nobody else knew about it. She put on a very good front for the rest of the world, and finally they *did* marry. My sister married before she ordinarily would have because—I think, she never said—because it was so impossible to put up with it any longer. *(sigh)* I suppose that is more at the root of mine than anything else because I knew at the time almost inevitably the same thing would happen to me. (C: uh-hum) And it is going to. She doesn't know anything about it yet. That's one of the things I'm so afraid of is to announce the subject.

C 16. Uh-huh.

S 16. But I have two prospects for marriage. One of them, a boy out here she is—I think she would accept much more readily than she did my brother-in-law, but (C: uh-hum) well, she'll find something to carp about. But he's not the one—the one I *do* want she has no use for at all, doesn't like at all for the same reasons. I think mostly reasons of—well, security and he isn't quite the catch that she'd like to see me have. And there is another fellow whom I've dated and whom she sees as the be-all and the end-all. He's the guy she wants to see me with and I can't see that.

C 17. Uh-hum.

S 17. I haven't said anything but even when I go home, I'm sort of— I'm forced into—not—uh—well, lying, fibbing, pretending that I hadn't planned to see him but it happened all of a sudden and I didn't see why I shouldn't go here or go there with him. And I had to tell him that I couldn't see him as much as he wanted to and I wanted to because I was afraid. I can't bring things to a head now. I'm, well, we'll have to wait until June, anyway, when I graduate. But in the meantime I—it's—I suppose it's this mainly that colors every time I look at her or talk to her I (C: uh-hum) feel kind of afraid of what's coming and, well, it comes out in other ways. She is dissatisfied with me, I think. Maybe not only for that, maybe for other things, but last vacation was pretty awful as a result. She was at first—the entire first week, there wasn't a single word spoken between us, and I still don't know the reason for that. I'm pretty sure it wasn't because of the boy because nothing new seemed to have been developing.

C 18. Uh-hum.

S 18. Nothing leaked out. I don't know the reason for it, but it didn't help. It made it much worse. She was—she's quite neurotic. She has a terrible temper and when she gets angry she blows up, yells, says almost anything, anything, it doesn't matter whether it's true or not. She knows because I'm her daughter where I'm vulnerable, where she can hit me the hardest, and she goes right for that point, things like attacking my friends (C: uh-hum) in stupid little ways that she knows don't count, but she doesn't care about me when she's angry. She's got to find some way to hurt me. I don't know why that is. I've—it makes it worse on me, I can't—I try to understand it. I try to feel pity for her (C: uh-hum) because I realize that I'm going to be an awful disappointment but stronger than pity is—the fear I feel, and what amounts to hatred.

C 19. Uh-hum.

S 19. I don't know how to deal with her. I don't know what to tell her or how to behave when she gets the way she is.

C 20. Uh-hum.

S 20. *(low)* And soon I'll have to tell her.

C 21. And so what it amounts to is that when she begins to act this way, you can't be untouched by it, and you can't keep from wanting to almost hit back for being hit. And yet you—that's something you really can't permit yourself to do.

S 21. I did. By mail. *(lower)* I don't know what'll happen with it. I wrote a letter hitting back. I suppose I really hurt. I got an answer from my father, who couldn't quite understand it and wanted an apology.

C 22. Uh-huh.

S 22. I wrote back and said it's stupid to ask for an apology. I might say I'm sorry but I'd still feel that way, so what are you solving?

C 23. Uh-huh.

S 23. And *she* finally wrote and I suppose it was a kind—she tried to defend herself and apologize to me, saying that if I were more mature I would understand why she was the way she was last Christmas, etc. And it helped. I felt better towards her and I have since. And the next—well, the letters are few and far between that I get from her and the next real contact I had was the phone call and the same old story.

C 24. Uh-hum. It was only a temporary relief to kind of get it off your chest a little bit.

S 24. It did seem to *(lost)*.

C 25. Uh-huh. Yeah, I see. *(low)* *(pause)* I have the impression that your relationship with your mother before this, that is before you went to college, hadn't—had not involved ever giving expression to any negative feelings toward her.

S 25. *(low)* No. It hadn't. *(pause)* *(sort of sigh and little laugh combined)* I'd keep my mouth shut as a rule and intellectualize, I suppose—my feelings.

C 26. I see. (*low*) What you seem to be saying is you had feelings but you didn't express them.

S 26. I couldn't really feel them, because I—even if I'd start to get angry, I would feel more pity than anger (C: uh-hum) and the feeling that I couldn't say or do anything to hurt her if I should want to.

C 27. Uh-huh.

S 27. I suppose they were there, but they were unrecognizable to me at the time.

C 28. Uh-hum. (*pause*) You were mostly conscious of feelings of pity.

S 28. (*pause*) Y-yes. Instead of anger.

C 29. (*very low*) Uh-hum. I see. (*pause*) Well, it seems like there's still a lot to tell here.

In this section of the interview we notice that the counselor's broadening of the task in C 11 and 12 seems to have been helpful. Miss Tir now begins to tell more about her relationship with her mother. She talks about the attachment between her mother and herself which she carefully says was "not too strong," "not an unnaturally strong one." Then she uses her older sister's experience to introduce an analogous problem of her own marriage plans. In C 21 the counselor points out that although she feels angry and aggressive in response to her mother's action and even though she feels justified in her anger, she must hold back from expressing it. In C 25 the counselor reacts to the implication in the previous communications, particularly in S 21 and the following, that expressing negative feelings toward her mother was a new experience to her. This leads to an exchange over how she has controlled her feelings. While avoiding an explicit interpretation, the counselor in C 28 focuses on her attempt to substitute feelings of pity for anger. At the same time, we observe that the client has begun to slow up the rate of expression. Notice that there was a pause after S 27 and another pause before S 28 and still another pause after S 28. One might speculate about the cause of this slowing down of communication. Is this a reaction to rapid acceleration in expression of her feelings? Is she still sufficiently uncertain of the counselor to slow up until she knows him better? With the amount of information we have, it is extremely difficult to answer. The counselor also is not certain of the answer, as indicated by C 29 which represents a relatively noncommittal invitation to talk more. The interview proceeds.

S 29. I—well, what would be relevant?

C 30. Almost any aspects of the situation could be relevant, what kind of a person your mother is, what kind of relationships you've had before, what kind of a person your father is, what the general pattern in your family is. Apparently one of the suggestions is that it's pretty much out of the family pattern for a child to in any way be critical of a parent, the way your father wrote back after—in other words, he—it wasn't an issue of whether your mother was—had really justified your criticisms. Whether your criticisms were justified. It seemed mostly a matter that you as a child were criticizing your mother.

S 30. (*very low*) Yes. That's what it was.

C 31. Uh-hum. (*low*) I see.

S 31. Well, I sort of expected that when I wrote. It ran true to form. They're—well, they've always demanded respect because they're older, respect because they're parents, not because they are what they are. But I have the idea that respect is *not* coming to a person because of an age or because they happen to have children and are one's parents, and I don't know whether I can expect—really expect them to understand that or feel that way, so I did expect the apology, and the request for an apology, and when I got it I had an idea in mind to say that they should be intelligent enough to realize that though I apologize I still have feelings. And then she did come off that high horse. So when she came—when she wrote back to me, she said something about, "I feel as though I'm putting—being put into competition with your friends. Hasn't a mother a right to criticize—to judge, if you will?" Because I had yelled at her for saying something particularly nasty about a very dear friend of mine.

C 32. Uh-hum.

S 32. And she wanted to know didn't she have the right to criticize, to judge. And I wrote back that yes she did have the right if she criticized because she—you really feel that something's there that ought to be corrected, but that I felt she was criticizing to try to drive some kind of a wedge between me and my friend—to— (*short pause*) so that I would have less liking for her, and that it was a criticism with evil intent and not with constructive intent and that that was what I wouldn't put up with. That was where it hurt.

C 33. Uh-hum.

S 33. And as far as that—this might be relevant. Well, we are only two of us, my sister and I, and she is older than I am by two years. So she never confided much in my mother. (*clears throat*) All the confiding she did was to me, and I was often the middle-man. I'd—my mother would want to know what Ann had to say and if I felt that Ann wouldn't mind my mother knowing, I would tell her. And I would always come home and give all the gruesome details, everywhere I had been and everything that I had done. We used to—I knew she liked it, and I could tell her most things. There are some things that one does not talk about to one's—not to my mother anyway. (C: uh-huh) The subject of sex, what happened to you when you're out on a date is for—I'd die of embarrassment before I'd ever mention it to her. Things like that would go to my sister or my friend. And this particular friend of mine is very close. She's at home. I've known her for almost ten years and she and my mother do like each—she likes my mother very much. I believe my mother likes her, but yet, a great deal of the criticism is directed at her. I came to the conclusion that it was a kind of jealousy. Because she realizes that Eve, my friend that is, gets more of my confidences than she does. She may even realize now that in case anything is cooking with me and my boy, Eve would know about it, and she doesn't. I don't know whether she suspects that anything is (C: uh-hum) but everybody else knows except my mother, even my father.

C 34. Uh-huh.

S 34. And I think that's the reason for the criticism leveled there. It's probably jealousy. Nevertheless it hurts.

C 35. Uh-huh. (*very low*)

S 35. And I would like to get things back where they were. I'd like to be able to talk to her again without feeling this—as threatened as I do (C: uh-hum [*low*]) as if anything that I have to say is not going to be met with any kind of approval. As if she feels me a fool—thinks that I am. I think she does think so. For she would consider me a fool for making the choice of the boy (C: uh-hum) that I have chosen because he is—of all the three, has the least of what she would desire for her daughter's husband.

C 36. Uh-hum.

S 36. (*low*) Or if she were picking her own. And she's not—she's not—I don't know what the word is—unselfish or broadminded enough to even think that somebody else's values could be as true as her own. Well, to her what she accepts as being worth while in life, everybody thinks is worth while in life, and only a fool doesn't go after those things. That's another thing that rubs—I don't like being thought of that way and though she never said so, it's pretty apparent in her attitude. (*this last bit a little sadly*) My father is—well, he's no difficulty. He'll take with a little bit of disappointment anything I do. He'll, if you talk to him long enough and pound it into his head, he'll understand—see your viewpoint and be sympathetic. I could, I suppose, get him on my side, but I don't ever expect to have him in the case of my marriage, being in active—in active opposition to me. I suppose if I worked at it I could get him to be on my side of the fence, but I don't want to—I don't want to (C: uh-hum) separate them. They usually—they don't know it, but they usually work together—want the same things, and I'd like it to stay that way.

C 37. You don't want to set him against her.

S 37. No. If I could—and I don't know if I could. (*low*) Well, where can I go from here?

C 38. Uhmm—it seems to me that as—as you look at this thing, you put the emphasis on the fact that there's something wrong with the way your mother is going about this thing, the way she looks at it, she's being irrational about it, and so on.

S 38. Yes. It's—uhm—

C 39. Yet, your approach to your reactions to the situation is the same. There's something wrong with me, that I fear, that I dislike her, that I'm in conflict with her. In other words, it's almost—in other words, on one hand, you develop the picture that there's every reason for you to feel the way you do toward her since she's just not reacting in a way that a person should react to this situation. Yet, on the other hand, you don't give yourself the right to feel the way you do toward her.

We see that the counselor finally reacts to the client's hesitancy by attempting to give her alternative tasks and, in addition, calls attention to one aspect of her relationship to her parents (C 30). More than anything else it is the latter idea which seems to lead to further action and eventually she is again, in S 31 and the following, talking about her relationship to her mother. The salient point seems to be her perception of her mother as competing with her friend. We notice also that she follows this with talking about her relationship with her sister and mother. She quickly returns to the issue of her mother's jealousy of her girl friend. In S 36 we notice that she is indicating and rejecting the impulse to drive a wedge between her father and mother and for some reason this once more stops her. The counselor attempts to deal with the halting of communication by elaborating his earlier interpretation of her irrational guilt feelings. The interview proceeds further.

S 39. Oh, I— (*slight pause*) I realize I suppose I have a right and I don't think you'd say one doesn't have a right to one's feelings, but I don't like them.

C 40. Uh-hum. (*low*)

S 40. I don't know whether it's something lacking in me, not enough tolerance or understanding.

C 41. Uh-huh.

S 41. But I haven't done very much tolerating. My ordeal, so to speak, hasn't even begun yet because she doesn't know, and I've already had more than I can take.

C 42. Uh-huh.

S 42. And I haven't got any more—any more pity left in me, nothing but negative feelings.

C 43. Uh-hum. (*low*) (*after slight pause*) In other words, what you're trying to do is to recapture the feelings of pity for her.

S 43. (*after short pause*) (*low*) Yes.

C 44. Uh-huh.

S 44. That would be nice. (*laugh*)

C 45. (*laughs*)

S 45. I never thought of it that way.

C 46. Uh-hum. Or if you had more feeling of pity, you feel that that might counteract and hold back some of these other feelings or neutralize them to some extent. I wonder why you don't pity her any more.

S 46. (*pause*) Well, she—she's a powerful woman.

C 47. Uh-huh. Too strong to be pitied.

S 47. I suppose so. But even her strength is a—a—I know she dominates things when she wants to, but she doesn't realize it. (C: uh-hum) She doesn't know her own strength. She's very insecure and I'm certain she's afraid of me because I go to college and she never went to college.

C 48. Uh-huh. (*low*)

S 48. And feels *inferior* for that reason, and then to *her* my doing what I want to do is going to be the end—the wreck of everything for awhile at least. I hope it won't stay that way because she—

C 49. Uh-hum.

S 49. She doesn't feel that way about my sister's marriage any more.

C 50. *(low)* Uh-hum.

S 50. But this is going to be the most awful catastrophe. Even when it happened to Ann there was still me she could—I could still give her what she wants from her children. *(getting louder somewhat)* I'm the last. *(louder again)* She doesn't know how ruinous she's being. She doesn't have any idea of what—how she makes me feel. To her I suppose I seem as if I don't care, as though I'm going on my own merry way. (C: uh-hum) As if I'm going on my own merry way. Actually it is the case. She can't do anything to me. She can't stop me. I've got the ace up—up my sleeve. Because if it got to the point where she shoos me out of the house, why I could go, and she stands to lose. I don't. There's room there for pity because from her point of view that's the way it looks. But then again, I—she just overwhelms me completely!

C 51. Uh-hum.

S 51. It's an awful thing to be afraid of my—her steps coming—she was away all day because she works with my father in his business, and when she comes, I feel as if it was—I—I—heard a burglar's step on the stairs—that same fear, the feeling your heart starts to pound—because my mother was coming up.

C 52. *(low)* Uh-hum.

S 52. And well, it does mingle with pity. *(little laugh)* I pity myself.

C 53. Yeah.

S 53. I pity myself.

C 54. Yeah. In other words, you're the one who's really so insecure in your relationship with her that there isn't any room for pity. Even though, looking at it rationally, she really can't stop you, she can't really stand in the way of what you want, she's still such a fearful figure to you. You're still so frightened of having to go ahead with this thing in the face of her opposition that you can't feel any pity for her.

In this section of the interview there is a mixture of thought and feeling in the young woman's expression which suggests some movement. From the recording we get the distinct impression that the client in S 39 has reacted rather thoughtfully to the preceding counselor reaction to her guilt feelings. She seems to be criticizing herself for not having any more pity left. In C 43 the counselor calls attention to her efforts to defend herself against her aggressive feelings by trying to recapture feelings of pity for her mother. In S 43, 44, and 45 even the typescript conveys the clear impression that an important chord has been touched. One wonders why the counselor had to respond at all in C 46. Perhaps he felt it necessary to spell out his interpretation more clearly, but one would still wonder why he had to end it with the question. It would seem as though she was already being sufficiently thoughtful to make it unnecessary for the counselor to encourage at this point still further cognitive emphasis. In fact, further encouragement seems to run the risk of draining off the emotion and of reducing the process to a purely intellectual one. Perhaps the counselor was reacting to the periodic blocks which had been occurring during this first interview and attempting to forestall another one.

Miss Tir in S 47 through 50 vacillates between emphasizing how much power her mother has over her and emphasizing her own powers. She seems to see her mother's power winning out and, in S 51 and 52, expresses her own strong reactions to this power and her pity for herself which the counselor reflects back in C 54.

S 54. (*low*) Uh-hum. (*pause*) Well, I just wonder how the—my insecurity to her could have come about. Where would that come from? What does it come from? Childhood?

C 55. (*low*) Uh-hum.

S 55. Is there any—uhm—

C 56. Well, there are lots of general formulae. I doubt (*laughing a little*) whether there will be any real answers.

S 56. Uh-hum. (*low*) I—

C 57. (*breaking in*) There certainly—the relationship between the child and the parent has lots of potentialities for insecurity and fear. When you think of the small child and the relationship between the small child and the parent, with the parents kind of the source of everything to the child, the parent can be a very fearful person, controlling your destiny. (*rather low*)

S 57. (*very low*) Uh-hum.

C 58. So you can very easily suggest general formulae. I don't know that that will give you the real answer. The real answer involves just kind of puzzling out your relationships as they developed, as they are, and try to see what it is in *your* situation, what it means specifically, this fear. Around what kind of issues have these fears developed?

S 58. It—it could be—what I am really saying—I wonder if it would be—she was always a strict disciplinarian as far as that goes. (*moderately low*)

C 59. Uh-hum. (*low*)

S 59. In our family we were talked about as always having been good kids, and my brother-in-law said maybe you were too scared to be bad.

C 60. Uh-hum. (*low*)

S 60. Which might be the case. I felt—but does the feeling insecurity come from the sort of a—it would be subconscious idea that maybe you're not loved (C: uh-hum) as—as much as you'd like to be.

C 61. (*low*) Uh-hum.

S 61. Does it necessarily come from that?

C 62. No. Not necessarily. It could come just as much from feeling that you've got a lot more hate than you'd like to have.

S 62. Directed at her—

C 63. Yeah.

S 63. (*very low*) Oh.

C 64. (*This whole response is delivered in a slow, fairly low tone*) There are lots of interpersonal relationships that can account for these. I don't know that there's necessarily going to be a very easy way. That is, I don't think it's going to be just a matter of my trotting out different formulae, and we're saying— well, does this one apply? Does that one apply? It is more going to be a matter of trying to put the pieces together in terms of the various—I mean—you have many feelings toward your mother (S: uh-hum) and they're tied up with many relationships with her. It's more trying to put the pieces together in a way that will be meaningful. It may not only be just your mother. It may involve your mother and your father and your sister. So that they're all kind of interwoven. Bound to be, as you yourself were describing.

S 64. (*low*) Uh-hum.

C 65. (*low*) The relationship between your sister and you and how she was confiding in you, and the differences—variation in your relationship with both her and your mother, as her relationship to your mother was somewhat different than yours.

Apparently you had more the need to please your mother than she did.

In this section of the interview we again have some slowing down of movement and examples of one of the kinds of situations that arise with psychologically sophisticated clients. We see that Miss Tir is still being thoughtful about her feelings of guilt for opposing her mother and is reaching for some pat explanation. She seems to be testing the counselor to see whether he will give her the kinds of explanations her brother-in-law has given her, but the counselor refuses to be involved in any simple explanation. In both C 58 and C 64 he tries to communicate the conviction that there is no pat answer. One should note in C 57 indications that concomitantly the counselor is trying to influence her thoughts in a particular direction. It seems evident the counselor is reacting to the client's apparent helplessness in the face of her parents, particularly her mother. He is also suggesting that such feelings imply certain parent-child relationships. We also notice that at the very end of the particular sequence the counselor is teaching, in almost a formal sense, rather than reacting to any specific aspects of the client's communication. After this, he makes a pointed interpretation, calling attention to the contrast in the client's story of her own and her sister's reaction to their mother's opposition.

S 65. (*low*) (*slight pause*) Yeah. (*slight pause*) (*ruefully*) It's my main maladjustment. I'd like to be able to say I don't care.

C 66. Uh-hum. (*short pause*) And yet you want to pity her.

S 66. I'd rather do that than say I don't care. That sort of thing would—

C 67. Yeah. (*pause*)

S 67. I just wonder how much I could do from my end. I mean she's of no help to herself or to anybody else. And I think I—I don't know whether it was a wise thing, but my brother-in-law and I got on the subject, and it wasn't smart. He has—he knew what was going on at the time—

C 68. Uh-hum. (*low*)

S 68. And he's far from objective about it though he tried.

C 69. Uh-huh.

S 69. He has absolutely no affection for her.

C 70. Your mother hasn't accepted him particularly.

S 70. Well she, she does. I mean I hear her talking on the phone to her friends, telling about all his wonderful exploits, that he has done this and done that with his studies and his career (C: uh-hum) and bragging about him. She is very nice to him now (C: uh-hum) and calls him Sonny. But yet, when she gets into a temper she attacks him almost as quickly as she does my friend.

C 71. Uh-hum.

S 71. It was a case of her attacking them both at once last summer. (*low*)

C 72. Uh-hum.

S 72. I don't think she feels any genuine affection for him. (*quickly*) I don't know if she ever will, but she puts on an act to others. I imagine to herself.

C 73. Uh-hum.

S 73. He's not as bad as she thought he was. She won't admit that my—that she realizes that my sister has made a good marriage and is happy so far. When other people tell her she expresses surprise—how nice he is—"You really think so?" (*mimicking*)

C 74. Uh-hum.

S 74. And—or she'll say that since he's been in our family, he's really improved, we made a man out of him with our good influence, and—well, he stands as much as he has to between my sister and my mother. Whatever sway my mother had over my sister he tried to eliminate in every way.

C 75. Uh-hum (*low*)

S 75. It isn't too much. She never dominated either one of us to any great extent. She never tried. He's—well—bitter I suppose. He doesn't even sound objective. I don't know whether he thinks he does when he talks about it. He isn't interested in winning her affections.

C 76. Uh-hum.

S 76. I mean he doesn't care, I don't suppose, if he ever lays eyes on her again in his life.

C 77. Uh-hum.

S 77. He's just interested in keeping her from interfering with my sister and her learning how to cook, and all these other things (C: uh-hum) that my mother knows more about. He doesn't want her to try and teach my sister.

C 78. Uh-huh.

S 78. And he regards her as a narcissistic personality, and I can see it. She—when we were younger she was a good mother. I suppose it's easy to be a good mother to little kids. Their needs are—if you love them— (*lost*). I mean with a minimum of common sense you can settle their little problems for them. Mostly up to the time that they are ten or eleven, but when they get older they conflict—their ideas are liable to conflict. That's where she is breaking down now. She can't understand either my point of view or my sister's. She's not willing to. She only knows what she wants, and she goes after it, every (C: uh-hum) way she knows how, consciously or unconsciously, I don't know. (*last three words low*) But he said that there was nothing I could do about it, because the problem didn't lie with me, that it lay with her, and that if she ever tried to help herself, then something might be done. But as it is she never looks at herself squarely. She's not willing to—to explore her own feelings, and to find out whether she is right or wrong. She sort of—keeps on running with her eyes closed.

C 79.   Uh-hum.

S 79.   Well I—I wonder (*short pause*) how much my talking will help.

C 80.   (*slight pause*) I have the impression that in this talk with your brother-in-law you have had the feeling as though you—well—almost of being involved in a conspiracy. Definitely he was against your mother, and that in that sense you were not being able to decide this for yourself, but were kind of working toward a foregone conclusion.

S 80.   Yeah. I think so. (*short pause*)

C 81.   Uh-hum. (*low*)

S 81.   It was—he wasn't soft enough. He was much too hard.

C 82.   Uh-huh. (*low*)

S 82.   And I—he always is when he talks of her. (*low and rather fast*)

C 83.   Uh-huh (*short pause*) Did you feel the need to defend her when he seemed so hard?

S 83.   (*pause*) Well, not—not at the time because it was—it was last Christmas when I had had about as much as I could take and there—that is—I wasn't (*both laugh*) as calm as I am. (*still some laughter*) So I didn't, but I would whenever I feel good toward her, and he makes a remark. (C: uh-huh) He's got quite a sarcastic sense of humor.

C 84.   Uh-huh.

S 84.   I don't like it. It seems too hard. (*pause*)

C 85.   I have the impression that you have some reluctance to try to talk this out. (*short pause*)

S 85.   How do you mean?

C 86. Well, I was wondering about your saying that you wonder if it's going to do any good to talk like this. (*low*)

S 86. Hmm. (*low*)

C 87. Just a minute ago. (*low*)

S 87. Well, for the reason that *he* had told me that there was nothing I could do about it, that it was something I had to put up with because the fault was in her and not in me.

C 88. Uh-huh. (*low*)

S 88. And he just said whenever you want to blow off steam come on over here and blow it off.

C 89. Uh-huh.

S 89. And I hope there's something more constructive than that I can do. I don't know.

C 90. Uh-huh. Well, I see. (*low*) (*pause*) And it's kind of a question. In other words, is this situation just going to be another situation where you'll simply blow off steam about her or will you be able to find out some constructive solution.

S 90. Uh-hum (*low*)

C 91. Uh-hum. (*low*) Well, I think that's what we'll try to work for, and see if it's possible.

S 91. Good. (*little laugh, sounding both anxious and happy*)

C 92. Uh-huh. I—again, I think that there are solutions. In other words, you're— what you're seeking for is some stable (*short pause*) solution, rather than one that involves your kind of getting worked up and blowing off steam and getting worked up again and blowing off steam again.

S 92. Uh-huh. (*low*) Also one on how to—how to face her, how to answer her when she's angry. (C: uh-hum) What kind of tack to take when the day comes that I announce that I'm going to marry Tom. What am I supposed to—should I try to reason with her?

C 93. Hmm.

S 93. Should I say you'll find enough in him to like if you try or should I just say, "This is it. If you don't like it," etc.

C 94. Uh-hum.

S 94. (*low*) I don't know how to go about it. Which she's more likely to respond to.

C 95. Yeah. Well, of course, I can't guarantee (S: uh-hum) any real answer here. About all I can say is that I think we can be optimistic about being able to find some answer. I'm not sure if we can do it within the time limits you've set. (*laughs*)

S 95. Oh. Until June then. (*laughs too*)

C 96. (*smiling*) Well, I was just thinking you're setting—you were thinking about April too.

S 96. No. (*low*)

C 97. (*still smiling*) I'm not so sure about that part of it.

S 97. Hum? (*very low*)

C 98. When do you want to come back? Our time is about up.

S 98. Oh! Well, if the frequency of talking has anything to do with getting it solved (*little laugh*) I'd like to come back real soon.

C 99. Uh-hum. Uh-hum.

S 99. (*smiling*) I know you're busy.

(Two meeting times a week are agreed on and the interview ends.)

In this last section of the interview we notice that something has caused Miss Tir to draw back. She seems to be equating this counseling experience with the experience she had with her brother-in-law. She wonders perhaps whether the counselor will be as biased and as involved as was her brother-in-law and whether he will be able to help her to any constructive solution. It seems difficult to determine just what has brought on this feeling. Perhaps it was something around the counselor's handling of her effort to find a general formula. Perhaps she took his response as indicating he didn't think he could do anything more than her brother-in-law could do. We notice also that the counselor helps her bring her doubts into the open, in C 86 and 87, and concentrates his attention on making clear that he does understand what she hopes to gain out of the relationship. He permits himself to make mildly optimistic statements. We notice that in C 98, the counselor has inferred she will want to continue, and the client's response suggests that his inference was accurate.

Summary. In this interview we are able to form certain definite impressions of this young woman. Even with the limitation imposed by a typescript, one gains the impression, which comes through more clearly in the recording, she is capable of a good deal of spontaneous and relatively controlled expression of affect. From this we can infer she has achieved a considerable degree of emotional maturity and integration. With clients of this sort it is possible for a counselor to proceed quite rapidly. This our counselor has tried to do. In order to proceed rapidly and still be effective, one must be sensitive to the conditions and signs of such progress. Speed of progress is partially tied to the level of affect at which the relationship operates. As the counselor responds in such a way as to increase the pace at which feelings are expressed, the intensity of feeling experienced by the client increases. To be effective, this intensity of feeling should not exceed the client's capacity to deal with it in constructive ways. When the feelings being brought forth exceed the client's capacity to deal with them in an integrated way, one may expect the client to fall back on regressive and less organized ways of reacting. This may take the form of introducing particular defenses of a relatively-well-organized sort, such as we associate with neurotic behavior or the more disorganized, more childlike response of the psychotic type. From most clients, one can expect the more organized types of regressive responses such as are involved in the process of intellectualization. In fact, in attempting to move too rapidly, counselors often fail to encourage any expression of affect at all. Their interactions with the client become purely intellectual discussions of ideas about the client without involving any real feeling.

Case of Mr. Bav [2]

The client is a twenty-year-old male senior premedical student.

C 1. Mr. ———— is my name.

S 1. What is it?

C 2. ————.

S 2. ————?

C 3. Won't you sit down? I'd kind of like to record this interview. We're sort of making a study of interviews here.

S 3. Oh. Okay.

C 4. What did you have—

S 4. Just what is this? I mean I didn't have any idea at all just what it is. One of my friends, well, called up and he told me about it. We were having a discussion in the house and he told me that, if I did come over here, perhaps, they could solve my problems.

C 5. Uh-huh.

S 5. But I'd never heard of it before.

C 6. Well, maybe you could give me more of an idea of what you had in mind.

---

2 The third interview with Mr. Bav appeared in Chapter 3.

The opening of this interview illustrates some clients' initial feeling of having gotten in deeper than they bargained for. This student comes on the recommendation of a friend, perhaps feeling this was a relatively casual step that he was taking. The fact that the counselor is recording the interview seems to make him pull up short and raise questions about the agency. The counselor disregards Mr. Bav's efforts to re-examine his decision about coming; instead he suggests that he tell what his problem is and the interview proceeds.

S 6.   Well, *(sigh)* I don't know. I'm sort of mixed up right now. I have been pre-med. And, well, I'm a senior now, but I have next year also. I have nineteen hours to take, still, and I'm not sure now whether I want to become a doctor or not. I haven't been re-fused yet and I haven't been accepted either. And, well, I'm not sure in my own mind whether medicine would be the best thing for me.

C 7.   Uh-huh.

S 7.   And I was just wondering if there was anything I could do to find out whether I have an aptitude for it. I have taken tests already in St. Joseph at the Board of Education but I don't think they prove anything. They're just tests of what you know about science and other related subjects. I mean I scored high in science because I studied it in high school. *(little laugh)* That's the only reason so I don't think they prove too much.

C 8.   You're kind of wondering—you sort of followed down this one path all your life and now you're beginning to wonder a little bit.

S 8.   Yeah. Well I'm just not sure whether *I* had made up my own mind about it or whether it was my friends. Because, well, all through high school and through college my friends have been interested in the same thing, medicine. I don't know. Maybe it was—it's just—I mean that that's typical of most of the people I've been going around with. They're all interested in it. Maybe it's because they're—all their—their parents—although I don't think *my* parents have really suggested it. I think I suggested it myself. And I think the first time I ever became interested in it was when—it was even before high school. One of my best friends was very interested in it also. And people ask you all the time what do you want to do? What field are you going into? What are you going to take in college? What would you like to do? I was just thinking that possibly, I said that—I mean—I wanted to become a doctor because I just had to say something. I had to give them some answer, and that seemed the most logical. I mean that being a doctor you have social status. People look up to you and you make money. Maybe that was just the only thing. And I have been toying around with the idea now of teaching, but my parents have practically forbidden it. They said that there isn't enough—that you don't get enough money out of it. And, well I think I'd be satisfied, but everybody I know says they think I'm crazy. My parents said they'd rather just have me graduate and possibly my father could help me out doing something else. (*little laugh*) But I don't know what else I'd be happy in. I've always done best in the sciences. I guess it's because I've been most interested in them.

C 9. Uh-hum.

S 9. And I haven't, well, I don't know. Since I've been going here I've concentrated mostly on science. I'm a zoo. major, and I haven't—this last semester and this semester—I've had a chance to take other courses. The reason—well, when I had my interview with the medical school dean he said my marks were all right. On the aptitude test I did all right except I did very poor on vocabulary. I've always had trouble in vocabulary. So I guess I could expect to be approved if I don't get in this year. I just don't know if that's the best thing. And also I've—well, I'm very unsure of myself. I'm just wondering if a person that's not sure of himself, not—I mean, very doubtful about himself would make a very good doctor. Because I'd hate to have a situation presented to me where I wouldn't be sure what I'd learned and whether I should do this or that and have a person's life in my hands and do the wrong thing. It still is—I mean it still isn't too late to change my mind. Now I have another year. This is my third year of college. I'm a senior because I went to summer school, twice, but I can still go to college for another year. I don't know. I know they're giving tests at the Test Service or someplace, they're giving an aptitude test, but I don't have much faith in that. I don't think that proves too much. It's—my roommate and some other people I know have taken it and they describe it as hooey.

C 10. It sounds like really the thing that has to be straightened out here is probably your feelings about things. In other words, to have clarified what your feeling is.

S 10. *(little laugh)* That's it. I mean I just don't know whether I'm suited for that or not.

C 11. You kind of have the feeling that—well—maybe you have some of the academic qualifications, but you're not the sort of person that belongs in the field.

S 11. Well, the thing that got me over here was that I—one of my friends, my best friend, got into med. school and I was talking to him. I told him I was going to take nineteen hours next term and graduate and I'd like to work for half a semester and then when I got into Med. School, I'd have money. He didn't quite understand why I wanted to do this. He—I mean he thought that—well—knowing me, he thought that the logical thing is to go on and get my Master's. But the way *(little laugh)* everything has shaped up now, I don't feel that I can do anything with my Master's anyway. I don't know if—if I don't do the thing I'd be happy in—well, I'd be happy at it but I'm used to—I mean my parents make more money than a teacher would, and I don't know what kind of—what I could provide for my family, if I had a family.

C 12. Sounds like you're pretty responsive to what other people think.

S 12. Yeah, that's why I'm afraid that maybe I—you know, I—being a doctor isn't my own decision. Maybe it's a decision of somebody else, I don't know.

C 13. You're not too sure of where you can draw the line between what you feel and what other people tell you you ought to feel.

S 13. That's right. Because it seems that I—usually I— *(little laugh)* feel what other people feel, rather than my own feelings. *(slight pause)* I don't even know if I'd be happy going into teaching. And if I did I'd want to go out and get my Ph.D. in zoology, but I don't know if I'd be happy at that.

C 14. You're really not too sure of how you feel about yourself.

S 14. Uh-huh.

C 15. You're kind of all tied up with what other people think and what other people—

S 15. Yeah, that's right. *(short pause)* I just don't know. *(little laugh)* I don't know what to do. I—is this the right place to go or—

C 16. Well, one of the ways in which we can help a person here is by helping him kind of clarify how he feels about himself.

In this portion of the interview Mr. Bav, starting with S 6 through S 9, gives a long summary of his thinking about medicine and alternative vocational choices. This is an interesting statement

in that it reflects the many different motivations which can influence vocational choice, for example, social status, economic
return, parental pressure, and self-doubt. The central theme
throughout his communication is his fear of an alien influence in
his choice of medicine. He is not sure whether it is a choice which
is being foisted on him from the outside and whether it will represent a role which is foreign to him. In C 10 and C 11 the counselor responds to his confused feelings, which leads to still further
interaction centering on his feeling of being overly swayed. In
S 15 we see the client's uncertainties about the counseling situation, which the counselor had earlier disregarded, once more
appearing.

During the next ten minutes of this interview the counselor
proceeds quite rapidly, attempting to point out to the client various aspects of his feelings of dependence upon others. At the same
time, Mr. Bav is talking about his confused feelings and his
impression that he may have chosen medicine because of his
mother's unverbalized interest in the choice. Yet he doesn't see
anything else for which he would be better suited. He has doubts
about teaching. He is afraid he would be trying to find an easy
way out. But he feels also he cannot postpone his decision much
longer.

The counselor's attempts to press certain views of himself on
the client can be illustrated by this series of consecutive counselor
responses:

You kind of have some—do have some feelings, then, about what
it is that you really want. But sometimes they bring you into conflict
with what you think other people expect of you.

And so you're unsure of whether you should respond to your
own feelings or kind of respond to the sort of expectations that other
people have of you.

It's not so much a matter of kind of picking one over the other.
It's more a matter of reaching a compromise, so that you can satisfy
everybody all the way around.

For you to be happy you have to have other people's approval.

You're kind of saying that you were pretty responsive perhaps to
your parents' feelings and that sometimes they might have led you in
the wrong direction.

In other words, there might be some issue here in terms of how much you can really depend on what other people say—what other people suggest.

Apparently partially in response to this pressure, the client has begun to express some of his negative attitudes toward his parents and their relationship to him. We pick up the interview at this point.

S 44. *(after short pause)* Well, I know that you can be independent and maintain good relationships. I've seen it done. Some—mostly—I know most of my friends I know are the same way I am. Although some of them are growing out of it now, they were quite dependent upon their families. And some of them—some of them aren't—some of them are very dependent on their families and yet they're very aggressive.

C 45. Uh-huh. *(pause)* Uh-hum. You're kind of saying this is a workable problem. You just have to find the sort of solution.

S 45. Yeah. I guess that's about it. *(low)* The best solution.

C 46. I wonder if that isn't pretty much the core problem that you have to deal with, the kind of arriving at a solution on this issue so that you'll know where you stand in relation to it. And then some of these other things will fit right in.

S 46. Possibly. I think that would be a help. I'm just wondering if that could be done.

C 47. Maybe it's kind of a matter of sort of clarifying what you really think and feel about yourself and about other people's feelings so that you can get a clearer perception of the relationship.

S 47. Well I just—the only thing is that takes so much time *(little laugh)* I'm just wondering how much time it will take.

C 48. You're kind of hoping that you can get sort of a quick decision.

S 48. Well, I *(little laugh)* I would like— *(little laugh)* That's what I—I *knew* that I couldn't get a quick decision and yet *(laughing)* I'd like one.

C 49. Yeah.

S 49. It's—it's sort of hard, I guess. In other words, you can't go on for ever and ever. I— *(little laugh)*

C 50. In a sense you are kind of saying maybe somebody could give me a decision in a hurry.

S 50. I think I did *(little laugh)* expect that. I mean I did—I don't think I expected it. I think I wanted it, but I didn't expect it.

C 51. Uh-hum.

S 51. I don't see—I mean I don't know how—I was just wondering how much a psychologist can do anyways. Because, well, I mean I don't know how long you've gone to school, but there must be, I mean everybody has a little knowledge. I know one of my friends had gone to a psychologist a few weeks ago. He's been going for about four weeks, and finally the psychologist just told him to leave because he was putting up too much resistance.

C 52. Uh-hum.

S 52. He—I mean both of us have gone through (*little laugh*) three psych. courses and both of us have just taken this third one and thought that we knew it all, and why (*little laugh*). I know he did. He (*little laugh*) thought (*laughing*) he knew more than the psychologist. I know he did want to go to one though. He is very neurotic.

C 53. Maybe you're kind of raising this sort of issue—you're kind of saying to yourself, well now can I accept this sort of relationship? Where I talk these things over?

S 53. Well, I think I—I *think* I can. I think I can see where it has its good points.

C 54. Uh-huh.

S 54. But I—the only thing is from what I have been, I mean, it seems as though it will take two or three years before you can finally get deep enough into the person's (C: yeah) personality to decide exactly what is good for him and cure him of all his— (*little laugh*).

C 55. Well, maybe on these issues it isn't important really that one kind of gets to the ground floor. Maybe it's just a matter of kind of reorienting right on top here how you see yourself. See?

S 55. Well, I don't understand how that—how it can be done, just by sessions like this where I just talk and you listen. And something can be done?

C 56. Well, let's kind of frame it this way, that generally when a person has a problem he's kind of involved in that problem, emotionally involved, so he doesn't see it from a perspective. He kind of sees it one way. Let's say that there's another person kind of working with this problem with him, but this other person isn't emotionally involved. Now he can take the same situation and see it in a different way. So he kind of communicates the way he sees it and that gives the person with the problem a chance to look at his problem in another way. See?

In other words, he has more angles to work on. He can kind of explore his feelings more completely, and in that way he can kind of understand himself a little better. He gets clarification. See what I mean?

S 56. Yeah. Well by doing this, do you think it would be possible to arrive at some conclusion? I mean—what I— (*little laugh*) what good I am or what—

C 57. Yeah, the conclusion or decisions *you'll* come to. I mean, you'll arrive at them essentially on the basis of seeing more of the issues involved and seeing them more clearly. See? In other words, our function here is pretty much to kind of help you see these issues more clearly. You will actually work with the problem and we'll kind of talk around the same problem with you. Talk about what you say, only in a different way, so that you have a better understanding.

S 57. Well, the thing is once I— (*little laugh*) once I do see myself, then, and try and arrive at some conclusion, won't all these forces that have been working on me from all sides—they're still going to be working on me, aren't they?

C 58. Maybe you will come to see these forces in a different light. See? In other words, you're kind of looking at them now as sort of having one meaning. They sort of push in one direction, but maybe there are other ways of looking at them? You see? That's the sort of thing that occurs. In other words, it's not that we change situations here. Maybe you kind of change a little bit the way you look at situations, and of course, that kind of makes for a different world. Your problem becomes a different sort of problem. It isn't a matter of going deeply into it necessarily for two or three years. It's just kind of a matter of sort of straightening out how you're looking at things.

S 58. I don't understand—what was this center set up for? I mean, it hasn't been publicized at all and for—I mean—for what purpose was it set up?

C 59. Well, our function here is to do essentially the sort of thing that I just described.

S 59. Uh-hum.

C 60. In other words, kind of helping people to see things more clearly; to see all the angles so that then they can come to solutions to their problem.

S 60. Well, is this attached to the University, isn't it?

C 61. Yes, a part of the University.

S 61. Well, what are the people that are here? I mean are—I mean are they going to the University? Or are they teaching at the University or what?

C 62. Some people are. Some people are on the staff of the University and some people are on the advanced graduate level here.

S 62. I see.

C 63. All of them have had considerable training in personality and behavior and the like, so that they have a pretty good understanding of these problems.

S 63. What's the difference between this and—well, one of the fellows in the house has been going to student health service.

C 64. Uh-huh.

S 64. I think that's what it's called. He's been going there for about two years. What is the difference between this and health service?

C 65. In many ways they're very much the same in that both kind of deal with problems that individuals have. But probably here we probably deal with decisions that an individual has to make which don't involve too long a process.

S 65. Oh. I see. Well, how can they go about—in a different way? I mean how can they go about it and take longer than you can? How can you shorten the process?

C 66. Well, maybe it's kind of a matter of dealing with issues that perhaps don't involve so much of the person. You see?

S 66. Where, there. At health service?

C 67. No. Here. And there you kind of get involved in a lot of different things, you see.

S 67. Oh.

C 68. And here we kind of relate ourselves to this one kind of decision that you have to make, here without kind of changing everything.

S 68. Oh. I see. (*short pause*) I was just wondering about it. I—'cause— (*little laugh*) I mean I never heard of it before. (*pause*) (*little laugh*) My—the first time that I had ever heard of the University doing *anything* at all like this was last term when they started publicizing the aptitude tests here, at the psychological services here, that somebody was giving.

C 69. Yeah.

S 69. And everybody clamored over to the building to see whether they were in the right thing or not.

C 70. That's also part of our function here. You see sometimes an individual decision involves getting more information. Sometimes he kind of knows pretty well what he can do, but it's mostly an issue of just clarifying how he feels about things.

S 70. Well, do you think it would be—in correlation with this, do you think it would be useful to take one of the tests that you give, or don't you think that would be of any use?

C 71. Maybe we can kind of decide on that when we sort of have a better picture of really what the decision is going to involve. Whether or not it's really going to involve getting more information (S: I see) or whether or not you have enough information. It's just kind of a matter of sort of clarifying the picture. You see. This is the kind of a situation that a lot of people can and do take advantage of. It's kind of helping them to get another person's point of view so that they can kind of restructure a little bit how they're feeling and seeing things.

S 71. (*pause, then in low tone*) Well, as long as I can take advantage of it, I don't see why I shouldn't. I don't know I— (*pause*). Can anybody go about giving counseling like this? You get special training, don't you?

C 72. Yeah. We're all trained in clinical psychology. In other words, it's our special job to work in this sort of thing.

S 72. I was wondering—do you think that the grades have any correlation, do you? I mean, well, some people will get good grades in everything. But I was just wondering if my grades do prove anything. I mean, there again I'm not sure of myself. I'm wondering if getting the—getting good grades in things like chemistry and zoology, things like that, (*lower*) do mean anything.

In this section we see the effects of the counselor having bypassed Mr. Bav's earlier doubts, suspicions, and ambivalences about the counseling situation. He starts by raising questions of time and of how much he can be helped. He also raises doubts about the qualifications of psychologists. Note that in S 51 and 52 he is in effect saying that his friend had really needed help from a psychologist but had only received criticism and rejection. This also the counselor seems to bypass. Eventually the student's questions and challenges become more direct, and we see that the counselor reacts to them by attempting to reason with him, to explain why what is being done will be helpful to him and to give him information about the process. One cannot help wondering why the counselor is so defensive and why he has to push the client so hard trying to convince him that counseling is appropriate for

him and that his suspicions about the process are ill-founded. Ordinarily, this sort of situation would be handled by acknowledging
the client's feelings of suspicion and doubt with more of an attitude of patient waiting while he tried to resolve these feelings. In
his process of trying to resolve them, he may ask for information
or explanations. A certain amount of this might well be supplied,
but the counselor should avoid overwhelming the client. Finally
in S 72 Mr. Bav either gives up the testing process or is satisfied
and returns to his problem and the interview proceeds.

C 73.   Well, sometimes the issue is more a matter of how a person
        feels about it. For instance, a guy can be pretty good in drawing,
        but that's no assurance that that's what he wants to do. You
        see. Grades kind of indicate the level of ability. That would
        be one part of the issue. The fact that a person has the ability,
        let's say, to do these things. But perhaps one of the bigger issues
        would be what does he want to do? How does he feel about
        it? You see?

S 73.   Do you think it would be good for me to take an IQ test, or
        something, to see just how much ability I do have.

C 74.   Well, do you feel that that's kind of an issue, or—

S 74.   Well, I don't know if it is an issue or not. I— (little laugh) I
        don't know why I brought that up. I mean—

C 75.   I wonder if you don't really have a picture from the fact that
        you have come this far. In other words, you couldn't possibly
        have made it up to now unless you have a pretty high level of
        ability.

S 75.   I don't know how much—how high a level of ability you really
        have to get you this far because I think that anybody with a
        normal amount of intelligence could get through school, (C:
        uh-hum) could get this far.

C 76.   You'd kind of like to—sort of find out more about that—sort of
        reassure yourself on that issue.

S 76.   I don't even know if it would reassure me. Maybe that would
        be further impetus for myself to (little laugh) want to give up
        the thought of medicine. I don't know if it would show me what
        to do but it would be either encouragement or discouragement.
        (C: uh-hum) I know I did take a test in St. Joseph last week.
        I was applying for a job (C: uh-hum) for the summer, and took
        a Civil Service exam. They gave me an intelligence test. I
        haven't had the results, but I was really—that was the only
        thing I really liked about the thing because I wanted to find

out the results. But still I don't know whether that would prove anything. If—I don't know how they—how they even go about marking it, whether they mark it on an ordinary range of people that take tests, you know, the Civil Service people (C: uh-hum) won't prove too much. (C: yes) Because college people naturally have more training, more—and they have more ability and they usually—

C 77. You really want to know how you function with people that you're working with.

S 77. Yeah. I'd like to know that and I'd like to know (*little laugh*) where I stand I guess with the rest of the people in my school.

C 78. Yeah. In a sense you're kind of saying I wonder if I really stand high enough in comparison with the people I have to compete with.

S 78. I guess that's about it. Because a lot of people have been going around the house wondering about their 140 IQ's and I know I don't have a 140 IQ. I was wondering if I just have an IQ as high as the average college student. I don't—if I was when I came here—I don't know. It seems that my study hall counselor in high school warned me against coming here and told me that I wouldn't do well. Well, as far as that goes, I have done all right. I have around 3.3 (B = 3.0) or something like that and (*little laugh*) I'm just wondering if he was right. I never found out how I did in the IQ test in high school. Possibly it's— I didn't have a high enough IQ to come to a school like this.

C 79. Uh-hum.

S 79. He told me I should go to a small school.

C 80. Uh-huh. Sometimes that concept of IQ is very much abused. You see what the IQ tells you is the possible level of potentiality the person has. But it also has to take into account and it can't very well other issues like motivation and things like that. So sometimes it's unfortunate that people kind of use it as a way of kind of labeling somebody and saying, well, you're 120. You can only do so much. But the issue would pretty much depend on what a person feels he can do and wants to do, and so forth. You see, the IQ is just a rough indication.

S 80. Yeah it is, but still I was wondering if it could be possible that I could have an IQ something like 110? Or I was just wondering if, I mean, going here I do have the motivation to work because I saw everybody else around me working and possible that's the reason I did well.

C 81. Yeah.

S 81. I was wondering if I could have an IQ that low and still be able to get A's and B's.

C 82. You could.

S 82. You could?

C 83. Yeah.

S 83. *(little laugh)* I'm worried. I'm just wondering if my IQ was that low.

C 84. That's why we don't depend too much on IQ you see. What we do is kind of get a comparison of how you stand with the people you're competing with. We don't give you a number, an IQ. See? *(short pause)* The more important issue would be what kind of work are you doing? And if you're doing work, why that's evidence.

S 84. Well another thing I was wondering. Why do you think I have such poor ability when it comes to subjects such as language? I did so poor. I stood in the tenth percentile group (C: uh-huh) on the vocabulary test on the medical aptitude test.

C 85. Uh-huh.

S 85. And also when I came here, I took Freshman English and I got a D in it. I took English 2 and I got a C in it. Those were the only marks I got (C: uh-hum) below B's. In high school, when I took Latin I flunked it. And do you think that ties in with the personality? Do you think it could be due to training? Or do you think it's just heredity?

C 86. Well, there are possible a number of issues involved here. You're kind of saying, well, I sort of want to know a little more about myself here. How good am I? I mean, that's really the problem.

S 86. Well, I think, well, do you think—don't you think—that's sort of normal because (C: yeah) I think my personality—I'm just trying to prove to myself—I mean that's one of the factors. I'm trying to prove to myself whether I have something on the ball or don't.

C 87. Yeah. First you'd like to know that you can do something before you (S: yeah) go on to these other issues. On an issue like the one you're talking about there would probably be different elements involved. Sometimes a person hasn't had very good teaching or training. I wouldn't say he hasn't had enough. It isn't the level, but the type of teaching, how good it actually was, and he might be handicapped later in his work. It would be—

S 87. *(breaking in)* but still it's, well, the school I went to, well, I went to the school—it was the same schools as a lot of other people did, I mean in St. Joseph.

C 88. Uh-huh.

S 88. And it seems that the other people had all ability when it came to English. Most of the fellows that I have gone to school with and the girls that have gone through all three schools that I went to and then came up here all could write. Most of them wrote for the school paper, and a lot of them right now appear in it. And they all got good marks. So I—as far as the training in school goes, I think I had just as much as they did.

During this sequence a little tug of war goes on between the young man and the counselor. Considering what has preceded this part of the interview, one wonders what is behind Mr. Bav's questions about his level of ability and his apparent pushing for some kind of testing to check on it. In S 74 he indicates some doubts as to his motives for introducing the question. Considering the fact that he has expressed negative attitudes toward tests in the earlier parts of the interview, one might wonder whether this represents a more subtle form of the resistance feeling he has just previously exhibited. The counselor reacts to all this primarily in terms of the pressure toward testing and tries to prove he has the essential information that testing can give him and that the question of his feelings is more important. In S 86 Mr. Bav gives us a possible clue about his insistence on the issue of his ability, namely, that he is feeling pushed into considering his personality with the possible implication that there is something abnormal about it. This tug of war between the client and counselor continues beyond S 88 until finally they return to the issue of the client's efforts to please others. We pick up the thread in S 99.

S 99. Maybe it's my—my dad is very responsive, I mean to what other people think. I mean, he tries to do as much as he can for other people, and possibly I—I resemble my father. I don't know. I know people always, when they talk about him, they always say what a good man he is and how wonderful he is and everything. He's a lawyer and he gives advice about—to so many people without charge and things like that. Maybe he was my ideal. I identified myself with him and I've become the same way. But he's, he's a lot more independent than I am. Of course he *(laughing a little)* has to support a family, and I don't.

C 100.   You're kind of saying that by pleasing people you're successful, and vice versa. You're successful when you please people.

S 100.   You're successful when you have the recognition of other people. Or they respect you. Maybe that— (*little laugh*)

C 101.   One of the issues might be—can you please other people and still be independent or does pleasing other people mean that you sort of have to give in to the way other people feel?

S 101.   Maybe that's it. Maybe I've always—I think I've always been submissive because that way I show that I wanted the friendship of people if I do what they want and try and follow along with them and not be a leader. Let them get a feeling of superiority and that way, they'd resp—they'd like me more. Maybe that's it. I don't know.

C 102.   You're kind of saying well, that perhaps is the only way that people can accept me. They kind of have this picture of me and sort of expect it so I'm going to sort of follow through. You're not allowing that possibly they would accept you more, if they—you were a more independent individual.

S 102.   Yes. That possibly could be it.

C 103.   This is something to think about.

S 103.   It—maybe it's just that it always seemed so easy to—not have to lead and always follow. Maybe that's it. Well, that (*little laugh*) is the easiest way, not to be aggressive, just to be submissive.

C 104.   You're kind of saying it's safest because then you're assured of a relationship. But on the other hand it isn't entirely satisfying either.

S 104.   No. It's not altogether satisfying.

C 105.   It kind of boils down to the issue of whether or not you can be yourself more than you are and still have other people accept you. In other words, do you always have to be a baby (S: yeah, that's it) in order to be accepted?

S 105.   (*after short pause—low*) I think that's right.

C 106.   How do people work out that sort of problem? The sort of thing to think about.

S 106.   I don't know. I don't see how people can work it out, themselves.

C 107.   Uh-hum.

S 107.   Well, I don't know. Maybe they can. I guess if they try hard enough, they possibly do get—they get deeper and deeper into themselves.

C 108.   Yeah. Maybe they kind of have to look into themselves a little bit to understand what it is they're really trying to do.

S 108. Well, I think it's really hard for people to look at themselves. They don't want to. I think they're afraid of what they'll find. They're afraid they'll find something there that they don't want to find. (C: uh-hum) They'd rather keep away from it.

C 109. Yeah. That might be one of the issues that you have to deal with here. This question of whether or not you really want to look into yourself, or whether you—

S 109. The point is I *know* myself! I never said that I don't know all the things that are bothering me. In my personality. It's just that I never do anything about it. (*little laugh*) (*short pause*) I guess maybe that means I don't know (*little laugh*) myself.

C 110. Yeah. Maybe you're saying that you kind of have different needs here. On the one hand you sort of have the need to rely on other people, which is kind of satisfying. You know yourself in that respect. You know where you stand. But on the other hand you also have a need for more independence, and that kind of creates a conflict.

S 110. Yeah.

C 111. In other words, you're kind of like two different people here going in different directions. See?

S 111. (*after pause*) So what are you supposed to do? (*little laugh*)

C 112. Well, maybe that's kind of something to think about, in order to try to understand why it is that you're feeling this way. Why it is that there are two different people here, rather than just one person that's kind of supplying a little of each need.

S 112. Another thing that seems very funny. For no reason at all I feel anxious so many times. When I—when I study I get not terrible pains, but I get pains in my stomach and my food seems to come up on me. Maybe I have guilt feelings and I feel that—maybe I feel that I'm not studying enough to please my parents. (*little laugh*) I don't know. To please somebody, I don't know who. It must be them. They're the only ones that I— (*little laugh*) care about pleasing I guess. I don't know where *they* come from. I don't want them, but at times when I just can't quite get rid of them. They especially occur at times when I have to spend time over at the fraternity house or something like that and I feel that it's purely wasted time. And that's why I can't understand why I don't like to spend time over there. I just don't feel like devoting my time to it. I wanted to join because it's an easy way for getting meals and having parties, and having people around and not have to go around hunting for people. (*little laugh*) Yet I don't like it so much because it involves spending time over there and I think it's so much a waste of time (*little laugh*). I don't think a fraternity's much good.

C 113. I wonder if there isn't an issue to think about there. On the one hand, you're kind of looking for social approval. You're kind of looking for social participation.

113. (*breaking in*) I think that's probably—I know I think I did join it because I wanted social approval. I wanted something to take a girl and be able to possibly say that I'm a fraternity— it seems that fraternities, being a fraternity man, gives you more social status on the campus. And yet, I don't know whether it's worth it.

C 114. On the other hand, you're kind of saying, well, really in order to get social approval I've got to drive myself to accomplish here. (*short pause*)

S 114. Well, you can get social approval from those outside a fraternity, but if you don't work for a fraternity you can't get too much social approval except from those that are your best friends in the fraternity.

C 115. Uh-hum. In other words, it's kind of necessary really to have this kind of social companionship, and yet there's this other trend to kind of seek social approval and social companionship by making good grades.

S 115. Uh-huh. And yet by making good grades you don't get the social companionship of those that don't get the same grades you do. Allows them to look up to you and think and, well, it's the natural reaction on the campus to call him a D.A.R. and tell him, I mean, that he studies all the time and the only reason I don't get good grades is because I don't study. The only people that will look at you are those that get the same grades as you. Another thing, my best friend and I have always competed together (*little laugh*) for grades. I can't understand why. We always get such satisfaction out of beating each other on a test or on a final mark.

C 116. Uh-hum. I wonder if throughout here you aren't kind of saying, like in this last issue you raised and some of these others, that it's kind of important for you to kind of prove that you are good.

S 116. I think that's it. I think what I'm trying to do is just to—try and prove to myself that I'm good and I can do better than I think. It is that I always want to do better than other people.

You see for that—by getting grades is the easiest way. You can do that without being aggressive. Maybe you can be submissive and just study and get the grades and show that you are better than other people.

C 117. I might point to kind of another issue here that, while on the one hand you kind of want to be with people and like people, on the other hand you sort of want to be better than they.

S 117. Yeah. Maybe that's the reason, I mean, that's sort of a compensation for my nonaggressiveness. When I'm (C: yeah) dealing with people, of course, I think that what—there are a lot of people that are the same way.

One of the big questions at this juncture would be how much of Mr. Bav's return to the issue of his dependence upon other people's approval is a response to pressure from the counselor. It seems possible he would feel the need to please the counselor in the same way that he needs to please other people. The counselor has made quite evident to him his desire and interest that he talk about this topic. Undoubtedly his discussions of his feelings are of some significance, but they represent a superficial and intellectualized effort which results in relatively cheap insights and does not have any appreciable effect upon a person's ways of behaving.

This is not to say that no part of this section of the interview was of any use to Mr. Bav. For example, in the sequence between C 108 and S 109, he does seem to be genuinely aware of the ambivalences one experiences in trying to analyze one's feelings as well as the illusoriness of the feeling that one knows oneself. He seemed to become particularly involved in S 112 as he begins to give expression to some of the intimate relationships between his anger at having to satisfy others and his feeling that there was something worth while to be gained by satisfying them. The interview now moves into its closing minutes.

C 118. You're not really sure of how you feel about it. You just recognize that this is the situation. (*pause*) Well, I think we're going to have to kind of leave it go for today. Maybe you sort of get a picture of the sort of help that we give here, kind of talking about these issues and trying to understand them more clearly—what's going on here.

S 118. Well, do you think that at the end though I'd be able to reach some conclusion? I still don't know what to—I still can't

make up—pretty soon I'm going to have to make out my program for next term and what I'm going to do is going to be
an important determinant in what I might take. Because I'll
have to take a language again next term and, knowing my
difficulty in languages, if I knew for sure that I wouldn't go
on for my Master's I wouldn't take French or German next
term and I'd just take a lot of courses that I personally want
to take and get them in.

C 119.   I wonder if you aren't saying, well, I'm kind of looking for
that immediate decision. Where is it? (*both laugh*)

S 119.   Well, (*laughing*) I mean (*laugh*) I've got to make it sometime.

C 120.   I'm not so—I'm not sure of how long it will take you to acquire
that clarification. But one way of looking at it would be this—
that maybe it would be better to kind of make sure how you
feel and take a little longer, than to sort of establish a decision
that you may not want to back up later.

S 120.   Do you think it will last all through this semester? It won't
extend down to next semester, would it? Do you think it
could?

C 121.   Well, that kind of depends on how we work this out. In other
words, on kind of how we're dealing with this situation. The
sort of understandings required.

S 121.   Well, what would happen I mean if I was lucky enough later
on to get a bid to Med. School. I was wondering if that's the
best thing. I think that if I did get accepted I'd go.

C 122.   Uh-hum.

S 122.   But I (*little laugh*) I'm wondering in the long run whether
that would be the best thing to do.

C 123.   Maybe that's one of the decisions you're kind of going to have
to work on here, to try to understand more clearly whether
that's really what you want.

S 123.   I'm afraid that even if I decided that that's not what I want
if I was (*laugh*) accepted. I'd go because I'd be sort of obliged
to go. See? But I know—my next door neighbor has gone
through two years of law school, has just stopped, gave up law
and gone into teaching. And I don't want (*little laugh*) to have
the same thing happen to me, to go through two years of Med.
School and decide that that's not for me.

C 124.   Maybe part of the value of this process is to kind of try to
arrive at a decision which you feel will really be inside of you,
so that you won't vacillate so much.

S 124. Well, I'd better not keep you. By the way, I don't know why but I forgot your name. What was it again?

C 125. ————.

S 125. Oh. Thanks a lot. What is it? Doctor or Mister?

C 126. Either one.

S 126. Oh, Doctor. Do you think I should make an appointment for the same time or (C: well—) does it matter when I make my appointments?

C 127. You can handle that any way you want to, that is, you can make appointments whenever you—whenever you want to and kind of call in. Or if you feel that you'd like to kind of keep this a continuing process, in other words, where you're sort of living with it (S: uh-huh) what we can do is kind of arrange to get together the same time every week, twice a week, or once every two weeks, whatever it is.

S 127. Well, I think it would be better to do it as much as possible. Do you think? In the beginning anyway, as long as I started it, I don't want to neglect it, put it off.

C 128. Well, shall we—do you want to make it once a week or twice a week or— (S: once a week?) what's your feeling.

S 128. Well, I'm just wondering—do you think I should make it twice or do you think I should make it once a week?

C 129. Well, how do you—how do you feel about it? Do you think that—eh—

S 129. I'd just like about—maybe—make it—I think it would be best to make it once a week, for next week anyways.

C 130. Okay.

(The rest of the time is taken up in arranging specific details for the next meeting.)

In the closing minutes we see an example of a frequent occurrence in first interviews. Mr. Bav faces the possibility of continuing the relationship but seems to want some kind of commitment from the counselor to correspond to his own commitment to continue. In S 119 he puts it in terms of the immediate decisions he faces, attempting to extract some kind of promise from the counselor. The counselor parries this and emphasizes the dependence of the immediate decision on a clarification of more fundamental questions. The appropriateness of the counselor's attitude is doubtful, because in this instance the client does have certain realistic questions which cannot be postponed. The counselor could commit himself to help him make temporary decisions even though the final decisions might depend upon a longer process. Mr. Bav shifts to the issue of time, but still cannot extract any pledges from the counselor. Now the client begins indirectly to establish certain limitations. By implication in S 121 and S 123 he is indicating that maybe the counselor is not going to have any effect on him and that he will proceed with his plans for medical school regardless of the counselor's opinion. Again the counselor seems to bypass this idea and in S 124 Mr. Bav shifts back to questions about the counselor. Notice that he repeats the difficulty he has had with the counselor's name at the beginning of the hour and notice how he attempts to establish whether or not the counselor is a Ph.D. Even though the counselor gives him a choice of which title to use, the client chooses the doctoral title. This seems to represent a further testing of his relationship to the counselor before deciding to continue.

Summary. Though not necessarily a good example of effective interpersonal relationships, this interview illustrates very vividly how quickly a client's problems are manifested in the kind of relationship he establishes with the counselor. There is evidence of concealed hostility in his general suspiciousness of the situation and his various resistances to the process. We observe that his needs for affection are great enough to outweigh hostile feelings. In this respect one thinks his reactions to his father, touched on in S 99, probably are very important factors in these ambivalent feelings. In fact, one feels the counselor's response at this point had the effect of turning the client away from his concern about his feelings toward his father by treating it in more abstract terms.

The fact that the counselor exercised so much domination over the interview and his apparent need to operate through highly intellectual processes would make one feel somewhat pessimistic about the future of their relationship and its effectiveness.

Case of Miss Vid

The client in this instance is a nineteen-year-old freshman girl.

S 1.   Hello.
C 1.   ———— is my name.

S 2. Oh—uh— (*little laugh*)

C 2. Would you mind sitting over here?

S 3. All right. (*sweetly*)

C 3. I would like to record our interview. We're making a study of it.

S 4. Oh. I see. Uh-huh! (*assent*)

C 4. What did you have in mind?

S 5. Well, my academic counselor suggested that he wanted me to take the battery of tests.

C 5. Uh-hum.

S 6. Because last semester I was in music school and I was a voice major.

C 6. Uh-huh. (*low*)

S 7. And I—actually I didn't know anything about music (*laughs*) I was just a singer, and I was just very—very lost and I just didn't seem to take to the basic mechanics of music as well as some of the other students. And yet I still love to sing and I always sing, and everything. (*getting lower*) I think I quite confused a lot of people in the music school. They didn't know quite what to make of it (*laugh*) and so I mean, I'm in Arts now, really much happier, much better situated, and everything, but I think Mr. Jones was quite curious as to what it all meant I mean, and what I was suited for after all. I mean since I've been in Liberal Arts though I'm quite interested in botany. And I love it, my botany course, but now (*little laugh*) so far as I know I think I'd like to major in that, make it my field of concentration. My family, rather, it's very far afield from what they had in mind for me. They think of me as something along more arty lines, (*little laugh*) I think.

C 7. Uh-huh.

S 8. (*still laughing*) So, I don't know. But that's the reason why Mr. Jones suggested that I— (*lower*)

C 8. (*low*) Uh-huh.

S 9. (*still low*) I think this ought to be a good idea.

C 9. Uh-huh. Sounds like you have some pretty good ideas as to what you want to do.

S 10. Eh, you think I do? (*registering surprise and ending in nervous laugh*) Well—

C 10. (*breaking in*) Or does there seem to be a lot of doubt?

S 11. Well I—as I see—as far as I know now, I'm a little bit hesitant to say, to throw myself into anything (C: uh-hum) again. Because I did that with voice and I mean I wanted to be a singer and that's all there is to it. When I got into it I found I just didn't—didn't have what it took to be a musician. I mean whatever a certain—it's very keen concentration and actually my mind is sort of abstract, I think. And (C: uh-hum) I can't pin things down like that, but I mean people think of science and music as being so—so— (C: far apart?) far apart that, I don't know, they just don't, I mean they just don't think of me as going into science. (*a few words lost*) And everything, and I think I could—I think I'd like it very much.

C 11. Uh-hum.

S 12. I don't think I'd like to teach it, but I'd like to (*slight pause*) be—oh go into some—it's a wonderful field for research. I mean, there's so many— (*this said quickly*).

C 12. Uh-hum.

S 13. In the middle of a lecture he'll say, well, we don't know what this means. We give it the term X or something. (*laughing*)

C 13. Yeah.

S 14. And I think, (*laughing*) why don't they know? I mean, you know— (*laugh*) (*low*). A wonderful field.

C 14. You kind of have some idea of what you'd like to do, but you're not sure that you can trust yourself again.

S 15. Yeah.

C 15. Uh-hum.

S 16. That's it. I mean, I don't want to get disappointed again in a sense.

C 16. Uh-hum.

S 17. And I think I can—there's this only thing, people—I've been— had it drilled into me. They say that when you have something, a talent given to you, it's almost a sin not to use it.

C 17. Uh-hum.

S 18. I mean once you very definitely know you should use whatever you have (*slight pause*) —my (*slight pause*) —my sister's going into writing. She wants to be a writer.

C 18. Uh-hum.

S 19. (*low*) I hope she comes up here for graduate work. I think that would be nice. But I've been told I have a flair for writing too, and then of course my main thing is my voice that I've been working on mostly. (*lower*) I don't know. It's very confusing. (*apologetic laugh*)

C 19. You kind of have some facilities that extend in a lot of different directions and you're not sure of which one you ought to do your work in.

S 20. Yeah, (*at the same time as counselor*) I know that I couldn't—
I wouldn't be happy writing. I mean as far as that goes, because
it'll make me too lonely. I mean I like people too well and
I like to be with them and talk to them.

C 20. Uh-hum.

S 21. And I think writers are—I think live apart a little bit from the
rest of the world. (C: uh-hum) Not quite real. And I love, I
mean my happiest, well, I'm almost my happiest when I'm
singing. But I wouldn't like the life of an artist because—it's
very irregular, and, I like, I like a certain amount of order.
(*lower*) I like things to be sort of systematic (*little laugh*) (*softly*)
I don't know why.

C 21. You'd like to have something pretty stable and yet on the other
hand there are certain attractions in fields that aren't so stable.

S 22. Yeah, (*vigorously*) I mean, I guess everybody has that in them.
They sort of like to let the cap off the lid, and (*little laugh*)—

C 22. And you kind of see this as a problem of either or.

These opening minutes of the interview provide us with an
opportunity for developing certain distinct impressions of this
young woman. Notice the ready emotional responsiveness indicated by the frequent laughing which seems to be more of a
bubbling rather than nervous type. The initial statement of the
problem, starting at S 6, seems to emphasize her dissociation from
responsibility for her actions. She talks about having confused a
lot of people in the music school and about her present advisor as
being curious and confused. In C 9 the counselor seems to interpret her uninvolvement as indicating that she knows what she
wants to do. Her surprise along with her direct expression of confusion and doubt a few minutes later suggests this was not the real
meaning of her behavior. It seems more likely that she is confused,
but also is obtaining certain satisfactions from using her confusion
as a means of confusing others, probably adults. Her surprise in
response to C 9 might then represent a reaction to an adult not
responding in the expected manner. In the juxtaposition between
botany and music and her way of talking about it, we begin to
suspect also she is somewhat distrustful of her bubbling emotions
while enjoying them. The counselor responds accurately to this
aspect in C 21 and C 22. One other characteristic of Miss Vid is

suggested in these initial interactions. Her communications in S 18, S 19, and S 20 give rise to a suspicion that feelings about her sister have some special relationship to her problem. Notice that her sister comes up as an association to people drilling an idea into her and to the idea that if you have a talent it is almost a sin not to use it. When she brings in her sister she shifts to expressing a longing for her, but rejects any identity with her.

S 23. Yes. As a matter of fact, it may sound funny but ever since I was a little girl I used to think of life being, the life of an artist, being terribly erratic and the other life as being very well organized and (C: uh-hum) calm and settled. (C: uh-hum) (*short pause*) And perhaps maybe botany offers to me something stable. Maybe that's why I think I'd like it.

C 23. Uh-huh. (*low*) (*short pause*) You kind of think of yourself as two different people, or putting it in another way, as a person with two different types of needs.

S 24. I think I am sort of a mixture because I do—I'm so fussy about it. Matter of fact, I just had an argument with one of my friends about that. I mean (*laugh*) she's sort of—she's in music school now. She's real, extremely disorganized. (*laughs*) Her room is so—always in a mess. I mean, (*still laughing a little*) she's—there's nothing derogatory to her character. I don't know, (*quickly*) but it's just something that I just can't take. I don't know why. And she wondered about rooming together next term and I (*softer*) didn't want to do it because of that reason. I just thought it would break up a nice friendship. (C: yeah) And (*laugh*) well, we've gotten over it now but I don't know. In some ways I wish I didn't have that because it bothers my sister too. (*laugh*) As I say it's a very queer mixture. I (*short pause*) —and (*short pause*) because when I—when I let my—when I sing I let myself go so completely and (C: uh-hum) and my writing certainly isn't—well it's been called deep purple, (*laugh*) you know, in parts but (*pause*) it's funny. (*reflectingly*) (*pause*)

C 24. You might say that—

S 25. (*breaking in*) But the thing is I see in botany, I think in a way it could be both because a certain amount of it is creative and, well, I love—I love to be outdoors, and one thing they said, to be a botanist you can't be scared of mud or anything. (*laugh*) (C: uh-hum) I love the work outdoors.

C 25. Uh-hum.

S 26. The (lost) and (lost) and things like that and then of course there's the very high organization to it, and a feeling of accomplishing something definite.

C 26. Uh-hum. (low)

S 27. That's it. (very low)

C 27. You kind of have a feeling that there really is a basic interest there. In other words, you're not just reacting to something else.

S 28. No. I really do. I feel that, of course, I suppose I am going through a very impressionable age. I don't know. I mean everything—I've responded terribly to everything here. It's been such a new experience. It's been wonderful.

C 28. Uh-hum. (very low)

S 29. But I don't think this is just whimsy. (C: uh-hum) Because when I was back in Junior High School, of all my courses (laugh) I just loved physiology. And I would drive my family wild. I'd come home, look, it isn't a balanced meal! (laugh) You don't have such and such and such and such. And I'd go off on things like that (laughing) and I was a wiseacre. And, well, what makes it do such— (laugh) everything like that you know and I don't know, I never thought of it as being, until just lately, as being something connected with it.

C 29. Uh-huh.

S 30. Maybe— (low)

C 30. You kind of have the point of view of a scientist who is asking why, but, yet, on the other hand you want to have the freedom of an artist who isn't controlled by these considerations.

S 31. I guess so. But well, I do have this—maybe it'll die down. I do have a tremendous drive, (lower) I don't know what to call it— (C: uh-hum) something driving. I think that I will find a lot of that used up. I mean right now for the past couple of years, things, physical things.

C 31. Uh-hum. (low)

S 32. I mean I've been—but I mean I can find that need answered in the outdoors work in botany. I was almost considering going to phys. ed., but I think I wouldn't find that work as interesting. It would be purely physical. (low) (laugh)

C 32. You kind of need a field in which you can get a lot of stimulation.

S 33. Uh-huh. I do. Very definitely. I don't think I could take a sedentary job. (little laugh)

C 33. So that whatever field you're in you feel you want to be pretty active.

S 34. Uh-huh. That's the reason why even here (*lost*) my four years while I'm taking the botany, the lab courses are actually—you're using your physical and mental resources all the time. You're right there, on the alert and you're doing—I mean if one part of me goes to sleep the other part doesn't. (*laugh*) If I'm using both of them you know it will (*lower*) keep me alive, awake, and everything.

C 34. Uh-huh.

S 35. I think I like the way they have it planned out.

C 35. You kind of have the feeling then that botany will satisfy a lot of these needs which you've been satisfying through music and other forms of expression.

S 36. Uh-huh. (*pause*)

C 36. It kind of sounds as if at least right now, the issue is pretty clear in your mind and the choice is pretty clear.

S 37. (*slight pause*) It is, it is right now, but you know how—you know how whenever you make a new discovery or you do something you think is kind of good, or something, you sort of want to go to somebody of *authority,* and sort of have them put an okay sign on it. (*little laugh*) I don't know what it is, human nature. (*little laugh*)

C 37. You'd kind of like a little support and a little reassurance maybe that you're doing the right thing?

S 38. That's right. I mean the thing is my family is against it.

C 38. Uh-huh.

S 39. I mean they're not against it because there's anything morally wrong with it (*little laugh*) or anything like that, but it's just that—of course they want me to do what they think I'll be happiest in—and my grandfather has always (*short pause*) —well, for one thing, he always says that if he had his own life to live over again he'd be a college professor.

C 39. Uh-hum.

S 40. Because he did have such a (*short pause*) narrow training himself, an engineer, and then he went into business. And he's trying to have me get—I mean, he didn't find until later life, what he had missed in literature and everything, and he's—terribly well read now, but he wants me to be sure and get it when I'm young. (*short pause*)

C 40. To some extent you've had to make an independent decision here, and (S: yeah) you have to have a little reassurance to make the decision, because (S: yeah) you're going contrary to the people who've always guided you.

S 41. That's right. I mean I always have pretty much taken what my grandparents have said (C: uhm) as right, because they are *older* of course, I mean, and I feel they (*low*) —they should know.

C 41. Uh-hum.

S 42. (*little laugh*)

C 42. And inasmuch as you're kind of, well, going in a counter direction you sort of want to make sure that when you do step out of this way, it's right.

S 43. That's right. (*low*) I know and I mean (*louder*) the thing is I just want to be sure that it—that it (*short pause*) —I don't know, this past year has just been so full. I mean this is my nineteenth birthday. I've just been thinking back and—eighteen, and it was such a full year. And I never lived so much in one year in all my life. (C: uh-hum) I mean I've been going to boarding school for three and a half years, and (*short pause*) of course it's quite a very small world, and then you come out to a place like this, and there's so much all at once. (*little laugh*)

C 43. You're a little overcome by it, huh?

S 44. Yeah. Very much so, and I just want to make sure that—I mean I've tamed down a little bit, but at first (*laugh*) this spring, I mean, this fall I was just *completely* (C: uh-huh) *too* exuberant, I mean, you know, just a little bit, and (*pause*) I don't know. (*lower*)

C 44. Uh-huh.

S 45. I just want to be sure that it isn't that. Just—

C 45. Yeah.

S 46. You know, I mean overcome with everything. (*quickly*)

C 46. Yeah. There's still a lot of this emotional reaction. You want to be sure you can trust yourself.

S 47. Yeah. That's right.

C 47. Uh-hum.

S 48. (*quickly*) And another thing I think that, I mean—I do have— well just talking to you will probably, well, I don't know, but I do have—it's very evident in my English themes that I don't feel like I'm going in definite lines.

C 48. Uh-huh.

S 49. I mean that I don't have a mind that goes out in lines, A-B-C, 1-2-3, and all that, and in science, when I'm working with anything scientific, I do think it makes me think like that. And it's very good and that is what I'm trying to acquire.

C 49. You kind of feel that maybe you're not as stable as you might be and anchoring yourself to something that is pretty stable will help.

S 50. Well, I mean, I know, (*pause*) well (*a little less assured than first part of sentence*) as a matter of fact I—as far as being stable (*short pause*) that has a lot of connotations. (*little laugh*) (C: yeah) During my time in boarding school I was (*lower*) sort of looked upon as very stolid and very conservative, very, well you know, just no thought (*laughing*) and I knew just where I'm going and I guess (*more seriously*) I guess maybe it was that, maybe all of this is sort of a reaction to boarding school. I don't know.

In this section of the interview we see an interesting confirmation and elaboration of our initial impression. In the first part of this section, Miss Vid has responded to the counselor's initial understanding of her dilemma by going into it more fully. In S 24 and S 25 she emphasizes the value of control and organization. However, when the counselor in C 27 comments that her interest in botany is not just another example of impulsive action, this seems to stimulate her to think about the impulsive aspects of her life, which she then does through S 34. The counselor's response in C 35, bringing botany in juxtaposition to music at the time that the client is emphasizing the internal pressures toward action and self-expression, seems to slow down the rapid flow of communication through which she was acting out her feeling of the need for expression. Instead, she turns again to the problem of control, now in the context of people. She talks about using the counselor as an authority, and we see that she now begins to bring out additional aspects of her relationships with adults, in which she indicates evidence of a great deal of attachment to them. At the same time, she evidences the need to oppose the particular set of adults, the grandparents, and to have someone else take their place when she does oppose them. Her uneasiness about opposing these adults, which is partially stated in S 41 and by the counselor in C 42, leads back again to the theme of emotional expression, for example, "This fall I was just *completely too* exuberant." The counselor's comment in C 49, referring to possible fear for her own stability, seems to slow her up a bit and turn her toward a more analytical kind of expression as though she decided she had better stop and look at what she was saying.

C 50. (*low*) You're kind of free for a change.

S 51. (*low*) Yeah.

C 51. People don't lean on you so much. (*pause*)

S 52. Well, (*pause*) well, maybe, (*short pause*) maybe that's it. I don't know. (*little giggle*)

C 52. You're not quite sure of how you feel about yourself really.

S 53. I'm still finding out. I think they say first know yourself and then go out to (*lost*), but every once in a while, I mean, as I say I'm sort of surprised.

C 53. (*low*) Uh-hum.

S 54. I mean I get these feelings, I mean I sort of surprise—right now I know I'm just a bundle of emotions (*beginning to giggle*) and probably not myself. (*giggle*)

C 54. Uh-hum.

S 55. (*laughing*) But (*now serious*) I don't know. I've never had any place have such a reaction on me the way this school does. It's so full of (*lost*), so (*lost*).

C 55. Uh-hum. I know. There is room in which to spread out.

S 56. Uh-hum. (*pause*) And (*pause*) I don't know. I just get the most— it's just the feeling of sort of *abandon* and a feeling of a challenge to. I don't know. I get the feeling of—well, it's here and— it isn't really ruthless or anything but it's very definitely a sort of a man's world and I have been living in a very feminine world all my life and everything is, well, if you'd really like to do it, you can. (C: uh-huh) But I mean otherwise we'll understand you know.

C 56. Uh-huh.

S 57. And here, it's (*pause*) well if you don't do it, you'll miss the boat, and that's all there is to it.

C 57. Thus you're saying that in one sense, you're kind of away from many of these implicit restrictions (S: yeah) you've had in the past, and here you're sort of on your own and—uh—

S 58. Oh! Terribly. (*giggle*) I mean as compared to what I have been. (*pause*) Oh I was *so* young when I came here. (*giggle*) So terribly, I mean, I still am, but I think I've, I've probably learned.

C 58. You're kind of feeling your oats, you might say.

S 59. Yeah. (*pause*) But, (*pause*) well, (*pause*) I don't know, it would just— (*pause*) of course in boarding school your mind, your whole life is planned for you. (C: uh-hum) I mean, every move that you do, and then when you come to a place like this. Everything—I mean it scared me. Because whether I ate or not—I never knew what time it was and there's no regular meals in the dorm. I'd have to eat out, and whether I ate or not depended on me. I mean, depended on whether I got up and took my money out and bought my meal. (C: uh-hum) Understand? And that was, even that little thing was (*giggle*) (C: yes) quite big at that time. (*pause*) And now I'm getting so that I'm almost intolerant of people that were like myself.

C 59. Uh-huh.

S 60. Last fall—I mean, there's this girl I just met in the dorm. And she's been sort of clinging to me a little bit, and I think I haven't been very nice. (*little laugh*) (C: uh-huh) I don't know.

C 60. You sort of have for the first time an opportunity to be independent, and you're taking full advantage of it.

S 61. I guess I think that's it.

C 61. And yet you're not too sure about it because it is so completely new.

S 62. That's true. I mean— (*short pause*) the thing is that whenever you look at something for the first time, I mean, it's sort of like a big chunk of chocolate cake. It is so wonderful, all of it. You don't really discriminate and I didn't discriminate last fall. I mean, the whole world was fun and all the people in it. And since then I've looked at some of the friends I've made. Or I thought they were friends that I'd made. They were just acquaintances.

C 62. Uh-huh.

S 63. And I realized that to meet—that they weren't really the people that I wanted for my friends and that after all what was I judging by? What standards was I using? And (*short pause*) I mean it sort of frightened me. (*giggle*)

C 63. Uh-hum. (*pause*) In that case you really didn't want people on whom you could lean or could lean on you. You wanted to be associated with people who were mature. Because you wanted to be mature yourself.

S 64. As a matter of fact, I (*pause*) well I don't know, my sister and I are terribly different. She's about twenty-three now, four years older, and she has always been the—terribly much older (*giggle*) than I. She's always felt a responsibility. I mean I've never been in a situation that (*short pause*) my family as much as my sister because she was older and my parents were divorced and I've lived all my life except about three years with my grandparents.

C 64. Uh-huh.

S 65. And so my sister always felt that somehow she needs to protect me.

C 65. Uh-huh.

S 66. And she's always, I mean, she's always—I always am, you know, her little baby. (*giggle*) The baby of the family and everything and— (*pause*) I don't know. I mean then I was and then my grandparents, of course I was certainly the baby to their eyes. And I don't know. Then you get up here. You sort of look back and realize how silly it is. You sort of get the feeling that, well, when you get home, you just want to shake off something. (*giggle*) I suppose it's only natural I should.

C 66. Sounds like the yoke is being thrown off.

S 67. Yes.

C 67. You have a lot of satisfaction from being on your own and yet there's just a feeling, a need for a little more support too because you've always had it.

S 68. I've had it.

C 68. Uh-hum. (*pause*) But—

S 69. But, oh, I don't know. My grandparents have been *wonderful,* I mean of course, and then it is a rather difficult job. I mean I—two generations older, to understand the problem of—of (*pause*) you know, younger—that much younger. But, oh, they're very young in spirit. I don't think I'd ever think of them as old or anything.

C 69. Uh-hum.

S 70. And they just get a big kick out of life.

C 70. Uh-hum.

S 71. (*laugh*) They're the two most wonderful people.

C 71. You've felt pretty happy with them.

S 72. Oh. Yes! But the thing is they aren't the kind of people—they're so terribly liberal in some ways, but they want me to find what I want for myself and they think eventually it will be the epitome of what they have lived, and what they believe in. But actually, now that I think back, they've never really given me anything concrete.

C 72. Uh-hum.

S 73. But it's a little confusing. I think I'm a very concrete individual. (*giggle*)

C 73. Uh-hum.

S 74. I mean very explicit. (*giggle*) Because after all you have to tell people what's right and what's wrong. I mean you just can't say well it's all relative. It's all, well, I mean you find out for yourself. You know what I mean. Just you—that's—you know the fire's hot and you shouldn't be there, it's going to burn.

C 74. Uh-hum.

S 75. And you are—you tell your kid that before he sticks his finger in. And I think it's very, very wise to do that.

C 75. You sort of need something strong to lean on, so you're not in the dark so much.

S 76. Yeah. (*pause*) I guess I do as a matter of fact. I really look for that in men, friendships. I don't know. I mean, I get *very* put out, oh, just on the date situation with boys that are, I mean, most boys seem terribly immature. I mean they—I get—I don't get as disappointed with girls as easily as I do with boys. I mean somehow I mean I expect more of them. But I—uh—well, it was last night the boy I was with I was thinking, "My goodness! What a freshman!" (*laughs heartily*)

C 76. Uh-hum.

S 77. And I don't know. I just (*pause*) he just seemed so—nothing to offer me, nothing to talk about.

C 77. Uh-hum.

S 78. We went to the movies and said so long. (*giggle*)

C 78. Uh-huh. You kind of look for a strong supportive person in order to give you more support—

S 79. Yeah. That's right. (*pause*)

In this section of the interview, she has moved more deeply into the dilemma she faces. After only a relatively brief slowing up of communication, she starts anew to talk about the burst of feelings which has accompanied her new experiences during the preceding year. While talking about this there is also another note which is introduced in a minor key in S 55 when she talks about the university as being a man's world, that is, in the sense of a person being expected to produce and to be competent and mature as opposed to a feminine world which in her eyes is a world in which weakness is accepted and other people are comforting rather than demanding. At this point the counselor chooses to disregard this theme and to react more to the feeling of freedom from restriction. This is shown by the counselor's responses in C 56, C 57, and C 59. Through this section, Miss Vid responds by giving emphasis to these feelings of loss of support. In C 60 and C 62 the counselor finally begins to acknowledge these other feelings. This stimulates, in S 63 and S 65, further elaborations of her relationship with her older sister as well as clarifying certain aspects of the family constellation. Her ambivalent feelings about her grandparents come to a focus on the attitude that one does need adults as a support to control one's impulses. The counselor seems to have helped move communication in that direction through his responses in C 66 and C 74 which then lead to a still further elaboration of her differential attitude toward men and women.

C 79. While on the one hand you want to be quite independent, on the other hand you also want to feel that you've got something to lean on.

S 80. That's right. (*laughs*) I don't know. I do think it's certainly a paradox. But then last year I went through this stage when I—well I'm not—I'm getting out of it now, but I was sort of— so terribly disoriented that I wasn't thinking really. I was just feeling. And I used to write this man lush poetry and—oh it was terrible! (*laughs*) Awful. And I don't know. I (*pause*) just sort of floating around and at—the people you know should act on their im— because all man's impulses you know were inherently good and he should act on his impulses and emotions and let his emotions go. (*laugh*) All very silly and I think I better get away from that, and I—I know I am.

C 80. I'd say that you still want to be free but you want to be realistic too.

S 81. Yes. (*pause*) I know that—I know that botany is sort of—I mean I look back at the times in my life when it was, when the situation was very real and I'd—like at camp. I went about six years to camp, seven years of camp. I don't know, I just—

C 81. Uh-hum.

S 82. I think that's where I got some of my love for being outdoors. (*short pause*) And I don't know, that same sort of feeling, you know, very real, very solid, in being busy.

C 82. Uh-huh.

S 83. And I don't know. As soon as you let yourself get lazy or anything—I think I can just—I think I can find so much in botany that—

C 83. You kind of feel that you want to be a part of things, that you're doing something important.

S 84. It is important. Yeah. I mean my little emotions and feelings when I go off and sing, well, maybe they'll bring some happiness to me I mean, if—I don't know, if they would like to hear sing—hear me singing, but I feel that a real job (*short pause*) is so much more important (C: uh-hum) than my singing.

C 84. You have to have something more basic, eh?

S 85. Yeah. (*pause*)

C 85. Uh-huh.

S 86. I like it best. (*laughs*)

C 86. You kind of see yourself heading in a direction here but you're still kind of fluttering around a bit too.

S 87. Yeah. Maybe. (*laughs*) I don't know, I just—I just hope that some of this stage is over with. Eighteen! (*laughs*) I hope so.

C 87. Hmm. You'd kind of like to settle down a little bit.

S 88. I mean, it's been wonderful. It's the first time in my—in my life where I think I really have fluttered so much.

C 88. Uh-hum.

S 89. Because I always used to get so disgusted with sister for—I mean sister has a very deep intricate mind, very philosophical, which makes no sense about basic things. (*laughing*) She couldn't cook a square meal if she tried. (*laughing*) And she can't keep any kind of order. (*laughing*) Oh, dear! She'll sit for hours and talk and miss a meal. Just talk, and I think that's terrible! And that's what I mean, we're so—you wouldn't know we're sisters. We're so completely opposite in some respects, I mean.

C 89. She's mature in one sense and not in another and maybe you're just vice versa.

S 90. Yeah. (*giggle*) I guess so. (*short pause*) Of course I think age makes quite a bit of difference. She's certainly lived a lot more than I have.

C 90. It's a part of the growing up process, isn't it?

S 91. Yeah.

C 91. Which you don't hurt or change.

S 92. I guess so. Another thing about her. She's always had this feeling she wanted to revolutionize any situation she came into. And I was the one who was a pacifist. I mean I—maybe too—sort of a cock-eyed optimist. (*giggle*) I don't know, (*giggle*) I sort of—I liked too much the situation that I'm in and people will tell me, well, just what do you see in this?

I mean, are you sure that this is all right, and (*giggle*) I don't know, it's— (*pause*)

C 92. You sometimes wonder what your real feelings are.

S 93. One time somebody called me a chameleon. And that made me—hurt more than anything.

C 93. Hmm.

S 94. Because I don't want to be like that.

C 94. Uh-hum. You like to feel that there's something pretty strong and pretty basic.

S 95. Yeah.

C 95. That you won't change so much.

S 96. But the thing is, I *used* to look at (*pause*) when I was in about the ninth or tenth grade I used to be looked upon as sort of a *prude*. I mean quite a bit of one, and I could look upon—take a girl with quite a bit of make-up on or something and completely reject her from my mind.

C 96. Uh-hum.

S 97. I mean she was just all alone. Even though I did (*giggle*) even though I did perhaps go to the extreme of being *too* understanding. I think maybe it's better (C: uh-huh) than shutting out from my—than not trying to see what was good in the other girl.

C 97. You kind of accept people's feelings more readily now.

S 98. Yeah.

C 98. You feel a little more like them.

S 99. Yeah. (*pause*) I guess so. I mean because the more *you* live and the more experience *you* have then the more part of other people you are.

C 99. Uh-huh.

S 100. And I had such a narrow life. I mean narrow in the sense that it was so guided in one way. That I still—I'm still a little bit (*pause*) well, I mean, at times sort of surprised—

C 100. Uh-hum.

S 101. —and sort of sorry too at the—at the— (*pause*) sort of atheistic attitude that I find in a lot of the students here.

C 101. Uh-huh.

S 102. And I—then I realize, well, it isn't their fault. They can't help it. It isn't anything. It's just—it's just something that maybe we were luckier in having than they were. I don't know.

C 102. Uh-hum. (*pause*) Well, I'd say you've kind of accepted other people to be a little bit fallible too, as you've gained more confidence in yourself.

S 103.   Yeah. No. Wait a minute. (*giggle*) Let me think. (*giggle*) Figure that one out. (*giggle*) (*pause*) Well, it's more a sense of (*pause*) understanding that (*pause*) my infallibility too. (C: uh-hum) (*giggle*) I mean after all we're—

C 103.   You kind of know yourself a little better.

S 104.   Yes.

C 104.   And so what people do, how they feel, don't affect you quite so much.

In this section of the interview the counselor seems to be more active and it is less clear what the client is doing. The counselor bypasses some of the implications in S 80, particularly those referring to specific incidents during this last year; consequently, she stays at the general level of talking about restrictions versus freedom, and turns back to talking about botany as though perhaps she were a little frightened that she had gone so far in talking about her emotions. This suggestion of fear is expressed most clearly in S 87. In C 89 the counselor seems to begin to press home certain ideas which he continues still further in C 90 and 91. He suggests the idea that being free to express yourself is part of being mature. In C 94 he introduces the theme that she wants something basic to rely on. He will repeat this theme several times. In C 97, C 98, and C 102 he is telling her that she is more certain of herself. In S 103 perhaps the client has become aware that the counselor is harping on certain ideas. Consequently, she stops to try to examine the interpretations he is giving to her words.

S 105.   Like in—in—uh—well as I say, I've had— (*pause*) I can remember sort of being like a cocoon in boarding school. And sort of—I mean, I didn't really *think* too much what I learned.

C 105.   Uh-hum.

S 106.   I made good grades. Better grades in about my tenth grade and—and then all of a sudden, a tremendous awareness began. I don't—you know, when I came here, and it was almost too much. That I could—I sort of lost my power of concentration and I was on probation. I'm on probation for the first semester. (*voice drops for last sentence*)

C 106.   Uh-huh.

S 107.   And that didn't go too well of course, with my family or (*giggle*) with me either.

C 107.   Uh-hum.

S 108. They were quite mad at me about it, but I think, well I am making a much better start in Arts College. But the thing is, I've never been—been so—this is so good for me, this university, because it's so impersonal and it's so much of a test, a standard test. I mean it's such democracy it's wonderful. And before it was already a sense of, well, such a personal thing. I know we understand her problems and we'll try to work with her according to *her* way. (C: uh-huh) That's what you get from going to a private school. I've been in a private school most all my life. It's not a good thing. (C: uh-huh) I don't think so, at all. In some respects, not in this way. Here I just sort of get this feeling of a vast army sort of marching along and— *(laugh)* and trying like mad to keep up pace with them. I don't know *(laugh)* but— *(pause)*

C 108. You're sort of moving on your own a little bit here.

S 109. *(after short pause)* Yeah. *(pause)* For one thing I supposed to find something materialistic as—giving me something to work for in a materialistic way.

C 109. Uh-hum.

S 110. I suppose I'm about the most audacious freshman that ever lived. While being on probation I applied to South Dorm.

C 110. Uh-huh.

S 111. *(laughing)* and I got accepted. I was accepted just on the condition that I bring up my grades by next June.

C 111. Uh-hum.

S 112. And in a way that gives me a sort of a goal. And some people say—I know she wrote me a little note and said I'm looking forward to next fall. And so I'll work to get those grades up. I hope it won't be a mutual disappointment.

C 112. You kind of have some direction here. You know where you're going.

S 113. Yeah. Uh-huh. I do. I—well, I mean much more so than last fall. *(giggle)* I mean I realize I—the thing is I'm not committing myself. *(short pause)* I'm being sort of in between about a lot of things because I had been going through a stage where I was so *(bursts into laughter as she says)* all over boiling, (C: uh-huh [*low*]) for one thing and the other and I'm just afraid to say any too *much* to learn, I have so much to—

C 113. You're kind of feeling your way very carefully here.

S 114. Uh-huh. The thing is people think of botany and oh a lot of sciences connected with it—sort of quiet people.

C 114. Uh-huh.

S 115. People that sort of observe but don't have much to say.

C 115. Uh-huh. Yeah.

S 116. But I don't know. I think you'll find all kinds of people in all kinds of positions and I think the profession molds you or makes you more.

C 116. You think it's pretty much what you make of it.

S 117. What you make of it.

C 117. That the field doesn't call for anything.

S 118. No. It doesn't call. I mean it's if you find something in yourself. Snatches, I mean, (*pause*) with me I just think it's just a feeling of, well, interest in nature and how it works.

C 118. Uh-hum.

S 119. And I mean that's a certain human—that doesn't come with the call of nature. That's a something humanistic because after all that is the basis of all life. You're interested in what makes it work, where life comes from, what it is.

C 119. Uh-hum. (*low*)

S 120. That's not anything.

C 120. You're getting at something pretty meaningful. You're kind of saying generally that even though you're being a little bit cautious, you're not sure of yourself, that you see a lot of reasons why you should go into botany and why you're going in your specific direction.

S 121. Well, I do. (*little laugh*) And actually I suppose it's sort of like taking a first step.

C 121. Uh-huh.

S 122. You know what I mean?

C 122. Uh-hum.

S 123. They have a picture of me all—some bright painter or something—had painted a picture of me taking my first step and I look so scared! (*laughs*)

C 123. Uh-hum.

S 124. (*still laughing*) I guess that that's the way it is, I mean, it is such a—oh! Isn't it such a tremendous jump?

C 124. (*pause*) Uh-hum

S 125. And the thing is that my grandparents had—if—my father had been a scientist or something like that, but see my mother sang.

C 125. Uh-hum.

S 126. And my father was on his way to be a very successful writer. He had a play on Broadway when he was about twenty-one. And (*short pause*) (*lower*) didn't go on with it—carry out what he—got married and he went into the advertising business.

And (*pause*) perhaps too I know that there is a side of me that does sort of want to go out and explode and everything. (*last three words said very quickly*) And (*pause*) and yet I think it would be just a little too heady (C: uh-huh) for me. And I think my—I don't know too much about my father but from what I do know he had a very—very sort of unsettled life. And I don't think he's very happy. (*lower*) And he is down in Florida. Has married again and (*pause*) I don't know whether I'm anything like him, but there probably—probably is just a little bit.

C 126. Uh-hum. (*low*)

S 127. (*short pause*) And (*pause*) he—if he'd gone in, I don't know, of course I don't know anything too much about it, but— (*pause*).

C 127. You kind of see yourself following the same pattern pretty much. In the sense that you've got the same problem, the same decisions to make.

S 128. Well, my—well, it's more a sense of being worried about my sister because of that. I mean she is *so*—I think she is supposed to be more like my father.

C 128. Uh-huh.

S 129. Very much and she is so terribly like him, so extremely so.

C 129. Uh-hum.

S 130. (*pause*) I don't know. I just wonder. I mean I'm afraid that well if I'm going to follow one path she sort of thinks of me as (*short pause*) oh, I was in the stage one time, I suppose everyone does, when I thought it would be— (*short pause*) I just sort of wrote this *long* epistle on the values of a society where the girls receive very basic education and they were married! I mean, after all, that was a woman's place in the world. That's —maybe that was a reaction against (*lost*), I don't know! (*giggle*) But she—oh! She wrote back and said she—this thing about you don't— (*short pause*) I mean I've always thought of you as something—something *higher* than just a *housewife* (*said with scorn attached to last word*) (*laughing*) I mean, something, something more artistic. She was thinking in terms of that and I know she's going to look on the science field as (C: uh-hum) something sort of drudgery.

C 130. Well, it's a question of what sort of values you set for yourself. Isn't it?

S 131. Yeah.

C 131.   Which path you follow. (*pause*) Or putting it another way, kind of deciding what is important to you.

S 132.   Yes. That's right. (*pause*) I mean that business about what you bring to the profession is very true because I—the very fact that I do find botany interesting and that a lot of people don't is something. I mean the very fact that I think it's fascinating. (*pause*) That the way the (*laughing*) spring fungi come out (*lost in laughter*) that must be as boring as heck to somebody else but (*laughs*) I don't know. (*pause*) Where if you can bring some enthusiasm to something well, maybe it's to the good. (*ends low*)

C 132.   You're kind of saying maybe this is important for me, maybe I'm good for it.

For some reason, the client takes another tack at the beginning of this section of the interview; perhaps because she is not sure of just what the counselor is getting at. In essence this new tack is another variation on the theme of the big change that has taken place in her since coming to the University. Again she emphasizes not being treated differently from anyone else, another version of the earlier theme of being treated more like a man than a woman, of being active and striving rather than passive. The counselor's responses at this juncture do not contribute much. They represent fairly general restatements of rather platitudinous ideas. The counselor's response in C 120 seems to lead into a slightly different direction, and the client now moves into emphasizing how different from the family pattern is her plan of going into botany. This may be the significance of talking about her father's backing away from a career as a playwright to enter advertising. In S 130 we get more clearly stated her notion of her university experiences as more masculine but at this point espousing the feminine side. C 130 to C 132 bypass the affective conflict around sexual identification to treat it as though it were purely an issue of rational choice.

S 133.   Yeah. I think so. (*pause*) And then right now too an education—I think of course when you're little—you think of college and all the fun and everything—you sort of think of it as a white image or something. (*laugh*) And the first time in my life, I look on Wisconsin as a (*pause*) as sort of, not an end in itself but as something to help me to make myself an independent person so that I can assert myself more or less.

C 133. Kind of an opportunity here to act as an adult and make your own decisions. (*pause*)

S 134. I have been babied, I guess, and I think about it—all my life. I mean, I'm trying so hard. I mean, I know it's going to get worse all the time, and I'm trying to get away from it.

C 134. In one sense you're kind of reacting against your earlier environment where you had an awful lot of direction, let's say, or at least were—kind of followed people's values and now you're kind of looking for your own.

S 135. Yeah. But they were very—it was good advice and everything.

C 135. Uh-huh. (*pause*)

S 136. (*low*) But, (*pause*) well, you can see something so good (*hesitation*) in what has been given you (C: yeah [*low*]) and add your own to that, I guess.

C 136. You just kind of build on top of it.

S 137. Uh-hum.

C 137. You're kind of in the process of building you might say and you're not sure of whether you're using the right blocks or not.

S 138. (*laugh*) That's right. And I'm still—still reaching around I mean. I think it's mostly this business about—well, there are these four seniors on our floor, and they've been sort of acting as my—they've taken quite an interest in how I react to new situations and how everything comes out. And they have been just wonderful. Perhaps you know some of them; some of those girls there and they're all in the English department and they know all grad students and everything, and they know lots of the people in the psychology department. (*pause*) Well, they've been very understanding and I know they think too that this botany with me is just a passion, that it will be very momentary.

C 138. Kind of a passing fancy.

S 139. Yeah. (*pause*) But I don't look upon it like that.

C 139. It sort of sounds like you have to think a little bit about the problem of—one problem is how you *feel* and the other is connected with it—is what's important to you.

S 140. Uh-hum.

C 140. You have to think through those two problems a little bit.

S 141. That's right. And Jane says too that I'm too prone to accept people on the same level and then afterwards wonder about it.

She says as long as I wonder about it it's all right. (*laugh*) She says that when I have, you know, too— (*pause*)

C 141.   While you want to make an independent decision you're still looking for a lot of direction here.

S 142.   I guess so. (*pause*) I mean you set up in your mind certain things. This is right. This is wrong. And you sit down and list them very—oh, in your mind—very—well, he lives up to such and such and such and such and maybe he drinks or something that you don't accept. It's not right or something.

C 142.   Uh-hum.

S 143.   And then you think, well, can I reject him just because he drinks? I mean, it seems so heartless and so sort of cruel, you know. And it doesn't seem human at all.

C 143.   Uh-hum.

S 144.   And then yet you have to make standards! And yet the standards that I have found that I judge people by aren't the ones that I've been told because (C: uh-hum) the things that I judge people by are most of all sincerity, honesty of person. I just can't stand a hypocrite. (*giggle*) And I'm nuts about them. (*laugh*)

C 144.   You're kind of deciding on just what those things are that are important.

S 145.   Well, I guess so. I mean if he drinks, I can forgive him. (*laugh*) Now, I mean. I wouldn't have been able to before because my family wouldn't.

C 145.   To some extent perhaps some of your feelings and ideas have changed a little bit and you're kind of feeling out these new ideas.

S 146.   I think so. And still there's enough of it hanging onto me so that I can't do what—put myself into a situation. I mean, I couldn't drink because it's been pounded and pounded and pounded into me so much and I couldn't smoke for the same reason. And things like that. But I certainly don't judge people wrongly about them any more.

C 146.   There's more freedom on your own part. You've come to be a little more tolerant.

S 147.   Uh-hum. Maybe that's it. (*low*)

C 147.   Yeah.

S 148.   But it's certainly a very wise thing that my grandparents did, bringing that about drinking, because it was evidently something in the Vid make-up that (C: uh-hum) doesn't take to it too well. And that's what ruined my dad's career and (*pause*) so I mean that's perfectly logical. I mean— (*giggle*).

C 148. In other words, you don't think, that even though you don't respond as much as you did to the values, that the values are wrong. They are really right for you.

S 149. That they're right in my case.

C 149. Uh-hum.

S 150. (*after short pause*) But (*short pause*) I'm not going to teach my children that (*short pause*) that drinking is all wrong. It isn't morally wrong. Because it isn't. I mean, even in the Bible it isn't! It isn't anything wrong. It's only if, it's when you do anything to an excess, if you get sort of lax in your (*pause*) anything. Well, I mean, you're—well, I mean—you're—well, that's wrong.

C 150. Uh-huh. (*pause*) I think we're kind of going to have to (*she giggles*) recess for today. Maybe you feel you'd kind of like to continue with these talks?

S 151. Okay, (*burst of laughter, and while laughing*) because it's fun. I'm a great talker. (*giggle*)

C 151. You can kind of explore your feelings a little bit and maybe find out a little more about what you really want to do.

S 152. All right. And we should make an appointment probably.

C 152. Yeah. That's kind of up to you in terms of when you feel you want to come in.

(The remaining minute or two of the interview is taken up in arranging for the next appointment.)

In this closing part of the interview the client gets to some very significant material. We now see that part of her feelings of change in attitude represent to some extent a change in attitudes toward her father. She has now revealed to us that her father was an alcoholic, that this had been a source of difficulty to him and that her grandparents had reacted negatively and quite moralistically about this. This gives special meaning to a number of her other communications such as in S 24, when she talks about her conflecting attitudes on self-expression; and in S 39, when she is talking about her family's attitudes toward the choice of botany; and in S 80, when she is talking about man's impulses being inherently good. In all of these we see evidences of conflict about standards. S 150 reflects the evolution of a relatively balanced attitude toward the issue.

Summary. This interview gives us the distinct impression of Miss Vid as a young woman going through a very important period of growth. It is a period of increasing awareness of herself and her impulses. She seems to be experiencing both exhilaration and fear. We find here a good example of the way that developmental issues can be expressed in the form of curricular and vocational decisions. Her vacillation between music and botany provides a specific arena for coming to grips with the task of reaching a workable pattern of impulse and control. In Chapter 14 we shall return to a more thorough discussion of the facilitating of such processes through vocational counseling. It is important to emphasize here that Miss Vid fits the class of client who is dealing primarily with an age-specific developmental problem fairly well. Despite the disrupted relationship between her parents, she appears to have developed considerable inner resources; facilitating further growth does not call for a long relationship. The freedom with which she expresses her feelings and the apparent constructiveness with which she reacts supports this impression.

The counselor appears to be of this opinion. His transition to the next hour keeps the focus on the question she brought in, namely, her indecision regarding botany, and there is no call for a lengthy commitment. Throughout most of this hour the counselor has been relatively inactive. He has tended to react quite slowly, permitting a number of pauses to occur without comment on his part. At the same time, we notice also that when he has reacted, he seems to stay away from any of the concrete issues brought up and encouraged their translation into very general ideas. Perhaps his belief that a brief relationship was indicated was translated into an effort to control the relationship by avoiding focusing on any of Miss Vid's specific feelings or past experiences. In Chapter 13 we will discuss problems of controlling the intensity and duration of counseling relationships.

CHAPTER 11

Test Selection and Interpretation[1]

COUNSELING DIFFERS most clearly from psychotherapy in the role played by psychological tests. Since psychotherapy typically deals with people who are aware of themselves as sources of their own difficulties, it places less emphasis on testing as a technique for discovering a desirable course of action. As was pointed out in our discussion of intake patterns, in most psychotherapeutic clinics diagnostic testing precedes treatment. The patient is promised no specific report on the results of the tests he has taken and is given only general explanations of the purposes in testing. He remains in the dark, feeling that testing is a somewhat unfathomable process. In fact, the kinds of diagnostic inferences drawn from tests are usually of a sort that would be either mystifying or frightening to a patient. In contrast, the counseling client usually comes oriented not so much toward treatment as toward getting information. He is usually fully alerted to the information-giving functions of tests and generally sees this information as one of the major benefits he will get from counseling. In this chapter we shall outline a rationale for the selection and interpretation of psychological tests in counseling and will discuss its practical applications. In the next chapter, counseling situations where test selection and test interpretation appear will be utilized to illustrate this line of thinking and its applications more specifically.

[1] This chapter incorporates, with some additions and modifications, the essence of two papers (Bordin, 1951; Bordin & Bixler, 1946).

USES OF PSYCHOLOGICAL TESTS

In our preceding discussion we have implied several uses of psychological tests. There are four such possible uses: (1) to provide information for the counselor; (2) to develop more realistic expectations of what is to be the purpose of counseling; (3) to give the client information; and (4) to stimulate self-exploration. Let us now consider these uses more fully.

To provide information for the counselor

This is the traditional diagnostic use of psychological tests. When the counselor is meeting a wide range of clients, sooner or later he will become aware that he is dealing with a client with an unusual degree of emotional immaturity and conflict. Like the therapist, he may seek the aid of diagnostic psychological testing as a reinforcement to his understanding of the client in the therapeutic decisions he has to make. A discussion of the psychological tests and related techniques for obtaining diagnostic information is not within the scope of this book.[2] It must suffice to repeat here that we are convinced that counselors should not undertake counseling responsibility without at least a rudimentary knowledge of diagnosis and diagnostic techniques.

To aid in developing more realistic expectations about counseling

Psychological testing is big business. As such it is one of the more advertised features of psychological services. Like anything involving a potentially great financial return, it draws quackery and exaggeration. From time to time there have appeared articles in popular magazines and newspapers overdramatizing the information supposedly derivable from such tests. It is not surprising, then, that clients who come to a psychological counseling service where tests are known to be used may have unrealistic expectations about how much such tests can contribute to the solutions of their

[2] For sources on diagnostic testing, the reader is referred to the following: Abt and Bellak (1950), Bell (1948), Rapaport (1944), and Schafer (1948).

problem. Some clients actually seem to conceive of tests as a scientific, and therefore credible, version of the soothsayer's crystal ball.

However, putting aside excessive and unprofessional promotion of tests, personality theory leads us to expect that clients will see the counselor as an expert and focus on psychological tests as tangible symbols of the power he wields. Clients, as they come to counselors, are most frequently persons who are having some kind of difficulty in making a decision. In vesting the counselor with great powers of seeing through people and of forecasting the consequences of their decisions, clients fulfill their wish to assume a passive role rather than depending upon what they feel are their own all-too-fragile decision-making capabilities. Furthermore, testing offers a tangible form of escape from the unpleasantness of examining their own threatening feelings.

Thus, it can be seen that clients' concentration on tests can represent an important obstacle to progress in counseling. In some clients, resistance to therapeutic endeavor may first express itself in this overemphasis on testing; other clients' preoccupation with tests reflects uncomplicated feelings that dispelling their ignorance will lead to a solution of their problems. In either event, it would seem important to remove this obstacle by discussions of what psychological tests can offer and by interpreting test results. Selecting and interpreting tests may be as important to the client who, for defensive purposes emphasizes information as a way of solving his indecision, as it is to the client who is blocked by sheer ignorance. Awareness that the information he gets from tests has not removed his indecision may prepare the defensive client for interpretations, leading to enlightenment concerning his true motives: that he is attempting to use the issue of information as a defense against having to examine himself as a possible source of difficulty.

To provide information for the client

One of the recurring themes in this book is that counseling is for normal people. Counseling, we insist, can play an important part in people's development and maturation. One can hold that our entire educational program is partially designed to expose the individual to those experiences which will enable him to become aware of his capacities and those aspects of his environment which provide him with opportunities for the fullest utilization and realization of these capacities. Broadly conceived, an individual's capacities are relevant to the part he plays in educational, vocational, social, and familial settings, as a learner, as a citizen, as a husband, as a parent, as a provider, and as a friend. To develop these and other roles of the individual is a broad and demanding task for the educational program. Inevitably, in respect to some roles it fails to provide him with the opportunity to develop maximum self-understanding and self-acceptance. Psychological testing, as part of counseling, can provide opportunity for the individual to become more aware of gaps or deficiencies in his life experience.

Some writers in the field of counseling, notably Williamson (1950: Ch. 8), have used the term *diagnosis* to refer to the process of analyzing and interpreting a client's test scores. "Diagnosing abilities and aptitudes," for Williamson, is the clinical interpretation of test measurements as distinct from interpretations based solely on the rigid application of regression equations. He stresses the use of background knowledge and direct observation of the client in addition to data from psychological tests as the basis for the predictions which form part of the information given to clients.

To provide a stimulus for self-exploration

Tests often reflect facets of himself of which the individual has not been aware or to which he has not devoted enough attention. Thus, even revealing to him through testing the possibility of exploring such facets may stimulate self-examination. Similarly, the interpretation of his own test results may set in motion an important sequence of reactions that may lead to clarification of his attitudes toward himself.

A THEORY OF THE FUNCTION OF TEST INFORMATION

We shall now describe a conceptual framework for the counseling uses of tests. Our conceptual framework will apply to the last three uses, the first having been treated in Chapter 9.

Testing the accuracy of our expectations of various aspects of our environment and of ourselves is known as reality testing. It includes verifying that boiling water is hot, that when father says "no," he really means no, and that I will fail to jump over the bar when it is set as high as five feet. Reality testing is a necessary part of all adjusted living. It is utilized in establishing a harmonious relationship between one's impulses and the outside world. Psychological testing is one medium through which the client can carry on a reality-testing process. It is a resort to instruments by which one can test the accuracy of his perceptions of his capacities, his interests and other personality traits, and the reasonableness of the goals he has set or might set for himself.

Whenever reality testing bears on the individual's expectations of what he might accomplish in some form of activity that is central to his wishes and aspirations, his emotional and motivational dynamics cannot be completely separated from the reality-testing process. My expectations of not being able to high jump more than four feet eleven inches may keep me from being able to jump any higher. Whereas, if my attitude were changed it might turn out that I could actually high jump five feet or higher. When you stimulate the individual to a process of reality testing with respect to his own psychological characteristics, you at the same time stimulate his emotions and motivations. Every time you describe a psychological characteristic which a test can reflect or you interpret the degree to which the test has shown him to possess a given psychological characteristic, you are in effect presenting him with a stimulus toward emotional and motivational expression. Thus, tests can provide a basis for helping the individual to explore his attitudes toward himself and toward the possible endeavors in which he might engage.

In summary, then, it is our conception that psychological testing, as it is typically used in counseling, provides a basis for reality testing and a stimulus to explore motivations and emotions.

APPLICATION TO TEST SELECTION

In order to accomplish the major aims of testing in the counseling process it is necessary, not only to permit, but to encourage the client to take an active role in selecting tests. Too frequently counselors are overly influenced either by their own needs for information of a certain sort which tests may yield or by a misconception of the dynamics of the reality-testing process. Since the problems posed by the counselor's need for information in early interviews have already been discussed previously, we will turn our attention here to reality testing. One of the major ways in which a counselor can misconceive reality testing is to assume that the client necessarily approaches it in the role of an unbiased scientific observer, ready to know the facts and to let the chips fall where they will. This is rarely the case, particularly where the client is in conflict over some decision. To be in conflict means that, far from being an unbiased observer, he is beset by impulses and counterimpulses. In this situation, every bit of information he accumulates counts as a weight on one or the other side of the conflict. In such circumstances, the reality-testing process is likely to become subordinated to the tugs and pulls of his conflicting feelings. In some instances, the conflict can become so intense that the individual cannot afford to admit certain factual information which might upset a hard-won and tenuously-maintained stalemate. The reader should recognize this last statement as another way of describing the dynamics of resistance and interpretation within psychotherapy discussed in Chapter 7.

It has been our experience that counselors who follow a procedure where decisions on testing are at best made with the client's passive concurrence, find that a large proportion of their clients do not return. Either they withdraw before undertaking testing or at some stage in the testing process. Our guess is that these failures to complete counseling arise from at least two sources. One of these is loss of interest in counseling where the counselor has failed to establish specific relationships between the tests assigned and the client's particular problems. The other is the client's unpreparedness for reality testing. Clients in conflict may not be emotionally ready to subject themselves to a realistic scrutiny. Such an appraisal must be preceded by giving them opportunity to air their fears and to become aware that behind their superficially expressed desire to get at the facts lurks a tenderness which makes any pressure to reach a decision exceedingly painful. Instead of forcing the client to evade this painful experience by finding, as he tells himself, that "testing is taking too much time," or "I cannot see how the tests I am taking can help," the counselor might better have postponed testing while he deals with the client's feelings about his immobilized uncertainty.

All this adds up to the conclusion that the client must actively participate in test selection if he is to test reality more efficiently. It is not sufficient for the counselor to realize that a particular test will contribute information useful to the client. It is necessary that the client see that this particular characteristic of his is relevant to some kind of plan which he himself must work out. The more thoroughly he is convinced of this, the better use he can make of taking tests and grasping the implications of test interpretations. Often overlooked is the insight obtainable by self-observation during testing. Where the relevance of a test to his goals has been established and his resistances to reality testing have been worked through or minimized, the client's self-observation during testing can become much more pointed and more meaningful. Moreover, he will be in a position to make more rapid and more effective use of test interpretations. Finally, it is a good principle of education that motivation becomes strongest when one is able to see the relationships between means and ends. When the client can see for himself that the tests are clearly related to the goals he is considering, he can throw himself more fully and more enthusiastically into the testing effort.

This position on the effects of greater client participation in test selection has been buttressed by experimental verification. In the earliest study, Seeman (1948) investigated the effects of increased participation by clients on the appropriateness of the tests chosen. In an experiment involving fifty clients of two counselors, he found that of all tests described to clients as available for actuarial or clinical prediction of something related to their problem, 93 per cent were selected. Seeman also found that clients having questions about technical curricula were more likely to choose a test of spatial relations than clients in social science curricula. Since spatial relations tests are more relevant to the former curricula, this difference is taken as evidence of the discriminating nature of the clients' choices. Dressel and Matteson (1950) investigated three hypotheses about those clients who participate more in test selection: (1) they gain greater understanding; (2) they are more satisfied with counseling; (3) they are more certain of their vocational choice after they make it. Forty recorded interviews representing seven counselors were used. All subjects were freshmen students who had taken a standard test battery. These students took a test of self-understanding and answered questions about their vocational satisfactions and their degrees of certainty before, immediately following, and two months after counseling. This study produced evidence to support the notion that those who participate more will gain more self-understanding and will be more secure in their vocational choices. This finding, however, was not completely unequivocal, since no relationship between participation and self-understanding or security was found[3] for the clients counseled by the same counselor. Also, no support was found for a relationship between participation and satisfaction.

To make it possible for the client to share in test selection, certain conditions must exist in the counselor's presentation of tests. First, the counselor should not burden the client with the responsibility for deciding which specific test is the best measure of a given psychological characteristic. This is a technical question which the counselor must be prepared to answer. If the issue is college aptitude, he must decide which of the numerous college aptitude tests is most appropriate. His description of the psychological characteristics involved should be in simple nontechnical language; for example, it probably communicates more to a client to tell him that one type of test compares his book learning ability with that of other college students, than to tell him that it is possible to take a test of his college aptitude. Similarly, telling him that there is a test which can probe his ability to work quickly and accurately in routine number- and word-checking operations will give him a more concrete psychological characteristic to react to than telling him that there is a test of clerical ability he might take. In fact, the phrase *clerical ability* is more likely to provoke his reaction to the idea of being a clerk than to the idea that he has some measurable degree of the ability to go through routine checking operations quickly and accurately. In general, the best

---

[3] Later studies (Forgy & Black, 1954; Gustad & Tuma, 1957 and Tuma & Gustad, 1957) have suggested that the personality of the counselor instead of his method may be the critical factor. Because of variations in the versions of method, conditions of counseling, and populations of clients, these studies cannot yet undermine our convictions regarding the influence of process, but they do keep the question open.

plan is to give the client a description of the psychological characteristics tapped by the tests, couched in behavioral terms, followed by some indication of the relationship of this psychological
characteristic to any decisions or problems that he faces. Since
these types of tests are most likely to be used in connection with
educational and vocational planning, the most frequently appropriate translation of a psychological characteristic would be in
terms of its occupational or curricular implications, for example,
"The test of one's ability to work quickly and accurately in routine checking operations is the sort of skill which is required in
paper work in an office. Such skill is vital for an office clerk or a
bookkeeper. It will probably be useful to an accountant, but
would not be so vital there."

To use this kind of procedure in selecting tests, the counselor
must feel comfortable with tests and be fairly well acquainted with
them. Otherwise he will find himself rapidly reciting the different
types of tests and in his anxiety to get this chore done he may not
give the client time enough for a real opportunity to react to the
tests. This limits the client's opportunity to struggle with the question of whether or not he wants to expose himself to a given test.
It is important that the counselor not see his test-proposal process
as a mere recital. Each type of test should be presented as a stimulus which may elicit significant responses. In this sense, the
process is very similar to the administration of the Rorschach
cards. The counselor must pause to give the client time to react
and to encourage his further reaction. Under those circumstances,
he will find that the client reveals a good deal about himself, his
life history, his attitudes toward himself, and his conflicts. While
they are talking about the fact that it is possible to get a measure
of his college aptitude, a student may reveal his suspicion that he
does not possess adequate ability to do college work and his strong
feelings of reluctance to admit this. He may reveal his reluctance
to face reality in the form of psychological testing by raising questions about the accuracy of tests. While discussing a mechanical
comprehension test, he may talk about the fact that his father is
an engineer and that his older brother has gone into engineering,
but that he has never felt he should try to follow in their footsteps.
He may feel uncomfortable about being asked to react to the tests
and to decide which ones he thinks would be helpful. This may

be incompatible with the passive, information-receiving role he had visualized for himself in seeking counseling.[4] The counselor's sensitivity in picking up these reactions, his willingness to interrupt test selection to discuss them and to encourage the client to elaborate, will be significant in achieving maximum therapeutic results.

The point at which test selection occurs and the form it takes will vary according to the client and his need. It may come early, involving a systematic survey of all of the personal attributes tapped by tests, or after several, even many, interviews and confined to one or two characteristics which have become the focus of attention. The kind of client who comes with no pressing problem and more for the purpose of gathering information for some future problem is likely to be quite test-oriented, and counseling will proceed fairly rapidly to the issue of tests. Many counseling agencies see a large number of high-school seniors who have been referred by their high-school counselors for vocational and educational planning as they graduate. Most of these youngsters are trying to decide whether or not to go to college and, if so, what curricular choice to make. With such clients, the orientation is toward a general self-inventory as a preliminary to moving into a new stage of development. Under these circumstances, a systematic view of all of the types of psychological characteristics that can be tapped by tests or other special measurement procedures will be useful. With clients of this type, who are set to hear predictions of future achievements and tend to assume a passive role in the counseling process, it is useful to discuss first general ability, special aptitude, and achievement measures before proceeding to interest and personality measures. Shifting to interest and personality measures can serve as an opportunity for further clarification of the possible uses of counseling. The counselor can convey to the client the idea that his feelings and emotions are important here and that the counselor is prepared to do something other than administer tests and give information.

Such statements as the following will serve this purpose:

The tests we have talked about so far are ways of getting predictions as to how well you would learn something, or getting measures

_____

[4] Seeman (1948) found that clients who showed indecision about selecting tests also exhibited indecision in other areas.

of how much you already know. We also have tests that reflect how you feel about things. People make up their minds as much or more by how they feel as by what they know or could learn. The main way we help people to take their feelings into account is by giving them the opportunity to talk things over with us in this kind of interview. With the kind of help we can give them we find that they can get a deeper understanding of how they feel. But we also have these tests which get at a person's feelings. Many times these tests can help a person get started on this process of thinking things through by giving him new slants on how he feels.

Discussing personality tests or inventories is sometimes difficult for a counselor. The personality inventory can usually be described in terms like this: "Another test gets at your general feelings toward yourself. What you can get out of this test is a personality description of yourself." If the test used is the Minnesota Multiphasic Personality Inventory, it is probably a good idea to cushion the client against the impact of the wide range of attitudes covered in this test by saying: "You will find that this test was intended to apply to a wide range of feelings that people have. Consequently, some of them will not seem very appropriate and some of them will refer to very extreme feelings."

APPLICATION TO TEST INTERPRETATION[5]

The problems of interpreting psychological tests to clients are unique to counseling. As we have already pointed out a number of times, the nature of the counseling situation is such that psychological testing is most frequently used for information-giving and reality testing. Therefore, the interpretation of test results must above all else make it possible to distinguish between the client's judgment of the facts, whether or not emotionally distorted, and the facts with which he starts. It seems axiomatic that the counselor's obligation is to give the client an accurate interpretation of test results. This implies that the counselor must neither overemphasize nor devalue the certainty of the predictions derivable from these interpretations. For example, when a prediction is

[5] See Bixler and Bixler (1946) and Rudikoff and Kirk (1959) for other discussions of test interpretation in counseling.

made of probable success in a given curriculum, it should be couched in terms such as these:

Out of a hundred people who present your pattern of test results we would expect to find that the largest number of them would fall around a B— average. There will be those who would do better and those who would not do as well. A very small group would get as much as B+ and, similarly, a very small group, probably no more than five out of a hundred, would fall below a C average. We have no way of telling in which group you will actually fall, whether you will be part of a larger group around B—, which seems most likely, or will be one of the smaller groups who do better or worse than the majority of people with this test pattern.

The above statement illustrates an attempt to convey to the client the range of probable outcomes associated with his test scores, so that he may understand his relative position in his group. The lack of finality in the statement allows the client to react to it in terms of his own expectations. One client is able to accept this statement readily, responding that he sees no particular reason why he should not perform at about the level most expected of his group. Another talks in terms of having always been overestimated by tests and of never achieving up to his expectation. Still another indicates his implicit faith that he will be part of the small group that does better than expected "because I am going to be working harder than I did in high school."

It should be evident that the effective use of tests for reality testing depends upon the adequacy and thoroughness of the counselor's training in test technology. The counselor's knowledge of the particular tests which he uses must go far beyond the information provided in a test manual. He must be acquainted with the accumulated data on each test which establish their validities for different criteria, each test's reliability and any special conditions which influence its interpretation.[6] Not only must he have this thorough understanding of the tests, but he must be sufficiently versed in the basic statistical tools used in test analysis to translate a test score into an accurate interpretation. The type of interpretation illustrated above would depend upon his having a grasp of regression equations and standard errors of prediction.

[6] Super and Crites (1962) offers an excellent compilation of the information needed for counseling.

The problem of test interpretation is not yet solved solely through mastery of the technical problems of securing precise inferences from tests. Just as educators have become convinced that the formal educational process cannot be reduced merely to the straightforward transmission of knowledge, so the counselor must recognize that, even when his sole function for the moment is to fill in a gap in the client's experience and information about himself, he is faced with more than a simple information-giving process. Whenever a person must learn something in which his ego is considerably involved, the learning process must be adapted to the motivational and emotional reactions engendered by the learning situation. The counselor must help a client see when he is doubting the accuracy of a test result because he does not like its implications; when his score suggests courses of action or describes characteristics which he finds unacceptable. The client who over-emphasizes the meaning of a test result, who goes beyond the counselor's interpretation, sometimes even in contradiction to what he is told, should be helped to differentiate the meanings supplied by the counselor from those dictated by his own motivations and emotions.

To help the client use test interpretation most effectively, it is important not only to give him the final predictions, where these are possible, but also to permit him to react to the combination of judgments on which the prediction is based. In the example cited above, the counselor, in the discussion leading up to prediction, might have said:

In trying to predict at the time he enters college how well a student will succeed, we find that there are two indices which when combined will give us our most accurate basis for prediction. One of these is rank in high-school graduating class. We find that this is the best single indicator of what a student will do in college. The other index is how well he does on a test of book-learning ability which compares him with other college students. This we call a college-aptitude test. Primarily, what it seems to tap is a person's ability to manipulate the English language in many subtle ways as well as his ability to manipulate abstract language such as might be involved in mathematical symbols. We find that high-school rank is about twice as important as a person's score on a college aptitude test in indicating how well he will do. According to our records, you graduated at the 95th percentile in your high-school class. In order to judge how this compares with other students in college, you should know that the average student entering this college has graduated at about 75th percentile of his class. So that in terms of this score you are considerably above the average of entering freshmen. On the college-aptitude test your score is just about average. So that, if we take into account that on the index that is given the most weight you were considerably above average and on the index that's given less weight you were average, we would end up with the over-all expectation that you would be above average.

In the case of many tests our knowledge does not permit too specific a predictive interpretation. When we interpret the significance of a test like the Bennett Mechanical Comprehension Test it is usually to a client who has not focused upon any one type of occupation. Even when the question is reduced to his probable achievement in a particular occupation, it may be one that has not been included in validation studies and the counselor is forced to extrapolate from studies of similar or approximately similar jobs. Interpretations under these circumstances are likely to deal with the test's relation to a wide range of mechanical jobs and will compare a client's performance with a relevant norm group.

One erroneous assumption often influencing counselors' interpretations of tests is that they can be certain when a test score will be threatening or satisfying to a client. This erroneous belief is based on half truths, namely, that there are general social pressures toward higher achievements, so that any test result which seems to predict lower than average achievement is per se assumed to be a threatening test result. This fallacy springs from the common failure to allow for the variability hidden behind most of our generalizations about people. Despite the existence of an over-all pressure toward higher achievement, there are subgroups of persons who find value in one type of achievement and who may devalue others that are usually highly esteemed. When we get beyond the standards of a subgroup and come to the individual, we are now faced with a complexity of motivations that can discover almost any meaning in the results of a particular test. For example, a student who feels he is too effeminate and, in an attempt to deny this effeminacy, is planning to go into engineering, may be considerably threatened and disturbed by a test result that shows he has superior verbal and artistic ability. On the other hand, a student who feels under pressure from his parents to stay in school but wants to drop out may actually be motivated to treat a slightly below average college aptitude test score as though it were a sign of certain failure in college. The counselor's interpretation of test scores should be free of such evaluative words and phrases as, "Your college aptitude is *very high*," or "You did *very well* on this test." What *is* important in this situation is not the counselor's valuation of various abilities and characteristics of the client but rather the values which the client attaches to each of them. When the counselor introduces his own values for social or other reasons, it may interfere with the client's freedom to express his own preferences.

The interpretation of personality scores also is frequently a difficult problem for counselors. This is not true when the personality inventory is simply a summary of the individual's expressions of dissatisfaction or satisfaction with various areas of his life, for example, the Bell Adjustment Inventory; the interpretation problem here is relatively straightforward. But when a test attempts to get at complex emotions, motivations, and behavior traits, the counselor's interpretive problem becomes more difficult. As has been indicated, this problem is best faced earlier when the counselor has arranged for testing. If he feels the personality test results should be reserved primarily for his own use, he should indicate this to the client at the time tests are being arranged for. Then there has been no promise to give test results as such to the client and the client may not expect them. However, the experience of taking the tests may have been sufficiently unsettling to the client so that now he does have some need to discuss the test results. Although this kind of effect is usually anticipated with projective tests such as the Rorschach or the Thematic Apperception Test, it has been our experience to find a similar disturbance in response to the Minnesota Multiphasic. It is important to recognize that the client's anxiety very likely arises from an uncomfortable suspicion of having revealed some mysterious, unfathomable attitudes and feelings. An interpretation of the test results which emphasizes some of the immediate and surface derivations of his feelings and motivations, those that have probably already appeared and been talked about in preceding interviews, will serve to quiet his anxiety and stimulate him to go further with the exploration of these attitudes.

Where extensive testing has taken place, the counselor will usually have prepared for the interpretive interview with the client by a thorough review of all test results and an analysis of their implications. As a result, there is a danger that the counselor will approach his task in somewhat the same manner as the teacher approaches a formal lecture. He will have laid out a series of items which he is prepared to transmit to the client and will proceed to do this somewhat in lecture fashion. But he must never lose sight of the fact that in most cases it is not the information per se but the client's reaction to it and his ability to incorporate it into his own system of thought which will be of value to him. Consequently, the counselor must proceed no faster than the client's willingness and readiness to digest the information permits. Instead of being able to transmit all the information in a simple hour's interview, the counselor may find that the first bit of information he gives the client leads to considerable interaction, so much so that the rest of the test results cannot be returned to until hours later. In some cases, they may not be referred to again until the end of the counseling process, when the client, having solved whatever problem or sets of attitudes have been blocking him, may simply as a matter of curiosity ask for a report on the rest of the test results. In presenting a particular bit of information, it is not sufficient for the counselor merely to pause to see whether the client has some reaction to it; he must actively invite some reaction from the client. In some instances it proves useful to encourage the client to match his own judgments about himself with those judgments provided by the test results. Such questions as the following serve that purpose: "Does this fit in with your own impressions of yourself?" or "Is this what you expected?" Incidentally, Young (1954) has demonstrated that college freshmen are able to judge their academic ability with considerable realism.

One of the procedures around which considerable disagreement has arisen is the preparation of test results, either for or by the counselor, in profile form, that is, on sheets upon which a wide range of aptitude, ability, and achievement tests can be entered to make up a single profile. This is a common practice. Such tests as the Kuder Preference Record, the Strong Vocational Interest Blank, and the MMPI have standard profile forms upon which test results appear. The question is, should the client be given the profile to react to? In general, proponents of this procedure maintain that this is the most effective way of stimulating the client to react freely to test results in terms of their meaning for him. In effect, the profile operates like a projective test. To allow the client to look at it affords him opportunity to attach special meanings of his own to the names of tests—or to distort the shape of the profile, etc. The arguments against this use of an all-purpose profile seem stronger. In an all-purpose profile, where one point may represent performance on a mathematics test as compared to entering college freshmen, and another point on the profile represents performance on a clerical ability test as compared to employed clerical workers, and still another point represents performance on a mechanical comprehension test as compared to the general population, the *shape* of the profile has little if any substantive meaning. Because this is so, it can only give the client a distorted picture of the facts. To present test results in this way is to abandon completely one of the important functions of this kind of testing in order to evoke the client's own interpretations, a purpose which can be satisfied in so many other ways. The arguments against presenting the client with a Kuder Test Profile are not quite so over-riding. Here all of the profile points are based upon the same norm group. However, in a particular profile a moderately high score, for example, one at the 70th percentile, may give the impression that it is an extremely high score. Take the example of the 70th percentile in a profile where the rest of the points fall as follows: two of them at about the 50th percentile, three more between the 50th and 30th percentile, one at about the 10th percentile, and two others between the 1st and 2nd percentile. The client looking at it might well assume that the 70th percentile point is evidence of a very intense interest, whereas our general knowledge of the occupational distributions of interests leads us to believe that the 70th percentile on the general Kuder norms may be exceeded by as many as 65 or 70 percent of successful men in an occupation reflecting this preference.[7] Here again the issue is whether at this point we should encourage emotional and motivational expression on the part of the client at the expense of accurate communication. Although the decision is not as clear-cut in the case of interest test profiles, our own impression is that it is in the client's best interests to maximize the accuracy of communication. In the Strong Vocational Interest Blank, where the main results are communicated not so much by individual occupational-interest scales as in their groupings, the visual presentation of the profile serves to distort this basic communication. The client is likely to focus upon a particular occupational name, taking this as evidence that his interests are high for that occupation, whereas in fact the over-all pattern suggests that some specific factor led to a high score in that occupational interest and that, taking the results as a whole, an entirely different interest grouping is significant. Too frequently the relatively inexperienced counselor presents the test profile to the client because he is uncertain in technical test interpretation. Before choosing his procedure, the counselor should carefully weigh the alternatives open to him and thoroughly analyze his reasons for choosing one alternative over the other.

In this chapter we have considered in a relatively detailed way many of the problems associated with the use of tests in counseling. In the next chapter we shall examine interviews or parts of interviews that illustrate in the living process the different ways in which counselors resolve some of these problems.

[7] This statement is based on Strong's data on the percentage of men in occupation who exceed given percentile points for men in general (1943).

CHAPTER 12

Illustrations and Problems

IN THE last chapter a rationale for the uses of tests in the counseling process was described. We shall devote this chapter to interviews or parts of interviews that will illustrate our point of view. In addition, we shall call attention through excerpts of interviews to the types of problems which may arise, to discuss the ways in which actual problem situations were met by the counselors and some other possible alternatives.

Ideally, all of the illustrations should represent the most sophisticated and the most polished examples of a particular technique for dealing with a situation. Unfortunately, even the most experienced and the most effective counselors lapse into ways which in retrospect they themselves would criticize. Regrettably, too, we sometimes found it necessary to choose an excerpt of a problem situation handled by a less experienced and therefore at times ineffective counselor in order to have that problem situation represented. Perhaps these less-than-perfect examples will help to reduce a prospective counselor's anxieties about his responsibilities by making him aware that others, even those considerably more experienced than he is, may make errors. We hope, however, that these illustrations will serve to emphasize the vast amount of information on test technology that enters into the process of test interpretation. Concrete examples of the applications of the sometimes dry and complex statistical reports on tests may serve to increase the counseling student's appetite for this dull but necessary fare.

FIRST INTERVIEW WITH THE TEST-ORIENTED CLIENT

Where counseling is carried on in an educational setting, the most frequent quandaries and problems brought in by clients are in the educational and vocational realm. These are situations in which psychological tests can be expected to make a realistic contribution. Consequently, first interviews in such a setting characteristically deal with a client who expects to be helped by interpretation of psychological tests. Indeed, the enthusiasm for psychological tests which has stimulated numerous popular articles, exaggerating their claims and oversimplifying the processes by which they can be helpful, causes many clients to anticipate that by an impersonal process in which they submit to testing all of their doubts and indecisions can be resolved. It is the problems and situations arising in first interviews with such clients that we shall attempt to illustrate in the following cases.

Case of Mr. Lav

This first illustration is almost an entire first interview with an eighteen-year-old freshman boy. The student is approximately six feet tall, strongly built but retaining a slight air of his adolescent gangliness. He is well groomed, neatly dressed, and in general is a handsome fellow. The interview begins:

C 1. Would you like to start by telling me what you want to talk about?

S 1. Well, I just want to find out whether I'm choosing the right vocation or not. And, I mean, whether it makes any difference which vocation I choose or not. (*polite and deferential*) If I'm going into the right one. (*little laugh*)

C 2. Uh-hum.

S 2. Probably I want to find out my best interest. I mean that'll help me find out what I want.

C 3. Uh-hum. Well maybe you'd like to tell me a little about the situation.

S 3. (*little laugh*) Well, I haven't got any situation. I just wanted to know if I'm going into the right vocation. Because when I first came up to the University here I chose engineering because my high school diploma, you know, just said technical. So I put engineering and I thought maybe I'd decide later whether I'm going to stay in engineering, but I found out that engineering is an altogether different school. I mean, I didn't know (C: hmm) that it was a different school.

C 4. I see. So you really only made a very tentative choice in engineering (S: that's right) and your experience so far has been such as to make you doubt very much whether engineering is—

S 4. Well, not doubt very much. Just doubting partially, that's all.

C 5. I see. Uh-huh. A certain amount of doubt has been created. Uh-hum. Apparently in your high school training you were—

S 5. Well, it was technical courses throughout high school.

C 6. Uh-huh.

S 6. And I just, well, my courses were such that I chose engineering. That's all.

C 7. Uh-hum. I see. I wonder if you'd like to tell me why you feel that you are in this kind of doubtful situation. What's kept you from focusing more definitely on something?

S 7. Well, I just haven't been able to decide in my own mind whether I should stay in engineering or not, see? It's all, (*little laugh*) (*short pause*) I just thought maybe the factor of time would tell me whether I wanted (C: uh-hum) —engineering or not, see?

C 8. Uh-hum. I see.

S 8. And still I didn't want to waste too much time because I—if I have to switch to another school, my credits wouldn't transfer so well, say in the arts college or something.

C 9. Uh-hum. I see. How about the sorts of things you've—the sorts of bases for the doubts that you have arrived at. What have they been?

S 9. You mean doubts for engineering?

C 10. Yeah— You kind of indicated that your experience in engineering has raised some doubts. (S: well) And I was wondering what they were.

S 10. Well, no I don't have real good grades. I just have average grades. (C: uh-huh) And, well, I imagine it's all right (*little laugh*) I mean there's nothing that—real doubts.

C 11. Uh-hum.

S 11. But I just wondered whether I was going I was going into the right vocation—because I'm not so sure (*little laugh*) I don't know how to explain it. (*pause*) Well—I—it's just that I'm just not sure (*struggling a bit to verbalize his thoughts*) whether it's the right vocation. I mean, whether I could do better at something else. In other words—

C 12. It's kind of a vague feeling rather than a very definite one? (S: uh-huh) Uh-huh— And apparently it's a question not so much of feeling that you couldn't do well in engineering, but perhaps you could do better at something else?

S 12. That's right.

C 13. I see. All right. Well, I gather from the way you're thinking about this that the main idea in terms of help that you thought you could get here was in terms of taking tests or checking your judgments about yourself.

In this first section of the interview we see a very good illustration of a client who is pretty definitely oriented toward an impersonal process. Notice how in the first statement he says, "I just want," indicating that he has a choice and is looking for confirmation. The counselor in C 2 simply gives a listening response to convey that there must be more to it and Mr. Lav, struggling, dredges up another goal for his counseling, to find out what his best interests are. Notice how sensitive he is to any implication that he is facing some problem as indicated by his balking at the Counselor's use of the word *situation*. Again in S 3 he emphasizes, "I just wanted to know if I am going into the right vocation." However, he then goes on to amplify some of the details of his present circumstances. In C 4 the counselor attempts to establish the fact that the client does have some doubts about his present choice and again Mr. Lav, very carefully trying to avoid any specific implication of a problem, attempts to water down the doubt and the counselor accepts this.

Right here we have a very specific choice point and one at which the inexperienced counselor often makes the wrong decision. One of the standard errors is too quickly to focus on the purely informational questions associated with a number of alternatives being considered by a client. In effect, this is an act of moving away from psychological considerations. The other alternative is to encourage the client to consider the origin of his inability to decide. Notice that our present counselor chooses the latter alternative by his comment in C-7. The client has difficulty developing anything in this direction and the counselor has to continue to press him. In

S 10 and S 11 the client struggles to dig up some reasons for his doubts and finds that outside of the issue of whether he might not do better at something else, he is relatively vague about them. This is verbalized by the counselor in C 12. In C-13 the counselor seems satisfied that this is the best basis for a consideration of tests which can be established at the present time and decides to proceed with the test discussion. The interview goes on:

S 13. That's right.

C 14. That sort of thing. Well, all right, then maybe we could start here by talking about what kinds of judgments about yourself it would be possible to check by means of tests and trying to decide which of those judgments it would be helpful for you to get a check on.

S 14. (low) Okay.

C 15. All right. Well, naturally one issue is usually an issue of a person's learning ability, how well he can learn. In thinking about college, and in general people usually tend to think in terms of—well, I want to know whether I can do better in this or in that, which of these things I'll be better at.

S 15. Uh-huh.

C 16. The sort of thing that I think you have expressed here and usually the idea that, well, one set of learning skills will apply to one situation, another set of learning skills will apply to another and so on. One of the things that we find is that you can divide college curricula in terms of just about two skills, types of learning skills that are involved.

S 16. Uh-huh.

C 17. Probably there are a lot more. But these are the only (laughing) ones we can get at by means of tests. One of them is—oh, we might characterize it as the ability to manipulate the English language in the subtle ways that are involved (S: uh-hum) in learning, let's say a social science course or the usual arts college type of course. The other one is the type of skill that's involved in manipulating the abstract language of mathematics, chemistry, physics, that type of thing. And that would apply for example to the physical sciences, engineering, physics, and chemistry. Those are the main differentiations in terms of learning skills that we've been able to find. So that you can arrange curricula as being this curricula involves more of one of these than the other, and then we can arrange curricula in terms of the level of competition that you're up against in terms of that type of skill.

S 17. I see.

C 18. So that's the picture there. Well, that would be one possible type of check or issue you might be interested in. That is what kind of a student do I stack up to be? In one field as compared to another. One way of getting at that is a type of college aptitude test. It's given when a fellow enters. That test contains within it these two aspects of learning skills although we have some question as to how well it gets at this nonverbal learning skill.

S 18. Uh-huh.

C 19. What we find is that you can usually bank a little more on, say, a test of a fellow's knowledge of high school mathematics as compared with others who've had about the same amount of high school math as he did. That would give a more accurate indication of what he's likely to do in say a physical science type of curriculum than what we get out of this college aptitude test. (S: I see) But we do have—I notice that you did take the college aptitude test. Had you—gotten the results of that? Have they been interpreted to you at all?

S 19. Well—I just took the engineering aptitude test. I think it was only mathematics. I mean, it was a half an hour or an hour test. That's all that we had.

C 20. Well, I think that was the college aptitude test according to our records.

S 20. Oh!

C 21. You—did you take a mathematics test?

S 21. I just don't remember. I think it was mathematics.

C 22. I see. According to the record we have—we have a record of you as having taken a college aptitude test, but not a mathematics test. (*laugh*) Now I don't know. That might be a mistake in the record.

S 22. Well, whatever they give the engineering freshman, that's what I took.

C 23. Uh-hum. You only took one test?

S 23. I believe so. That's right. One test.

C 24. Uh-huh. Well, the record we have—did you know how you came out in these tests?

S 24. No. I just took them.

C 25. Uh-huh. This was in the fall of '49. Well, according to this record, the only record we have is of a college aptitude test and there we compare you with the general run of entering freshmen at the University. And you did relatively better on the nonverbal part than on the verbal part. There on the nonverbal part you were in the top 20 per cent of entering freshmen. You were almost as far below the average on the verbal part as you had been above on the nonverbal part so that you can—

S 25. Well, that's the way it's—I mean that's the way it's been.

C 26. Right along?

S 26. Right along. I mean, we had these in prep school.

C 27. Uh-hum.

S 27. And I always fell way below and pretty far above (C: uh-huh) and not too far above, (C: uh-huh) a little better than average anyway.

C 28. Uh-huh. Yeah, so that in terms of the total test you came out about equal with the average. Now, as I say, we don't have a great deal of confidence in how accurately that nonverbal part predicts how a fellow will do in engineering. I think another factor, by the way, in predicting what a fellow will do—when we're trying to predict as accurately as possible, what we do is combine what a fellow does on a test like this with what he's done in his previous academic work, in other words, his high school rank.

S 28. I see.

C 29. How—how would you rate on that?

S 29. Well, I did, on most of my high school in math I did better than average.

C 30. Uh-huh.

S 30. And in chemistry I did better than average.

C 31. Uh-huh.

S 31. And English was always just passing, I mean, you know.

C 32. Where did you rank in your high school graduating class? Over-all? (*slight pause*) Did you go to a prep school rather than a high school?

S 32. (*at same time as C's last question*) It wasn't too high. I went to a prep school and—

C 33. Uh-huh, what school was that?

S 33. St. Paul's.

C 34. Uh-huh. Oh yes.

S 34. It was in the top two thirds, but I don't know exactly whereabouts.

C 35. I see.

S 35. The number.

C 36. I see. (*pause*)

S 36. It wasn't too high, anyway. (*little laugh*)

C 37. Uh-huh. Apparently it wasn't far above the middle.

S 37. No.

C 38. I see. In trying to judge what that means, I suppose we have to figure how the students at St. Paul's compare with the general run of high school students.

S 38. Yes. I think that—

C 39. I think they might be a little more selected. Did you feel that way?

S 39. Well, you see in our senior class we had students that had already graduated from high school.

C 40. Most of the students are pointed toward college?

S 40. That's right. I was at St. Paul's three years.

C 41. Uh-hum.

S 41. But I probably should have been fairly high, but well I think you have to figure that some had already graduated from high school (C: I see) and they had a year or two ahead. In fact, some graduated from high school and go there two more years.

C 42. I think it's probably—if we are trying to make a prediction for you at the point that you entered in engineering, taking into account your high school record—your prep school record and what you did on this test, we probably would predict somewhere around C or C+ work in engineering.

S 42. Hmm. Well, that's about right. A C+. Well, I have a 2.4 something average.

C 43. Uh-hum. So in other words you—that would have come pretty close to indicating that you have been achieving at about where one would expect you to (S: that's right) on the basis of your high school record, your prep school record, and what you've done in the college aptitude test.

Notice now that the counselor is trying to give the client certain information as to how the various judgments which are available to him through tests will bear on the kinds of decisions and conclusions he is trying to draw. Mr. Lav adopts a very inactive role, mostly giving listening responses. Finally in S 19 he gives a more definite response, but only in answer to a question from the counselor. The counselor's act, in C 25, of interpreting the college aptitude test scores can be questioned. In this kind of situation, where the counselor has previous test results, it is usually a good idea to make certain that the client does want these test results interpreted to him. Otherwise the ambivalences with which clients often approach tests will not have the opportunity for expression, even though they will still play their part in blocking the full utilization of test information. There is no indication here that such ambivalences have been present and are blocking a use of test information. This leads us to wonder whether the counselor had any cues from the nonverbal aspects of Mr. Lav's behavior which led him to conclude that Mr. Lav did want him to interpret the tests.

Notice, also, that the counselor does not interpret the tests solely in terms of a final prediction but interacts with the client around the two different bases used in arriving at an interpretation.

S 43. Uh-huh.
C 44. Have you had more difficulties with one type of course than another in your engineering work?
S 44. Well, only with the English.
C 45. Well, that part fits in with the general expectation.
S 45. That's right. (low)
C 46. Uh-hum. So if we were to take these indications as they now line up, it would seem as though you're more favorably placed in a physical scientific curriculum than you would be in, let's say a social scientific curriculum.
S 46. That's right.
C 47. Uh-huh.
S 47. But it's—what makes me wonder is that sometimes, I mean, my interests change so much. I mean, we read a book or we read a play or something, and I become really interested in it. (talking with more animation)
C 48. Uh-huh.
S 48. I don't know. It makes me wonder whether, I mean, I'm really interested or it's just a passing phase or—
C 49. I see. In other words it's your interests that you're thinking about here as much as the issue of your abilities.
S 49. That's right.
C 50. Uh-huh. I see. (pause) The picture looks pretty clear as to how your abilities lie, doesn't it? Or clearer anyhow than the issue of where your interests are.
S 50. (low) That's right.

C 51. Uh-hum.

S 51. I think probably though in arts, I mean, I can take some of their courses and still get a C+ average. I mean—I'd still run the same no matter what. Maybe the first year in their English course, I'd have to work a little harder, but I'd still run about the same.

C 52. I think that's very possible. In terms of how you feel about this, which seems to be the issue here, in other words, it seems to come down as much to an issue of your feelings, being able to take your feelings into account, as it is an issue of what you're able to do. And one of the main ways that we help people take their feelings into account is through what seems like a kind of an indefinite process of just talking it over, (S: I see) helping the person to kind of examine his feelings and puzzle it out, just what it means. But one of the ways we can help people get started in that kind of puzzling out process—or one way in in which we can use tests is as a starting point in puzzling it out. For example, we have a type of test where you would indicate how you feel about yourself in terms of a wide range of occupational activity or occupationally related activities. The way it works is that your likes and dislikes are compared to those of successful men in various types of occupations and see which ones you resemble most in your likes and dislikes. You might speak of it as a way of checking your impression of yourself, how you feel. Whether you see yourself as the promoter type of guy, the teacher type, the scientific type, and so on.

In S 47, Mr. Lav begins to be a little more active, apparently in response to the counselor's statement that the test results seem to favor slightly a physical-scientific curriculum. He seems motivated to point to contraindications revolving around the issue of his interests. The counselor takes up the question of interests tests and uses his introduction to the interest tests as an occasion for communicating the idea that the counseling situation does offer opportunity to deal with one's feelings directly.

We shall not reproduce the next section of the interview where the discussion revolves around the interest test and where the client is trying to get a clearer idea of it. He expresses concern that the interest test will consist solely of asking him what occupations he prefers but is satisfied when the counselor assures him that the questions refer to much more specific activities. It may be of interest to reproduce how the counselor discusses a general information blank and presents it to the client.

C 74. In terms of other tests which would have a bearing on a person's feelings another one that we have is really not a test, but just a collection of the kinds of questions about oneself that a person usually asks himself when he is trying to make up his mind about this kind of an issue. Things like what have my experiences been? What kind of people have I associated with? What kind of work experience and so on? What have I thought about in the past, and things like that. If you felt that, I mean, going through a whole collection of things like that and answering those questions might lead you to take into account certain aspects of your own experience that you hadn't considered before, that would be another possibility.

S 74. Well, I think they both would be helpful.

Mr. Lav, who had not yet indicated whether he would like to take an interest test, now indicates that he feels that both the interest test and the information sheet would be helpful. It may also be of interest to reproduce the discussion around the personality tests which proceeds immediately afterward.

C 75. Sounds like they might be helpful. All right— (*short pause*) —still another—I don't know how much you'd want to go into this. This one would be a collection of questions dealing with your feelings about yourself more generally, not just in terms of occupational activities or occupationally related activities. What you would get out of that, for what help it would be, would be a personality description of yourself. (*pause*)

S 75. Well, does— (*short pause*) in that—do you mean that the personality test would help determine whether you'd be fit for a certain, I mean, whether you'd be out for a certain type—I mean whether a certain type of job wouldn't be any good for you.

C 76. Well, this test wouldn't be a basis for predicting how well you'd learn. The main place where this test would come in would be if you had some question as to how your personality would fit into different occupations or how your feelings about yourself more generally fit into this issue of satisfaction with one type of occupational choice as compared to another.

S 76. Uh-hum.

C 77. That would be.

S 77. (*fairly low tone*) I think that would probably be good. I mean—

C 78. (*low*) Uh-huh.

S 78. I have some characteristics. I mean I have (*lost*). I guess every-one has, but—

C 79. Yeah. Many of these characteristics that this test gets at wouldn't have necessarily a direct relationship. They might be kind of indirect. They (S: uh-huh) are more of the general background for thinking about what you want to do. All right. (*pause*) Well, that would seem to cover the possible starting points in the way of tests dealing with your feelings, in other words what you feel like doing, rather than the issue of what you're able to do.

The counselor very carefully tries to delimit how much direct bearing on the client's choice the personality test will have. Mr. Lav becomes a little more active and one wonders whether in S 78 he was struggling to indicate some doubts he may have about his personality and behavior. The counselor's response in C 79 seems to pass over this possibility.

S 79. Yes.

C 80. We have lots of other tests that get at different kinds of learning ability. Most of those are not so vital as far as a college trained occupation. Some of them might be good to have in a college trained occupation, but they're not going to make the difference between success and failure. I don't know whether you'd want to discuss those or not. (*pause*)

S 80. Well, (*pause*) I don't—well, why don't we take those tests first and then see what they—

C 81. All right.

S 81. —tend to do. And then, if I have any doubt myself whether my interests are that and whether I can do well at whatever those tests come out, I don't—

C 82. Start with these and then—

S 82. Yeah. See what that turns out to be, first.

C 83. All right. We can do it that way. Okay, well, are there any other angles of this situation that you feel we ought to talk about? Any questions you have. (*pause*)

S 83. I can't think of any right off hand. (*low*) (*a little louder*) I could probably think of millions some other time, but (*little laugh*) I mean, when I'm not talking to you or anything, but—

C 84. (*smiling*) If someone asks you directly, (S: yeah) something like that, you just kind of get blocked and—

S 84. That's right.

C 85. You can't think of anything. Uh-huh. (*long pause*)

S 85. I wonder if my home environment would have any—weighing to one side of it. You see my father is a doctor, a physician—

C 86. Uh-hum.

S 86. My mother wants me, I think, wants me to become a doctor, but my father tells me that I make my own choice, you see.

C 87. Uh-huh.

S 87. And (*clears throat—short pause*) I put engineering down as my own choice, see?

C 88. Uh-hum.

S 88. I didn't know what I was getting into. I mean, not that I don't like it, but I'd never been in contact with anyone who had been an engineer until I came up here. Most of them had been doctors and lawyers and business men. (*pause*) The reason I did put engineering down is because I thought that the first year up here was all the same (C: oh—yes) I mean Arts College and engineering and everything.

C 89. Do you have the feeling that your putting engineering down was in relation to your home environment was kind of an expression of independence?

S 89. That's right.

C 90. Uh-huh.

S 90. I think so.

C 91. Uh-huh. I see. Maybe you've neglected to think about medicine as a reaction to wanting to make an independent choice.

S 91. That's right.

C 92. Is that the way— (S: [*breaking in*] Yes. I have that kind of a feeling—yes) Uh-huh. I see.

S 92. I wonder whether I would, I mean, whether I should go into medicine or (*sigh*) business or something like that. See?

C 93. Uh-hum. I see. (*pause*) And so that becomes an issue for trying to think out. That's one of the issues.

S 93. That's right. (*pause*)

C 94. Now you talked about your mother having a definite feeling of wanting you to go into medicine, of urging you, and your father says it's up to you.

S 94. Well, she doesn't definitely state it, but I know that she does.

We see that when the issue of the tests is disposed of, the counselor in effect gives Mr. Lav a new possibility for starting on his problem and we see that this is productive. Now for the first time he seems to begin to think a little more freely and a little more responsively about himself. We notice that the counselor must be patient, must allow him to struggle with it a little bit as happens in S 83, S 84, and after C 85. At this point, Mr. Lav has returned to the issue of why he is in doubt. He begins to amplify the possible influences on his choice, bringing out particularly the conflict with his mother around a possible need to establish an independent decision. Notice that the counselor did not attempt to stimulate a directed effort at examining more fully what lay behind the client's choice of engineering. Chapter 14 will consider more thoroughly issues in vocational counseling.

The next section is lost because of a mechanical difficulty in the recording, but we know that Mr. Lav tells the counselor that his father is not really his true father but a stepfather. His mother had divorced his natural father prior to this new marriage. He tells this with relatively little emotion, so that there is no particular clue as to what it meant to him at the time or what it means now. However, one cannot help wondering to what extent his resisting his mother's pressure toward medicine reflects a reaction to her possible effort to pattern him after his stepfather.

The rest of the interview is characterized by increasing freedom in the client's interaction with the counselor. Here he discusses medicine quite seriously from many different aspects, particularly from the point of view of whether he can get into medical school. He also brings up the issue of his interests, indicating as he did earlier his concern about this transitoriness of his interests and, in this connection, discusses his feeling that he does not know enough about either engineering or medicine to be sure of his choice. The counselor tells him of occupational pamphlets which are available to him and this first interview closes. We shall follow this relationship further when we discuss problems of ending counseling in the next chapter.

TESTS AS THE FOCUS OF INITIAL RESISTANCES TO COUNSELING

Clients who have come for counseling as the result of someone else's pressure or with considerable ambivalence about it are likely to embody their negative feelings in the way they react to tests and the emphasis they put on them at the very beginning of their counseling contact.

Case of Miss Cil

The following portion of a first interview with a music student illustrates how tenuous the counseling relationship can be.

C 1. This spring weather always kind of sets up a lethargy, doesn't it?

S 1. Yes. Spring fever.

C 2. Uh-hum. Well, what did you have in mind?

S 2. Well, Mr. Smith sent me over here from the School of Music and he said that I do not have the musical ability to keep on in the Music School.

C 3. Uh-hum.

S 3. And he wants to know exactly what I am suited for, but I know I'm (*outside noises drown out the rest*).

C 4. What's that again?

S 4. I *know* I still love music.

C 5. Uh-hum.

S 5. But anyway he wants to be satisfied.

C 6. Uh-huh. (S: *little laugh*) As far as you're concerned there's no problem. (*little laugh*)

S 6. (*smiling*) No.

C 7. He's the one that has the problem. (*Miss Cil laughs at this*) (*pause*) You kind of feel then that you're sort of fulfilling a responsibility or obligation to him, more than anything else?

S 7. (*low*) Well, partly, yes.

C 8. Can you tell me a little more about it, in terms of what you had in mind for yourself?

S 8. Well, it's just that I've always wanted to be a musician, and I did fairly well until I got up here and I do all right in everything but theory. (C: uh-huh) Over here in the Music School (*lost*) and it seems that does take native developing. I mean, it's not something you can actually learn unless you have the musical ability behind it.

C 9. Uh-huh.

S 9. So I made a very poor grade on that and Mr. Smith looked up my score on the Seashore test (C: uh-huh) and that I really didn't have any. So he could see why I didn't do well. And then I asked him could I continue Music School and not take that course. He said, "no," but that I probably could transfer to Arts College and take Music School subjects.

C 10.   Uh-huh.

S 10.   But I still love music. (*with a little sigh*)

C 11.   Uh-huh. Sounds like it's pretty important to you to stay with it.

S 11.   It is. (*slight pause*) Since I've got up here, I've been a little confused, (*little laugh*) I don't know if it is worth the struggle.

C 12.   Uh-hum (*short pause*)

S 12.   He said that maybe I could have a few tests to see if I'm fitted to anything else.

C 13.   Uh-huh. It's more or less his feelings that you ought to be going into something else, but you feel pretty strongly in terms of music.

S 13.   Uh-huh. (*pause*)

C 14.   You kind of wonder then how we might be of help to you.

S 14.   (*low*) That's right.

C 15.   Or what it is that you feel you would get out of this situation.

S 15.   (*short pause*) That's—actually there's not too, much. I mean, I do feel I'm wasting time— (C: uh-huh [*low*]) wasting your time, because I *know* I want it. And I also know that I'm just average. I mean I could never be great (C: uh-huh) and I don't expect to be. But then there's nothing else I actually *care* about.

Thus we see how Miss Cil at the very start of her interview makes clear to the counselor that she has come under duress and that she knows what she wants. Her response in S 7 gives the first indication that she may have some goals in counseling other than placating Mr. Smith. Then she begins to explain the long duration of her interest in music and even to indicate as she does in S 11 some doubts as to whether she should be continuing in music. The counselor possibly makes a mistake in C 13 when he assumes that the client is reasserting her lack of responsibility or desire for counseling. This misunderstanding may account for S 15 in which the client rather strongly rejects any basis for counseling.

C 16.   Uh-huh. You sort of put all your chips on that one pot, huh? You want to follow it out as far as it goes. (*short pause*) Well, if that's Mr. Smith's feelings, I'm wondering what you've sort of planned or what you had in mind then.

S 16.   Well, I'm definitely getting out of music school (C: uh-huh) and I'll go into Arts and take as many—I'll take my piano course and everything but the theory course.

C 17. Uh-huh. Then you do have in mind continuing in music and continuing here at the University, even though it won't lead to a degree in music at the School of Music.

S 17. No. That's right. I'll have an Arts College degree and major in music, I suppose.

C 18. How do you feel about that?

S 18. I don't know. (*little laugh*)

C 19. Haven't quite made up your mind whether you like it or not?

S 19. I suppose it's the best thing. Well, Mr. Smith feels that maybe I would be better in something else altogether—I suppose that's what he thinks. That's why he sent me over here.

C 20. Sounds like you're really not too happy about the situation.

S 20. Well, no. The main trouble—I'm really not too happy that he discovered I don't have the (*little laugh*) musical ability. That's what's eating me. I *believe* it! I actually *do!*

C 21. You mean that you—

S 21. I believe that I don't. (C: oh) He said I know that I don't. But I'm still (*little laugh*) not too happy about it. (C: uh-huh) I'm just sorry that I don't have it.

C 22. You kind of recognize you don't have the particular facility that apparently you need, but yet you're pushing on anyhow.

S 22. Yes. But is that wise?

C 23. I'd say on the one hand it doesn't seem to be wise when you take into account the rational considerations, but on the other hand, it does seem to be pretty important to go right ahead. (*pause*) I wonder why music is so important to you.

S 23. It always has been. (*low*)

C 24. Uh-huh.

S 24. Well, now it's dying off a little bit. That was really a *passion* with me (C: uh-huh) until about three years ago.

C 25. Uh-huh.

S 25. I guess it's fading a little bit ever since I got into college

C 26. It doesn't have quite the fascination it did?

S 26. No. (*pause*)

C 27. You kind of recognize that, but yet you want to push ahead with music anyhow?

S 27. And sometimes it's not even too pleasant. In fact, most of the time it's not.

C 28. You might say it's sometimes a chore for you. (*pause*) Kind of taking into account these things, I wonder why it is that you push yourself so hard, when apparently you too have some doubts in your mind? (*pause*)

S 28. It's a good question. (*little laugh*) I really don't know.

C 29. Uh-huh. (*pause*) You're sort of pushing yourself in one direction, but maybe you haven't stopped to think of why. Huh? (*long pause*) Sometimes kind of understanding or clarifying why one feels the way one does, or why one is doing whatever one is doing, is just as important as getting such as how good you are at a thing. Do you think it's worth your while to kind of look into the—the "whys" here? Sort of look into these questions we've been raising or—

S 29. (*very low*) I don't know—

C 30. —or would you sort of like to leave it all. (*low*)

S 30. Well, it may be easy to (*little laugh*) look into it.

C 31. Well, that's kind of hard to say at this point. All we can do is sort of speculate. (*pause*) Sounds like you're kind of interested in getting by this requirement, so to speak, (S: uh-huh) take the tests and go. Well, maybe I can indicate to you the sorts of tests we have available and you can decide on those that you think you might want to take. At the same time that you're kind of fulfilling somebody else's requirement here this is kind of an opportunity to get information about yourself which might help you. (S: uh-huh) So I'll mention the different possibilities of getting information and you can decide on those that you think you might want to take. They might give you information that you can use.

Notice how Miss Cil vacillates back and forth during this section of the interview. The counselor's response in C 16 seems to be a counteraction to her rejection of counseling in the preceding response. It attempts to call her attention to the reality she faces. Once more she begins to talk about her feelings about having to give up the idea of music and her doubts about the wisdom of giving in to her reluctance to give up this dream. In C 23 the counselor, by his question, clarifies the intensity of her feelings and indicates his awareness of them. This enables her to examine the feelings and even to indicate that perhaps she is not feeling quite as strongly about music as she had earlier. In C 27 the counselor again through a question has confronted her with the fact that her dogged persistence in the field of music does not necessarily arise from any zest for the subject. The counselor utilizes her long, thoughtful silence to suggest that perhaps here they have the basis for a counseling relationship. Unfortunately, in C 31 the counselor undoes the good work he has been doing toward establishing a possible basis for counseling by bypassing it and returning to the previous topic of the pressure on her. There is no indication that the counselor had to go ahead in the way that he did. It would have seemed much more appropriate to have allowed her to struggle longer with her perplexities and with her fear of submitting her desires to more searching examination. Instead this was bypassed by introducing the discussion of tests. This seemed to have the effect of emphasizing once again the outside pressures to force her to give up her irrational impulses. Whatever must have been involved in this issue of music must also have been connected to feelings about the imposition of the will of others upon her. She resumed her passive resistive attitude, agreed to take additional tests, but also insisted that she wanted a retest on the Seashore. She completed taking the Seashore but did not complete the other tests; instead she arranged for another interview with the counselor. The results of the retest were pretty much like those of the original one, showing definite deficiencies in aural sensitivity. In spite of these results, she reaffirmed her determination to continue in music. Having made this decision, she felt it unnecessary to take the other tests and terminated the relationship. In retrospect, it seems quite clear that the counselor's unwillingness to let her struggle with the question of whether to submit to a counseling relationship was probably the deciding factor.

One of the ways in which the resistance to counseling shows itself is in the client's reactions to various types of tests and to the issue of deciding whether the information they have to offer will be of use to him. A good example of this is from an interview with Mr. Fab, a freshman who had matriculated in engineering and then had transferred to the Arts College, but still was confused as to his college goals. He tells the counselor he had started in engineering because his father was an engineer and because he did not want to take a language. Languages are not required in engineering. He quickly decided that he did not want to go further and shifted to the Arts College. He vaguely mentions business administration, journalism, and architecture, but feels his ideas are indefinite and hopes that tests will provide a more definite basis for choosing. The counselor has just finished describing college aptitude tests and says:

C 25. This one that I was just describing, these ones, really are measures of just your general ability.

S 25. Yeah, I suppose that would be a good test.

C 26. Uh-hum. Yeah. (*pause*) You understand that you're free to decide whether or not you want to take these. That is, I don't have any reason to try to sell them to you.

S 26. Oh, no.

C 27. But—

S 27. Probably wouldn't do any harm though. (*mumbled*)

C 28. You're free to if you want it (*rather low*).

S 28. Uh-hum. (*pause*) I suppose it would be good to take one now. My grades are sort of slipping. I'd like to (C: [*low*] uh-hum) know if I should be up there or not.

C 29. You're not sure whether you can do better than you really are.

S 29. Oh, I know I can do better than I'm doing!

C 30. You want to know how much better.

S 30. Yeah. (*pause*)

C 31. You're kind of deciding whether you want to take these. Is that it?

S 31. Well, I just want to take something. I don't know—don't know what.

C 32. Yeah.

S 32. I'd just take them all! I don't know. (*little apologetic sort of laugh*)

Here we see that although Mr. Fab has talked about tests as a possible answer to his indecision, he is unwilling to commit himself to the possibility that the particular test could be helpful to him. Finally in S 32 he implies that he can escape the problem by taking them all. This happens many times when the counselor and client participate in the process of test selection and where the client has antagonistic feelings. A client will express his antagonism by deciding that he is going to take all of the types of tests that the counselor discusses with him. In most cases when this occurs the client does not return.

Many times the client greets the counselor with a direct request for tests as in this example where after an exchange of greetings the counselor says:

C 2. What can I do for you now?

S 2. Well, I'd like to take some tests or find out what kind of job I'd best be fitted for after college, after I get out of college.

C 3.   We do have tests and they are helpful sometimes in this type of situation, but could you tell me a little more about what ideas you have on the subject?

Appropriately, the counselor has not acceded to the client's demand for tests. It is hard to conceive of the situation where it would be appropriate. In this instance, the counselor's response might have been a little more pointed in the sense of saying that it was not yet clear what types of tests could be helpful to the client or whether tests would be helpful at all. As it was, the client interpreted his more ambiguous statement as meaning that the counselor wanted him to tell him about the possible alternatives he had been considering. In general, when a client starts with such a specific orientation, it is important to clarify that tests are not a panacea for doubts and to help him begin to focus upon the origins of these doubts.

Clients often express their resistances to tests and the process by such questions as "Do you think this test will do any good?" In most instances, it seems most effective for the counselor to recognize the client's doubts of the test's value and to encourage him to talk about this. Sometimes, however, this type of question may be accompanied by feelings that the counselor ought to be more helpful in deciding which tests will be useful. Many times the counselor actually does convey the impression to the client that the client is pretty much on his own and struggling with these decisions. In such instances, it may be more therapeutic to indicate to the client that the counselor is willing to participate in this process rather than simply sitting by as a distant, uninvolved figure. He might say, "I would give you the answer if I could tell whether it would provide helpful information. From what you have said so far, I can't decide. Perhaps we should talk about it some more and between us we might be able to come to a decision."

TEST DISCUSSION AS A STIMULUS FOR EXPRESSION OF CLIENT MOTIVATION

In the preceding chapter, we pointed to the importance of test discussion as a way of stimulating the client to give expression to his desires and as a stimulus to self-exploration. Now we shall try to present a couple of illustrations of this.

In the first one, the counselor is discussing tests with a Mr. Dem, a passive fellow who was enrolled in engineering. He graduated from a teachers college and worked for one year as a teacher. He had originally planned to transfer to an engineering school, and had taken a pre-engineering program in the teachers college. However, when a job came up, in his passive way, he let the circumstance decide for him and taught for a year. We turn to the interview at the point where the counselor has begun to describe the kinds of information available from a clerical aptitude test.

C 75. Uh-huh, yeah. Well, let me review some of the different types of skills that we can get at and see whether any of them would be of any value to you. One would be a test that would get at how fast and accurate a person is at routine checking operations as the sort of thing that would be involved in paper work in an office. That would be pretty vital for an account clerk or a file clerk to have. It might be useful for someone who was going to be an accountant or an office manager to have even though it wouldn't be vital to them. *(short pause)*

S 75. I'd like to take—I don't know. I thought at one time too probably of entering accounting. *(weak, hesitant)*

C 76. Uh-huh.

S 76. When I was in high school I was quite interested in accountmg and that field. At one time I thought that I might like to enter accounting.

C 77. Uh-huh.

S 77. But I didn't know. And there's been quite a little pressure at home on different things, (C: uh-huh) and they've said quite a little on engineering and when *(low)* I was teaching why they thought it was quite a laughable role. But I don't know *(louder)* and there was definite against accounting.

C 78. Did you say there was pressure *against* accounting at home?

S 78. Any business course.

C 79. Uh-huh. I see.

S 79. But I don't know. And at one time I was thinking of accounting.

C 80. Uh-huh.

S 80. I was thinking of going into business administration.

C 81. Uh-huh.

S 81. And trying for an accounting (*very low*) job.

C 82. I see.

S 82. I wanted to do public accounting. (*very low and indistinct*)

C 83. Apparently your family pressure discouraged you.

S 83. (*laughing*) I did find it a little bit discouraging—

C 84. Uh-huh.

S 84. At times. But I never knew. I always thought that I would take an accounting course in college to see.

C 85. Uh-huh.

S 85. —if I'd like it there.

C 86. Uh-huh.

S 86. (*low*) I don't know— (*whispered*)

C 87. You've always had kind of a sneaking suspicion about it.

S 87. That I might like it.

C 88. Yeah.

S 88. And I've never yet—I've taken very few courses that I've really liked so well at college.

C 89. Uh-huh.

S 89. —that I've wanted to dig right into 'em (C: uh-hum [*low*]) and stay.

C 90. You kind of had the feeling that maybe accounting *would* turn out to be something like that.

S 90. Well, I was wondering if it was (*little laugh*) something like that.

C 91. Uh-huh.

S 91. That's what I wonder.

C 92. Uh-huh.

S 92. Really I haven't (*laugh*) many opinions on the subject, that's what I'm trying to—

C 93. Yeah—

S 93. (*low*) find out a little about it.

C 94. Uh-huh. I see.

S 94. I don't know. My English (*low*) grades are bad. I've got mostly C's in English. (C: uh-huh) I mean (*low*) and (*short pause*) the, foreign language, history—

In this excerpt Mr. Dem reveals a great deal about himself and of the degree to which he is controlled by his family's pressures in spite of rather definite interest and desire to move in the direction of accounting. Notice that the counselor throughout is immediately responsive to the fact that he has stimulated an involved expression and responds mostly by listening and saying just enough to encourage the client to go further.

A second example is taken from a first interview with Mr. Par, a predental student, who is wondering whether he should give serious thought to medicine or engineering as alternatives. In discussing the issue, Mr. Par indicates that he feels relatively satisfied with dentistry as a choice but wants to be more certain that it is a better choice than the other two. The counselor decides that it is appropriate to begin discussing tests. He has just gotten through saying:

C 9.   . . . one of the kinds of things that students are sometimes interested in finding out is some indication of the quality of work they might expect of themselves, that is, some prediction of the grade they might get in terms of their ability to learn. I don't know whether you're at all concerned about that issue, that is, whether you feel you're doing about as well as you could do or if maybe you could get better grades than you are or what. What do you think?

S 10.   I think I'd like to find that out. (*little laugh*) I think personally I could do better than I am doing. I mean, in my own opinion, so I don't know. I'm doing fairly well as is. I mean I'm not doing that poorly. My parents certainly think I could do better. (*laugh*)

C 11.   Some pressure on you then?

S 11.   (*recovering from laughter*) Well, not pressure. It's just that, I mean, once in awhile you take home a C and for me that isn't the usual mark so they—but it's no—I mean they don't actually harp on it, or drive me to anything because of it. A lot of times I know I can do better and I, at least, I feel I can do better, and maybe something that would test my real ability would be—

C 12.   You wonder how realistic these expectations are.

S 12.   That's what it is. (*slight pause*)

One notes here that the issue of his general ability touches off some reactions in Mr. Par, reactions of dissatisfaction with himself but perhaps more reactions of feeling that others, notably his parents, are dissatisfied with him. However, he is not very ready to talk about this, and when the counselor shows perhaps a little too definite an interest, he begins to modify his statement and to minimize his feelings. As we shall see, in the next interview when he becomes readier to confide his feelings, he shows that he feels that both his older and younger brothers are much better and much more effective readers than he is. We discover that his older brother is in medical school and that medicine is apparently the main alternative being considered by him.

THE TEST-INTERPRETATION PROCESS

As in the interactions which occur in deciding which tests will be helpful to the client, the client approaches the interpretation of test results with a cognitively dominated set. Usually he is actively attempting to integrate the information he is receiving from tests into some rationale of himself and of his life plans. When the information is sufficiently divergent to resist integration, the client becomes more involved and usually expresses his emotions more freely. Yet the expression of emotion under these conditions is not of the free flowing sort, the open-ended kind of expression that characterizes the more therapeutically-oriented client. We shall try to convey the flavor of a test-dominated interview by a detailed presentation and then follow with additional small excerpts to round out the picture.

For our example we choose a second interview with Mr. Par, the predental student in the preceding illustration. He has completed a battery of tests and the counselor has before him the results shown below.

TEST RESULTS FOR MR. PAR

		NORM GROUP	PERCENTILE
ACE *Psychological Examination*	Q	All University Freshman	91
	L	" " "	75
	T	" " "	88
Co-operative General Culture Test:			
Current Events		Arts College Sophomores	22
Science		" " "	95
Mathematics		" " "	99
Mechanical Comprehension Test		Engineering Freshmen	45
Revised Minnesota Paper Form Board Test		" "	40
Scholastic Aptitude Test for Medical Schools		Fresh. Pre. Med	97
Minnesota Reading Examinations		U. of Minnesota Upper Classmen	73
Minnesota Speed of Reading Test		" " " " "	80

		STANDARD SCORE
Crawford Spatial Relations Test	Ind.-Technical Pop.	5.15
(Remarks: **Trial and error behavior**)		

		LETTER GRADE
Minnesota Spatial Relations Test	General population-men	A
(Remarks: Calm intelligent approach, excellent performance)		

		PERCENTILE
Crawford Small Parts Dexterity Test:	Unselected job applicants	
I Pins and collars		99
II Screws		25
(Remarks: I—Adept with tweezer, calm, pleasant, co-operative;		
II—Good eye-hand co-ordination, a bit hasty).		

Study of Values	NORM GROUP	STANDARD SCORE
Theoretical	Adults & Undergrad.	35
Economic	" " "	30
Aesthetic	" " "	20
Social	" " "	40
Political	" " "	39
Religious	" " "	16

Strong Vocational Interest Blank (Scored for selected occupations)

GROUP	OCCUPATION	SCORE
I	Artist	C
	Physician	B—
	Dentist	B
II	Engineer	C
	Chemist	B
III	Production Mgr.	B
IV	Carpenter	B—
	Forest Service Man	B
V	YMCA Phys. Dir.	B—
	Personnel Manager	B+
	Soc. Sci. H.S. Teacher	A
VIII	Accountant	B
	Purchasing Agent	C
IX	Sales Manager	C
	Life Insur. Sales	C
X	Lawyer	C+
	Author-Journalist	C

Minnesota Multiphasic Personality Inventory

SCALE	NORM GROUP	STANDARD SCORE
L	General Population	50
K	" "	70
F	" "	53
H_z	" "	47
D	" "	56
H_y	" "	55
M_f	" "	67
P_a	" "	53
P_+	" "	42
S_c	" "	43
M_a	" "	37

These test scores seem to indicate that Mr. Par is close to being a top level student in ability. His performance on achievement tests must be considered against the fact that his predental curriculum emphasizes mathematics and science at the expense of the social sciences. The findings suggest that he has talents in either the physical or biological sciences. His scores on mechanical comprehension, spatial relations, and performance tests indicate that he has adequate supporting skills for either engineering or dentistry. One would say that on the ability and achievement side, neither engineering, dentistry nor medicine, all of which he has mentioned, are contraindicated. The picture is not so clear with regard to interest and personality inventory. If we take the Allport-Vernon and Strong together, we find a clustering in the social or welfare area. This kind of interest can be consistent with certain specializations in medicine, but is contradictory to engineering and perhaps dentistry. However, there are secondary indications in scientific and subprofessional technical fields strong enough not to rule out dentistry. The results on the MMPI, in so far as they suggest, even allowing for differences between college students and the general population, that he is more on the feminine side, would also contraindicate engineering. This inventory also suggests that while he may maintain an appearance of being calm, realistic, and nonintrospective, underneath there are tendencies in the opposite direction which can only be maintained by careful vigilance (High K).

After the usual greetings accompanied by both getting settled the counselor has asked Mr. Par what he will want to talk about today and we start with his reply.

S 4. Well, I want to mainly find out the results of the tests. I completed them all last Friday. (C: uh-hum)

C 4. Well, they're all set here. Is your situation still about as it was when we talked?

S 5. Well, it's about the same.

C 5. Uh-hum.

S 6. I still don't know how things came out. (*low*)

C 6. Uh-hum. No changes or new items of information or anything of that sort?

S 7. No. Nothing special.

C 7. You were kind of reacting to some doubts about your pre-dentistry (S: uh-huh) course. You're still feeling kind of doubtful.

S 8. Well, as far as that—I'm still planning to go ahead with it. (C: uh-huh) I mean it's just that I want to see if this reinforces the way I feel.

C 8. Uh-hum.

S 9. And just, well, what the tests say more or less, but I still am planning on dentistry.

C 9. Uh-huh. Your doubts apparently aren't so strong that you're seriously considering stopping or anything of that sort.

S 10. Well, no. No. I just want to find out how I stand.

C 10. Uh-hum. Well, I suppose it would be safe to start in with a general statement that there doesn't seem to be anything in the tests that we can think of that is really arguing against your going on in your predentistry program. That's kind of a general statement. Maybe you'd like some more—

S 11. Well, I knew they'd be more or less telling me that, (C: uh-huh) especially on the medical aptitude and mechanical.

C 11. Well, the medical aptitude that you mentioned, you were compared with first year premeds and, since you're a sophomore, why that would make it just about right for you and you place up in about the top 5 per cent of the group you were compared with. So on the basis of that test, we would be inclined to predict superior work in any studies like the premed or predental program.

S 12. What about mechanical aptitudes?

C 12. In the one that was designed to measure your mechanical comprehension, where you were looking at wheels and gears and things like that, you're compared with engineering freshmen there and you come out right about the average line. You can expect half of them to do it better, and half worse. And you seem to have about the average engineering freshmen's mechanical comprehension.

S 13. And what about on the screw driver, (*little laugh*) the manipulation?

C 13. Those manipulation tests right around here. (*pause*) It's in looking these over, it's safe to say that your scores place you in a superior group. You came out somewhat low on the one where you were putting the screws into the little holes, and might have gotten them mixed up or something, but—

S 14. I thought I'd become a little wrong. (*low*)

C 14. But in general, this seems to show considerable co-ordination above average manipulative ability, which is just about as definite a statement as we can make from the test.

S 15. Uh-huh.

C 15. It's not the sort of thing that we can just apply directly to dentistry and say that you can be a skilled technician or something of that sort. But at least as far as these tests go, they indicate that you're not only not clumsy, but you're quite adept in your finger movements.

S 16. I see.

C 16. Does that seem to—is that clear?

S 17. Oh, I was— (*breaking in*). See, I had taken a mechanical aptitude test once before when I was in high school. (C: uh-huh) And well, but that test was more—it wasn't a manipulatory test. It was more like the test I had on comprehension.

C 17. Uh-hum.

S 18. And I had done very poorly on it. So that I was wondering. I wanted to see just about where I would come out now. Whether I progressed any, because I was below average at that time.

C 18. Uh-huh. There really doesn't seem to be anything to suggest that you're at all poor in that ability. (*short pause*)

S 19. What about the results on the achievement test? (*low*) In chemistry?

It is to be expected that in the interview following a program of testing the client will be oriented to discuss the results of tests. Nevertheless, it is a good idea to start such an interview as our counselor does with a general invitation to choose what topic he wants to talk about. This type of opening plus the indication that other aspects of the client's life are important can often be productive. The counselor's response in C 10 is an interesting one in that it appears to be an effort to test the meaning of the client's doubts about dentistry by indicating that the tests offer no basis for contradiction of his choice. Apparently this is not enough, since the client has already anticipated it and asks for more detailed interpretation. We can see here also that Mr. Par is taking an active and alert part in the discussion of the test results. Notice how in S 17 and S 18 he attempts to relate these test results to previous test scores. This is part of the process of fitting the results into his operating framework. This also continues during a process of

discussing the results of the Co-operative Achievement Tests, and
we pick up the interview again as the counselor is saying:

C 22. ... the only other kind of—well, there are two of them here. One
of them is your—just the general college aptitude tests which
you took. It seems to place you in about the upper 10 or 15
per cent compared with university students. So that I would
be inclined to predict something along the lines of B or B+
average in grades.

S 23. And what about the personality test? I was wondering— (low).

C 23. There was one other abilities test here that I wanted to mention
before we got side-tracked and that was that you took this reading test and it indicated no reading difficulty at all. You're in
the upper 25 per cent, in your general reading skill. So unless
you feel that there is some other kind of problem in reading,
why—

S 24. I don't know. Maybe it's just that (laughing) everyone else reads
as poorly as I do.

C 24. Uh-huh.

S 25. Maybe, it's just that I read very slowly, that I know, and although my comprehension, my ability to bring out facts, usually
is pretty good. I mean, if I read it once I can usually remember
things pretty well. (C: uh-huh) But I do read, I know, very
slowly.

C 25. I was wondering how you get the impression that you read
slowly?

S 26. (low) It takes me a lot of time, (louder) I don't know. Things
that, like reading a—well, ordinary light reading, like a novel or
something. I know I haven't done too much reading now. I
don't usually, I haven't had the time, but I know when I was in
high school and well, last summer or so, it took me quite a bit
of time to get through, well, light reading like a novel, let's
say (C: uh-huh) compared to, well, I have a younger brother
who reads faster than I do. Well, I know a lot of people in
general who read fast. (C: uh-huh) Maybe it's just that I happen
to be in contact with people who happen to be very good at it.

C 26. I was curious to know how you developed the impression of
yourself as a slow reader since this seems to indicate at least so
far as this one test goes that you probably read faster than 80
per cent of the college students.

S 27. It was more just a matter of comparison between (C: uh-huh)
myself and other—

C 27. Other specific individuals.

S 28. That's right. And you see I have an older brother who is very adept at reading. (*little laugh*) I mean I didn't compare myself with him. I wouldn't mind being able to read as well as he does (C: uh-huh) but—uh—as I say, I have a younger brother who also—who reads very well, when it comes to speed and remembering. (C: uh-hum) And most of my friends read, I think, better than I do, which is why I was under that impression. Maybe it's just that, as I say, they happen to read very well, (C: uh-huh) and I'm just average.

C 28. Apparently certain comparisons that you've made of yourself with other individuals have given you rather an unnecessarily discouraging picture of yourself.

S 29. Well, I— (*little laugh*) I don't know. (*little laugh*) In some instances, yes. I guess so. (*ends low*)

C 29. Uh-hum.

S 30. I haven't tried to keep up with anyone in particular, but it's just that, well, as far as reading goes, I was under the impression that I don't read well.

C 30. Uh-hum.

S 31. I know my vocabulary is—that I am pretty sure of. (*low*) Because (*louder*) At least it was in high school. My vocabulary test in high school was, in general, I believe, low. (C: uh-huh) I mean at—well, they were, I think just a little slightly below average. So that's why I think my general over-all intelligence test probably—there's a lot of reading on that. And, of course, I don't know how much you're expected to finish on that, but (*little laugh*) I don't think I finished as much as I should have. (C: uh-huh) I don't know most of the vocabulary parts.

C 31. On the general abilities test?

S 32. Yes.

C 32. Well, I—

S 33. I was wondering. (*breaking in*) Do you know the relation of marks of the certain parts of it?

C 33. No. It doesn't show us how you came out on specific parts, but your scores place you up, as I said, in the upper 15 or so per cent. So that maybe you were expecting more than was necessary to expect.

S 34. (*little laugh*) (*pause*) (*low*) I was—maybe it's just that (*louder*) I do think that I have too high a standard that I go by.

C 34. Uh-hum. I'm beginning to get the impression that you tend to jump to conclusions which are usually kind of uncomplimentary to you. (*short pause*) Is that something that you maybe have always done or—

S 35. Well, not necessarily, but I do push myself. I—

C 35. Uh-huh.

S 36. That I know. I mean I always—if I'm good I do try and usually get better, even if it is high, and that's why more or less if I don't know whether it's a matter just personal satisfaction or what, but I do try and get still more ahead than I am. So I don't know. Maybe that's why I feel that in many of these things, by comparison, I actually am up pretty high (C: uh-huh) but I feel that I'm not doing as well as I can.

C 36. Sounds like you might be a little afraid to be satisfied with yourself.

S 37. (*lower*) I don't know. I don't know. (*louder*) I—I've done well in school. I mean, I always have had good marks, better than average marks.

C 37. Uh-hum.

S 38. Well, I guess it's just a matter of thinking I ought to do better. (*little laugh*) I don't know whether that's good or bad. (*laugh*)

C 38. I think I'm still kind of thinking of your saying that you kind of push yourself, and as soon as you said that, why it really occurred to me that you really kind of push yourself down a little bit, in the sense of always under-rating your abilities.

S 39. Well, I've done that at times, (*low*) (*louder*) as far as school work and other things too, I imagine I do underrate myself at times. (C: uh-hum) Sometimes I overrate (*laughing*) myself too. (C: uh-hum) I think that's true to a certain extent. (*short pause*)

In this section of the interview we have the recurrence and elaboration of the theme from the first interview of Mr. Par's dissatisfaction with his own achievements. We have here the indication that his standards of achievement are set by the examples of his older and younger brothers. Notice here also that, although earlier the counselor had followed the direction of the client's interests in the choice of tests to be interpreted at this point, he goes against Mr. Par's expressed interest in his personality test results by holding that up until he has interpreted the reading test. Presumably, he did this because of his awareness of Mr. Par's feelings about his own achievements which were expressed in the first interview.

Where a client has started with an orientation toward making a decision and begins to become involved in emotional issues, an important choice point is reached. The counselor must decide what modifications, if any, will best fit the client's present orientation and needs. He must choose either to keep the focus on the decision, helping the client to apply insights from more general explorations to it, or to propose a more open-ended effort directed at the personal anxieties which have been uncovered. It is possible to temporize by testing the degree to which the client is ready to carry further the expression of the particular set of feelings revealed. Our present counselor seems to have assumed that it is not appropriate to attempt any reorientation of the counseling task and apparently interprets the short pause after S 39 as indicating that the client is waiting to move to another topic, so that in the next section we see that the counselor shifts to the topic of the personality test.

C 39. Well, that kind of covers the abilities tests that you—that you took, and, as I indicated right from the beginning, there isn't anything in the pattern of findings to raise any question at all about your capacity to handle the dental curriculum or any other curriculum that you might take a fancy to. So then you asked about the personality test. (*pause*) About all I can do with this is to make some guesses and then see what you might say about it. Your findings are all within—are all well within the normal range, so that any guesses that I might make would be in terms of normal variation. I wouldn't be trying to make any kind of a peculiarity out of them or anything of that sort. One guess that I might make is that perhaps you're inclined to be—to think of yourself as a pretty realistic person. That is, you'll always try to—to be down to earth and make plans of a concrete nature, rather than building castles in the air or any kind of wild ideas. Does that seem to—

S 40. (*low*) I think so. I have my times (*laugh*)—(C: uh-hum) when I guess everyone probably does too. (C: uh-hum) I think in general I— (C: you probably—) I do.

C 40. You probably don't take what daydreams you have too seriously.

S 41. No.

C 41. That's kind of reflected too in the sorts of things we've even been talking about up to now. You tend to focus yourself on trying to beat certain marks that are already there and to meet standards that you set for yourself right on the spot, rather than sitting back and someday reaching a certain wonderful distant goal. (*pause*) I don't want to—don't want to give you the impression that I have very many comments to make. I have enumerated one of a number of guesses because nothing very spectacular comes out of this. You're perhaps (*clears throat*) the sort of person who is (*short pause*) well oriented to the finer things. You probably appreciate music and art or both. Maybe literature. In general, I'd say that your cultural appreciations are perhaps above average. Is that a—is there any validity in that guess or am I?—

S 42.   I don't know. I don't know how you mean that. If you mean as far as ability to recognize things that are?

C 42.   No. I was thinking just in terms of maybe an emotional response. That you feel that the arts are important. But I'm guessing about the content. I don't know whether it would be art, music, or literature or (S: well, I—) or none of those.

S 43.   That I don't—I don't know— (*short pause*). Literature I've never really done so, much. I've done very little reading as far as that goes. And I used to have to be driven to read books. So I don't know. Maybe I like to think that I'd like to be able to sit down and read a lot more. I don't know. I don't always have the time. But as far as reading goes or books in general, I don't know. Music I do enjoy. (C: uh-huh) I—

C 43.   Well, that would not be enough to support this guess, because as I say, it is such a tentative guess that it's a little bit hard to feel sure of it at all. I think that I'll have to bid a pass for any more guesses. There isn't anything more on the results that I would feel sure enough of to make any comments about it.

S 44.   Uh-hum.

C 44.   The variations of this wavy line aren't enough variations to make any bones about it. (*pause*) No, I think that's about all I can pull out of that. Were there some other ones that you remember that you wanted to ask about?

Here we have an example of the interpretation of the Minnesota Multiphasic Inventory, an instrument that attempts to get at personality traits which may have deeper meaning for the individual than inventories which reflect only the individual's feelings of satisfaction or dissatisfaction with various aspects of his life. Notice that the counselor avoids any technical terminology or use of trade names in his interpretation. We notice also that other than an allusion to the characteristics noted in our interpretation, the counselor is unwilling to make very definite statements because the test profile is so relatively undifferentiated.

The interpretive process proceeds with the Vocational Interest Inventory and the Allport-Vernon Study of Social Values.

C 45. Oh, yes. The vocational interest picture. As I probably described when I talked about this test before, it's designed to compare your pattern of likes and dislikes and how you feel about a lot of different things with the patterns of men who are doing various types of jobs and are successful in those jobs. (S: uh-huh) It's supposed to give some kind of a picture of how you see yourself in relation to jobs. It—for instance, it compared you with successful dentists and shows a high degree of similarity between your patterns and those of other dentists.[1] Along the same lines, there's about the same degree of similarity between your pattern with chemists as with dentists. Now, actually, there isn't an awful lot of difference between those two jobs except that they are—the dentist is a little bit more oriented towards mechanical kinds of things and the chemist is a little more oriented towards theoretical things. But certainly you have to study a lot of chemistry and other theoretical subjects to prepare for dentistry, so the two kind of go along together as far as that's concerned. Seems to suggest that you—that you like to work with your hands. Now that's a guess based on the fact that there's considerable similarity between your pattern and most carpenters. It certainly doesn't say that you'd be happy as a carpenter (*S laughs*) but it does suggest that you'd be happy working with your hands and tools. You also seem to indicate some liking for the outdoors. I don't know just how that fits in here.

S 46. Well, I— (*fairly low*) that's a side interest of mine.

C 46. Uh-hum. That's shown in a fair degree of similarity between your patterns and those of men in the forest service, who are pretty basically outdoor people.

S 47. My scouting training. (*laughing*)

C 47. Uh-hum. You have a pattern of activity apparently that gets you into the outdoors. Then another area of this is evidence of your having a pretty strong reaction to yourself as a person who likes to deal with people, a person who likes—who is interested in social welfare and social activities helping people, having lots of contact with them, getting to know them.

[1] An inaccurate interpretation.

S 48. (*low*) I think that's pretty much so. I've always done a lot of work with, well, with children as (C: uh-huh) now. I've always enjoyed working with people in general. (*short pause*)

C 48. One sort of speculative question that we might raise in that connection is whether some of your doubts about dentistry might grow out of a feeling that the courses and the training and everything are all kinds of impersonal, kind of abstract and technical. And that you don't have enough contact with the social sciences and studying about people as people rather than as cases.

S 49. Well, I don't think in my, well, my desire about people is so much to study them. Like as you say social sciences. Aside from psychology, if you class that as a social science—I don't know, I really don't find too much interest in them. (C: uh-huh) I mean, I do—I enjoy working with people more so than studying them. Psychology interests me a lot because well, I like more or less to know why people tick.

C 49. Uh-hum.

S 50. (*low*) I feel that I'd like to know more psychology than I have. (*louder*) But as far as just things as maybe sociology and anthropology, that sort of stuff, (C: uh-huh) doesn't really interest me. I'm more interested in more working with them than with studying the background and the history.

C 50. Uh-huh. Well, then the only place where this would apply then would not be in your course material, but in perhaps your— just your daily living. Perhaps the years of training in dentistry might seem a little demanding in terms of the time required. Maybe you wouldn't have enough chance to do other kinds of work. I don't know whether that's anything that you have thought about.

S 51. Well, one of the—one of the reasons why I took dentistry, well, why I'm more interested in dentistry than medicine was that I felt I would have more time.

C 51. Uh-hum.

S 52. That I would have the chance to work on the outside and I feel that a doctor doesn't really have his own time.

C 52. Yeah.

S 53. And that was one of the considerations why I didn't take medicine.

C 53. Uh-hum.

S 54. I really felt I'd like to have the chance for outside work.

C 54. Yes. Well, then, these findings tend to once again support rather than detract from the idea of dentistry, since one of your motives for, going into it is to be relatively free to do other kinds of things. And certainly dentistry itself has some contact with people, although you would hardly think of it as a social service kind of job.

S 55. (*laughs heartily*) That depends on how much I would charge! (*laugh*)

C 55. Depends on whether you'll be working in a welfare clinic or in a plush office somewhere. (*pause*) About the only other that we haven't said anything about here is this little study of values. Do you remember that? One that asks you whether you'd rather— (S: whether I would like to look at a painting or sell it, that sort of thing?) (*pause*) I don't know whether I can tell you anything very exciting or not. It seems to indicate that your main values are theoretical and social and political. And that's what we've been saying right along here really is that you have this scientific interest, dentistry, chemistry, that sort of thing, plus a sort of a human interest outlook, social activity, leadership, something of that sort. (S: uh-hum) And the values that you don't seem to place too much stress on are religious, esthetic, and economic. Those would be the less personal and less scientific areas, abstract and philosophical kinds of things. They don't seem to appeal to you quite so much as these ones that involve either scientific study, a search for truth, or human contact, social activities. Does that seem to—

S 56. Yeah. That fits me.

C 56. Uh-huh. Well, I think that I've kind of run out of things that I could raise spontaneously from the tests. I must confess some feelings of still wondering how you developed your doubts about dentistry. Maybe they weren't really strong enough to matter anyway.

Mr. Par continues to be quite active in the process of dealing with the test results. The counselor's statement in C 48 would seem to arise from a somewhat inaccurate conception of the meaning of the welfare pattern in the Strong Vocational Interest Blank, as indicated by his emphasis on the social sciences as compared to the correct emphasis on working with people in a helping relationship. In general, the results of the interest test are interpreted as also supporting his choice of dentistry. We shall see that Mr.

Par, himself, later makes use of the more accurate conception of the social-welfare-interest pattern.

After the interpretation of the scale-of-values test, the counselor ends the interpretation of the tests by raising a very important question of just why the client does have doubts about dentistry. This is a well-timed and important step for the event where a client finds nothing very unexpected from test results. It is important to point out that his doubts must rest on something else than an informational issue and this is the essence of the counselor's interpretive question.

S 57. Well, I don't know. It's just—I've always—it's more or less been a fight between medicine and dentistry more probably than anything else.

C 57. Uh-huh.

S 58. It has been a certain amount of, I guess, outside pressure. (*little laugh*) I mean not that my parents or anyone would force me either way, but well, my older brother is getting his M.D. this June, and I know he'd like very much to see me go into medicine. He feels that I do definitely have the ability for it, and he thinks that possibly I'm going into dentistry because, well, my parents suggested it, or something like that. And, well, more or less that to a certain extent well, you know what I mean, more or less thinking that maybe—when he brings it up, naturally I think maybe it would be— (C: uh-huh) And then sometimes I think that I might enjoy medicine more than dentistry because it's probably a little more personal, a little more, well, social contact, I mean, a doctor has than a dentist has. The doctor usually gets a lot closer to his patient I think than a dentist. There's, well, more satisfaction probably from medicine in helping and things like that than there is from dentistry. (*past few sentences in lower tone*) (*now louder*) Things like that more or less give me my doubts. And then, well, even though my marks have been good, I really wanted to see if my ability to retain things and to hold on to my knowledge was good enough, something which I definitely think is absolutely necessary in either one of those fields. So that I felt that I'd like to, well, test my general ability to have knowledge and keep it from the past. Those more or less were the things which kept me, well, not exactly definite either way. Because as I said, I did have this mechanical ability test in high school which, although it wasn't manipulatory, it didn't show me *(short pause)* that way, and I did want to find out a little more. Because in dentistry I guess that is probably one of the important things. I did want to find out more or less see if I could get a better judging of my abilities in that field by taking some of these tests. *(lower)* And more or less if they could tell me what I should do.

C 58. Well, there certainly doesn't seem to have—it doesn't seem to have turned out that there is anything in any of the tests to discourage you from either course, really, medicine or dentistry. Our tests really aren't good enough to discriminate between the two. They are so much alike, you see. The only semi-significant thing that I can say would be that there is a slight evidence of there being more similarity between your patterns of interest and those of dentists than there is of your pattern and those of doctors. But the difference isn't so very great that I would consider it a basis of choice. I wonder if perhaps your brother is inclined to overlook or not be aware of some of your other interests, since the doctor's life certainly does tend to be a dedicated one in the sense that he'd better not have any side interest because they don't get attended to.

S 59. Well, he—I guess he knows me. As far as that goes I think he knows pretty well. I've always been extremely active outside of school, and in school and everything else. He knows that. (C: uh-huh) And I don't know maybe—I don't know why he feels that I really might want medicine and just be going into dentistry for other reasons. (C: uh-huh) But as I say, he—well, when we do talk sometimes and he brings up the question of whether I really feel that I want dentistry, I don't know, I think he may do it to a certain extent to make me think more often.

C 59. I was just going to ask you if you had any idea of what might be involved in his trying to sell you on his own career.

S 60. I don't think he— It isn't a matter, I don't think of his trying to sell me on medicine because, as I say, I do have an interest in it. I mean I—it wouldn't take much selling actually. *(little laugh)* (C: uh-huh) I think though it is more or less an interest to see that I'm—I do what I want. And not just take something and—the other thing has been the question that he feels to a certain extent that I may not want to go into it because of the financial expenses, that he's drained the family treasury quite a bit, and I might not have wanted to go into—take medicine and because of the added financial expenses, (C: uh-huh) to my parents but I don't think that that's so. I mean, you see, that's one of the things. You see, he says if I do feel that way it's very foolish, and that as far as that goes, although it probably would be a little more expensive, by the time I would get to that point, he certainly would be—

C 60.   He doesn't—he doesn't want to feel that you're making a sacrifice (S: that's right) because of him.

S 61.   I think that's more his motive than anything else, to see to it that I don't try and sacrifice myself because of the fact that he's been ahead of me and possibly prevented me from doing what I want. I think that's more his idea to try to get me to come to medicine and—

C 61.   He just wants to make sure that he's not going to be a barrier to your doing what you want to do.

S 62.   Do what I want to do, yes. (*low*) I'm certain that it's more that than anything else. (*pause*) That's about all, I think that I can—

C 62.   You also mentioned that he was perhaps concerned that you might be going into dentistry because your parents wanted you to. Is it that he's afraid that you're under their thumb, or—

S 63.   Well, no, I don't think he feels that my parents would—our parents (*little laugh*) would stop me from doing anything, I mean, either way. I think my parents feel that dentistry is a better profession for me. They have always felt that way because of my mechanical interests more than anything else. (C: uh-huh) They feel that I'd make a better dentist because of, well, like my outside work than I would be a doctor.

C 63.   Uh-huh.

S 64.   Because of my mechanical ability things like that I have always been building things, and things like that. I have always been interested in it. And my dad especially because I have mechanical ability, I probably might make a better dentist than a doctor. But more or less they have thought that dentistry is my field, but I don't feel that there's been any pressure put on me either way— (C: uh-huh) from my brother or from my parents at all. If I choose one or the other it wouldn't (*lower*) make any difference to either one of them. I mean, the decision is completely up to myself. (C: uh-hum) I don't feel any compulsion.

C 64.   Uh-hum. Well, our tests seem to have observed some of the same characteristics in you that your parents observed, and come to the same conclusions that you do seem to have more interests than the pure scientific professional interest of the physician, and you do seem to have some mechanical and manipulative interests and abilities, though you certainly wouldn't want to use those as positive proof that dentistry is *the* field because actually these tests don't discriminate too well between two fields that are so similar. But there is the additional evidence there that certainly does tend to raise some questions about how completely satisfied you would be with the relatively limited life of that of—a doctor leads. *(all this in fairly low tone)*

S 65. That has always been one of the things that has I guess pushed me more towards dentistry (C: uh-huh) *(this is quite low)* in my own—my own feelings. I would want more time for myself, and I think that dentistry certainly offers it. At least a dentist he has his office hours and when he's done, he's done.

C 65. They're not going to call him in the middle of the night very often.

S 66. *(laugh)* That's it. To pull out a tooth or something. While a doctor doesn't have that, (C: uh-huh) I mean, he goes someplace and someone has to make sure that if a call comes, that he can be contacted and I don't feel that I really want to be tied down that much. (C: uh-huh) so that I feel that I'd get more out of dentistry myself. It's my own feeling. *(low)* *(pause)* That's about all, I guess. *(little laugh)*

C 66. That seems to be the ground you wanted to cover?

S 67. Yeah. I think so. *(pause)* I guess that's fine. *(laughs)*

C 67. Okay, well, it might be that later on some new questions might come up or—you might meet unexpected difficulties, not that we foresee any now, but you can never tell. But the situation now seems to be pretty—pretty stable.

S 68. I think it bears me out a little more *(low)* (C: uh-huh) Gives me, well, some sort of foundations to—

C 68. Seems to have confirmed a lot of impressions that you really had already, rather than adding anything really new. *(pause)* Well, maybe I'll see you again sometimes.

S 69. Yeah.

C 69. I hope your plans work out well.

S 70. I hope so too.

C 70. Goodbye.

S 71. So long.

In this section we see that the counselor's interpretive question stimulated the client to bring out and discuss more of the intangible reasons for his doubt. As he discussed it through this last part of the interview, one gets the picture of his surface feeling. One sees that he feels a little caught between his brother's urging and perhaps both his parents' and his own attitudes toward himself. We would judge that he also obtains a better understanding of his brother's motivations in pushing him and reinforcement in his own impression that it would not be appropriate for him to go in the direction of medicine.

SUMMARY ANALYSIS OF INTERVIEWS WITH MR. PAR

In such brief contacts as this case, it is often difficult to judge how much has been accomplished and how much more could have been accomplished. From the indications in these two interviews Mr. Par has feelings of inability to satisfy himself and his parents with his accomplishments, accompanied by feelings of being inferior to his brothers. One cannot help suspecting that there are emotional origins in this client's doubt about his vocational choice. These emotional origins would lie in his feelings of rivalry with his brothers for his parents' affection and his defenses against these feelings. Indirectly, from the client's responses in S 60, we get indications of the possibility that the client viewed his older brother as being in a position to deprive him of certain satisfactions by virtue of being older and more able to compete.

Even if these suspicions are justified, it is also fairly apparent that this is a relatively limited emotional conflict because the client is able to operate in a relatively undistorted way. Consequently, one has the impression that having been reinforced in his own thinking he will be able to go ahead and follow through with his plans. Perhaps as a result of being successful in dentistry, he may gradually be able to resolve the conflict surrounding his feelings of deprivation and the hostility toward his brothers which is associated with it. We are beginning to know more and more about the therapeutic resolution of conflict, but we know relatively very little about the resolution of such conflicts as a function of the growth process itself. It would seem as though, if one had the facilities for it, it would be fruitful to follow up persons like Mr.

Par, who have had a relatively brief therapeutic contact, to see to what extent the growth process itself, facilitated through this brief contact, can lead to the dissolution of such minor conflicts. Ten years later will this client still be carrying around his conflict?

INTERPRETATIONS OF INTEREST AND PERSONALITY INVENTORIES

The interpretation of interest and personality inventories is singled out for additional illustration and discussion because there are special problems of technique associated with the complex information derived from these sources and the resulting difficulty there is in communicating it. Another reason for this special attention is that these instruments deal with aspects of an individual which are less readily digested and incorporated into his view of himself. To a considerable extent, the problem of conveying interpretations of interest and personality-inventory test results bears a great similarity to the general problem of interpretation. There is no fundamental difference between transmitting one's view of the client gained from personal conversations with him and discussing with him the significance of his scores on interest or personality inventories. Where the client feels a need to defend himself against awareness, the information will be rejected, resisted, or distorted. Information derived from testing has one advantageous difference. The client is less able to rationalize it away as a biased view based on the counselor's attitudes and needs. However, this similarity with therapeutic interpretation is great enough to suggest that the usual principles of interpretation apply. The interpretation of personality-inventory results should be paced to the client's readiness to accept and utilize the interpretations. Those results which are already closest to his awareness should be interpreted first. In many cases, encouragement to react to these interpretations will prepare the way for additional test interpretation. Where the device touches on material far from awareness, it may be necessary to withhold discussion of that particular phase of the results until readiness has been created. Though projective tests are less frequently used for purposes of "feedback" to the client, the same principles will apply.

Case of Mr. Ril

As one example of this interpretative process we choose a portion of a second interview with a freshman student who was trying to establish a vocational goal. In his first interview, the student, Mr. Ril, mentioned as fields he was considering law, medicine, and the ministry, but said that he was now fairly sure that he would exclude the last alternative. During this first interview he also indicated that he was responding to his family's expectation that he would get a professional education. Although Mr. Ril seemed to be accepting this pressure rather passively, the counselor noted some evidence that there was an underlying unconscious rebellion against this authority. Mainly, it became evident through his critical reactions to his professors. Most of the first hour was devoted to a discussion of tests in which he participated quite actively.

At the very start of the second interview, Mr. Ril was ready to plunge right into the results of tests. Almost as soon as the counselor greeted him, he was asking whether the tests had shown that he was inconsistent. However, the counselor did not turn immediately to test results. Instead, he asked whether there had been any change in Mr. Ril's thinking. When he replied that the issue of the ministry was reopened, they discussed briefly what could account for this shift. During this discussion, Mr. Ril indicated that his father disapproved of the choice because he did not think that he had sufficient religious faith to become a minister. Mr. Ril showed that he shared his father's doubts on this score and confessed to the feeling that the ministry's main attraction was its central role in a dramatic religious service. It is at this point that the counselor begins to introduce the interest and personality inventory results shown below.

INTEREST AND PERSONALITY INVENTORY SCORES FOR MR. RIL

Allport-Vernon Study of Values

SCALE	NORM			STANDARD SCORE
Theoretical	Adults and Undergraduates			29
Economic	"	"	"	31
Aesthetic	"	"	"	43
Social	"	"	"	24
Political	"	"	"	23
Religious	"	"	"	30

Kuder Preference Record

SCALE	NORM			PERCENTILE
Mechanical	General Population Males			0
Computational	"	"	"	75
Scientific	"	"	"	42
Persuasive	"	"	"	90
Artistic	"	"	"	50
Literary	"	"	"	60
Musical	"	"	"	85
Social Service	"	"	"	72
Clerical	"	"	"	60

Strong Vocational Interest Blank (Scored for selected occupations)

GROUP	OCCUPATION	SCORE
I	Artist	C
	Physician	C
	Dentist	C
II	Engineer	C
	Chemist	C
III	Production Manager	C+
IV	Carpenter	C
	Forest Service Man	C
V	YMCA Physical Director	B—
	Personnel Manager	A
	Soc. Sci. H.S. Teacher	A
VIII	Accountant	B—
	Purchasing Agent	B—
IX	Sales Manager	A
	Life Insur. Sales.	A
X	Lawyer	B
	Author-Journalist	B

Minnesota Multiphasic Personality Inventory

SCALE	NORM		STANDARD SCORES
L	General Population		50
K	"	"	61
F	"	"	50
H_s	"	"	42
D	"	"	46
H_y	"	"	55
P_d	"	"	37
M_f	"	"	71
P_a	"	"	35
P_t	"	"	42
Sc	"	"	45
Ma	"	"	50

The scores on the values and the two interest inventories present a formidable problem for integration. It is often difficult to differentiate disparities that reflect different traits appearing under the same, or similar, designations from those that reflect invalidities or unreliabilities of one or both of the scales. The Kuder and Strong are in agreement in reflecting dominant promotional or persuasive interests and rather clear rejecting attitudes toward scientific and mechanical activities. However, the Strong also indicates another area of primary interest in the welfare field which, in the Kuder, is only a secondary interest. The outstanding positive valence shown on the Allport-Vernon is in the esthetic sphere which is reflected in the Kuder Musical scale but not in the artistic one. The "feminine" inclinations indicated in the MMPI are consistent with the Allport-Vernon and Kuder results. Other than this there are no clear trends. Although there are little data to support or reject this interpretation, many experienced users of the MMPI report that low scores on a number of the scales are significant. In this case, the low psychopathic deviate and paranoid scales might be interpreted to suggest conforming tendencies and a readiness for a naive, uncritical acceptance of others. The slightly elevated K score would lead one to move a number of the below-average scores closer to the average.

Now comes the discussion of these data in the counseling interview.

C 24. These things that we're talking about here are all ideas about yourself that are pretty well supported by the tests that you took. That is, you were consistent in that sense that the things we're talking about here also showed on the tests and that you seemed to have quite a lot of reaction to the whole idea of having contact with people.

S 25. Uh-huh.

C 25. Of having influence or putting on some kind of a— (S: show) Well, I don't want to say a demonstration or a show either, but at least it adds up to putting something across.

S 26. Uh-hum.

C 26. I think that's the main idea.

S 27. Uh-hum.

C 27. That seems to be one of the most important pictures of yourself that seems to come out from these tests that you took. Does that help you feel more sure that—

S 28. Well, I'm positive of that.

C 28. Uh-hum. There isn't—wasn't any doubt in your mind.

S 29. No.

C 29. Uh-hum.

S 30. But there is just about the end of my own picture of myself.

C 30. I guess you're saying that really isn't definite enough—that you want something of which you can be (S: yes, [*with little laugh*] sure.)

S 31. If there is any possibility of getting something like that.

C 31. (*short pause*) Well, perhaps it would be of some value if, instead of unraveling the thing in such a general way, that we try looking at it more specifically and see what we can come across. A little while ago you suggested that I begin at the beginning but I've never been able to figure out where the beginning is. (S: oh. I see) I just wander along into it. This measure here gives some indication of your feelings about yourself in relation to different kinds of activity—as what you prefer to do and what you prefer not to do, that kind of thing. For instance it suggests that you have a very strong negative feeling towards anything along mechanical lines. Is that?

S 32. Uh-hum.

C 32. So that pretty much excludes a number of occupations. For instance dentistry (S: uh-hum) might be excluded on that basis since there is quite a lot of mechanical work involved there. But I guess you never included that as a possibility anyway.

S 33. No.

C 33. It might conceivably apply to medicine too but more indirectly. There is an awful lot of laboratory work involved in a medical training program. That might be something to (S: uh-hum) stop and think about.

S 34. I was hoping to go into psychiatry when I got through Med. School.

C 34. That still would include the necessity of going—

S 35. Going through it.

C 35. —training and this indicates that it might be something pretty unpleasant.

S 36. Uh-hum.

C 36. Not for sure, but just points. That's a question that you have to answer, (S: uh-huh) whether you want to put up with that much practical work, lab. work.

S 37. Well, it's funny. I have a funny attitude about that now. I don't mind working in a laboratory or something like that. But when it gets out to making something, I don't want to do it unless it's something that I actually want myself. I mean, if I'm working on a photographic project or something and I want a gadget, I'll go ahead and try to make it. I can't make it very well. But I'll make it. I'll enjoy making it. If I have to make something for somebody else, I wouldn't enjoy it at all.

C 37. You sort of use it as a way of—

S 38. A means to an end.

C 38. Uh-hum. Well, I guess there's no point making too big an issue as you seem to understand the idea. You don't seem to have any—well, you—it's kind of a mild feeling of liking for dealing with numbers. Apparently you don't have any great ambitions along those lines but you also don't seem to mind computing or working with figures.

S 39. Uh-hum.

C 39. That kind of thing I think we talked about that last time. Didn't we?

S 40. Uh-huh.

C 40. I've already mentioned one here that seems to stand out as the strongest feeling about yourself as somebody who is a persuader, somebody who influences other people. (S: uh-hum) That kind of preference seems to be the strongest with you, that you like to make an impression. (*pause*) The other one point that seems to indicate some preference is a musical one, that hasn't fitted in with anything except perhaps just for fun.

S 41. Uh-huh.

C 41. But at least you seem to think of yourself as a person who likes music and enjoys it, maybe knows something about it. I don't know about that last part. At least you have a positive feeling about music is the most this can tell. (*pause*) You also seem to have some positive reactions to the idea of being in sort of a helping position, a welfare role or having some concern for—for helping other people, doing some good for other people. Does that fit in at all or—

S 42. Well, it depends. It's very hard for me to analyze that. Because I want to help some people and yet there are other people I don't want to help. I don't know. It's very peculiar. I think what it actually amounts to is that if I get into contact with somebody that needs help I want to help them. People I don't know about and the general class. I don't want to help.

C 42. Uh-huh.

S 43. I don't know where it comes about. It just seems to be that way.

C 43. You mean it's sort of a limited conception of yourself as a helping person. (S: uh-hum) It's not so much a feeling of wanting to help humanity as if wanting to help specific—

S 44. Individual people.

C 44. Uh-huh. But at least we can say that you don't want to think of yourself as a person who doesn't care about anybody. That is an issue with you.

S 45. Uh-hum.

C 45. Apparently though you might like to help somebody. (*pause*) This scale here is one that gives some indication of how your patterns of interests are similar to those of people who are already doing different kinds of jobs. And I've already presented generally the ideas, the same ones, that you seem to be the kind of person who is like men who are doing promoting kinds of work. In this particular test, it seems to come out as a combina- tion between people who do promoting types of work along business lines and people who do personal contact work along welfare lines. Do those (S: uh-hum) two ideas fit together? It seems as if they still are describing you as the same kind of per- son we were talking about all along.

S 46. Do they have individual professions running down this column?

C 46. Well, it just has the names of the ones that they use as (S: I see) a criterion, but they don't mean anything specifically.

S 47. I see what you mean.

C 47. We think of them more as groups rather than individuals.

S 48. Uh-hum.

C 48. It doesn't seem to indicate that there's much similarity between your patterns of interests and those of people who are success- ful doctors or who have taken any kind of training along the specific professional group of that kind. That particular kind of profession—at the present time you don't seem to be like those people. (*pause*) There seems to be some similarity between your patterns and those of people who are in intellectual work, something more like lawyers and writers, that (S: uh-hum) kind of dealing with words. I'm inclined to feel that perhaps some of the work of a minister fits into that area too, as well as the field of law. (*pause*) That to me seems to be saying the same thing we've been saying right along.

S 49. Yes.

C 49. Does this make you think of anything?

S 50. Well, no. It doesn't make me think of anything. It just makes me feel a little bit, oh, not very much more certain but I'm pretty well decided I want to limit to those three, but it—there was always the possibility at the back of my mind for teaching but (*sounding doubtful*) I don't know.

C 50. Well, that would still—

S 51. Still, it would be all contained within the same group. I want to find out how to isolate that group.

C 51. You seem to be having a little difficulty really deciding for yourself which one. (S: uh-hum) As if you kind of would like some outside—

S 52. (*breaking in*) I'd like to have two jobs. Yeah, sort of, I'd like to have outside pressure and also I'd like to have two. I'd like to have—be trained for two jobs. (*lower*) It's kind of foolish but I would like to be trained that way.

C 52. Would you care to say more about what it is that makes you want to do that?

S 53. Well, I don't know. I'd like to do two things. That sounds rather ridiculous, but I've always had the idea in back of my head to run a restaurant. I've always had little projects of trying to make money out of something, and they've always more or less failed, but I've enjoyed doing them, and I was at one time thinking of teaching and then trying to run a restaurant too. But I always like to be dabbling in something different. That's why I'd sort of like the ministry because I would be—I wouldn't be able to have a private business or anything, but I would always be able to start some new project in the church or starting some new project somewhere. Usually you can have—ministers have notorious kinds of gardens that they can putter around with, things like that. I'd have a chance to, well, I'd have a chance in my opinion to get some of my music worked out. I'd get an access to an organ. I'd like to take organ lessons. I don't know. Maybe I'm basing my opinions on just one particular minister. I don't know. But he seems to have enough time to do those things that I'd like to do. He can, if he wanted to, take organ lessons. But he doesn't particularly care about that. But he has enough time to read. He has organized a book club within his church and he does a lot of reading for himself. He has organized a book club. He has organized a lot of other things for the church. He sponsored a lot of clubs. He's active on the Labor-Citizen's Committee which is supposed to settle labor disputes in the home town and he gets time to do a lot of different things. And that's what I'd like to do. I always want to do a lit of different things. I don't want to be confined just to one little narrow field where I can operate. I want something new and different coming up all the time. I sort of like to organize things, get them started, and pull out and let somebody else take over.

C 53. There isn't anything still that changes the picture. (S: no) it's almost as if we still have this picture of you as a person who likes to promote things, who likes to have a variety of things going on, who likes to contact people, make things run, things of that sort. It seems almost as if it's pretty much up to you what particular area that you decide to do it in. The—the business area is indicated here. The intellectual area is indicated. That would include the ministry, and that would also include this helping kind of thing, promoting for the benefit of others. Starting a book club is an example. I think there may be some questions about the field of law. That is, it tends to suggest that it might become pretty busy in one kind of thing, but that would be a matter of individual planning. That is, it's still a pretty confining and demanding profession. It would be contrary to this (S: uh-huh) minister who has time to putter. It's more a matter of the size of church and things of that sort that you got into. Does that seem like a—

S 54. Uh-hum.

C 54. —realistic consideration? There's also the matter of the training. That is, the training for a lawyer is a tough grind for several years, whereas the training either as a business type of promoter or a minister—a religious type of promoter or even a teacher includes a kind of liberal education, allowing changes for (S: uh-huh) extracurricular activities and side interests (*short pause*). I'm doing a lot of talking. Maybe you have some—

S 55. No.

C 55. —reflections on all this?

S 56. I can't dig anything out.

C 56. You understand of course that most of this during the last few minutes has been speculative (S: uh-hum) stuff. We really can't get much more definite with the tests than this general picture of you will keep coming back to you.

S 57. Uh-hum. (*pause*)

From this illustration we can see how the counselor brings in test results as they are relevant to the discussion and involves the client in trying to assimilate those results. Notice how various interpretations of the test results are punctuated by discussions. The counselor encourages these discussions with comments such as the one at the end of C 41. It seems also that Mr. Ril resists the counselor's interpretations in C 48 that the test results are not so favorable to medicine. Notice that in S 50 he reaffirms by implication his interest in medicine, even though he also begins to think in a somewhat different direction. There may be some question here about the appropriateness of the counselor's apparent sloughing off of the incompatibility of the choice of medicine with the results of the two interest tests. Except for the one statement alluded to, he keeps talking as though the results of the test are pretty consistent with the client's thoughts about himself.

In the discussion that follows this section of the interview, Mr. Ril goes on to indicate that there is some home pressure to go into law and that with regard to medicine, he would be primarily interested in psychiatry. Then he reveals that his father is a psychiatrist. He has wanted to be a lawyer for a good many years, whereas the idea of psychiatry is of relatively recent origin. The counselor and the client go on to discuss the fact that among the ministry, teaching, and law it isn't absolutely necessary to make a specific choice at this point, since all three curricula are rather broad in the first two years, whereas medicine does require a much more restricted curriculum. In the process of this discussion Mr. Ril decides that the restrictive nature of the premedical curriculum makes it a less desirable choice. This seems to give him considerable relief.

There still remain a number of unanswered questions. In the first interview we saw intimations of passive resistance to authority figures. One might speculate that the femininity shown in the MMPI and the overconformity and naiveté were also reflections of passive relations to others. At the same time, we also note that his occupational choice may reflect identification problems. Law, his earlier choice, seems far removed from his father's profession of psychiatry. On the other hand, his later interest in the ministry has considerable potential overlap with psychiatry, but seems to carry the flavor of the substitution of an alternative compensatory identification for a longed-for but blocked identification with his father.

While the information available in the above illustrations did not make possible any definitive statements about outcomes, the excerpts did provide representative illustrations of interpreting interest and personality instruments.

Having discussed the process of forming a counseling relationship and the special problems associated with the use of psychological tests, we will turn our attention in the next two chapters to the kinds of issues that arise in the course of the relationship. We will consider in the second of these two chapters the general patterns of the relationship which adapt it to the developmental aims of counseling and the intention to offer a more time-limited service.

CHAPTER 13

The Process of Counseling: General Problems

In the foregoing chapters of this section we have considered certain problems that are inevitable concomitants of counseling. Questions of getting the process under way and of the use of tests will arise no matter whether counseling is brief or of long duration. These questions come up whether counseling stays close to one specific, concrete problem or ranges far into many aspects of the client's life history and current relationships. In this chapter we shall consider for the most part some of the features of extended relationships. In our terminology, extended relationships are those that go beyond three or four contacts, those that open up a broad area for discussion, including many problems usually considered in the practice of psychotherapy. Our aim will be to select those issues which appear to have special relevance to the task of the psychological counselor.

LIMITING COUNSELING RELATIONSHIPS

The adoption of a dynamic theory of personality in counseling carries with it the danger of some distortion of counseling functions. The role of the counselor has been differentiated from that of the psychiatrist and psychotherapist on the basis that he is concerned with contributing to the fuller emotional development of persons in general, rather than working with more extremely maladjusted individuals who are subject to incapacitating emotional difficulties. To achieve this broad coverage, the psychological counselor must concentrate on relatively brief relationships with large numbers of people rather than intensive relationships with a few.

Both economic and theoretical grounds support the conclusions that counseling processes can and should be brief. It is self-evident that society is neither willing nor able for economic reasons to devote more than a limited amount of its resources to this one kind of social service. A college or university might be willing to allot funds sufficient to make it possible for 20 per cent of its student body to receive an average of four or five counseling contacts in any given year. This would indeed be a generous allotment, and a sufficient budget would be found in only a minority of colleges and universities. It is unlikely that counseling services will expand far beyond this level of operation. Eight to ten contacts for the same proportion of students would probably be unrealistic and bring the budget for counseling staff into critical competition with that for teaching and, in some institutions, research also. It seems unlikely that colleges or society in general will conclude that mental health services are so vital that other types of services must be sacrificed to them. Mental health practitioners themselves would hardly be willing to argue that they should be.

Even if sufficient economic resources were available, it still can be argued that it is unnecessary to get the kinds of people who will make up the bulk of the counselor's clients involved in a more extended process. When counseling services reach the intended segment of the population, the typical client will be a person who has achieved considerable emotional maturity. He will be a person who has some capacity to deal with anxiety and he possesses many resources for achieving satisfaction. Under those circumstances, whatever problem situation brings him to the counselor is likely to have more limited ramifications than would be the case when a person is considerably less mature. The pressures on the individual who is seeking counseling are sufficient to support only a relatively limited effort on his part. If it comes about that special satisfactions in the relationship convert it into an end in itself, he may continue in it over a much longer period, though progress will have ceased a long time ago. Quite definitely, we are assuming that a relatively-well-integrated person can make use of a brief counseling experience to set in motion a learning process that carries far beyond the relationship itself. His high level of integration insures that he has demonstrated considerable capacity to develop and change in the normal course of living. If counseling helps to remove some immediate obstacles to further development, then the process of learning and modification can be expected to continue with renewed vigor. With the right clients, then, it is feasible for the counselor to depend on a brief experience having an effect far beyond its duration.

THE PRESSURES TOWARD EXTENDED RELATIONSHIPS

The duration of a counseling relationship is necessarily a function of both client and counselor. As long as a client retains confidence in the counselor, his continued anxiety or feeling that he has not yet achieved closure on the problem that brought him to counseling serves as a realistic stimulus for wanting to continue. However, and not infrequently, the client's pressure for continuation may reflect his residual regressive desires to retain the relationship as a specific source of gratification, rather than as an instrument for dealing with his problem. Sometimes this transformation of the counseling relationship from a means to an end has been inadvertently fostered and encouraged by the counselor, when because of his own needs he substitutes gratifications derived from the counseling relationship for those he might otherwise obtain through his personal life.

Counselors and psychotherapists who have dynamically oriented views of personality may take satisfaction in their own work and find an enhancement of their feeling of professional worth through their sense of having appreciably influenced their client's personality structure and development. They gain assurance that they have achieved their goal by establishing an intense counseling relationship in which the client has confided a great deal and has expressed deep feelings which are of central significance for his behavior. In short, there are certain pressures on the counselor also to measure his accomplishments in the terms used by the intensive psychotherapist.

Pressure toward intense counseling relationships may arise also from the set that the counselor develops in helping clients seek personality goals in counseling. Since the typical counseling client comes to talk about a very specific problem situation, he comes with a relatively limited personal commitment to the counselor. But because the counselor wants most to help the client at a psychological rather than an informational level, the counselor learns ways of interacting with people which encourage them to look at themselves. We have discussed many of these ways in the preceding chapters. Eventually the counselor develops skills in interpersonal relationships which help to foster feelings of trust and confidence in him. He evolves definitions of the therapeutic task which draw the client into a closer relationship and focus his attention on his own personality and learns how to help the client overcome his own resistances to this task. The uncontrolled utilization of these skills is bound to lead to intense and extended relationships whether or not these relationships are appropriate to the particular goals of counseling.

FACTORS CONTRIBUTING TO CONTROL

It is clear that to retain his functions distinct from those of the more intensive psychotherapist, the counselor must study methods of controlling the duration and the intensity of counseling relationships. This is a realm of therapeutic practice in which our knowledge is especially meager and where principles must of necessity be tentatively stated.

Keeping to the reality problem

As we have pointed out, psychological counseling usually involves a shift of the locus and definition of a problem from some specific decision or situation to the personality of the client. However, the personality of any individual has unfathomable depth, so that if it is not further delimited, the goal of achieving complete understanding of a personality postulates an endless task. It is in keeping with the restricted goals of counseling to attempt to establish a much more limited conception of the task. What this implies is that the counselor should react in such a way as to facilitate the client's coming to terms with the many wishes and fears that are brought to bear on a specific problem situation. His personality is dealt with only as it bears on the decision or problem situation and the client is not encouraged to go much farther afield. Naturally, the more intense the conflict, the more widespread its ramifications through the personality, and the less the likelihood that the problem situation can be resolved through only a restricted excursion into the client's motivations and feelings.

This process of staying close to the external problem will apply to the many transitional difficulties and decisions that occur during the life span. In our own experience which concentrates on adolescents, attention necessarily focuses on the area of vocational decision. Expanded understanding of vocational choice requires extensive discussion of the counseling of clients with vocational problems which will be presented in the next chapter. As a briefer example solely illustrative of narrowly focused counseling, we present the following résumé of a two-interview relationship with a college student.

The intake interview with this man was one of the most fascinating I have ever had. He is a neat, compact, boyish looking junior of 19, who is in the business administration school and definitely does not like it. He plans to go into his father's business, which I believe is a machine shop. He does not want to handle the financial end of the business, expecting to hire someone to handle that part of the work. In short, he wishes to do management engineering, so we talked about Harvard Business School's sort of training, and about the client's wish to take a program where he would register in courses like psychology of management, but not go through the regular business-administration curriculum which requires so much study of finance and accounting. He would really love to major in history, but his father objects to this. His father complains that his son is bucking him. He also must take three hours of naval ROTC in each of his remaining four semesters, since he wants to shift out of his former military program. He wants to study navigation so his years in the navy will be in that field rather than in supply, which he has found rather dull.

I picked up the talk about the father and he mentioned that his father had wanted him to go into medicine, but just cutting up animals he had shot while hunting had convinced him he didn't like that. An alternative to the father's business is a job he has been offered if he finishes law school. I talked very rationally with this man, noticing definite tendencies to isolate and extreme nervousness in the beginning. We decided on some tests. But having already gotten somewhat developed in this direction, the topic broadened to include his difficulties in studying and his anger at himself. He slapped at himself several times and at the desk. He showed an amazing number of insights which he seemed to have arrived at during the hour with the aid of some restatement, reflection, and a slight amount of interpretation, such as my pointing out that he didn't really know whether he himself wanted to study until he didn't have to after he got out of high school. Another one was that he doesn't know whether he himself wants to go with girls because he has always been forced in this direction by social pressures from boy friends.

What is not recorded in the counselor's summary of the first interview is his judgment that in spite of his conflicts about dependence-independence, the client is a relatively mature and well-integrated person. Notice that the discussions in the interview keep pretty well oriented toward the decision which is to be made, even though the client is encouraged to deal with its emotional aspects. One indication of his emotional maturity is his capacity to move to relatively intense and yet controlled emotional expression without any special help in unbinding these emotions. From this observation one would assume that he is neither very frightened of his emotions and impulses and need not expend great effort to keep them from awareness and expression, nor is he so poorly organized that emotional expression will run away with him. With a client of this sort it is neither necessary to go through a long process of free associative or semi-associative communication to help him reach the stage of bringing his feelings rather fully into his communications, nor is it necessary to foster the vivid projection of his feelings and attitudes upon the counselor as is the case in transference and transference interpretation. True, there are many aspects of this client's feelings which get bypassed without such processes. But the measure of the effectiveness of our counseling is not how thoroughly or how completely the client's feelings and emotions have been brought into the counseling relationship, but how much flexibility, increased integration of feelings, and better ability to handle life situations for his own satisfaction and productivity have been achieved.

The second interview, coming a little over a week later, suggests that some movement in this direction has already occurred. The counselor's notes follow:

He described a series of changes he had made in his life since our first interview. He did this, however, only after talking about the tests and discussing their implications with me. He said that the tests of interest came out as he expected. He then described having discussed with the fraternity president going on inactive status and moving out but he did this only after he had "on an impulse" gone into a place which advertised rooms and "on an impulse" chosen a room. He then moved out of the fraternity. He now feels this was definitely the right thing to do as a trial. He told the fraternity people that if he found that it was not the study conditions that made the difference but his own attitude toward studies then he would move back into the fraternity knowing that he could study there too. It was my impression that he felt as confident as he said he was that he would now be able probably to handle the study situation so as to get the kind of grades he wants and is capable of. He had a long talk with an accounting instructor whom he admires because he is quiet and intelligent and so on (I think this was a description of his perception of me also) and decided to leave accounting and business administration after this semester and transfer into the Literary College. Despite the fact that his father prefers that he go into medicine or dentistry or accounting, he told his father of his plans for a change and the father at one point, after expressing his own preferences, veered in the direction of insisting that his son should make up his own mind. His father added he knew he would do the latter, being a stubborn "Swede" like himself. To his surprise, his mother was the one who seemed more doubtful about his making up his own mind.

He arranged to have an academic counselor in the Literary College in history and is planning to major in history because he knows this is what he likes. He also is going to look into the possibility of teaching as a career. Though his father seems to feel he would make more money in medicine, he himself sees that his father's business, which he can enter, could be built up so he could make much more money in that; so his most clearly formulated alternative is to go into this production management kind of job. He is not settled whether he will transfer out of naval supply because he feels an obligation to the supply training officer and a switch into navigation would be awkward. But he is much calmer and less worried about this minor decision since he has these other things temporarily settled. At the end, he described beautifully what has happened as he saw it, namely, that he had been very confused and in doubt and had come in and had needed to talk about it so that he himself could see it all more clearly. This he has done and as a result he now feels much more settled. He is proud of his decisions to come in, to choose a new counselor and to leave the fraternity room, thus achieving a degree of financial independence. His effectiveness while discussing his decisions with his father and the fraternity president is a source of new confidence in himself. He praised our kind of service. I think this man still has dependent needs but he is now really testing out which are his own wishes and which are responses to others' wishes.

In the record of this interview we seem to have three kinds of evidence of progress. First, we have the client's reports of his own attitudes, indicating a considerable shift in his feelings of well-being, adequacy, and confidence in the future. A second line of evidence is the counselor's observation of changes in the client's behavior which accrue with the attitudes that he is expressing verbally. The final source of evidence is his report of the concrete steps he has taken. If we are to believe his report, he apparently was able to react both to the fraternity president and to his father in a much more mature way. He was able to maintain the integrity of his own desires without having to break his relationship with the other persons involved.

Selecting a critical facet of the conflict

Often clients come to counselors with no very completely focalized concrete problem or sense of needing to decide something. Sometimes their conflicts are of a more intense and long standing sort and are so diffused in effect that it is not very easy to initiate the therapeutic process by centering on one particular decision or problem situation. The client's view of his problems does not provide a basis for keeping discussion centered on some external view of his situation. Under these circumstances, the counselor faces the task which most nearly approximates that faced by the psychotherapist. In such a case, one rule of thumb for staying within the more modest aims of counseling is to select certain critical aspects of the inner conflict to be worked through. By centering attention on a particular aspect of the client's inner life, the counselor limits the probable duration of their relationship. The counselor does this by selective responsiveness and by helping the client to establish greater intellectual control over other conflicting impulses.

The process of centering on one aspect of the client's motivations is not one that can be carried out mechanically and inflexibly. The counselor feels his way, testing out what can work for a particular client. At one point he may have to encourage an expression of feeling and a certain amount of working on areas of feeling other than the selected one. He will also have to modify from time to time his conception of the appropriate area. The process is guided by a general orientation rather than a rigidly applied mode of action.

The following set of five interviews can serve as an approximate illustration of a process in which the counselor focuses on one set of conflicting feelings. In this instance, we happen also to have another illustration of the preceding type of control where the counselor has also focused on the making of a decision. Again we will rely upon the counselor's notes.

First Interview

The client was interested in knowing more about the kinds of work she would like to do and stated that she did not have a clear idea as to what this might be. She described her high-school experience as being very pleasant and expressed some concern about not knowing her rank in her high-school graduating class in which there were 157 members. However, she estimated that she probably fell in the upper quarter. She mentioned the fact that she was accelerated in the 12th grade, combining 12-B and 12-A, and graduated last February. She enjoyed extracurricular activities and expressed a particular dislike of science and mathematics. She said that she took them only because one was supposed to if one wanted to go to college. Evidently, when she graduated from high school, she was quite uncertain about what course of action she should take. She felt that her parents laid down the law in telling her that she would herself have to pick out a school and decide what to do afterward. She said that although her whole life has been built up around going to college, her parents evidently felt that she might not go to college just then.

She spent a couple of months in Florida after graduation from high school and returned home in April and worked through July in an office. The outstanding feature of these experiences seems to have been meeting people. She talked particularly about the possibility of doing switchboard or secretarial work. She expressed considerable concern about Ohio being too large a school and expressed the feeling that the buildings were so large that they looked as though they might swallow one up.

Fear of reciting in class was something that evidently had concerned her for a good deal of time and she felt that it tended to lower her grades to some extent in high school. She expressed concern over the fact that a number of other students in the class were probably superior to her and that maybe when she said something it would make her feel inferior. She then talked about the fact that this feeling about being concerned about her ability and feeling inferior had been of long standing. However, she localized it solely in the school situation.

Business had occurred to her as a possibility, since her father and her two brothers were in business but this did not particularly appeal to her. She talked about her choice of Ohio in terms of its being a large school in a trio of schools where she had applied. She described the three as a small school, a middle-sized school, and a large school. She felt that she might not be in Ohio too long because it was too impersonal and that she never got to feel close to anything. However, she then began to point out that the students were swell and that she had settled down and was able to study now but felt that she just wasn't the kind of person who should go to so large a school.

In talking about her feelings up to the present time, she stated that she liked to work with people but probably not entirely with people and said that her work probably should involve things too. She has done considerable thinking about designing and interior decorating but has not been too interested in following this because it required a long training program. In selecting the tests, she felt that the general ability test would help her in knowing more about her concern over how she compared with other people and was particularly interested in the interest and personality measures.

Second Interview (9 days later)

The client was able to estimate quite accurately her test results and felt that they were what she had known but that she wanted some added confirmation of her belief that she was really pretty good in a number of things. She stated clearly that support was very important for her at this particular point. She felt that she had been talking to professors, academic counselors, housemothers, and girls in the dorm, but that this had not been helpful because they really could not understand what she was going through. When I commented that she was probably feeling some tension, she used the example of the Purdue

Pegboard where she felt her performance was lower because of the amount of tension she was experiencing.

She is going home for the Thanksgiving recess and is going to discuss the matter with her parents. She feels that she is getting poor grades, and although she tries she is not able to do very well. She expressed considerable hostile feeling toward her parents, since she said they continually tell her that she has to do well but that they really do not understand her. She then talked about her brother who dropped out of school and went into their father's business and spoke of this in a disparaging way and she had the feeling that he gave up the fight, that he had given in. She said that she had been very curious just as to why two children with the same common background, mother and father, had resulted in two different kinds of personalities. I commented that maybe this might be some of the reasons why she was experiencing some confusion at the present time. She immediately responded to this and there was a sudden gush of conversation on her part. She expressed the feeling that she had never been able to talk about these things with another person who did not try to impose upon her some of his own feelings. In the hope of giving her some support for her visit home, I commented that sometimes parents have the tendency to put their own goals in a child's life although they aren't aware of this and are doing it for what they think is the child's own good. She felt that this was exactly what had happened in her case and wanted to arrange to see me as soon as possible.

Third Interview (10 days later)

The client talked a great deal about the confusion she was experiencing at the present time, part of which seemed to revolve around whether she should stay in school or not. She gained considerable satisfaction from the job she had last year and felt that it did not require a college degree and wondered if this might not be one type of solution. When I asked about any discussions she had had with her parents over the Thanksgiving recess she said that they want her to stay in school, particularly her father. Since her vacation at home, he has evidently telephoned her and asked her if she likes it any better. She stated that she got a big bang out of his call and there certainly was the indication that she enjoys seeing him upset. In talking about her school work proper, she felt that in the classroom it was very hard for her to express herself or even defend any point of view, even though she might know the answer or feel that she was right, because of the presence of some person who was evaluating her in some sense. She felt on the spot, both in oral recitations and examinations. In informal social groups she feels that she is able to express and defend herself quite easily and with no hesitation. She remembered that a family-relations class in high school was a situation in which she felt much at ease and was not afraid to express herself. In this particular situation she felt that the teacher was one of the girls because of her age and also felt there was a real lack of intellectual competition. In defining what she thought was a superior person, she realized that there was no real difference between these people in each group, but that is one group she feared them and in the informal group she did not. She talked considerably about her father, who appears to be a person who stresses individualistic thinking and not being pushed around by anyone. Although she admires and almost idealizes this philosophy, she is unable to carry it out in a situation where there is an authoritarian figure and where she is surrounded by her contemporaries. This latter point became apparent when she said that she felt that if she had a tutor she could get along all right because in class if you make a mistake the other students all laugh or make a remark. As a result, in classroom performance she feels that she has to produce at an all-or-nothing level.

She talked about herself as being more like her younger than her older brother who has gone back into business with their father. There was a very definite indication of a fear of rivalry situations with sibling substitutes in any large classroom situation where there is evaluation by an authoritarian figure. She realizes quite well that changing a school will not help the situation and that it is something that evidently resides within herself. I commented that we talked in our last session about her strivings to be independent and maybe she operated in a different way than her brothers in reacting to the original family situation. There certainly seemed to be a real will on her part to do something on her own. She felt that this was exactly it but expressed some concern about making a move and afterward being sorry for it. I suggested that maybe the thing that she felt was important was that she get some support or someone who might approve of her action just as she wanted others to regard her intellectual ability highly. She had realized that she had good intellectual ability, but wanted someone to confirm this fact for her. She readily stated that she felt that was what she needed because many people had been telling her so many things and not really understanding how she felt.

Fourth Interview (one week later)

The client told me she had visited a mental hygienist at the Student Health Service and had been told it was unnecessary to consult another place. She had also talked with her academic counselor who had evidently talked a good deal to her about going to a vocational school and had told her that it would be necessary for her to make a choice now since the time was getting late for deciding on a career. She talked about the possibilities of Antioch College, and Fenn College in Cleveland. I commented that it seemed she had made a decision as to what she was going to do. At this point she felt that she had, and said that after she talked with people who knew a good bit about it, she always felt that was what she wanted to do, but when she went home she began to waver a bit. I commented that it seemed where some authority told her what to do she temporarily wanted to do it, but then sooner or later wanted to do something on her own. I pointed out that this seems to be the situation in classroom discussions also. She saw this as indicating again her wish to be independent. When I asked her what her parents' reactions might be, she commented that she had called her parents last Sunday and that her mother refused to say anything about the situation, but her father said that if he had the information from schools and so on, he would be willing at least to talk about it with her. She felt that going to college meant a good deal to her parents, particularly since her older brother, Bill, did not finish college. She said that now if she stopped it would be up to her younger brother to finish, to do what the two older children had not done. She expressed the feeling that she would feel guilty if she had to talk and talk and talk to get her parents to see that she needed to transfer to another school, but did not indicate that this would change her decision.

She evidently has thought considerably about marriage and in fact thought about it in lieu of college. I pointed out that this could certainly be a practical goal for a woman. At this point the client became quite vehement in talking about the fact that so many women got out of the home and went into a job. It is rather apparent that she talks considerably about her father and makes identifications with me, and therefore appears to be seeking a very dependent role in the relationship with male figures, although at the same time she feels a need to be independent. For her the one positive feature of the situation here at Ohio is the personal relationships she enjoys with the girls in the dormitory and which she says is almost a substitute for home. At the end of the interview she expressed the feeling that she was much clearer in her thinking since she had had the opportunity of coming in and talking and I suggested that there really was a pull toward Ohio as well as away from it. The pull in terms of the personal relationships and the push away from it in terms of the lack of a concrete goal toward which she would strive. She felt this was the crux of the situation, and that she had not made a decision and was wavering.

Fifth Interview (one month later)

The client expressed some concern as to whether she had understood about coming back to see me. She revealed an attitude of ambivalence and felt that it had made her understand that she would come back toward the end of the semester at which time we could both evaluate how the situation was going. In response to my comment that things had evidently been going pretty well since she had not felt it necessary to come, the client felt that the reason that she did come was to tell me how well things were going. It had been decided at home over the Christmas vacation that she would finish the entire year and that this summer she and her family might look into the possibilities of another school. As she described the conversation with her parents it seemed that the father was quite understanding and willing to give her a chance to think through the situation for herself. She commented on the fact that she recognized the change in herself after vacation and felt that one of the indicators of this was the fact that dorm life was no longer the totality of campus life for her. She commented upon the fact that it was always a problem as to whether she was to have a single room or a double room but now it didn't seem to matter because after all she felt she was in school to learn something. She expressed some guilt about the fact that she anticipated having rather poor grades this semester and felt that this was part of the general process of not understanding herself and not knowing what she wanted to do. She felt that she had probably worked too hard getting grades instead of gaining the knowledge and interest that her courses have to offer. When I encouraged her to talk more about the influence that the Christmas break had upon her feelings, the client expressed the feeling that she had found her father more understanding than she had anticipated. She then commented upon the fact that her coming here and talking with me before Christmas helped her a good deal. I commented that she seemed to have been going to a number of different sources for help and wondered what this meant to her. She felt that she was needing some sort of authority to tell her what to do but that this had not happened here but rather she had been given support and mentioned specifically the fact that her abilities were that of a college student. She expressed some hostility in talking about the academic counselor to whom she had gone who suggested to her that she go to a vocational school. She commented that this had shocked her into realizing that this wasn't what she wanted from him and that really she was getting support in a different kind of way from her interviews here. I commented upon her relaxed expression and manner during this session and she felt that this was something that was characteristic of her now and that she didn't feel as upset and on edge as she had before. I commented upon the fact of her calling in to have another interview and she felt that it really was just an opportunity for her to tell me how much she appreciated the help I had given her and to report that things were going well.

As the session was ending she commented that she was pretty optimistic about the next semester but that if she had difficulty she would get in touch with me.

Throughout this series of meetings, the counselor has tended to concentrate his responses around the client's feelings about asserting herself and about receiving help from others. It appears that the counselor correctly perceived her ambivalent feelings about receiving help and advice from others as an important conflict area. While continuing to encourage her to interact around these various decisions, he quite carefully refrained from taking a position on them himself. A measure of the client's progress in this regard would be the contrast of her action prior to coming to college and her decision at the end of this series of counseling interviews. Before coming to college she had opposed her parents by leaving home and taking a relatively routine job. However, she gave up this momentary revolt and came to college; but her oppositional feelings come to the fore once more in the thoughts of leaving college.

At the end of the counseling series, she seems to have been able to separate the issue of asserting herself from that of leaving college. Consequently, she is able to deal with the issue of leaving in a much more independent way, because her desire for independence does not force her to go against others' apparent desires that she remain in college. Thus, she is able to make the decision to continue through the end of the year without now feeling that this decision represents giving in to pressures from her parents and losing her independence.

Giving more cognitive emphasis to interactions

If the counselor is to keep a relationship limited, it is necessary for him to avoid fostering a vague and ambiguous conception of the trend of the relationship and its accompanying discussions. In intensive psychotherapy there is relatively less need to be concerned with this. A patient approaches each interview without any very specific task except to talk about whatever comes to his mind or whatever has been troubling him since the last interview. At the end of the hour he may not see much relevance to his problem in what has occurred. We suggest that by giving more direction and a clearer shape to the client's interactions with him, the counselor can limit the relationship. This is not direction in the sense in which Rogers has used it, where the expected outcome is increased dependence. Actually the expected outcome is the direct opposite. By giving the client more perspective, one encourages him to be more responsible for the direction the process takes. Where he is vague about what is going on, the client must of necessity depend on the counselor to judge which way lies progress. One way to foster greater activity is to call attention through summarizing responses toward the end of each hour to the direction the interactions have taken and to discuss possible new directions that succeeding hours might move in.

Another way to foster active, purposive effort is by controlling the level of intensity and complexity of feeling at which the client works. As was suggested in Chapter 7, this is best brought about by encouraging rational analysis at the expense of free-floating communication. This, however, is a matter on which there are strongly divergent opinions. There are those who feel that the inevitable outcome of such action on the part of the counselor would be simply to reinforce and increase the client's neurotic efforts to dam up his feelings and desires. The danger of this outcome should not be minimized. It means that careful attention must be given at every moment to the degree to which the affect expressed is appropriate to the content of the client's discussion. Indications of inappropriate affect, for example, where the client becomes angry at a time when he is discussing something which hardly seems adequate to create this amount of feeling, or seems unusually calm and detached when discussing something of great emotional significance, suggest that the cognitive processes are not moving in the direction of greater integration. This should serve as a warning that the effort to encourage more rational control is misfiring.

THE OPENING OF HOURS

The start of the counseling hour is likely to present a special problem to the inexperienced counselor as indeed it does to the inexperienced psychotherapist. This period is not only a problem, however; it also has considerable significance.

The counselor must always keep in mind the therapeutic orientation of his relationship with a specific client in handling the initiating of an hour. Some of his clients will have accepted therapy as a goal. With these clients, the social interchange in the greeting phase of the meeting will be minimized, at least so far as the counselor is concerned. In essence, he will be reacting to the greeting phase, especially if there is any effort to extend it, as he reacts to all of the behavior of the client, that is, trying to observe and to understand the meaning of what is happening with regard to the specific therapeutic needs of the client and to respond to these needs. Therefore, his dominant set at the beginning of any hour will be an alert attempt to understand the first communications of his client. On the other hand, with the large numbers of his clients who have not yet or never will arrive at a definite therapeutic orientation, it may be necessary and appropriate to conform a little more to the conventional social phases of a greeting. Even here, however, the counselor will neither initiate nor encourage this type of interaction. To some extent he will react in a manner to differentiate their relationship from a social situation. He will be showing that socially instituted greeting forms are not considered necessary by him even though he may remain tolerant of them in the client.

No matter how the counselor deals with the greeting stage of the opening of an interview and no matter what the orientation toward therapy of the client, the general rule should be to wait for the client's lead as an indication of the direction the discussion is to take. For various reasons, clients will not conform or comply only reluctantly with this implicit demand from the counselor. In some cases, the client will start by telling the counselor that he is not going to start. The neophyte counselor may be sufficiently threatened by this to fail to see that by saying he is not going to start the client has in effect started, and that the appropriate next steps are likely to be those involved in trying to understand why it is that he feels a need not to start. What attitudes and thoughts toward the counselor and the counseling process lie behind this behavior? For one thing, this kind of reaction is quite frequent following a first interview in which a client who has not been particularly prepared for relatively personal and confiding discussions suddenly finds himself in a situation where they seem to be called for. At the end of the first interview, he has the feeling that he had confided a good deal, with a certain amount of concern about what the limits of this confiding are going to be and what the counselor's reactions are. A client who has had this kind of first hour will often begin the second hour with some comment like, "I guess I did all the talking last time, now I want to hear what you have to say." The counselor has several choices of reaction to this, depending upon qualitative differences in the characteristics of the first hour as well as differences in the personality and needs of the client. He may simply greet it with silence, although it would be an unusual client with whom this would be appropriate. Another possible appropriate reaction would be to verbalize the client's implicit statement that he has revealed a good deal about himself. A variation on this reaction would be to add to the previous response some slightly more generalized statement of the view of himself and his problems that the client came up with in the first interview. This communication will serve as a symbol of the counselor's promise to contribute to the process himself and will give the client a concrete opportunity to test the fact that he has nothing to fear from having imparted these confidences. Obviously, the counselor's response must avoid departing from the client's perception of himself in a direction which will be sufficiently threatening to stimulate defensive reactions. On the one hand, departures in a direction toward which the client had shown he was definitely groping may prove useful and stimulating to him. On the other hand, failure to avoid deep interpretation will communicate to the client that he has something to fear from counseling before he has a definite conviction that he has a great deal to gain from it.

Another way of responding to the counselor's waiting for him to begin is for the client to remain silent. It is important for the counselor to treat this act as a beginning in the same way that he would treat a verbal communication. The counselor's problem is to understand what this silence means. Silences are well differentiable in behavioral terms. One client's silence is marked by deep thought; another's silence is accompanied by leaning forward in his chair toward the therapist with a questioning look. In such a silence as the latter one the client is saying to the therapist, "I am waiting for you to begin," "Where shall we start?" It is important for the counselor to discriminate between different silences and to react appropriately. The counselor must be sufficiently secure to be able to wait calmly and patiently when the first kind of silence occurs. Inexperienced counselors and counselors with problems which are tapped by this kind of response sometimes find silence hard to meet. When silence becomes extended to such a point that it indicates some obstacle to communication, it may be appropriate for the counselor to comment on the client's thoughtfulness and on his difficulty in getting on with the task. Where through mutual agreement communication has been clearly established as the major task, this inability to communicate can become a concern for both the counselor and the client.

When the client by his silence is asking the counselor to begin or to tell him where to begin, the counselor must beware of a too-ready acceptance of his behavior as a sign of resistance to the therapeutic process or of dependence. So many times in counseling it may simply indicate that no definite orientation to the counseling task has been established, or that the full implications of the counseling task have not yet been communicated. Under such circumstances, the counselor will probably not want to enforce any extended silence but will respond almost immediately in one of two ways. He may ask, "Where do you want to start today," or he may say, "For some reason you are looking for me to suggest where you should start." In general, the counselor's response should communicate the idea that part of the counseling task involves the client's acceptance of the initiative in the communication process, particularly at the beginning of interviews. At the same time, the counselor should guard against feelings of annoyance or frustrations over the apparent evidence that the client has not learned and is not accepting the counseling task. Such feelings will distort the communication into a figurative "back of the hand" for not being a good client. Many times these kinds of feelings are reflected in long structuring statements by the counselor, for example, "Perhaps I should explain again how we go about things here. We find we can help people best when they take the initiative in talking over the things that bother them, the sorts of things that have happened in between the last session or other things that they want to talk about." The farther along in a relationship this type of statement occurs the greater the likelihood its translation is, "You stupid oaf, how long does it have to take for you to learn what you are supposed to do?"

Often the counselor will believe that the feelings dealt with toward the end of some hour are extremely significant and will get the impression that, if only he could have kept the process going, tremendous strides would have been made. Under these circumstances, and where their schedule permits, counselors often extend hours. In a similar mirage-seeking vein they yield to the temptation at the start of the next succeeding hour to invite the client to continue with the topic. Often this has been preceded by a suggestion that the client think about this general area in the intervening period. Such efforts on the part of the counselor will likely result in defeat. As was suggested earlier in this chapter, this kind of action can be useful when the goal is to limit the process; but its stimulation of specific purposive action will also stimulate defensive processes and will not result in exploration. Not only are the client's ego defenses activated by such efforts, but, in addition, he is likely to experience these suggestions as irritating pressure and demandingness on the part of the counselor. It is just when the client is relatively free of the pressures to be realistic that the more significant rationale of his emotional organization with its impulses, its fears, and its efforts to escape the fear can come to the fore.

Keeping on the surface

The general therapeutic dictum of staying with the client and of interpreting only slightly beyond his present level of awareness applies as well to the beginning of interviews. Perhaps at the opening of the interview greater emphasis is placed on staying *within* the client's present level. It is important for the counselor at the beginning of the hour to be able to see in what terms, from what point of view, and at what level the client is reacting and thinking about himself. The counselor's initial responses test his understanding of the client's current level. Instead of attempting to convey *his* impression of the client, the counselor encourages the client to talk more about whatever it is that he has started on.

An approximate illustration of this can be taken from the early parts of two later interviews with Miss Tir, the twenty-year-old girl whose first interview was presented in Chapter 10.

First we take the beginning of the tenth interview.

S 1. I'm very sorry about last week; it was very stupid of me. I had intended last Tuesday to go on in that direction. I don't know whether it will amount to anything, but since I couldn't decide what course to pursue in regard to what to do with my mother, I thought I'd like to talk about what has happened. Something I almost forgot which didn't seem connected with this more recent explosion. I felt that this first started two years ago. I mean I remember when I came away from home in 1945, I took, I think it was Psych. 31, and in the lab they had us do a—some kind of a personality test, I suppose it was a survey or something, and one of it was incompletion. (*obviously referring to an incomplete sentences test*) He said just the first thing that popped in your mind to put down and I remember there was one thing that said, "My mother is all right, but—" and I put "but nothing" and I wrote it so hard that I broke my pencil point and a thought at the time did pass through my mind, "Well, she does have a terrible temper, but she's such a good mother it would be false to her to put that down and here I am eight hundred miles away, I should only think of the good." And, it's funny, I just happened to think, if I had seen anybody else do that, I knew enough at the time to realize there was something wrong there but I didn't apply it to myself and nothing happened for a long time. Then there was, last year, all this at the beginning, I was a junior, I got interested in the young progressives on campus and I think I told you about—I went to a convention in Cincinnati, a convention and at night there was a dance. We only arrived that night, my girl friend and I, (*mumbles*) (*slight pause*) and when I arrived at the dance I discovered that the population there was primarily Negro—it must have been about 60 or 70 per cent, and I went through the whole gamut of feelings inside, didn't know what to make of it. At the beginning I didn't know how I felt about it; by the end of the evening I was perfectly at ease and felt as if I had learned more in that one night than ten years of classrooms could do for me. And, well, the whole thing went on over the weekend, it was the beginning of a new attitude. If I could hang on to the feelings I had gotten that night, I had come a very long way along the road I wanted to travel. And when I wrote home about it, I got back this letter from my mother that I would get locked in with rabble-rousers, that's the term she used. It seems I could have gotten that way quietly and peacefully—why don't you start at home, first, and then some more about anti-Semitism. Well, I answered that letter and I said, and I never heard any more from her about it, but my brother-in-law wrote to me about it and gave me quite a bit of satisfaction. And I realized that in the back of my mind, I suppose, the beginning of feelings that I had been taught things all my life, my mother had been teaching me things—she didn't really believe (*stammering*) that, what, sh—people should believe in them, and now that I was beginning to be exposed to the carrying out of these ideas she had taught me, I was beginning to really take them to heart and believe them. That didn't—sit too well. And it was all right. Then, well I was going with Dave at the time and I—at the time I hadn't made up my mind, I honestly kept telling myself that there was a chance, that someday I would fall in love with him and marry him. And we talked about what we wanted out of life, what the future ought to be like and he, well he's a very alert kind of person, he's shrewd, he knows how to get along with people, very sociable and extroverted. He's never at a loss for what to say—he's well—the—people like him, he's a good Joe. And, I had noticed and particularly my father said it and I think I, I had heard it elsewhere, and I think my father meant it, he said something about, "There's a boy who will get places; he's a hustler." Sort of implying that he would have a Midas touch and know how to turn things into money and, and he's always being offered jobs. He helps his uncle. A salesman comes in and wants him to work for his company. In retail business he's, he's a salesman, I suppose from way back and he's not afraid, or shy or anything—he's very friendly. And that didn't appeal to me somehow. I had pictures of myself in twenty years being a very "house-first" middle-class wife whose husband makes a real fine living, maybe I could even strut around in a mink coat and he being an architect would build us a beautiful house and we would be surrounded by material prosperity of a kind and in the acquiring of it, would have lost the taste, the uh, ambitions in any other direction and I know I'm sort of between the devil and the deep blue sea. I have that—I've learned that, well I read somewhere that the acquisitive view of life which a great many middle-class people have—I've learned it and I have learned more and wanted to reject it—what were the others?—oh, the—the esthetic. I don't know whether that applies, anyway its something to property. Something more concerned with ideas than with property. And I feel that whomever I should marry, if I married a person with the acquisitive view, I would, I would go wrong eventually—it would defeat me. And when I found someone like Tom who doesn't have it, who has the other view—its strong in him, that I would follow him and be led along the way I want to go. And so I suppose I tried to extract from Dave a couple of statements to the effect that he didn't have these acquisitive ideas—that the dollar was not so almighty to him as it sounded and that he wouldn't devote all his energies to acquiring more and more. And he said yes. He talked about—that he had already begun, that in architectural school he very often took a C instead of a B or an A, because the approved way of designing a thing, the way the professor would want him to design it, didn't suit him. He had his own ideas and he would sacrifice the grade for the sake of the little principle he believed in. And he talked about carrying out that pattern into life, sacrificing more money for the things he wanted to do and, the things he wanted to do with architecture wouldn't necessarily bring him money, might get him into a lot of difficulty; new idealistic (*mumbles*) which I suppose a lot of young architects start off with. And he tried to impress me with the fact that money was not that important to him, that other things were more important. And he said it so many times and I never, I never quite believed it because I always bring it up again in my old belligerent attitude. I, it—starts arguing with him as if I were trying to convince him that he's wrong about feeling that the only way to be successful is to be rich, very rich. I remember one night we were talking about it and he said, "You know I've told you this so many times and you don't believe me. I wonder why you don't." And—I said, "No, I suppose I don't." And he said, "Have I ever lied to you that you should think I'm lying now? You probably think that I'm telling you I'm that way." He says, "You ought to know me well enough that if I'm not what you want me to be, then

I'm not and I'll tell you so." He said, "Somebody, it's almost as if somebody did lie to you once, that you can't believe anymore." And that was really the first big, big breakdown. I—I uh, sort of, you know, a blinding flash of lightning. And I told him yes, my mother did. Betrayed, I suppose, is the word. It still hurts. And the worst of it was that, well, I began to cry and he didn't see what I was crying about—what was so terrible and what seemed so terrible to me was that I should be saying: imagine a mother betraying her own child. It didn't help any. (*mumbles*) And that is the same thing that popped up again, but that was the beginning of it. I had forgotten for some reason. I got over it in some way. I just stopped thinking about it. And, the only, the best I could think of—when I went home after that I noticed a million things I never noticed before. I notice the little bits of bigotry popping out and things she said. I remember her saying once, we had seen a movie and it was very good, I don't remember the name of it, but she was telling somebody to see it and she used a very harmless, maybe, sentence: "It's the story of an Italian family, but it's very good." In spite of the fact that it's about Italians. And I, I suppose things like that have been going on in my house all my life and I never saw them before, never noticed them, never made any difference, maybe I said it myself, I don't know. There's an expression Jewish people have: *die yiddische kopf,* the Jewish head. And it sort of, every time we talk about a man, figuratively it has got to be a Jew of course, who has done something remarkable, they'll end up with "Well, *die yiddische kopf*—he's a Jew, he's smart; what else do you expect? Nobody else could do it." It's along the same pattern. That's one of my father's blind spots even. He'll argue that if you take one hundred Jewish children and one hundred any other type of children you'll find the IQ among the Jewish children is much higher—considerably higher. It's as if they were born with better heads. Well that's so much bilge to me, but I can leave that alone—that wouldn't be so bad, but that sort of habit, feeling like, I can see where it comes from and of course I—the despised and persecuted race has to do—has to fight back and that's the way Jewish people fight back, not from the defensive but in an offensive approach, not only are we not worse than others, we're considerably better. And that's it—it can't be helped and it isn't too harmful, but the rest of it, well, I've never wanted to reconcile myself to it. I think it's all wrong. As I said I don't ever expect to convince them. We had a knock-down-drag-out fight with my father last vacation, so my brother-in-law answered this statement about the hundred children with the fact that investigation has been made if there is any difference in intelligence between different ethnic groups, and there hasn't been anything proved to the fact that there is. My father answered that he doesn't agree (*chuckling*) with all this psychological bunk. Tests! How can you prove by tests? That was sort of the parting of the ways.

C 2. It was the parting of the ways but you didn't get it out of your system completely.

S 2. No. The funny—it seems to me that if I could have then I could believe them and I still don't to this day, which seems to me to indicate that it's still (*mumbles*) that I'm still emotional about it, and that I can't believe them both. I'm curious to see what he's going to do when he gets out in the world. I don't think he's going to do the things he talks about.

C 3. I think there may be another kind of evidence too: your need—last time when we talked, at the end of the hour you ended up by saying, "Well, this was something that bothered me two years ago, it doesn't bother me now." I don't know if you recall that (S: no, I don't) —but that's what you said at end of the hour. Of course it does bother you. (S: yeah) It's even possible that you got mixed up on the time of our next meeting partly because you were thinking about this.

S 3. I had planned to say what I was (*covered by outside noise*) (C: uh-huh) —so I was very disappointed when I had to wait a little while. I had forgotten about it, I didn't think about it (*mumbles*) particularly. Well what's the difference; it's always going to be there. They can't ever get out of their way of thinking. I'm just lucky that I did.

C 4. I think possibly one of the reasons it bothers you is that you're not sure just how much you've gotten out of their way—how much of your mother you've still got.

S 4. Well, I'm sure that intellectually I'll never want to go back. (C: oh, yes) But I know that I haven't erased all that—I never will.

C 5. Well, you talk about the fact that if you're with an acquisitive person, you will become acquisitive and will—I think that represents to you your mother, being that way. And so, in other words, what you're saying is, "This is something that could come back in me, if I'm not careful. If I don't marry the right person, I could come, become like my mother."

S 5. Yeah. That is the way I feel.

C 6. Uh-hum. In other words, you still feel you have these potentialities—becoming that way—you still have your mother in you.

S 6. I think it would take another twenty years of experience within
the other world, before I could —

C 7. Yuh. But that would be something that would keep you worried
about this thing and kind of fighting it. You don't trust yourself.
You think you've got this undesirable aspect of you—undesirable,
well, undesirable aspect in you that you've got to fight. (S: yeah)
Just as you don't trust yourself to face your mother directly, you
don't trust yourself to be able to overcome your mother in you,
her influences in you.

S 7. That's right. Well, I, I, it seems to me the only way to make this
complete, the way with her way of life. (*mumbles*) That's probably the reason too that I never could make up my mind to
marry Dave. And the one time that I was close to it—well, he—
seems to represent to me—I've looked at that the way my mother
has. Even the family he comes from—it's just like mine and
though it—come to think of it, quite unreasonable—I was saying
to myself the other day, "Coming from such a family, why should
I expect him to be any different?" But I'm different, and (*chuckling*) I suppose it would seem—at least I'm trying to, see, and he
could be trying too. But I just don't believe him.

C 8. Just as you don't believe yourself.

S 8. About what?

C 9. About being different from the influence of your family.

S 9. I believe in myself that I want to be (C: yes) and that I'll try
and that I need help. I, I suppose I'll lose out because I have
very heavy odds. That's the main reason I'm going with a person
who didn't (*mumbles*) I wonder if there's any connection—just
now occurred to me—to—Dave seems to more or less belong to
my mother's category, in that I expect that same kind of betrayal
from him, that he isn't telling the truth and this terrific sense of
obligation I feel to leaving my mother happy. I feel the same
towards Dave, only in a part I should, I consider what I've done
to be very bad and, I look at it from a moral point of view, it
was stupid and wrong. (*sighs*) But, I have excuses enough; when
I first started down the road I've been traveling these three long
years, I didn't know what I was doing. I mean the first time he
told me how he felt I had no conception of what I was dealing
with or how deeply I could hurt myse—how bad it is to play
around with things like that. And so I went on and then for the

first two years I had all kinds of illusions. I did think he really had a chance, and so I was justified in hanging on. He chose to hang on to me. But now that I have made up my mind that it's not him, I realize he's going to be unhappy when I write him a "Dear John" letter which ought to happen a month from now. (*sighs*) I also realize that being the sort of person he is—he's got a lot of bounce in him, he's not going to pine away in grief—he's never going to find another woman. I don't think it will be more than a matter of months before he's over it. Maybe it'll be a matter of weeks because he's been led to expect this to happen; it isn't going to be a bolt out of the blue. And, well, how many girls in the lifetime, well, of quite a big percentage refuse one or more boys who are in love with them and want to marry them. My sister did two or three, four. And I suppose she spent a couple of nights crying, but that's about all. And I feel as if though, as if it, it is necessary to me, that not only will he be very happy, if anything much happier with another woman where I am with Tom, but I don't want to give him that feeling that I know you get when you're rejected that way, that lonely feeling—sort of being left out in the cold. I keep getting awful pictures of this other person running around with somebody else and—well, the feeling of rejection. And I would want to— crazily, I never could—eliminate it by keeping him assured all the time that I do love him and even if I do marry somebody else, I won't forget about him, it won't be as if these three years haven't existed. He, he just never will be the "old flame"—he'll always be very important to me, and even when I have great dreams about the future, he always worms his way into them and he's always got a wife; he marries before I do and very happily, not on the rebound or anything like that. And we're just great friends and the only trouble is that his wife might be a little uncomfortable about the whole thing and my husband might. I try to ignore that. It's almost sort of necessary ingredient of my happiness that he be part of my life and that he be very happy in this part of his—namely, as a friend. I feel more of an obligation to him perhaps than it is normal to feel. My girl friend also had, this girl, a friend of mine's that's engaged now— well, she went around with a boy, Jasper, almost as long as I have with Dave, and it was the same mistake; he wanted to marry her. He was in no position to do anything about it, so maybe he figured he'd stick around and he would tell his friends well, she'll come around eventually—she'll marry me. And she used to say, "I think it's this attitude that if I don't find anybody else I will marry Jasper." And true, I never felt that she felt as deeply about Jasper as I do about Dave, because I don't think he was as smart a guy, he didn't treat her as well—wasn't as good to her. But when the time came, she, hearing of my constant grief of what am I going to do, what am I going to do, I feel so guilty, told me that she didn't—I remember she wrote me a letter saying, "What in the world am I going to do; how shall I tell him?" and she broke it to him by degrees that she was seeing this guy and was too busy to see him, the next time, she was doing this and that with him and then finally she was going to marry him and by the time she got around to the stage of telling him, never mind Jasper, I'm going to marry somebody else, she didn't feel any obligation—didn't even feel any pity for him. Felt absolutely nothing; just a little uncomfort—discomfort at the idea that he might call again, and she had to put a stop to it —sort of an unpleasant business. Well I would expect to feel more than she did, because I think I felt more for Dave—feel more for Dave. But such a terrific amount; she did the same thing—had him hanging around about the same number of years, but the same idea's in her mind. Maybe she would, maybe she wouldn't, probably she wouldn't. My sister did the same thing. I remember my roommate at college did it even worse; finally said he just flunked out of school, but before that she just kept her mouth sh—I'm (laughing) not the only one. It happens to a lot of people and when it's over it's over, except I—I can't think of it being over. I mean it's going to be easy for me. I do it long distance, I don't have to look him in the eye and say it. And Ed, my brother-in-law was saying, I suppose realizing how I felt last time, he, he said, he'd be surprised, after he hasn't seen you for a couple of months, why by next October or November, he says it won't hurt him half as much because he's used to being without you, and you don't have to worry about it. And I do. I worry about it as much as I worry about leaving my parents. It seems to me that he has a connection there. It doesn't seem to be a very, a very reasonable way to feel.

The client's long communication at the start of this hour tells us that something important has been happening in the relationship, namely, that she has now reached the point where she can permit herself to become aware of strong hostile feelings toward her mother. In this process she also becomes aware of previous instances where these feelings have either momentarily slipped out and been repressed, such as was the case in the sentence-completion test, or appeared in more subtle derivative form, such as was involved in her inability to accept Dave's claim to have values similar to her own. From other sources we know that the counselor had already inferred that she could not express her hostility or allow herself to be aware of it because of her extremely dependent feelings toward her mother. He was not yet absolutely sure as to the specific dynamic relationships which had created this fixation upon dependent feelings, but he was quite aware of the fact that there was such a relationship. Notice that his first response in C 2 goes only slightly beyond the client's communication in focusing on her need to remain angry with her mother rather than accepting this difference from her mother. The rest of the interactions through C 9 involved the further elaboration and clarification of her uncertain differentiation from her mother and its ramifications. During the rest of this hour the client and the counselor continued to clarify and to point up the implied dependence in the client's behavior.

Now we return to the start of interview 11.

C 1.   Shall we start?

S 1.   Yeah. Let's start now. Oh boy. I left my little umbrella at home. (*it started to rain*) Well, it seems to me—I've been thinking it over since last time—that, the thing, the place we left it was this feeling of obligation I have to Dave that probably stems from the same root, the same feeling of my mother and it's so, uh, so it seems to me quite impossible for me to find out where it came from. Must go way back which I can't do—a thing. And I wonder, would it be possible to find out the root of it? And even would finding it out get rid of it? I don't know. I thought not and I also thought that it has been my habit, I discover, to very often, to watch the feelings I have by being reasonable about, my intellectualizing about them. But I—that's probably the best answer for this feeling. That's about as well as I can do with it and I think I could, I'm pretty sure I could.

C 2.   That the familiar way of dealing with this feeling kind of appeals to you.

S 2.   Yeah. Well, I think it's the only possibility. I don't know if there is any other way. Except to, I mean, how far back can you look or can you remember? To find an occasion for my beginning to feel that way, I can't.

C 3. It seems pretty impossible to do it any other way—to do it this other way.

S 3. What do you mean?

C 4. That is to go back, to try to figure out (S: yeah) why it is you feel this way.

S 4. I can't call to mind anything I actually remember at this point, and, I doubt—a thing like that wouldn't be one incident, it'd be illustrated I suppose (*mumbles*) but I can't even remember anything to account for it. And it seems to me if I'm dependent, I never acted like I was or go on acting like I would. (*chuckles*) And I think as far as Dave goes, I can get rid of it. I had a little sample yesterday; and I have been trying to keep things away from any serious talk, because I have nothing to say that can make him or me feel good and he brought it up anyway. He said some of the boys in his house have been asking him again why he doesn't get pinned and there's going to be a big dance, a formal and they think you ought to do it then. He asked me if I would and I said, "No," that I couldn't. He said you could if you wanted to. He says, "You know you could always send it back to me." Yeah, I could do that but I only lied a little more than I already am, lying to a lot more people. And he was rather unhappy about it, but on the occasion we had the talk, I only had a certain amount of time—I had to be somewhere so I left and I decided not to think about it, not to think how unhappy he was which is the thing that makes me unhappy; thinking of what I've done to him, not what I've done to myself. And I didn't think about it. Every once in a while it would sort of pop into my mind. I have that way when I sort of worry, I only worried that the next time I saw him he would bring it up again and as long as he didn't I was going to be happy. He didn't and I was happy, so I can do that all the more easily when I get home, when I can make myself forget how he feels.

C 5. How about your mother?

S 5. I think I could do that too. (*slight hesitation*) I hope. I, I've been away—I don't know how long, it's been a month now, I guess—and I sort of, forget how I felt at the time.

C 6. You're not as sure about being able to do it in her case.

S 6. No, I'm not— (*short pause*) I guess I, I could. I guess the logical thing to do is do what I can while I'm home, like I always have been trying to almost. (*sighs*) Do a little. (*very softly*) They have

to be left alone to find their own way, and if I feel as though
I'm being selfish or anything, I don't—I don't think I'm being
any more selfish than other people are. Just not being so dependent which is what I want. I think I could— (*short pause*)
there's a change in my own behavior and my own attitude that
I would like to make because of what it's indicative of. I don't
know how I ever got this way. My sister isn't at all.

C 7. It's really a pretty puzzling thing about yourself, kind of a
source of a, well, of lack of ease to think that you are this way.

S 7. Yes, very much so. (*softly*) I don't like the idea at all.

C 8. Sort of saps your confidence in yourself.

Notice that the client starts this hour in a somewhat different
vein from the preceding one. In the preceding hour she had been
able to become aware of certain feelings she had toward her mother
and had come to terms sufficiently with them to want to communicate them quite fully to the counselor. By contrast she starts
this hour with considerable doubt about the possibility of doing
anything constructive about her dependent feelings. The counselor in C 2 and C 3 confines himself to acknowledging these feelings. In S 4 the client expresses her resistance in another way by
implying that she will be able to handle the problem anyway. She
does this in the context of talking about Dave. The therapist
gently indicates his doubts in C 5 and her response in S 5 conveys
her awareness of her own doubts. The remaining interactions in
this excerpt indicate that this is only a momentary resistance and
the client is ready to communicate further. The interview continues.

S 8. Well, disappoints me. (C: hmm) (*pause*) It's, (*chuckles*) it's sad,
I, it's always, I think such a stupid way to be; it's so wrong. I
don't know how, it can happen. My sister and I always got
equal treatment, with neither of us feeling more favored than
the other. And yet, my sister doesn't have any of that that I can
see—never had it. In the same situation she didn't feel any
obligation to my parents—more than the normal obligation
and I don't see why I—she went off and left them unhappy. Oh,
then every suggestion—the time, the time I used to come back
to school, each time my mother was, would say, "Well, next
year you won't go. You'll go to PU and you'll stay home with
us." And I wouldn't consider it for a minute, and I knew that

she would love something like that she would never ask me to, the only way it would get done was if I offered to, and I knew I wouldn't. And I told my sister about it—never did anything that made me feel a little bad that they were lonesome, but I didn't for a second dream of not coming, so I realize it's a dangerous path to go down and the next request: "Well, please don't run away and get married and leave me" and then I won't be able to do that either. And my, well, my sister would always say, "Don't for a minute think about it and your mother won't insist on it and if she does she's very wrong. You are entitled to it as I was," she said. She never displayed any of that behavior and after we brought up, she did equally, I realize that we're still going to be different people, because she's a different—born a different person, whatever you're born with, and is the older while I'm the younger—but how could such a tremendous difference come about that you get one normally independent child and one dependent? There's something pops into my head; I don't know. I've discovered lately—I've never felt myself inferior in any way to my sister; in a few ways I feel myself a little *superior,* stupid little things like, she was never domestically inclined, she was always all thumbs in the kitchen and I always liked puttering around. I learned a little more about it; I'm more at ease there. And, well probably the way things are going now, when I get married I'm going to have a considerable better reputation as a cook than she would ever have. She doesn't, she doesn't—but it doesn't interest her as it does me. As far as taste in clothes, she never had any—she does now, but only since she's gotten out on her own—before my mother and I used to choose for her; my mother never chose for me, I always did my own. But when she went, graduated from high school she graduated with a scholarship. I never did, never even came near getting a scholarship. And if she went to a smaller university—she was a tremendously big wheel in the small university. She's got into *Who's Who in American Colleges and Universities* and she was every single kind of officer in her sorority. She was an officer in Hillel Foundation. She ran for election and she won. Well, I've never done any of these things. Her marks have always been a little better than mine, not—there's not been a considerable amount of difference in that. But she has left an imprint where she went to schood. I've got the excuse that where, where she went was three thousand strong, this place is fifteen—that's a little higher to get anywhere and then, there's always the rationalization that she needs that kind of—she needs the recognition that she gets from people. She needs the actual pat on the back you get when you're elected to something; they really tell you that they like you and that they want you for this, that and the other thing. And she had insecurities in her own, so that she gets peace of mind in getting approval of all kinds. I never needed, I've never gone out for things like that. For some reason or other I made absolutely no marks here and never made the effort to. I never wanted a scholarship. Then I also discover that though we look alike, I think my sister is three or four times as good-looking as I am. Things I never realized before and have only come to lately. I also believe that as far as the question of looks are concerned, my parents knew that I was sort of the ugly duckling. And someone only told me recently that when I was a baby— we have another little baby in our family right now, a cousin, who is not too good looking, and the relatives talk about it, they call her funny-face and mean it and sometimes in spite of her—well, they did when she was younger and couldn't understand and my mother always objected very strongly, saying that, "Don't say that in front of the child. I know she can't understand, but don't say it. It might catch hold somewhere." And I've gotten the feeling from that and from people telling me, Ann was a beautiful baby. I was not such a beautiful baby. They were conscious of the fact that they had one pretty little girl and one not so pretty little girl and there's room there for, for danger. And they arranged it in such a way that I never realized, that Ann was never described as being particularly gorgeous or beautiful, they didn't pay too much attention to our looks, even when, when my sister was adolescent she never had, she never gained weight, or she never got acne or anything. I was spared the acne, but I got fat and I was fat until—still not skinny. And every once in a while I would remark something to the effect that, "My sister never had any trouble with her figure. Look at me—I do." But it never rubbed—it never bothered me to any great extent. I was never self-conscious about it or self— simply, always, I was always going to go on a diet, but I was never bothered that much but I would stop eating what I liked to eat and they never—they never bothered me about it. My father used to tell me how he was, he preferred my kind of shape to these "rails" that walk around—skinny women, and they wished Ann would put on a little weight and I really had a much nicer shape than she did. And, well it's almost a joke to the family, in fact that I know darn well that I have a long nose. *(laughing)* He's always telling me *(overcome with laughter)* —just saying not to get a complex about it and it's a little too late for me to start worrying about it. And I get the feeling that maybe because of these obvious ways, I was not quite as good as my sister. They covered up so well that it—I mean Ann wins the scholarships, so my mother tells me that with my kind of mind she expects me to go places and she never said anything like that to Ann. Maybe I depend on them more for things like that.

C 9. You depend on them to kind of support you in that way, to help you not see the discrepancy (S: yeah) for it not to hurt.

S 9. Yeah, it might be part of the answer and if it is so I'm just as glad they did it anyway, because I'd be pretty bad off anyway if I did—the result is—I doubt very much if she'd ever been jealous of me—I never have of her or any of the things she had. And as I say, a lot of the things—a few ways, not, true, not in a lot of ways, I feel slightly superior. Well, I've used the matter of cooking which doesn't really amount to a hill of beans, but they've even given me security in my own personality, sometimes I feel as if I outshine her in a room full of people. And my friend told me that the last time I was home, that she really did feel, always have felt, that, my social personality is more outstanding than my sister's. I felt quite smug about it which showed me that I didn't think it was so much hogwash, maybe she's got some truth there. And, and I've seen in my roommate who also has an older sister, who got a very different kind of treatment, what it did to her and how much better off I am. I know that her sister—well, in matters of scholarship, her sister did outshine her a long way, and she was quite heavy, her sister is a little—thing. And they did everything my parents didn't do. They worship their older daughter and they make no bones about it. And Betty, well, Betty is the younger child, Betty is the baby. Her mother will reproach her for eating too much in front of company which I can imagine, I don't know if they would even dream of doing, even in private she doesn't. Well, I don't think she's dependent at all. On the other hand, she wants to break away completely now because she feels if she goes back home she'll—she'll never win out over herself under their influence. So they don't force her into dependency in her, but she's pretty bad off and I'm not, I feel very privileged and sort of grateful and I suppose that I can see in spite of the harm, I have many more blessings.

C 10. This—you see this dependency as really having been a good thing for you.

S 10. Yeah, I suppose the—in a way it is.

C 11. Rather than having been a negative thing—

S 11. I don't like looking at myself in that light, I mean I'm unwilling to accept it as completely the truth. If the facts stand there, I know they are, but I don't have that feeling of inferiority it sort of—I keep on thinking of all the ways in which I'm better. But I suppose it was, in a way, sort of helping the crippled child keep up with the good one. And it was a good thing. But the thing is I've grown up without any of the—the feelings of inferiority and even now when I can see that there was room for feelings and where I was inferior—I'm putting it in the past where I am inferior—I still don't have the feelings that go with them. Sounds sort of as if they've set me up on my own two feet, I can go ahead on my own steam now, I don't need the support from them and then I don't want the dependency to go along with it.

C 12. You don't have to be dependent now, you think.

S 12. No, I don't feel as if I do.

C 13. But at the same time you have the feeling that maybe it's going to stay with you, even though you don't need it.

S 13. Yeah. I wouldn't want it at all. I think it is a sort of awakening —it comes between my—the way my sister has performed and the way I have. In some ways I've—caught up with her. Well, no, important numbers I haven't. I was just thinking of one of the—the thing that was always amazing to me, has always been, I never could understand it, was that there's only two and a half years between my sister and me and we were both at home in high school for a year or two years or something. We were both old enough to be going out. My sister was going out; I was not. I never dated at all in high school, I was stupid about it. I developed a crush on one boy who didn't like girls and I spent my senior year in high school chasing around after him, never getting anywhere and I left—the few chances I did have, I let them go by. And Ann was quite popular; by the time she got out of high school she had the two boys both madly in love with her and they kept her quite busy along with a few of the others. When I think of it, those boys now are younger than Dave and just about as old as Tom, who are, neither of whom are out of my category as far as age is concerned and that made a difference between us. And when I was in high school, I was always eligible—I was a little young, but not very young— now they take out girls that are still unmarried, well, there are some younger than I am. And I never competed with her for them. I always played the role of the little sister and I could never look on them as possibilities; feel sorry enough because they were Ann's and they treated me as a kid sister. I was a great favorite with both of them; they used to write to me from the army. And there was my sister running out every Saturday night and I was sitting home. You'd think that all kinds of jealousies would arise, I would have terrible feelings about the whole thing. I didn't. I don't know why I didn't and anyone, every once in a while my mother would, I might say something, my mother would worry that I was worrying about it—I really— I remember her saying, "Don't you worry. Your day will come when you get a little older. It happened the same way with me. Boys never liked me, so I got to be 18 or 19 and I was very popular." And she would attempt to console me with that; I wouldn't even need the consolation. I was satisfied with the few crumbs I got from this guy, who happened to be a friend, a brother of my friend, and that I saw him and if he said a kind word I was happy for weeks. It seems to me they must have done that some way. I don't know how they did it.

C 14.   It seems as though you leaned over backward to avoid competition with Ann.

S 14.   Yeah. Finding this little—I remember last summer my mother and I were waiting for father at the train and one of the boys, George, that Ann went with when she was in high school— haven't seen him for two or three years—and well, I think he must be now around 24, which is as old as Tom is, and he's younger than Dave is. And he stopped and leaned in the car window and said, "Hello, how are you?" this, that and the other thing. When he left, my mother looked at me and said, "You know, George is a very nice boy, would you ever consider dating him. When Ann sees him sometime, maybe she could have both of you up to her house or something." And the first—I was just about to say, "Why, no, he's liable to—" (laughs) which is kind of silly, but I couldn't. I—I realize he was perfectly eligible, he doesn't seem in the least eligible to me even outside of the fact that I'm not interested in finding new faces. I couldn't; he doesn't belong in my category. It's quite a strong thing, you know.

In S 9 we see that the client has very definitely overcome the initial resistance she was feeling at the beginning of the hour. However, even while talking of her discovery of feelings of inferiority to her sister, she unconsciously strives to minimize them. She is also discovering how much she is dependent upon her parents' support in order to be able to face these feelings of inferiority. With this discovery come a mixture of feelings that are expressed in S 9, 10, 11, and 12. She feels that it has been very helpful for her parents to be protective of her but at the same time she feels that she wants to and should now be able to proceed without this dependence. As one might suspect, this mixture of feeling arises partly from the fact that she still exerts some efforts to defend against her feelings of inferiority in which the dependence is an important bulwark. This comes out a little more clearly in S 13 and S 14 when, with the help of the counselor's interpretation in C 14, she sees that there had been a kind of awareness of the difference between her sister and herself and that this had operated to influence her behavior mostly through the medium of avoiding competition.

Reflections of problems in the counselor-client relationship

In most cases, both therapeutic progress and therapeutic impasses tend to polarize around the relationship between counselor and client. One important sign of the current nature of the relationship is the way the client begins the hour. We have said that he may begin by talking how bad he feels; or how undecided he is; or how unpleasant or unhappy his situation is. In these instances he may be complaining either with an intent (perhaps only dimly conscious) to express his annoyance with the counselor for not having made things right or to draw the counselor's pity and support. On other occasions the client may talk about the fact that nothing has happened in the interval since they last talked as a way of expressing a bland, uninvolved attitude toward counseling. On still other occasions clients will come with carefully thought-out and selected material to transmit.

When an impasse appears, it usually represents some form of the client's distrust of himself or of other people which he has transferred to his relationship with the counselor. In order to be able to make full use of this kind of behavior, the counselor must be prepared by anticipating such possibilities and by drawing on his own security as a counselor and a person. When he is prepared, he will be able to avoid being stampeded into action before he fully understands the meaning of the client's behavior. Instead, he can wait calmly for the behavior to spell itself out more clearly while he tries to understand its meaning. Incidentally, the counselor should not exclude the possibility that the client's behavior is a realistic reaction to those ways in which the counselor has failed to meet the client's needs or to misinterpretations by the client of the counselor's behavior and communications which have some realistic grounds.

Case of Mrs. Neb

One example of the handling of a beginning of an interview in which a block appears comes from counseling with Mrs. Neb, a 35-year-old married woman. She came after her husband had received counseling. She wanted to decide whether to end the marriage and also what kind of career she should take up. This is the twenty-sixth interview. During most of the preceding interviews she has dominated the situation, talked constantly, but has not really examined herself. The interview begins:

S 1. Tired and wondering about *just* why I don't have to work tomorrow. (*giggles*) This is what I have been waiting for. (C: hmm) (*audible sigh*) Ah, as soon as I get out of here (*several words unclear*) see if I can't get one of those books that deal with real estate, law and so forth. Um. Ah, wondering about, ah, these visits here, and whether it makes any difference as to whether there's a break in them for awhile.

C 2. Well, I don't know. What do you mean?

S 2. Well, I mean whether it will interfere with your setup or (C: uh-hum) you know, because after all—

C 3. Will it be inconvenient to us?

S 3. You have a schedule and so on (*C and S speaking simultaneously*). Yes. Does it matter to you one way or the other?

C 4. No.

S 4. Uh-huh. And when more or less and for what period? (C: uh-hum) Or does that matter either?

C 5. No. What are you thinking about?

S 5. (*laughs*)

C 6. Let's see what it's all about.

S 6. OK. Ah, I have too many things on my mind (C: uh-hum) and I think that *that* for one thing is probably detracting from what I'm trying to do here. What you also are trying to accomplish here, and, ah, I was thinking, maybe I could do away with a lot of these things that are cooking at the time, and, ah, once I've got those organized, then I can come back to this. Also, ah, I want to read a book. Do you have any objections to my reading books on the subject of psychology? I never have, and I have purposely stayed away from them because ah, you know I don't want to "set" certain ideas (C: uh-hum) as a result of something that I've read.

C 7. Uh-hum. Well, I'm not sure, here. Why are you changing your mind about it now?

S 7. Changing my mind about what?

C 8. About reading a book. Your—we were—you avoided reading a book before—

S 8. Oh, because on your desk out there—the receptionist's desk (C: uh-hum) I saw "Uses of the Past" by Walter something, Muller I think. Are you familiar with the book? Would it do me any good?

C 9. I doubt very much that it would.

S 9. You are familiar with the book?

C 10. No, but I—

S 10. You're not.

C 11. I still would doubt very much that (*amusedly*) that a book like that would—

S 11. Um. Well, ah, also, have you any suggestions, you know, I, if you have no suggestions, am inclined to feel that perhaps if I just relax on thi—this subject of trying to get anywhere here, for the time being, because I find that more and more I come up here and all I think of is just the current things (C: uh-hum) and I found that as a result of having made those visits to Morton's office (*a previous counseling interlude*) that I started thinking of my mother whereas prior to those visits I forced any thought of her out of my mind, (C: uh-hum) and a lot of that came about automatically just on its own, I mean, little by little

I no longer had the habit of pushing her out, and, another thing too, ah, —w-when first Ron and I were married I—I used to harp on the past and how—how good it was to be away from it, you know, but still just, you know, just constantly (C: uh-hum) think about it and thinking about it feeling something of what I felt then, you know, and then finally well, he says, "Look, that's behind you. That's past. You're living now and for the future." So there's the wall. And I honestly don't *want* to go into the past (C: uh-hum) when it comes right down to it. Ah, you know, to review it as such, but I know that it's necessary and for the purpose of accomplishing what I want for now and in—for the future, I want to refer to it (C: uh-hum) but is there a possibility that just like with this business of mother, I will also come to openly think of the past in relation to why I react to this and that, now as I do?

Notice that Mrs. Neb starts the interview with expressions of lassitude and then comes forth with the question of interrupting counseling. The counselor makes clear that there are no restraints against doing this but in C 5 and C 6 focuses on it as a process issue. In S 6 the client gives relatively superficial reasons for stopping counseling, accompanied by the question about reading psychology books. The implied criticism of counseling stands out. The counselor is definite on the usefulness of reading. In S 11 she moves a lot closer to the issue when she talks about her feeling that she did have to deal with the past yet of not wanting to do it. The interview continues.

C 12.   I would have the—the general expectation that the passage of time alone wouldn't change the—
S 12.   Wouldn't change, now—
C 13.   No.
S 13.   What then?
C 14.   Somehow we would have to work out here together why you—
S 14.   (*interrupting*) But we're not. (C: uh-hum) I can't see that we are anyway. (*giggles*) (C: uh-hum) I could, I don't know—I just don't *see* it. I don't *see* it and I don't know what to think, but of course that's why I'm asking. (C: uh-hum)
C 15.   Well then you're asking because you're kind of dissatisfied with what we've been doing and you're kinda trying to use this (*word unclear*) as a way of—of seeing what—something that happened.

S 15. Well I don't know what to expect, you know (C: uh-hum), nor do I know what is expected of me, nor do I know how to go about, ah, falling into line as it were, you know, oh, I don't express it well. It seems to me that at some point (*brief pause*) after a certain number of visits that I should, ah, develop some sort of a working order (C: uh-hum) Something, you know, I mean everything has been too helter-skelter, too *nothing*, too pointless too, just (C: uh-hum) and I just can't see that it's getting anywhere, and I wonder too whether, ah, all these other things that have me cornered; all these things that I want to do that I want to get into, ah, whether they have a bearing on the fact that—that nothing is coming out of it in the present and the same old harp, harp, harp, you know (C: uh-hum) because after all, the—the thing that I'm feeling now is that there are these things that I have to do; there are these things I have to do—I have to get started—and now's the time to start. (*pause*) I don't know, now I thought, well, if that is what's, ah, tying up things. If that's the reason why I can't concentrate on the thing at hand here to the extent of developing some systematic working order or something that—that will bring things freely, (C: uh-hum) well, maybe I ought to organize all that and—and then I will be able to do more about this. I don't know.

C 16. Usually when a person has these difficulties we—we expect to find that—one of the main obstacles that keeps them from being able to think of the things around them (*one phrase unclear*) is usually that they are trying to avoid it.

S 16. You know, that has occurred to me and I asked myself what am I trying to avoid? (C: uh-hum) What—from what I had told you could I, just—just in a general way, be trying to avoid? See, I can't see even that (C: uh-hum) or maybe I just won't see it, I don't know.

C 17. You surely aren't a person who is trying to avoid a situation like this—it's some reaction you are having to the situation.

S 17. To what situation?

C 18. To this situation.

S 18. I don't know— What is my reaction to this situation? I don't know. (*pause*)

C 19. All you can do is talk about it. Try and find out. (*short pause*)

S 19. I know one thing, I wish it weren't necessary. I wish I (C: uh-hum) I *had* it, this knowledge of myself that I want without going through all this (C: uh-hum) rigamarole. Ah—I don't know. I want to see myself. Could it be that because of the fact that I have always kept myself to myself and not allowed—any other individual to know me, ah, just—just, you know, I mean they see me as an open, frank, honest me, and I think I am, without being completely so.

C 20. Always want to keep control of the situation.

S 20. Yes, always, always, always and I asked myself the other evening after having left here the question you asked me, why must I? (C: uh-hum) Because if I have control I have the edge on the other fellow. I've already stated that. (C: uh-hum) What other reason could there be? (C: uh-hum) It's a matter of self protection. I suppose I just don't trust the other fellow *not* to hurt me. If he's going to hurt me I want to see it in advance. (C: uh-hum) And put up my guard. But of course you knew that, and you knew that I know it. What else is there?

C 21. This sounds like, ah, it could be a pretty good explanation of what you're afraid of then.

S 21. What's that?

C 22. Afraid of the other fellow, here.

S 22. I'm afraid of being hurt, (C: uh-hum) hurt by *anyone* (C: uh-hum) And I know that as long as I have control of the situation I won't be hurt. It's altogether possible that you fall in the same classification with everyone else. I don't know. You shouldn't—you shouldn't—

C 23. (*unclear*)

S 23. You shouldn't, should you?

C 24. But I think I do.

S 24. You probably do. (*short pause*) There's an exception to everything isn't there? (*giggles*) You should be it. (C: uh-hum) Well—

C 25. I don't think you're—you're going to really settle this by telling yourself that I should be, and that you should trust me.

S 25. I have to tell myself (*voice drops to whisper*) I want you to be. (*giggles*) (C: uh-hum) I have to tell myself (C: eh) you *are*, hm?

C 26. You have to satisfy yourself.

S 26. That you are, but I don't know you, see? (C: uh-hum) And I—I'm just like, who is it?—Thomas. I have to see.

C 27. You're not going to see by not coming in.

S 27. I'm not going to see by coming in either (*amusedly*) (*laughing*) except to stick my neck out and ultimately find out that my head didn't get chopped off (C: uh-hum) (*giggles*) but by then, it's too late, huh? But, of course, now, now I *know* this, see. Ah, this reminds me of the doctor who delivered the second child. (C: uh-hum) It reminds me also of the priests and the nuns and so many other general classifications of people, who are this or who are that. I'll tell you something—

C 28. Who are supposed to help you.

S 28. Yeah. Help me, not necessarily as an individual but just as a human being. (C: uh-hum) All this noble stuff. *Baloney.* It depends upon the individual with whom you are dealing. That goes for the man you work under—that goes for the man who is your physician, who is your dentist, who is your anything. It goes for marriage too I find. (C: uh-hum) It's not all sweetness and light. You can *live* in a dream concerning it for just so long, and then one day comes the rude awakening. And you realize that things do *not* materialize into what you have wanted it to materialize, or them to materialize, just because you want it so desperately and you go on pretending that it *is* so although within you know that it is not *yet* so. It doesn't work that way, and you know it. The dream concerning priests shattered. The dream concerning nuns shattered. The dream concerning physicians shattered—husband, shattered. Shall I dream with you long enough to open up and let go? I guess I'm afraid to, hm? (*pause*) And there's no point in a break is there? If I can eventually do it I can start now, (*giggling*) can't I?

C 29. Certainly I don't see a break as increasing the (*unclear*) that you're here.

S 29. All right. That's what I want to know.

C 30. Seems to me that all we can do is talk about it until you either decide that you—can't do it, or find that you can.

S 30. I can do anything I *want* to. (*giggles*) That's another thing, too, ah, after I had got out of school and worked part time here and there and then got a full time job—four dollars a week. Five and a half days. Some deal, hm? Permanent, full time job. Boorish employer, constantly belittling you and your work and everything because if you get the impression—and this by the way I got from Verne, and she is *right*. If the worker gets the impression that they are valued—that he or she is valued he or she is apt to get the courage to request more pay, and she says, look, you are probably worth more to him than anyone else he could have got because these days jobs are hard to get, and if he selected you, you can *bet* that he selected you out of at least twenty. That was during the depression. Building Manager Wrigley said even their elevator operators have no less than a master's degree, and stuff like that, you know? All right. She says, "Why don't you take a Civil Service Examination?" Thousands take them in this area. That was the tenth and what have you, the tenth U. S. Civil Service District at that time. I think they've broken it up somehow since. But it was quite a large area then. Thousands take that examination. You are rated on a competitive basis. The examinations are stiff. They require not only proof—pardon—ability to do the job, but proof of your intelligence. Why don't you see how you stack up against other people? Why don't you figure the percentage who pass and with what grade, because they *do* let you know the grade that you made and what your standing on the list is, for an opening, and the newspaper always tells how many hundreds took this exam and that exam here and in other places. Rate yourself on a percentage basis. See how you come out. I found out I was pretty darned good after all. Far better than average. And I practiced and I drummed away, and I hated typing and I hated shorthand. Well, I—I didn't take the shorthand test, I took just the typing, but anyway, I drummed away at it, until I was quite good, just to prove to myself that I *could* do it, and after I found out that I could, that was it. Then I went into bookkeeping. I wouldn't admit defeat in it. I wouldn't admit that anybody was better than I was in it. So, if I can do that I guess I can do this. I didn't *want* to but I did because I had to know whether I could. (C: uh-hum) And there's no reason why I can't here.

C 31. Maybe it's a question of whether I can be—

S 31. Whether you can what?

C 32. Whether I can be the person I have to be for you to trust me.

S 32. I thought about that a little while ago, and was about to mention it, but I didn't know how to put it, ah, because of the fact that it is recorded. Because of the fact that certain people know certain other people. The ones who might hear this, however—

The counselor's comments in C 12, 13, and 14 help to bring out the fact that the client is bringing up the issue of interruption as a solution to her apparent inability to make progress and also as an expression of her dissatisfaction with counseling. In S 15 we get intimations of specific defensive factors in her resistance. We see in such phrases as, "I don't know what to expect or how to go about falling into line, everything has been too helter-skelter, too nothing, too pointless," evidence that the ambiguity of the situation bothers her, probably because it makes it difficult for her to keep control. In C 16 the counselor reacts by pointing up the avoidance elements in her reaction. Eventually, in S 19, the client comes to an even more definite statement of her avoidance. The counselor, taking into account not only a number of the implications of the preceding remarks in this interview but also material from preceding interviews, calls attention to her desire to keep control of the situation. S 20 indicates that the interpretation has found its mark and the counselor, in C 21 and C 22, helps to get the discussion focused on Mrs. Neb's reactions to him. The next interchange illustrates how an interpretation leads to the dissolution of resistance. Mrs. Neb sees that her desire to control and her distrust of the counselor are contrary to the purposes for which she wishes to use the counselor. Thus, she sees that these feelings of wanting to control are irrational because they do not lead toward her goal. In C 27 the counselor gives a final touch to the issue of interruption, and the client by her subsequent behavior indicates that that form of resistance has now been resolved. In S 28 Mrs. Neb relates the feeling she has been having about counseling to many other relationships she has had, including those with her husband. In the remaining exchanges in this excerpt we see the issue of interruption finally resolved and counseling progressing.

ENDINGS, INTERRUPTIONS, AND FOLLOW-UP

The characteristics which distinguish counseling from other forms of psychotherapy also lead to special problems of ending, interruption, and follow-up. Throughout our discussions, emphasis has been placed upon counseling as a process which is most frequently carried on with minimally anxious people whose orientations toward help are likely to be limited to the resolution of specific problems. For such clients there are many choice points for either the interruption or ending of the counseling relationship. Which one is finally chosen by the client is a function of the interaction of such factors as the massiveness of his conflict, his success in alleviating the discomfort associated with the conflict, the potentialities for both immediate relief and long-time development offered by the resolution of the particular problem situation, the fullness of the counselor's understanding of the conflict and its ramifications, and the adequacy with which he relates to the client. In many cases, the client's commitment and involvement in counseling is so limited and his contact so brief that the counselor can only formulate the sketchiest kind of understanding of the client, the needs which brought him into counseling, and what counseling has meant to him.

We can illustrate this characteristic of many counseling relationships by the three-interview process with Mr. Lav, the freshman engineering student whose first interview appeared in the preceding chapter. In the first interview the youngster behaved in a deferential and relatively passive fashion, particularly in the early stages while he talked about being uncertain of his choice of engineering. At the same time he went to great pains to deny that he had any particular problem, and he attempted to maintain a fairly impersonal relationship with the counselor. During the discussions he did give slight indications of doubts about his personality and also revealed that his mother wanted him to enter medicine, his father's profession. He was ready to admit the possibility that his choice of engineering had been an expression of desire for independence and that because of this he may have too quickly overlooked medicine as a choice. Also during the interview, while seeming to become somewhat freer of his distrust of the counseling situation, he indicated that his mother had divorced his father and that the doctor is his stepfather. This communication was delivered unemotionally.

The second hour seemed to reveal the crystallization of an interest in management and business, apparently with a plan to shift to business administration. His scores on an interest test seemed to further crystallize this interest, although the over-all test results did not strongly contraindicate his registration in engineering. On the personal side, there was some increase in interaction with the counselor. There were a few signs of feelings of hostility centering around the interest test as was illustrated by the following excerpts. The counselor had just asked Mr. Lav what reactions he had to the tests he took.

S 7. I didn't quite see the first one though. I mean the one where they asked would you rather do this or do that?

C 8. Uh-huh. I see.

S 8. The second one was pretty good though. *(low)* Uh—

C 9. The reason I—oh, go ahead.

S 9. The—I guess the personality test it was.

A little later in talking about his welfare interests the counselor has described it as a mild interest.

S 18. Well, a mild interest, I mean, that's something that, I may have a mild interest in almost anything.

Shortly thereafter the counselor has been talking about the fact that doctors do not ordinarily exhibit welfare interests.

S 21. You—you mean you think in personal practice the doctor is objective? Well, I mean, not to his patient though. I mean, he couldn't be.

C 22. Yeah.

S 22. He is? Or—

C 23. Well, he—

S 23. Then he is to himself, but not to the patient.

C 24. He is in the way he feels about himself. That's the objective—

S 24. *(breaking in)* Yeah, but the patient feels just, I mean it's (C: uh-hum) subjective to the person, (C: yeah) to him.

C 25. You—you figure a doctor who didn't seem kind of subjectively interested in the patient wouldn't be a very satisfact—

S 25. *(breaking in)* good doctor—

C 26. —very satisfactory doctor—

S 26. No. I don't.

A little later, in the interpretation of the Multiphasic Personality Inventory, we get certain indications of other aspects of Mr. Lav's personality structure; particularly we understand a little better his behavior in the counseling relationship itself.

C 44. Yeah. *(short pause)* Another kind of possibility here is some possibility that along with this keeping a distance of yourself, (S: uh-hum) I mean, this keeping a distance, there's kind of quite a bit of sensitivity that goes along with it, quite a good awareness of people's attitudes and reacting very much to them.

S 44. *(very low)* That's probably true.

C 45. And kind of a little bit of not trusting them, what their attitudes are and kind of watching.

S 45. Yeah, well I think that (*low*) might be true.

C 46. Uh-hum.

S 46. To see what their attitudes are, (C: yeah) I yes them. (*indistinct*) Well I think I stay a distance from people. In other words I don't discuss things until I'm sure what their policies and ideas are.

C 47. Yeah.

S 47. Then if mine are in disagreement with them, I just, you know, I just keep away from them, I mean, not keep away from them, but I mean, don't express my attitudes.

C 48. Yeah.

S 48. Unless, I mean, it's someone I'm around all the time. Then I have to get in an argument with him, so— (*laugh*)

C 49. (*smiling*) Uh-hum. You're pretty careful whom you argue with.

S 49. Well, no. I argue with my roommate quite a lot.

C 50. Uh-hum. I mean if you don't know the person, you kind of hold back.

S 50. That's right. I mean, not because of physical needs, but I mean just because I don't want to make enemies with him, probably. (*short pause*)

Mr. Lav terminates discussion of this topic and they turn back to his decision. There is considerable discussion of specific details involved in various training programs. Gradually they begin to talk about the demands of a business curriculum upon verbal skills. It is at this point that we get an illustration of conflicting responses to the idea of undertaking a therapeutic effort.

S 79. What about this idea of expressing, I mean, you know, expressing my own ideas on certain things. I mean, I have a tendency to hold back on (C: uh) certain things. You know, I mean, I'd rather, I wouldn't rather, but, I mean, I'd hold back and watch rather than show a person how to do it. Maybe it's because,' I mean, he knows how to do it better than I, but well, I mean that's just something else. (*little laugh*)

C 80. Th—that wasn't something right on this topic. (S: no) But you were kind of wondering about it. That was something you were curious about, (S: uh-hum) about yourself.

S 80. I mean how I could, well, overcome it a little, you know, which is some—

C 81. Yeah.

S 81. *(low)* and yet, taking—I mean, if I was born into something like that, I mean it's important probably—

C 82. Yeah. Uh-huh. Probably that would be a—that would take a lot more talking in terms of figuring out how to overcome it.

S 82. Well, it's like this, see? I mean I'm not sure if a person—in other words, if a person asks me how to do it, then I'll go right ahead. I'll do my best, you know, I'll show him how to do it and everything like that. But, if he just happens to do it, you know I mean start doing something, and he doesn't ask any questions or anything I'd just let him do it his own way. I mean rather than try to point out something he's doing wrong.

C 83. Yeah. Kind of a case of having to be sure what your relationship is to the person before you can take the initiative.

S 83. *(reflects a second or so)* Maybe.

C 84. Uh-hum. *(pause)*

S 84. Well, that was just an idea.

C 85. Yeah. Well questions like that are questions that we do help people puzzle out if (S: uh-hum) they want to try to find answers for it.

S 85. I mean I feel sometimes I might be trying to butt in on something that (C: uh-hum) you know, well I mean, I guess that's just something that comes with more self-assurance. You know?

C 86. Uh-hum.

S 86. As you get older I guess you develop, I mean, that (C: uh-hum) you're—feel like your way of doing something is better than another person's. I mean, or as good or experienced or something like that (C: uh-hum) than the other person.

C 87. You feel that maybe it'll work itself out.

S 87. Yeah.

C 88. And not have to try to work at it.

S 88. Well, I mean work at it whenever I can, I mean, keep it in mind and not just toss it aside.

C 89. Uh-hum. Yeah. I gather that you kind of want to leave that and go back to this other thing that we were starting to talk about. Is that?

By this time certain definite impressions begin to emerge. One is inclined to put together Mr. Lav's initial behavior, which expressed polite distrust, and his later statements about not trusting people and particularly not trusting himself to oppose people unless he knows them. One gets the impression that he was talking particularly about adults and about authority figures. Again in S 79 one gets the flavor of oppositional attitudes toward adults, and in this context he refers to men, or at least uses the male gender. Putting this together with the fact of his mother's divorce of his father, with his attitudes of opposing his mother, particularly when she tries to suggest in effect that he use his stepfather as a model for occupational choice; this all has the flavor of considerable feeling about his mother's remarriage and of possible conflict and distortion as a result of it. Note how in S 83 and 84 he begins to back away from further exploration of these feelings and to try to belittle their significance. The counselor tries to explain that it is appropriate to talk about these feelings in counseling, but our client's efforts are only sporadic and are quickly deflected into reassuring ideas that the problem will resolve itself. With this he returned to his feeling that business was probably his best choice, though he still had some doubts about it. The need for discussions with his parents seemed to contribute to these doubts, so he decided that he would like to come back after he had talked to them. He was planning an early visit home.

The third interview takes a surprising turn. At the very outset, Mr. Lav declares his intention to stay in engineering. He tries to belittle and dismiss his problem by talking about the fact that he was "just confused" and talks about concentrating on chemistry. The amount of shift in the attitudes he is expressing can be illustrated by comparing this with his comments on chemistry during the preceding interview. At one point he had said: "All this chem and stuff I've had this year, oh, it just floats away"; then: "Rather than [chemistry], I mean, something I see and do is much easier." He reiterates the firmness of his decision and indirectly tells the counselor that he does not want the question of decision reopened. He emphasizes the concreteness of engineering and the vagueness of business as vocational choices.

The counselor then asks what has brought about this sudden decision, and Mr. Lav's hurried response indicates he was anticipating such a question. He exhibits a need to justify his choice and, in addition to stressing the definiteness of engineering and his reluctance to give up something definite, emphasizes his impression that the other fellows in his class were equally undecided about their choices of engineering. In general, he talks about the problem as not being so serious as he had thought. At no point does he mention any contact with his parents, which was supposedly one of the reasons he wanted this additional interview. Finally the counselor brings up this issue.

C 48. Yeah. I was wondering whether you'd gone home and discussed this with your folks too.

S 48. No.

C 49. Uh-hum. You haven't discussed it with them yet, huh?

S 49. Well, my mother called me up and—and I told her that I was going to stay in engineering.

C 50. I see. There wasn't any real discussion there. It was just your having told her. *(low)*

S 50. She said— *(laugh)* she said she thought I would make a good personnel man in business. She doesn't—I don't think she sees me as I really am. I mean, because I think she'd even be kind of shocked if she saw the way I dressed up here. *(little laugh)* *(C: laughs)* I mean just running around in dungarees all the time.

C 51. Uh-hum.

S 51. I don't know. When I went to St. Paul's, you know, we had to wear ties and coats as a matter of fact, and everything else.

C 52. You don't go for that very much.

S 52. Well, not too much. No, I don't. I like to dress up once in a while but *(low)* I like being comfortable too. *(little laugh)*

C 53. *(low)* Yeah. *(pause)* It sounds as if she's kind of favorable to the idea of you shifting.

S 53. Yeah, to business school. (C: uh-hum) Although I think that's just because that'll affect some of the people we know, in her circle. *(little laugh)* I mean a lot of the people we know are in personnel (C: uh-hum) and a lot of people are in business that we know (C: uh-hum) in Jackson; *(mumbles)* is head of a lot of business *(indistinct)*. (C: yeah) He founded a corporation.

C 54. Uh-hum.

S 54. He founded a fixture corporation, pardon me, a fixture corporation company. (C: uh-hum) I don't know, but anyway, and the Michigan Pattern company. We have neighbors in business, and things like that. And she [his mother] would like personnel.

C 55. Yeah. Did she know when she called that you were considering business?

S 55. No. I told her that, (C: oh) that I had read a business manual, and that the results of the tests were, showed that, that I had an interest in (C: uh-hum) industrial management or sales and process and things like that. *(low)*

C 56. Uh-hum.

S 56. And at once, as soon as I said business, she said, "Oh, personnel!" *(both laugh)*

C 57. Uh-hum. She kind of jumped then, huh? Had you kind of figured she would.

S 57. No. I didn't know what she'd say. *(little laugh)*

C 58. Uh-hum. One of the things I'm wondering about there is, you know, when you told me about how you chose engineering, you told me how your mother said, kind of suggested medicine, and you kind of, a little feeling as though you were kind of—to what (S: well, I said—) extent you were being influenced to do something different.

S 58. Well, I *(laugh)* told her that my interests, the tests show that my interests didn't have much of anything in medicine. (C: uh-hum) She just said, "Oh, pooh!" *(both laugh)*

C 59. She still wasn't giving up on that, either, huh?

S 59. No. Well, then when I said, well, I'm going to stay here, she said, "Okay. Anything you want." And I'm going home this week-end because of my grandmother. *(pause)*

From this excerpt we were able to get the impression of the sequence of events during the telephone call, namely, that the boy had started to tell his mother about taking tests and that he was considering business administration. This seemed to fit in quite well with the mother's social framework, so she jumped at the idea of personnel work, the specific aspect of business being considered by Mr. Lav. Somewhere at the same time they also discussed the interest tests from the point of view of medicine. It was after these two reactions, when the mother aligned herself with the results of the interest test, that it seemed as though the client made his decision to stay in engineering. Notice that he tries to avoid telling about the first part of the telephone conversation, acting as though he had started by telling his mother that he was planning to stay in engineering. His response in S 58 seems to be an acknowledgement of the counselor's implied interpretation in C 58, but we also see that he seems to have no disposition to really explore the issue which the counselor recognizes in C 60.

The whole flavor of this relationship seems to suggest that there is some possible conflict in this young man. At the same time, one also gets the impression, reading the whole record, that he is undoubtedly a reasonably mature youngster and that whatever conflicts he has are of only a mildly neurotic nature. Many counselors would have felt the impulse to keep him from leaving, to ask probing questions in order to create anxiety and the motivation to deal with his problems. Our own experience leads us to believe that this sort of procedure will be ineffectual in most instances. It would probably result in the client breaking off the interviews in any case, but it would leave him with much less positive feelings and perhaps much less able to make use of whatever contributions the interactions already made. In this particular instance, we have a little follow-up information. About a year and a half later, the counselor was eating in the college cafeteria when Mr. Lav approached him in a very friendly manner and informed him that he had, in fact, shifted to business administration and that everything was progressing quite nicely for him. Without a great deal more information, involving more contact, perhaps more intensive psychological testing and considerably more information about this youngster, it is extremely difficult to make any final judgment about his present status and the possible effects and contributions of counseling to it. This lack of closure is an inevitable characteristic of our knowledge at the end of many counseling relationships.

Interruptions

Interruptions are a frequent occurrence in the relatively superficial and transitory relationships that characterize counseling. There can be considerable variation in the nature of these interruptions. One client leaves saying he will probably return within some specified period of time. Another decides suddenly that at this time he does not want to continue with counseling, even though he acknowledges that his problem has not been resolved. Most interruptions do not have the sense of completeness, or at least definitiveness, inherent in a direct client statement that he wants to terminate counseling even though he has not reached his goal. Where the interruption has taken place through direct acknowledgement by the client, it is more likely to have the character of the sessions with Mr. Lav.

When a client has not returned when there was either a definite or implied expectation that he would, the counselor is faced with a difficult judgment. Should he made some effort to bring the client in or should he assume that the client knows what he is doing and has the right to decide unmolested whether he should or should not continue counseling? If the counselor decides to contact the client, which mode of communication should he use? Should he telephone, write, or visit him in his home?

The most important basis for these decisions, perhaps the only basis, must be an analysis of the meaning of the interruption and its relationship to the client's needs. One interruption may represent an act of hostility, whether stimulated by some inadequacy in the counselor or by irrational attitudes on the part of the client. With one client, the counselor may decide that a letter will be enough, one which makes clear to him that he has no obligation either to come back or to stay away and that the way is open if he should decide to come back. With another client, the counselor may decide that it is pertinent and appropriate to write to him acknowledging that in retrospect the counselor realizes that there was a certain kind of possible help he might have given that he had overlooked and now he is inviting the client to return and see if he can be helpful. In still other cases, the counselor will be convinced that any effort at communication with the client will only widen the breach and decrease the likelihood of his returning at some future time. More frequently than the inexperienced counselor imagines, the correct follow-up response is simply patient waiting.

There can be at least four different sources of error in the choice of follow-up method. First, the counselor may anger the client by appearing to be overprotective and overconcerned about his welfare. Secondly, he may frighten the client by conveying the impression that he thinks that his problems are so serious that it is dangerous for him to try to get along without further counseling. Third, he may appear to the client either too diffident or too uninterested in his welfare. Sometimes a phone call in place of a letter will counteract any tendency to view the counselor in this light. Fourth, an attempt at follow-up may seem to be evidence of the counselor's personal or professional need for the client to continue counseling, and if this occurs it shifts the motivation for counseling from the client to the counselor with inevitable detriment in the process.

Preparing for endings

The ending of counseling is a problem for everybody, clients on the one hand, counselors and psychotherapists alike on the other. When the therapist tries to decide whether a particular client has reached an ending point, not only are his professional knowledge and theories tested but also his professional and personal motivations. It has been our experience that counselors and psychotherapists tend to be perfectionistic in their thinking about their clients. Whatever weaknesses or immaturities they see still present in the client, whether or not the client is himself aware of them, take on considerable importance and persuade the counselor that his professional job is still not done. One cannot help thinking that these attitudes reflect a counselor's security in his own professional contribution and his suspicion that he has not done enough for his clients.[1]

The fact that counselors and their clients are each a relatively mobile population gives special emphasis to the problem of ending as it appears in counseling. The forced ending is a frequent occurrence. This is particularly true of college counseling. Student clients are about to graduate or leave for the summer vacation. Counselors move on to posts in other colleges. Many counseling positions are either internships or minor staff positions from which the incumbent will transfer to a position of greater responsibility in the same or in another college. These are among the many situations which occasion short processes. But, of course, counseling often is of only brief duration simply because the client is subject to such slight pressure from anxiety that he is motivated to make only a limited effort to solve his problem.

When a forced ending impends, the counselor must be able to judge what its nature will be. When the client is leaving on a

---

[1] An insightful reading of Freud's discussion of problems in the termination of psychoanalytic therapy (47: pp. 316-358) will show the reader that such feelings are not found only in the relative neophyte. In spite of the fact that one of Freud's major purposes in this article is to warn against psychoanalysts' tendencies to encourage interminable analyses, we find Freud himself fluctuating between his warning and seeming to feel that after all analysis does have to be interminable!

summer vacation, will this only cause an interruption? Will the counselor be in a position to resume when the student returns? Perhaps there will have to be a transfer to some other counselor who will be available when the student returns. Perhaps at this time it is to be a true ending. Naturally, the client's state of mind is an extremely important factor. The counselor must be sensitive to the client's reaction to this future event. This means he must make sure the client understands that he will not be back when the client returns after the summer vacation, or the other conditions the client will find. If he decides that an ending should be worked for, rather than an interruption or a transfer, he will need to help the client focus and restrict his introspective efforts in such a way that the client may experience closure.

Counselors often overlook the therapeutic value of a forced ending. We have already discussed the Rankian conception of the therapeutic advantages in setting limits. The forced ending may have special value because it is set by circumstances rather than by the counselor. It has been our experience that this tends to maximize the value it possesses as a limit. The recognition by a relatively mature client that a limited time is available can lead to a rapid acceleration in counseling progress. Many times with such clients it is possible to proceed at a rapid pace almost to the very last interview. On the other hand, many clients will feel threatened by the imminent separation. They will be fearful about opening up new problems, knowing that they will not have a later opportunity to rely on the counselor's help in coming to grips with them. Although the counselor need not be unnecessarily fearful for the client, he will also want to respect the client's judgment in this regard. It is most important that the counselor be sensitive to the client's reactions to separation. Anticipating significant feelings, he will want to call attention to a date of separation early enough to give time for a proper working through of such feelings.

One possible mistake of counselors may appear in any ending, whether forced or otherwise. The counselor's perfectionist attitude, his concern about his professional adequacy, and his apprehensiveness about the client's adequacy often lead him to send the client away with vague feelings of fear, with expectations that he will not be able to handle his problems in the future and will have to return for counseling or psychotherapy. Communications that convey the idea that the client should look forward to future upsets, communications which attempt to make sure that he is thinking about future counseling or psychotherapy, set the stage for the client to leave his present counseling with feelings of fear and of impending trouble or even a crash. In general, it would seem to be more therapeutic to communicate the attitude and expectation that the client will be able to deal with future situations competently and will achieve satisfaction of his needs. It seems appropriate also to assume that, if he should fail, the present experience will have made it easier for him to return for future help.

With clients whose problems have been only partially dealt with and who are fearful about them, the above approach will not be therapeutic. Their fears and insecurities, which apparently have a real basis, have to be accepted and dealt with. They must be given aid in planning for future difficulties, those already anticipated. As in all other aspects of a counseling or therapeutic relationship, there is no one approved way of dealing with endings. The key to them still lies in the depth of the counselor's understanding of the client's needs and in his own capacity to meet these needs.

CHAPTER 14

The Process of Counseling:
A Model for Vocational Counseling

MAN WORKS IN ORDER TO LIVE, and at the same time can take pleasure in productive activity. Whether rich or poor, fully or scarcely educated, productive activity is likely to take up a significant portion of a man's waking time. Earlier chapters have defined the goals of counseling in developmental terms and have argued that one way to prevent crippling psychological conflicts is to facilitate personality development by intervening at transitional points in the life cycle. Most of these transitional points are junctures in the evolution of the individual's motivations and capacities as they are directed toward his ultimate destination as a working member of his community. Through formal education, from nursery school on up, society supplements the socializing work of the family. Accompanying each step in education, e.g., movement from nursery to kindergarten, is a greater separation from the family and a greater opportunity to clarify one's growing capacities. The existential anxieties (those inherent to living and growing rather than arising from neurotic conflict) stirred by the challenges of change and growth provide the base for a counseling effort in which the counselor is willing and able to participate with the client in his efforts to clarify his work identity and struggle toward the integration of the impulses, ideals, and controls that most fully express him.

At many points such self-confrontations and self-clarifications can occur—the entrance to junior high school, high school, or college, or transfers and promotions within one's vocational career. At each of these points, some individuals will encounter inner obstacles, provoking anxiety and blocking growth which counseling can remove. The comparatively light inner pressure exerted by the combination of existential anxiety and small inner obstacles does not provoke the state of mind that leads a person to embark on psychotherapy, but does interest him in seeking help focused on the vocationally-based decisions he faces.

Preceding chapters concerned with initiating counseling relationships and with the use of tests in counseling have already dealt with many aspects of such processes, but only from the general stance of psychological counseling. This chapter will consider the nature of career development and its implications for counseling.

STAGES OF THEORY DEVELOPMENT AND MODELS

The form of vocational counseling has reflected prevailing conceptions of the nature of the process of vocational choice. Until this century conceptions of vocational choice were rooted in a relatively static society in which most men followed in their fathers' footsteps. Environmental pressures, limitations, and opportunities were the primary determinants. Whenever anyone thought about vocational choice, attention was concentrated on the point at which the adolescent stood on the threshold of the adult work-a-day world (Brewer, 1942). Choice was seen as essentially a process of becoming informed regarding available entry positions into various occupations, educational requirements, the conditions of work, and rates of pay. The implicit model for vocational choice centered on extrinsic motivations for work and vocation. Thus vocational counseling initially called for an older, more informed person acquainting an adolescent with the nature of the occupational world and offering him fatherly guidance as he took the initial steps to enter it. Many of the group counseling methods currently in use at the junior and senior high school levels preserve this process. Today this process relies heavily on the many pamphlets and monographs now available which describe various groups of occupations. The student searches through these materials, aided by a guidance teacher, and prepares a report of several occupations reflecting his professed interests.

The next stage in thinking about vocational choice introduced a mixed, extrinsic-intrinsic motivation model by matching the psychological demands of the occupation with the tested characteristics of the adolescent. Vocational interest and personality testing were intended to insure that satisfactions intrinsic to the occupation were considered. The major spokesmen for this view of counseling were the University of Minnesota trio of Patterson, Williamson, and Darley (Patterson, Schneidler, & Williamson, 1938; Williamson & Darley, 1937; Williamson, 1939). More responsibility was placed on the guidance counselor. The client was seen as motivated to maximize his returns and his chances of succeeding. The counselor's task was to interpret his client's test results in such a way as to make clear which occupation fulfilled this requirement. This view of counseling suggests that the process might be reduced to a mammoth computer operation, applying a comprehensive prediction formula. The Minnesota group was, however, sufficiently sensitive to the human process to suggest that predictive equations could not fully replace the clinical function of making use of more subjective and intuitive data and of helping the client to incorporate the results into a plan of action. The assumption still remained that the counselor, on the basis of his technology, was the important source in formulating the plan of action. He must aid his client to overcome any irrational tendencies he may have to reject the plan. This conception of the process of vocational counseling is still prevalent on the junior and senior high school levels.

An increasing emphasis on personality theory and personality dynamics marked the late thirties. Psychologists were becoming more actively engaged in working with persons who had moderate to severe emotional problems. Psychoanalytic theory became more influential as one means of trying to understand severely disturbed persons; and many modifications on psychoanalytic thinking were developed. Rogers' views represent a particularly influential example. Out of this came a third phase. Difficulties in making a vocational choice were viewed as symptoms of an emotional or neurotic problem. When a client came to discuss his difficulties with vocational choice, his attention was directed to the anxieties and perceptual confusions which appeared to underlie his difficulty and he was encouraged, sometimes even seduced, into making the alleviation of these emotional problems the goal of his counseling relationship. We call this the symptom model. In other words, vocational counseling was transformed into personal counseling. Vocational counseling was not obliterated because, in the event that the student clung to his desire to deal with the question of choice, or was unwilling to confide sufficiently so as to uncover a neurotic basis for his difficulty, he was offered vocational counseling, either by the same person or by another person sometimes in the same agency, sometimes in a different one, and the process returned to the earlier model. In this sense, the third phase implied a dual model, the extrinsic-intrinsic choice model and the inner dynamics symptom model.

For more than a decade a developmental conception of vocational choice has been emerging. Super (1953) crystallized the tentative searchings of a number of theorists and investigators when he pointed out that a person's vocational career consisted of a whole series of choices, first at educational transition points and later at occupational ones. Many others have elaborated and extended this point of view through theoretical and research contributions. Concentrating on the self-concept as a central construct, Super (Super et al., 1963) and Tiedeman (Tiedeman & O'Hara, 1963) have tended to treat vocational development as a late stage, appearing mainly in adolescence. In this sense they stayed close to the earlier tradition. In a series of pivotal studies begun before Super's landmark paper, Roe concerned herself more thoroughly than any previous investigator with development and personality as associated with occupation. She used personality tests, particularly of the clinical variety, and conducted intensive clinical interviews dealing with life histories. Roe examined in this way the life history events which might have shaped the careers of her scientists. Her investigations culminated in a developmental conception of vocational choice in which warmth or distance of parents from children is seen as the main determinant; and occupations are differentiated in terms of their closeness to persons (Roe, 1957). Toward the end of the fifties,

Holland (1959), while laying the foundation for a comprehensive theory of choice, offered an essentially cross-sectional or type theory of choice, centered around his efforts to develop a new interest test. He described a set of types into which all occupations and persons could be mapped. Although he left a place in his scheme for the development of these personality types, he has hardly begun to fill that gap.

Psychoanalytic theory suggests that a developmental approach to vocation should examine the full sweep of influences shaping personality from birth, even from conception. To prepare the way for this we must make a more searching analysis of the gratifications to be obtained while engaging in the activities comprising the occupation. The author and his associates have attempted to do this by outlining a framework for vocational development (Bordin, Nachmann, & Segal, 1963). Our pivotal assumption is that insofar as he has freedom of choice an individual tends to gravitate toward those occupations whose activities permit him to express his preferred ways of seeking gratification and of protecting himself from anxiety. In an open-class society dedicated to minimizing the social and environmental obstacles toward maximum individual development, this gravitational process must be assumed to exert an appreciable influence. The individual's preferred ways of seeking gratification, the kinds of gratifications he seeks, and his modes of protecting himself from anxiety are the subject matter of personality theory and research. Thus, this view of vocational choice joins theory and research on vocational development to the study of personality. In essence, it leads to the assertion that one form of expression of the individual's personality development and its vicissitudes will be reflected in the vocational choices he makes over time and in the difficulties he encounters in this process.

With the foregoing in mind we constructed a framework of modes of gratification and methods of seeking them or of reducing anxiety into which occupations could be mapped. The vertical axis of this framework is made up of the various physiologically based sources of gratification, those centered around the activities of the mouth, i.e., nurturant (feeding and fostering) and aggressive (cutting, biting, devouring); manipulative activities designed to exert physical and interpersonal power; sensual activities, not for information but for pleasure; activities derived from anal impulses, acquiring, timing-ordering, hoarding and smearing; derivations of phallic and genital impulses, erecting, penetrating, impregnating, and producing; exploratory activities, seeing, touching, and hearing; and finally the activities of flowing-quenching, exhibiting, and rhythmic movement. The vertical axis contains five different ways in which these activities may be expressed in an occupation. One aspect refers to the importance for the occupation of a particular variety of activity. A second indicates the means through which the impulse is expressed. The possibilities range from the physical actions of the body to tools, words, abstract concepts and symbols, e.g., the expression of oral aggressive desires by means of cutting words. A third part of the vertical axis, "objects," indicates the person(s) or thing(s) toward which the activity is directed. The range of possibilities is from human beings or body parts to animals, plants, inanimate objects and abstractions. The next aspect is whether the activities appear to be patterned after a masculine or feminine model. Finally the question posed is whether the affective component of the activity is accepted or repressed. In the actual investigation of an occupation it would be necessary to determine the particular mechanism of defense or mastery employed.

The present form of this framework is the result of a process of refinement in which cruder forms were applied to the study of differences between occupations chosen because they were assumed to differ materially in one or more ways and, in turn, the more refined form provided a basis for later studies. A summary of some of our studies will illustrate what features of occupations are highlighted by this view. In examining the differences between creative writers and accountants, Segal (1961) noted the latter occupation's concern with precision and with records of the flow of money. The need for analysis and accuracy dictated a dispassionate unbiased stance. The accountant's position of being privy to the financial secrets of other persons and, more particularly, of corporate bodies without power over them, his being subject to routines and deadlines to be met, all converge to demand social conformity. In contrast, the creative writer is the observer of other persons and of society, able to draw on his own feelings to empathize with others. His freedom from conformity, which is often outright rebellion, permits him to examine the inner meaning of social patterns and their meaning for those persons whom society accepts or casts out. His femininely oriented involvement with words enables him to communicate these feelings and understandings in the sensitive style that marks great literature. Similarly, Nachmann (1960) saw in the practice of law a concern with justice as a formal process, an opportunity to fight your brother's battles using words as weapons, and the exercise of a privileged curiousity into the lives of others. When Beall and I (Beall & Bordin, 1964) examined the occupation of engineering, we were impressed by the engineer's involvement with producing concrete products, buildings, bridges, machines, etc. He relies on the abstract to produce the concrete. His mode is the epitome of masculinity. The engineering method combines orderliness, objectivity, and foresight. In his modes of relating to people, the engineer emphasizes again the concrete and the practical. He usually is a good follower in the beginning of productive enterprises and often rises to positions of leadership.

This developmental conception of vocational choice translates into a new model for vocational counseling which departs from the extrinsic-intrinsic choice and inner dynamics symptom models, though incorporating some of their aspects. The developmental model is a version of vocational counseling which treats it as a self-confrontation which an individual is able to experience at various junctures in his life cycle.

PROCESS ISSUES IN THE DEVELOPMENTAL MODEL

When a client seeks counseling at a transition point in his vocational career, the counselor must decide how to go about facilitating an optimal self-confrontation under conditions of minimal anxiety. We see three stages in this process: an exploratory, contract-setting stage, a stage of critical decision, which often blends almost imperceptibility into the third stage, working through problems indigenous to that stage of his development or, where present, dealing with long-standing chronic problems. The major problem is to avoid either overly superficial abortive self-examination or seduction into an equally abortive psychotherapy. As a vehicle for illustrating how one treads this fine line, we will use the case of Kenneth, who was seen for twelve interviews. Kenneth was a moderately obsessive character whose chronic difficulties may ultimately force him into intensive psychotherapy. He asked for counseling near the end of his freshman year saying that he was not certain of his vocational preference and expected to be helped by interviews and tests. Kenneth was casually but neatly dressed, held himself rather stiffly, and betrayed his initial anxiety by the tightness with which he kept his hands clasped. His speech, simultaneously rapid, tense, and halting, betrayed little of his early years in England other than his pronounciation of "dog" as "dahg." With respect to his long standing character problem and his initial anxiety Kenneth was not a typical vocational counseling client. At the same time he was oriented to deal with a circumscribed problem—vocational choice —rather than with any sensed feeling of personal inadequacy.

Exploration and contract setting

At the outset the vocational counselor must tread a fine line between two major pitfalls. On the one hand, the client may have a very restricting set toward what is relevant to his choice. He may see counseling as no more than obtaining the results of tests and examining their implications in terms of possible occupations. He sees all of the impact coming from outside, supplied by the counselor. His, the client's, role is a passive and compliant one. Looking inward is not part of his task. The other pitfall of inappropriately offering or demanding a therapeutic effort flows from the counselor's efforts to counteract this restricting set. Somehow he must strive to disclose to his client that the question of his vocational choice deserves a closer, more painstaking look at the kind of person he is, his ways of seeking gratification and protecting himself from anxiety, and the images of self that go along with it. But this effort must not become an ultimatum to acknowledge personal inadequacy and to commit oneself to unlimited confiding that a long term psychotherapeutic effort implies. Unless the latter pitfall is avoided, clients with little anxiety are likely to leave counseling rather than comply and those with more than developmental problems may be seduced into a therapeutic effort without the necessary commitment.

How can the counselor facilitate a meaningful self-confrontation without forcing a therapeutic contract to confide without limitations? He does this, we believe, by staying with the client's focus on the issue of vocational choice. Our view of the personal issues involved in the choice of vocation raises questions bearing on the individual's doubts and hesitations, which disclose to him the relevance of coming to grips with himself rather than confining his efforts to an examination of the externals of a vocation. Almost everyone has thoughts and feelings about occupations which are intimately related to his reactions to and observations of himself. Even if these reactions are not on the surface, they are usually readily available and reflected indirectly in comments about the occupations he has considered, how he came to be interested, and the hesitations he may feel about choosing any one of them. Eliciting such reactions and probing for the kind of future he imagines for himself in an occupation often serves as a means of establishing communication regarding the individual's desires, his needs, and his anxieties about fulfilling them. To be able to sense the self-struggle that lies behind a client's talk about the occupations he has considered and to make contact with these struggles within the occupational context, the counselor must become thoroughly immersed in the above described way of viewing occupations. He must, in addition, have given thought to the developmentally based conflicts that might be provoked by particular vocations. For example, our analysis of the role of a strong, firm, but loving father in shaping the engineer prompted our conclusion (Beall & Bordin, 1964) that a likely focus of difficulty for the prospective engineer will lie in the incompleteness of his identification with his father. An overly stern father, one who is unable to balance his demanding and controlling ways with warm friendliness and willingness to share his interests and enthusiasms with his son, can induce a strong but highly fearful identification. Such a son will fear the task of following in his father's footsteps, yet be reluctant to reject father's demand that he emulate him. Deans of engineering schools are familiar with the timid, reluctant boys dragged into their offices by domineering, unrealistic fathers. Sometimes anger and rebellion, covertly expressed, is the son's response. He may be capable of functioning as an engineer and under freer circumstances would have chosen the profession of his own accord, but finds that the only way he can express his rebellion against his father is by failing out of the training program. With this general framework in mind the counselor will be able to react similarly to occupations not yet the objects of formal investigation.

Returning to Kenneth, he described himself in a brief fifteen minute intake interview as leaning toward medicine and having become more certain of this choice as a result of recent talks with a physician and a visit to a hospital. Earlier he had been interested in engineering because he meant to follow in his father's footsteps, but after a recent conversation had discovered that his father really would have preferred something else. A preliminary information sheet question, "How do you think we can help?" drew the response, "by finding the results of interviews and tests," a reply representative of clients who seek vocational counseling. In the extrinsic-intrinsic model such clients are often given a standard battery of tests surveying a wide range of issues. In the "vocational choice as symptom approach" there is an effort to convince the client that testing is unnecessary and to try to immerse him in concern with what is wrong with his personality. We advocate neither of these actions.[1] When a client himself raises the question of tests, the counselor should explain that there are a great many kinds of tests, and that we need to examine where his doubts about himself occur to ascertain which tests, if any, might contribute to the clarification of the decision he faces. In addition, the counselor should indicate that we will not necessarily have tests which bear on all of the client's uncertainties and that it is unlikely that tests by themselves will help resolve his doubts. However, test results could contribute to the helpfulness of their discussions.

In the first interview Kenneth and his counselor began by discussing the status of his problem, mainly that he seemed to have pretty much made up his mind about concentrating on medicine, but wished to validate this choice. They embarked on an examination of the relevant issues. Kenneth was eager to please

[1] See Chapters 11 and 12.

and as he warmed to his task, he seemed to relax and unclasp his hands and then to move them in coordination with the rest of his efforts to communicate. We take up the interview at this point.

C 9. Well, I think that the way you can do that is to get a clearer idea about yourself (S: Yes) as well as a clearer idea about what medicine might represent. Umm, we might start with how you see medicine, what it is that attracts you, what you think you're going to be able to capitalize on in yourself in medicine (S: Uh-huh) ; what gratifications you think you can get out of medicine.

S 9. Well, first, I'm very interested in science, *applied* science, not just theoretical science. And I'm also interested, very interested, in working with my hands, doing things. I think I'm mechanically inclined, because I always read articles on inventions, and things like that (C: Umm), cars, things like that. That's why I—for a while I wanted to be an engineer, because I was using my hands and using my scientific knowledge, and then I attended to—well, my father was talking one day and he said he was satisfied being an engineer but the time when he had made his decision he really wasn't sure whether he should go into medicine or engineering, or another profession, and he said he would probably be equally as happy. I started wondering, because I didn't just want to follow in my father's footsteps, and I started wondering, where else could I use this same knowledge. And I thought that medicine was probably the better choice than an engineer (C: Uh-huh), and I just more or less went along with that for a while, and I don't think I really realized what it was until I've been trying to read articles, more articles about it in magazines and books and talking to a lot of pre-med students and also doctors on how they feel and what they do. But basically it's because I'm interested in science and I like to work with people. I just don't like to work with machinery as an engineer would. I like the personal contact. (C: Uh-huh)

C 10. (*Pause*) How do you see yourself as similar or different from your father? You were talking about not wanting to follow his path.

S 10. Well (*short pause*), the main difference, I think, is that (*short pause*) things that are more human. I mean certainly he works with people, that's part of his job, but when he gets right down to what his work actually is, designing,—he's an engineer for Caterpillar Tractor—designing farm machinery in volume; I don't really like that kind of work. I'd rather be helping some other person with his problems (C: Uh-huh) rather than be working with my own problems. (C: I see.)

C 11. *(Short pause)* Can you think of places in your past experience where this kind of feeling on your part has expressed itself? This desire to work with someone? People?

S 11. Well *(hesitates)*, in going out of my way to really help somebody in a situation where I really didn't need to?

C 12. Well, just where, in effect, this was a way of showing where you get your satisfactions.

S 12. Well, I can't really think of any right off, now. I mean, as far as I feel myself, I think I'm kind of shy. I *know* I'm kind of shy, you know. I haven't been a real terrific joiner of clubs in high school. I'm only a freshman, so I haven't joined anything up here yet. I haven't been a real leader of anything. (C: Uh-huh) I like to follow, yes, but not a leader, so I never really—like in work. Everything I do, though, I always throw myself into whole-heartedly, and accomplish it. But I, uh—well, we've had dogs for a long time. I always enjoy having a nice dog, we have a little dog now, I don't like him, but when we have a dog I really like to take it for walks. One of my sisters takes care of it because she enjoys animals more, but the dogs kind of like me. I think that's a good sign. *(Laughs)* But I also *(short pause)* grow things, I like to throw things in a garden (C: Uh-huh), plant a couple of vegetables, and I like to work in the lab, help my dad, things like that. I don't look upon hard work as drudgery, I really enjoy it when I get some hard work. It's a challenge *(pause)*. I can't really think of any instances (C: Uh-huh) like you asked me to point out. *(Short pause)* I mean going out of my way to help somebody. *(Short pause)* I don't *(mumbles, starts again)* I don't really consider it going out of my way, I mean I would have helped them anyway.

C 13. I don't know if 'going out of your way' was the central issue in my question, I was wondering what kinds of experiences you've had in the past that involved being in this kind of relationship to other people so that you had a chance to see what kinds of satisfactions you *could* get out of it.

S 13. *(Pause)* I can't think of anything right now.

C 14. Uh-huh. Is it perhaps that as you think about medicine and this characteristic of it that you think of it as something you would *like* (S: Uh-huh) to be characteristic of you (S: Yeah) rather than it *has* been characteristic of you in the past? (S: Yeah.

I—yeah. Sure.) Is that it? (S: Yeah.) (*Half a minute of si-lence.*) Have you had any experience with illness?

S 14. I had a bout with measles a couple of years ago, I was pretty sick for a couple of weeks. (C: Uh-huh)

C 15. When someone else was ill, someone that you were close to or anything of that sort?

S 15. Well, over here, no. I was born in England, and all our relatives are over there still (C: Uh-huh), and of course I haven't seen them. I haven't really been too close to them, as close as I'd been if they'd been over here. I remember them a long time ago, maybe ten years ago. Well, two of my grandparents just recently died, and—I mean it's only natural that you feel 'I wish I'd been there and known them,' I really did wish I'd known them better, I wish I could have been there when they were dying, and helped them if I could. But we don't have any rela-tives over here, no one in our family. Well, my dad *was* sick, a couple of years ago, he had ulcer trouble, he was pretty sick with that.

C 16. (*Both talk at once*) Recently?

S 16. (*Inaudible*) He was in the hospital for a while. Course you feel bad about that, you don't know what to do, so you just trust in the physician. The physician my father had, he said he was exceptionally competent. He said as though he gave him a com-plete feeling of 'here is my life, I can trust you with it.' (C: Uh-huh) As the (*mutters—inaudible*) not fear, but 'I'll do my best and I think it'll be good enough. I'm sure it'll be good enough.' (C: Uh-huh) Any doctor's like that. They always act so con-fident. Even when the odds are against them, they always think they're going to win. (C: Uh-huh) It's a noble—kind of noble in them that brings this out.

C 17. This is something you admire in them?

S 17. I think it's different. I realize there are a lot of people *are* just as smart and they have just as much training as doctors, that's medical doctors, but they don't always seem to be competing quite as cut-throatish as maybe business (C: Uh-huh) workers do. Not that I fear competition. I enjoy it, but they don't seem to really mind it if there is some competing among them (C: Uh-huh). Because they realize there's just as much work even if they don't compete. I mean they are competing. I realize there's so much work to be done they don't really bother to go out and see how much business they can round up. (*Pause*) There's so many things I *could* say about it I could probably go on for a long time about it (*smiling*). I mean for other things I think you're in business for yourself, that's one thing in your favor. You figure there's always going to be a need for doctors, no matter where you are, no matter what's going to happen or what it's going to be. Even if worse comes to worse, that's when the doctor's needed most. So I say there (*short pause*) is always going to be work for a doctor. (*Short pause*) And like I say (*mumbles*) could go for hours. (*Pause*)

C 18. Does the independence appeal to you?

S 18. Yeah. I could make decisions for myself (*chooses words carefully*) and not just be another part of a big production.

Our framework for vocational development makes its presence felt at this point. It sensitizes the counselor to the personal relevance of the choices being considered. A thoughtful application of concepts of personality development provides a basis for helping the client break out of his restricting set of responding only to such stereotyped questions as what courses he liked best or what hobbies he pursued. We see that at the very outset the counselor uses such expressions as, "What are you going to capitalize on in yourself?" and "What gratifications do you think you can get?" Kenneth begins by turning to the familiar questions of what courses he liked and what hobbies he pursued. But soon he is associating to his father and to his thoughts about following or not following his pattern. Notice how the counselor is quick to respond to this association by inviting an examination of how much of his identity incorporates his father's characteristics (C 10). We would expect that one important difference between engineers and physicians is the latters' more intimate involvement with people, to which Kenneth responds in comparing himself with his father. The counselor takes up his theme of working with people and the kinds of experiences Kenneth has had. Kenneth interprets the question as referring to working with others in a helping relationship and seems to find his cupboard of experiences fairly bare. He finally rather lamely comments on dogs liking him and that he grows things. Being confronted by this gap in his experience seems to slow him up and eventually brings a halt to communication which the counselor breaks in C 14 with his question about experiences with illness. Kenneth's response exhibits his admiration of the physician as an independent person fighting battles with illness and death, supremely confident despite great odds. The counselor participates actively. His questions are designed to bring to Kenneth's attention that his present interest in medicine, to be meaningful, must have connections to past experiences and their effect on him. The counselor aims to facilitate Kenneth's active collaboration in a process he understands. The questions asked are evidently associated with medicine and with his uncertainties about emulating his father. They are the kinds of questions which can lead to a more searching examination of inner promptings and self-concepts.

In the next section, which we will summarize, the counselor asks what, in his experience with his family, has made independence of special importance. Kenneth does not respond much, first equating independence with financial security and then dismissing it with some conventional comments about being in control of one's destiny. Discussion then turns to the contrast between his earlier interest in mechanics and the physical sciences and his present turning toward the biological sciences. Kenneth's remarks, seeming to lump biology, medicine, sociology, and psychology, suggests that he sees all of these subjects as differing from the physical sciences in their concern with people. Kenneth finds communication difficult at this point. He finally launches into an extended report of his visit to a hospital under the guidance of a surgeon who is a family friend. As he ruminates over the various specialties in medicine and the differences in the opportunities afforded for working directly with patients, he remarks that while he would enjoy working with his hands (referring to surgery and pathology), he would miss personal contact.

A brief excerpt of the interview at this point shows the counselor aiding the client to connect his reactions to medicine with his concerns about his capacity to relate to others.

C 28. What's kept you back from personal contacts up until now? You've told me that you're shy and the implication is that perhaps you have not had as much close personal contact as you would prefer. (S: Uh-huh) I'm wondering what kept you back. I know you are "shy," yes, but if you could talk a little more about that.

S 28. It's very basic, kind of hard to understand sometimes (*short pause*) because I don't have a tremendous number of friends. But the friends I do have I consider very good friends, and I get along with people very well. But a lot of people, I think decisions are made right away, and I think, well, I don't really want to know this person, and I won't go out of my way to go and see him at his house. I just (*inaudible*) I ask him, "Let's go out tonight and see a movie or something." I don't really do that. I just (*short pause*) well, for many reasons I don't do that. I think mainly it's a feeling of inferiority, I'm not really sure that I have enough qualities that would be a success with this person (C: Umm) to enjoy my company. It's funny, if something goes wrong at the beginning of the relationship I usually take it as being my fault (C: Umm), I made a mistake and I can't get along with this person too well. (*Mumbles*) Well, we can't understand each other and it doesn't really matter that much, but so often I look upon myself as being inferior. I'm not as good as I should be. It causes quite a bit of tension and makes for inattention while studying. I don't think I always use it. I just wander from one thing to another and am not really sure if I'm not really concentrating the way I should.

C 29.   Are you implying that this kind of self-criticism and uncertainty about yourself carries over into intellectual activities also? (S: Um-hum. Very definitely.) Uh-huh. One of the reasons I reacted to it was I noticed we have the kinds of information, preliminary information that's available on you via your high school record, and tests you took during orientation here, and I noticed your high school rank was out of line with what (S: Yeah) one would expect of someone of your potential.

They go on to discuss Kenneth's level of achievement in high school, its low level, which he ascribed to his participation in sports and other activities and to a general increase in academic motivation when he came to college. His grades are now more in line with his abilities. Around his report of dissatisfaction with his roommate, there ensues a discussion of his greater need for organization and neatness than either his father or his mother. As the interview approaches its close, we find the counselor saying:

C 40.   I think our time's about up, we might talk a little bit about where we're going and so on. I was wondering about what you had said on the face sheet, how you expected to be helped. It seems to me that you mentioned taking tests; is that what you—?

S 40.   Uh-huh. I took a lot of tests in high school, the Kuder test (C: Yes) for one, the personality (C: Yes)

C 41.   Now of course we haven't been talking about tests at all here. So I was wondering whether you were seeing what we were doing as different from what you'd been expecting.

S 41.   Well, really, what it boils down to is that I would like to know more about myself. (C: Uh-huh) I'm in physical science because I can tell right away if this thing is such—remember what I was saying way back that when I look at *myself* it's very hard to get any idea of what I am, what my values are? (C: Yeah) Because—well, since I've been up here they've changed, of course. And I have a hard time, if a person asks me—well, on our sheets to come up here we had to describe our own personality. (C: Hmm) I have a hard time seeing what kind of person I'd be, and I'd like to know more about myself.

C 42.   And you don't care whether it's (*laughs*) via test or anything else.

S 42.   (*Breaking in*) No, I don't care, as long as it's actually the truth. (C: Uh-huh) If it's bad I can do something to change it, and if it's good I can strengthen it.

C 43.   Um-humm. Well, I think at the moment it seems to me that we ought to proceed the way we're going. There may well be and probably *will* be points at which we might decide that tests would be useful (S: Uh-huh) to bring additional information into the picture. I think in the long run if you're going to get an understanding of yourself in a way that will help you to make these decisions and be more certain of the decisions you *have* made, it's likely to be via just doing more than getting the test and having the results reported to you. So I would propose that we proceed this way if that sounds— (*pauses as S voices assent*) Is that what you want to do? (S: Um-hmm) All right, is next Friday at this time a good time for you? (S: Yes) Fine.

In this first hour Kenneth has become involved with the counselor's questions about the bearing of his experiences and his personality on the occupational alternatives he contemplates. We see inklings, which are probably also visible to him, that his difficulties with his decision reside partly in incompletenesses in his identity and also reflect his dissatisfactions and conflicts over how intimately he can relate to others. The counselor wisely calls attention to the difference between the kind of help he is offering and what Kenneth had expected. Kenneth's interpolated "Uh-huh" when the counselor refers to points at which tests might prove useful tells us that he is still attracted by that kind of help, but the boy has become sufficiently involved in the self-examination process to be relatively flexible in viewing ways to achieve self-discovery.

The stage of critical decision

A more than superficial examination of an individual in the throes of vocational choice usually uncovers a struggle for growth and change. The occupations he considers will reflect both his views of himself as he is and as he would like to be. As the client becomes increasingly aware of his struggle, he also begins to see the counseling process not only as a means for effecting a decision but also, if he desires it, as a part of a process of personality change. He then begins to struggle with the question of whether he should retain his more limited original objective or seek broader goals in counseling. The counselor must be alert to the appropriate time for offering explicit statements of this choice. He must be sufficiently aware of his own motivations, whether of therapeutic ambition or of extricating himself from a relationship in which he has little investment, to allow the client to experience unhampered his own conflicting wishes and to arrive at whichever resolution is most meaningful to him. If the client opts for change, the counselor decides whether his own competency is adequate for his role in the change process, or whether referral is indicated.

In Kenneth's case, his obsessiveness gave him little choice but to come to grips with some aspects of his conflicts. Out of the initial exploratory period, continued for the next two hours, the conflict gradually emerged between his concern for precision as represented by the physical sciences and his desire for greater involvement with people. His concern with precision was surely a reflection of his obsessive-compulsive pattern and medicine represented an expression of his desire to take at least a partial step in the direction of closer and more intimate personal relationships. As Kenneth discussed his family, a picture emerged of an emphasis on closeness coupled with strong prohibitions against hostility and aggressive reactions. Toward the end of the third hour, when Kenneth expressed some of his doubts about being able to meet the personal demands of medicine, the counselor suggested that he take a Strong Vocational Interest Blank as a preliminary to further exploration.

Kenneth's Strong presented an essentially flat profile. There was an A for President of a Manufacturing Concern and a B plus for Osteopath, but there was no primary pattern or even a well-defined secondary pattern, and at the same time no rejection pattern. During the hour in which the Strong was discussed they talked about his difficulty in saying he either liked or disliked any activity. Similarly, in writing papers he found it almost impossible to take a clear-cut stand on any topic. These discussions directed attention to his inner obstacles to decision-making. If the counselor were willing to serve as a decision-maker he might well have been the external force that Kenneth usually used to push himself toward decisions for which he was not responsible and which he could then covertly oppose. Since there was no possibility of Kenneth committing himself at this time to an extended psychotherapeutic effort, the counselor had some misgivings about the usefulness of counseling focused around Kenneth's difficulty in making this vocational decision. Despite this hesitation, he accepted Kenneth's desire to work further in this way.

Working for change

In the preceding chapter we have discussed how counseling for limited goals is conducted by keeping the realistic problem in focus and by directing attention to a strategically selected conflict. Applied to counseling growing out of problems of vocational choice, these ideas suggest that relevance to vocational identity be kept as a central theme.

This Kenneth and his counselor did with secondary attention to conflicts over dependency. In the eight meetings they had before the end of the school year, they both understood that in order to work on the problem of vocational choice they must roam over the full scope of Kenneth's experiencing and functioning. At the start of an hour the counselor might begin by asking what thoughts Kenneth had at the close of their preceding hour. How had he felt, what thoughts had run through his mind while approaching this meeting? During the hour Kenneth generally had the opportunity to initiate whatever topics he wished. His thoughts often roamed in various directions, but most often had to do with current relationships to his parents. In addition he touched on his feelings about the past, as well as his reactions, both overt and covert, to the counselor. Thus, while retaining the purpose of helping him with his vocational choice, the counselor stimulated him toward a wider, more elastic examination of himself. Their focus on vocational choice meant that from time to time the counselor related what Kenneth was experiencing, what he was remembering, and his new awareness of their significance to his problems of choosing a vocation.

Proceeding in this way, it became clear to the counselor, and we believe to Kenneth, that his father's migration to this country had somehow created a difficult problem in identity formation. He talked about his feeling that his father's family was of more consequence in England than his father was in the United States. Apparently he felt that he would have developed better had he been brought up in England because he would have been made to work harder. He appeared to see his father's leaving England during its bad time in the immediate post-war period as a failure to live up to his obligations. One senses underlying this feeling that Kenneth, on entering this country, had experienced a discontinuity between his family and himself. The necessity of adapting to new customs and new standards seemed to have blocked the use of his father as a model.

When his father returned from a short visit to England, Kenneth was astonished to hear him say he was happy to return *home*. He seems to have misconstrued the nature of his father's attachment to the two countries. Another realization was that, although his father had been a champion quarter-miler in England, Kenneth's time for the same event, while competing for his high school track team, was actually faster than his father's. As the interviews were coming to a close, Kenneth was finding that his father had more to do with people in his work than he had supposed. Kenneth was beginning to entertain the possibility that some area of industrial or personnel management might provide a satisfactory mode of self-expression. It is possible that in freeing himself of his conflict over his English background, Kenneth was able to see things in his father that he had not seen before.

Although the major issue was that of vocational choice, other issues appeared and were partially worked with during the counseling process. There was the problem of separating himself from too close a tie to his family which was intimately related to the artifically tight adherence to his parents' standards which made him vulnerable to crippling guilt reactions. However, during the course of their interviews he seemed to begin testing out a greater maturity in his relationships to his parents and to their standards. He made unilateral moves toward planning his own living arrangements. Previously he had done this only after very close consultation with his parents. He began to talk of the possibility of dropping out of school and enlisting for a period of military service. The closely related theme of aggressiveness and competitiveness was explored. He became increasingly aware that his parents had seemed to emphasize prohibiting overt anger toward or even criticism of others and that patterns other than such strict prohibition were possible. He realized that his father had kept him from being openly expressive of both his competitive and his disappointed feelings in connection with his participation in track. He became aware that he had had feelings of disappointments, feelings of wanting to win, but that his father had demanded a British "chin up, good show" response in which one acted as if winning were not of any importance.

It would be neat and gratifying to be able to report that Kenneth, following this counseling experience, clarified his identity and achieved self-integration and independence. As the series of interviews closed, it was understood that following the intervening summer Kenneth would be stopping by to retake the Strong as a way of seeing what had happened in the intervening period. Although he did register for the fall semester, he did not appear to take the Strong. As the end of that semester he left school and there is no record that he returned. So we can only speculate as to what ensued. The counselor was inclined to think that leaving school was an expression of his desire to achieve more independence. Perhaps he did join the service. We can feel certain that important issues were opened up and partially clarified. There were other issues, of course—revolving around the pathological aspects of his character formation which were hardly touched and which may be taking their toll.

To summarize, Kenneth's case illustrates how the developmental model can be used in vocational counseling. It illustrates the close link between personality and career development which provides a basis for eliminating the spurious dichotomy between vocational and personal counseling without reducing one to the other. It permits us to relate a person's difficulties with his vocational choices to the viscissitudes of his personality development and, through helping with these choices, to influence the fullness of that development.

CHAPTER 15

Case Records[1]

EVERY JOB and every project usually has both an interesting and a dull side. The time has come for us to turn from the intrinsically interesting counseling relationship to the less interesting responsibility for making a record of that relationship. Most counselors treat the process of record-keeping as the least interesting and therefore most-to-be-postponed or avoided aspect of their work.

There are probably many reasons for this feeling, some rational and others irrational. One reason is that it is natural for the counselor to see his relationship with his client as the sole medium by which his mission is accomplished. In so far as the relationship is the primary and crucial medium through which the goals of counseling are reached, this is not an unreasonable notion. It relegates case notes to the department of bureaucratic red tape far from those operations that possess a functional relevance to living counseling. Many times the organization of a counseling agency unintentionally provides another reason for avoiding case-recording by so overloading counselors with cases that they have little time or energy for recording. Undoubtedly another contributory factor is the counselor's fear of his own case records as potentially self-revealing. It would be interesting to compare, in terms of the counselor's satisfaction and security about what he has been doing, the interviews which are either meagerly recorded or not

[1] For two excellent articles on this topic the reader is referred to Little (1949) and Sarbin (1940).

recorded at all with those that are very fully reported. Whatever motivates the counselor's resistances to records, it is important to aid him to overcome them. The most important way by which he can be aided to overcome his resistance is through becoming aware of the purposes of case records and how he can use them functionally, with a client's welfare in mind, and in other more extraneous but important ways.

FUNCTIONS OF RECORDS

Case records have four major functions, each of which will be described below. They are used for: (1) supervision and consultation; (2) the aid they give to the counselor in counseling situations; (3) implementation of agency policies; and (4) evaluation and research.

Supervision and consultation

This is one of the major uses of case records. They are one of the important media through which it becomes possible for the counselor to share his responsibility for the client. The value of this shared responsibility to both the counselor who is an intern and to the client is self-evident. However, even when a counselor has become a full staff member, consultation and often supervision are useful. No counselor, no matter how long his experience, is so broadly trained, so equally skillful in understanding all the varieties of situations that confront him, so uniformly free from personally distorting or conflicting feelings, that he can always function without help.

The counseling intern and his supervisor will undoubtedly want to have as full a record of his interviews as possible. Ideally, recordings and transcripts should be available. At this early stage of training, the perceptions and recall of the counselor should not be trusted not to omit or distort some of the most meaningful parts of his interaction with his client. Furthermore, a playback of a recording or a transcribed record of his interactions with the client serve as concrete and dramatic reminders of how he reacted, what aspects of his client's behavior he has so far overlooked, as well as the general meaning of the whole process. Ordinarily, the degree to which the counselor in training becomes increasingly motivated to make use of complete or at least extensive records is to a considerable extent a function of the effectiveness of the supervision he is receiving. An understanding and accepting supervisor will help the counselor to feel confident he can master the demands of the counseling situation and to look forward to the help toward achieving this goal that a supervisor will give him.

Similarly, where staff morale is good, members of the counseling staff will be able to lean on each other, staff consultants, staff supervisors, or directors for aid with knotty counseling problems.

General counselor uses

Apart from their uses for supervisory or training purposes, a counselor finds many other ways in which a case record can be useful. Many times in an extended series of interviews he will find it necessary to acquire a fresh perspective on the progress of counseling through rereading or rehearing the case record. In this way he may become aware that he has lost sight of certain important goals which loomed large at the beginning of counseling. With this new perspective he may also pick out patterns in what the client is trying to do to him or what he is trying to do to the client to which he has not been sufficiently sensitive and which he would have missed completely without this review.

In earlier discussions we said that a series of counseling sessions is likely to be interrupted, sometimes extensively so. Case notes can help the counselor refresh his memory of a client and the way things had been going, especially the client's reactions prior to an interruption.

Frequently, some current situation in counseling has a dynamic connection with interactions at some earlier point. It may be the description of a dream or an account of a particular relationship. Sometimes it is related to what the counselor himself has said or done. Ideally, the counselor should be so attuned to the client that all these events are carefully and meaningfully interwoven in his understanding of the client. Then he can instantly remember the event and tie it to the present. Unfortunately, this is not always the case. Naturally the counselor cannot always understand the client fully. When he is carrying a fairly heavy case load, there are possibilities of interference and transpositions in his memory from one case to another. To have the record available enables him to clarify and correct his recollections. Obviously this is only helpful when a particular event has further ramifications, permitting the counselor to complete the verification process after the interview

Uses by the agency

The counseling agency has many good reasons for wanting case records. One of the most important reasons is that staff members leave or go on a vacation but the agency's responsibilities continue. For the purpose of transferring a case effectively the new counselor must have available the record of previous contacts. He will want to be able to compare how a client reacts to him as compared to the previous counselor. Quite often it is illuminating to discover that the client's behavior in the initial interview represents a repetitive pattern. The new counselor will then be able to make use of the previous counselor's experience with the client to understand his present needs. He will also be in a better position to judge what progress, if any, has taken place following the previous counseling experience and possibly will decide to shift his approach to avoid a previous stalemate.

Apart from the issue of transfer, many other occasions for the exercise of agency responsibility may arise while a counselor is away or after he has left the agency. There will be requests for communications about the client, actions will be taken by some other agency in which the counseling agency is expected to participate. The staff member acting for the agency must have available to him a record of the client's relationship to the agency sufficiently complete to permit him to act on it.

Evaluation and research

Every counseling agency has a responsibility to undertake some research. At the very least it is expected to make an effort to assess the effectiveness of its service to clients and to discover in what respects it succeeds and where it might be improved. A case record which describes the process of counseling and notes the counselor's diagnostic analysis provides an indispensable link in the chain of evidence on the effectiveness of the agency's work.

Many agencies will not be satisfied with this minimum of research and will undertake investigations of the many theoretical scientific and practical questions that arise when the effectiveness of a particular form of counseling is scrutinized. Case records are, of course, a most important source of data at every point.

THE FORM OF CASE NOTES

Whenever case notes have been surveyed, the greatest heterogeneity of practice has been found. In size they range from no notes at all to voluminous, detailed, almost word-for-word records of each interview. In form they range between a shapeless chronological account in one long paragraph, without further identifiable subdivisions of the material, to highly structured summaries in which the interview has been broken down into a number of content areas with main headings and subheadings, a method which almost completely obscures the chronology. One system of categorizing the form of case-recording is according to the major line of emphasis in the notes, whether upon diagnostic judgment or upon the process.

Diagnostic recording

A crucial part of the process of helping a client is the gradual understanding of the dynamics of his personality and the part that his environment plays in his life. Whether the early stages of this analysis consist solely of an intake interview or include an extended diagnostic testing process, the counselor starts with initially formulated hypotheses about the client, some of which he feels highly confident about, others which he knows are highly tentative. As counseling progresses, some of these hypotheses become fully confirmed; others, even some of those most confidently held initially, are plainly contradicted and must be discarded. Still others are held in abeyance while new hypotheses are reached for.

In diagnostic recording, the record of this process is made explicit. This kind of recording can be useful to the counselor, the supervisor, and to later research workers, who are able to examine the kinds of hypotheses and judgments upon which counseling proceeded. They seek to discover to what extent the crucial points in the process were anticipated by the counselor. To what extent, they ask, were his initial hypotheses likely to be confirmed in a later relationship? What was his impression of the client at the end of counseling? Such are the kinds of questions to which diagnostic recording provides an answer.

Considering the various kinds of research and service uses that are likely to be made of diagnostic recording, it would seem desirable to identify different types of judgments by inserting appropriate headings in the script, probably underlined to help make them stand out. They might refer to such general categories as general level of ability, special abilities, vocational interests, family relationships, history of the complaint, treatment formulation, progress evaluation, or prognosis.

It is particularly useful in the training of counseling interns to be able to inspect their interpretations of tests as well as the general judgments upon which they are operating. In the case of elaborate individual testing, as represented by such special clinical instruments as the Wechsler-Bellevue, the Rorschach, or the TAT, a fairly complete diagnostic analysis and evaluation ordinarily make up the report of testing. On the other hand, only a test score or a test profile will appear in the folder for the typical pencil-and-paper tests or inventories. In the latter instance, it is only through diagnostic recording that the counselor is able to give evidence of the meaning he has drawn from these test scores and of what he has transmitted to the client.

Process recording

As contrasted with diagnostic recording, which deals with the over-all understanding of the client, process recording emphasizes the sequence of interactions that represent the counselor's efforts to meet the client's needs. It is here one finds the greatest variability. One important factor here is the counselor's level of understanding. If he has little or no understanding of what is going on between him and the client, he has no choice but to try to reproduce a verbatim record. If he is pushed for time, the task may become insurmountable and the result may be no record at all. Thus, both the counselor's ability to recall what occurred and the way he organizes his report depend upon his understanding. One counselor must reproduce step by step, and in detail, the topics the client introduced in the course of the hour. Another counselor is able to point out that "during this hour the client seemed to be trying to convey indirectly his dissatisfaction with the counseling process. He did this by talking about his dissatisfactions with doctors, with teachers, and with older authoritative adults."

Naturally, where the counselor's skill in understanding is still in the formative stage or where because of personal or other obstacles his understanding is momentarily blocked, a more complete reproduction of the interview will be necessary. In fact, it has been the experience of many who have supervised the training of interns in counseling or psychotherapy that recordings and typescripts are highly necessary adjuncts to the process of developing ability to understand and tc embody this understanding through case records. Even a more experienced counselor, when he hits a particular snag in the relationship, can profit through recorded reproductions of his interviews for later study.

Thus, the size of the process record will be expanded or condensed according to the particular needs of the counselor in each specific case. In many instances, a high skillful counselor working with a client whom he understands well may be able to condense several interviews in a brief summary. The following represents an example:

During these three meetings the client found it necessary to test whether I would really let him take the responsibility for controlling himself. He tested it by bringing in reports of impulses which he had either just barely avoided expressing or had actually expressed in some minimal fashion. Similarly, during our hours he threatened me with possible actions such as breaking the relationship, getting angry enough with me to break something in the office, and so on. I think this is a very crucial point in the relationship and, though at times I have had slight misgivings, on the whole I think he is justifying my conviction that he does have the ability to control his impulses and, I think, through my confidence he will be able to achieve the confidence for himself.

At other times, a confused counselor may need four or five typewritten pages for the record of a single interview. He needs consultation and supervision.

Summaries

After about five to ten interviews, it becomes desirable for the counselor to prepare a case summary after the counseling session. Running notes become too voluminous to serve many of the later purposes for which they might be used, e.g., to send a requested report to another agency. This summary, to be most useful, should combine the characteristics of diagnostic and process recording. It should show the presenting problems, the relevant history, what testing was done, how the counselor assessed the client's characteristics and his problems, and what his status was at the end of counseling. In addition, it should sketch the major events in the process of helping the client. One rule of thumb is for the counselor to ask himself what he would want another counselor to know if the client were to return for more treatment.

Problems of accuracy

Our general experience indicates that counselors can be highly variable in the accuracy of their reports. Covner (1944a, 1944b) reports a series of studies in which the completeness and accuracy of counseling interview reports were compared with phonographic recordings of the corresponding interviews. He found that while the materials included in the reports were 75 to 90 per cent accurate, 70 per cent or more of the actual interview material was omitted. He concluded that not only unimportant material was omitted but also important material, and that these omissions often resulted in a rather distorted picture of the interview. Since for the most part Covner was working with either counselors in training or relatively inexperienced counselors, we can assume that these results are more extreme than would be found among experienced practicing counselors or psychothera-pists. On the other hand, even these counselors are often so pushed for time that the difference in results may not be as great as one might presume. In any event, on both logical and empirical grounds, there is good reason to believe that the reports of inter-view processes are subject to a number of distorting influences. We shall review the sources of these influences in order to suggest ways in which their unfortunate effects can be diminished.

Laboratory research in learning and memory has demon-strated that we are able to learn or remember an extended sequence of stimulus events better when such a sequence can be given a meaningful organization. For example, I would not remember the number sequence 5–9–13–16–30, as readily as when I see it as the subway station stops on my daily trip to work. Where the chronological sequence contains such a meaning we are less likely to transpose the order of the events or to distort their character in a way that might change the meaning.

In our previous discussions we have talked about the coun-selor's lack of understanding as a function of either his inex-perience or of countertransference. This lack of understanding may take one of two forms. First, he will be completely confused and have to approach the events of the interview as a series of discrete, unconnected happenings, with the result that he will have considerable difficulty in being able to keep them in their chronological sequence or in remembering all of them. In addi-tion, he will tend to forget as many of the important as the unimportant events in the interview. Secondly, although the dis-torting effects of countertransference may take this form, they may also induce a reorganization or modification of the events in the interview to fit some meaning which has defensive value for the counselor. As has been suggested, supervision offers one im-portant means for furthering a counselor's understanding. Ideally, recordings and typescripts should provide the media through which the supervisor can know the actual events of the interview and hence they vividly demonstrate to the counselor repetitive themes which pervade the interaction and carry a special meaning. Where recording facilities are not available, both counselor and super-visor must fall back on an effort by the counselor to separate his inferences from the data which gave rise to them. This means that in addition to taking note of the fact that the client at a certain point or points "was trying to control the interview and show me that he is boss," the counselor must also try to note and describe the specific events which to him seem to require this inference.

Another source of inaccuracy in process records is the lapse of a lengthy period of time between the interview and the recording process. When other activities and especially other interviews have intervened, the obstacles to accurate reproduction become great. It is important for the counselor to strive to keep at a minimum the time interval between the end of a counseling interview and the recording process. To facilitate this, many counseling agencies provide dictating equipment for their counseling staff. Often it is useful to arrange counseling schedules so that there is a minimum of a ten-minute interval between appointments which can be utilized for the dictation of an interview summary. Either preliminary to that dictation or for purposes of later recall, it is often helpful if the counselor immediately after the interview jots down a brief chronological outline of the significant events in the interview. What follows here is an illustration of such an outline.

> "Counseling isn't helping"
>   "fight with her husband"
>   "mistreating her children"
>
> "depression"
>
> "I am not helping enough"
>
> Her feelings of dependence
>   Her relationship to mother
>   Relationship to father
>   Her first job

In these brief statements the counselor has recorded a brief notation to himself that in this hour Mrs. L., his client, had started with an indirect expression of dissatisfaction over the help he was giving her. She did this through the medium of recounting a number of different current events, all of which added up to the same thing: instead of getting better she was getting worse. The counselor has then recorded his critical interpretation, namely, that she felt she was not getting enough help and that this in turn led to an examination on her part of other important helping relationships she has had and her attitude toward them. The effort to establish a connected picture of the interview after it is over will, it is hoped, induce the same set during the interview and will help to increase his sensitivity to the meaning underlying his interactions with the client.

Our analysis of the purpose and form of case records has indicated that they have no single purpose and come in no single preferred form. Instead, we have called attention to the many different forms that case notes can take and the purposes they serve. We have also discussed some of the problems of insuring the accuracy of notes. There is one rule we can be sure of: The counselor ought to take seriously the responsibilities he has assumed in encouraging another person to try to use him and the relationship between them in realizing his own ends. A counselor's concern about case notes and his responsibility for deciding carefully what form they should take reflects the fact that he never extends this offer of help lightly.

Bibliography

ABT, L. E., & BELLAK, L. (Eds.) *Projective psychology: clinical approaches to the total personality.* New York: Knopf, 1950.

ADLER, A. *The practice and theory of individual psychology.* New York: Harcourt, Brace, 1924.

ADLER, A. *Superiority and social interest.* H. & Rowena Ansbacher (Eds.) Evanston: Northwestern University Press, 1964.

ALBEE, G. W. *Mental health manpower trends.* New York: Basic Books, 1959.

ALEXANDER, F. The influence of psychologic factors upon gastro-intestinal disturbances: a symposium. *Psychoanal. Quart.,* 1934, *3,* 501–539.

ALEXANDER, F. *Psychosomatic Medicine.* New York: Norton, 1950.

ALEXANDER, L. S. Employment counseling program of the United States Employment Service. *J. clin. Psychol.,* 1946, *2,* 123–126.

ALLEN, F. H. *Psychotherapy with children.* New York: Norton, 1942.

ALLEN, F. J. (Ed.) *Principles and problems in vocational guidance.* New York: McGraw-Hill, 1927.

American Psychological Association. Annual Report of Policy and Planning Board. *Amer. Psychologist,* 1948, *3,* 187–192.

ANSBACHER, H., & ANSBACHER, Rowena. *The individual psychology of Alfred Adler.* New York: Basic Books, 1956.

ATKINSON, J. W. *Motives in fantasy, action, and society.* New York: Van Nostrand, 1958.

BANDURA, A., LIPSHER, D., & MILLER, Paula. Psychotherapists' approach-avoidance reactions to patients' expressions of hostility. *J. consult. Psychol.,* 1960, *24,* 1–8.

BEALL, Lynette, & BORDIN, E. S. The development and personality of engineers. *Pers. and guid. J.,* 1964, *42,* 23–32.

BELL, J. E. *Projective techniques.* New York: Longmans, 1948.

BENEDEK, Therese. Dynamics of counter-transference. *Bull. Menninger Clinic,* 1953, *17,* 201–208.

BERDIE, R. F. Counseling—an educational technique. *Educ. psychol. Measmt.,* 1949, *9,* 89–94.

BETTELHEIM, B. *Truants from life.* Glencoe, Ill.: Free Press, 1955.

BINDMAN, A. J. Mental health consultation: theory and practice. *J. consult. Psychol.*, 1959, *23*, 473–482.

BIXENSTINE, V. E. Student attitudes and college counseling. *J. counsel. Psychol.*, 1959, *6*, 280–283.

BIXLER, R. H. Limits are therapy. *J. consult. Psychol.*, 1949, *13*, 1–11.

BIXLER, R. H., & BIXLER, Virginia H. Test interpretation in vocational counseling. *Educ. psychol. Measmt.*, 1946, *6*, 145–155.

BLOS, P. Psychological counseling of college students. *Amer. J. Orthopsychiat.*, 1946, *16*, 571–580.

BLUM, G. S. *Psychoanalytic theories of personality.* New York: McGraw-Hill, 1953.

BORDIN, E. S. Diagnosis in counseling and psychotherapy. *Educ. psychol. Measmt.*, 1946, *6*, 169–184.

BORDIN, E. S. (Ed.) *Training of psychological counselors.* Ann Arbor: University of Michigan Press, 1950.

BORDIN, E. S. Four uses for psychological tests in counseling. *Educ. psychol. Measmt.*, 1951, *11*, 779–781.

BORDIN, E. S. Ambiguity as a therapeutic variable. *J. consult. Psychol.*, 1955, *19*, 9–15. (a)

BORDIN, E. S. The implications of client expectations for the counseling process. *J. counsel. Psychol.*, 1955, 2, 17–21. (b)

BORDIN, E. S. The ambivalent quest for independence. *J. counsel. Psychol.*, 1965, *12*, 339–345.

BORDIN, E. S. Personality and free association. *J. consult. Psychol.*, 1966, *30*, 30–38.

BORDIN, E. S., & BIXLER, R. H. Test selection: A process of counseling. *Educ. psychol. Measmt.*, 1946, *6*, 631–637.

BORDIN, E. S., NACHMANN, Barbara, & SEGAL, S. J. An articulated framework for vocational development. *J. counsel. Psychol.*, 1963, *10*, 107–118.

BRAATOY, T. *Fundamentals of psychoanalytic technique.* New York: Wiley, 1954.

BRAYFIELD, A. H. Report of the Executive Officer: 1965. *Amer. Psychologist*, 1965, *20*, 1018–1027.

BREWER, J. M. *History of vocational guidance.* New York: Harper, 1942.

BRODY, E. B., & REDLICH, F. C. (Eds.) *Psychotherapy with schizophrenics.* New York: International Universities Press, 1952.

BUTLER, J. M., RICE, Laura N., & WAGSTAFF, Alice K. On the naturalistic definition of variables: An analogue of clinical analysis. In H. H. Strupp & L. Luborsky (Eds.), *Research in psychotherapy.* Vol. 2. Washington, D.C.: American Psychological Association, 1962. Pp. 178–205.

CAIRNS, R. B. The influence of dependency inhibition on the effectiveness of social reinforcement. *J. Pers.*, 1961, *29*, 466–488.

CANTOR, N. F. *Employee counseling.* New York: McGraw-Hill, 1945.

CAPLAN, G. (Ed.) *Prevention of mental disorders in children.* New York: Basic Books, 1961.

CARTWRIGHT, D., & ZANDER, A. (Eds.) *Group dynamics: Research and theory* (2nd ed.). Evanston, Ill.: Row, Peterson, 1960.

CLARK, K. B. Desegregation: An appraisal of the evidence: the role of social scientist. *J. soc. Issues*, 1953, *9*, 2–8.

COLBY, K. M. *A primer for psychotherapists*. New York: Ronald, 1951.

CORRELL, P. T. Student personnel workers on the spot. *J. counsel. Psychol.*, 1962, *9*, 232–235.

COVNER, B. J. Studies in phonographic records of verbal material: Written reports of interviews. *J. appl. Psychol.*, 1944, *28*, 89–98. (a)

COVNER, B. J. Studies in phonographic records of verbal material: III. The completeness and accuracy of counseling interview reports. *J. gen. Psychol.*, 1944, *30*, 181–203. (b)

CUTLER, R. L. Countertransference effects in psychotherapy. *J. consult. Psychol.*, 1958, *22*, 349–356.

DARLEY, J. G. The conduct of the interview. In A. H. Brayfield (Ed.), *Readings in modern methods of counseling*. New York: Appleton-Century-Crofts, 1950. Pp. 265–272.

DIBNER, A. S. Ambiguity and anxiety. *J. & abnorm. soc. Psychol.*, 1958, *56*, 165–174.

DICKS, R. L. *Pastoral work and personal counseling*. New York: Macmillan, 1951.

DITTMANN, A. T., & RAUSH, H. L. The psychoanalytic theory of conflict: structure and methodology. *Psychol. Rev.*, 1954, *61*, 386–400.

DREIKURS, R. The Adlerian approach to psychodynamics. In M. L. Stein (Ed.), *Contemporary psychotherapies*. New York: Free Press, 1961, Pp. 60–79.

DRESSEL, P. L., & MATTESON, R. W. The effects of client participation in test interpretation. *Educ. psychol. Measmt.*, 1950, *10*, 693–706.

DVORAK, Beatrice J. *Differential occupational ability patterns*. Minneapolis: University of Minnesota Press, 1935.

ELLIS, A. *Reason and emotion in psychotherapy*. New York: L. Stuart, 1962.

ERIKSON, E. H. Identity and the life cycle. *Psychological Issues*, Vol. 1, no. 1, 1959.

Ethical standards of psychologists. Washington, D.C.: American Psychological Association, 1952.

FENICHEL, O. *Problems of psychoanalytic technique*. Albany, N. Y.: Psychoanalytic Quarterly, Inc., 1941.

FENICHEL, O. *The psychoanalytic theory of neurosis*. New York: Norton, 1945.

FIEDLER, F. E. The concept of an ideal therapeutic relationship. *J. consult. Psychol.*, 1950, *14*, 239–245. (a)

FIEDLER, F. E. A comparison of therapeutic relationships in psychoanalytic, nondirective, and Adlerian therapy. *J. consult. Psychol.*, 1950, *14*, 436–445. (b)

FIEDLER, F. E. Factor analyses of psychoanalytic, nondirective and Adlerian therapeutic relationships. *J. consult. Psychol.*, 1951, *15*, 32–38.

FLESCHER, J. On different types of countertransference. *Int. J. Group Psychother.*, 1953, *3*, 357–372.

FLIESS, R. Countertransference and counteridentification. *J. Amer. Psychoanal. Assoc.*, 1953, *1*, 268–284.

FORD, D. H., & URBAN, H. B. *Systems of psychotherapy*. New York: Wiley, 1963.

FORGY, E. W., & BLACK, J. D. A followup after three years of clients counseled by two methods. *J. couns. Psychol.*, 1954, *1*, 1–8.

FRANK, J. D. *Persuasion and healing: A comparative study of psychotherapy*. Baltimore: Johns Hopkins, 1961.

FREEDMAN, M. B., LEARY, T. F., OSSORIO, A. G., & COFFEY, H. S. The interpersonal dimensions of personality. *J. Pers.*, 1951, *20*, 143–162.

FRENKEL-BRUNSWICK, Else. Intolerance of ambiguity as an emotional and perceptual variable. *J. Pers.*, 1949, *18*, 108–143.

FREUD, Anna. *The ego and the mechanisms of defense*. New York: International Universities Press, 1946.

FREUD, S. *An outline of psychoanalysis*. New York: Norton, 1949.

FROMM-REICHMANN, Freda. *Principles of intensive psychotherapy*. Chicago: University of Chicago Press, 1950.

GARRETT, Annette. Historical survey of the evolution of casework. *J. soc. Casewk.*, 1949, *30*, 219–229.

GOLDSTEIN, A. P. *Therapist-patient expectancies in psychotherapy*. New York: Macmillan, 1962.

GORDON, J. E. Project cause, the Federal Anti-Poverty Program and some implications of subprofessional training. *Amer. Psychol.*, 1965, *20*, 334–343.

GREENACRE, Phyllis. *Trauma, growth and personality*. New York: Norton, 1952.

GREENSPOON, J. The reinforcing effect of two spoken sounds on the frequency of two responses. *Amer. J. Psychol.*, 1955, *68*, 409–416.

GUNTRIP, H. The schizoid compromise and psychotherapeutic stalemate. *Brit. J. Med. Psychol.*, 1962, *35*, 273–287.

GURIN, G., VEROFF, J., & FIELD, Sheila. *Americans view their mental health*. New York: Basic Books, 1960.

GUSTAD, J. W., & TUMA, A. H. The effects of different methods of test introduction and interpretation on client learning in counseling. *J. counsel. Psychol.*, 1957, *4*, 313–317.

HARTMANN, H., KRIS, E., & LOWENSTEIN, R. Comments on the formation of psychic structure. *Psychoanalytic study of the child*, 1946, *2*, 11–38.

HARTMANN, H. Mutual influences in development of ego and id. *Psychoanalytic study of the child*, 1952, *7*, 9–30.

HARTMANN, H. *Essays on ego psychology*. New York: International Universities Press, 1964.

HELLER, K. Ambiguity in the interview interaction. Paper read at third APA sponsored Conference on Research in Psychotherapy, Chicago, 1966.

HILTNER, S. *Pastoral counseling*. New York: Abingdon-Cokesbury, 1949.

HOLLAND, J. L. A theory of vocational choice. *J. counsel. Psychol.*, 1959, *6*, 35–44.

HOLT, R. R. Psychotherapy as an autonomous profession: an alternative to the Clark Committee proposal. In American Psychological Association, *Preconference Materials*. Washington, D.C.: American Psychological Association, 1965. Pp. 81–82.

HULL, C. L. *Principles of behavior*. New York: Appleton-Century, 1943.

IVEY, A. E. Role conflict in counseling: its effect on college student attitudes. *J. counsel. Psychol.*, 1962, *9*, 139–143.

JACOBSON, Edith. Transference problems in the psychoanalytic treatment of severely depressive patients. *J. Amer. Psychoanal. Assn.*, 1954, 2, 595–606.
JAHODA, Marie. *Current conceptions of positive mental health.* New York: Basic Books, 1958.
Joint Commission on Mental Illness and Health. *Action for mental health.* New York: Science Editions, 1961.

KASIUS, Cora. (Ed.) *A comparison of diagnostic and functional casework concepts.* New York: Family Service Association of America, 1950.
KELLY, G. A. *The psychology of personal constructs.* (2 Vols.) New York: Norton, 1955.
KRASNER, L. The therapist as a social reinforcement machine. In H. H. Strupp & L. Luborsky (Eds.), *Research in psychotherapy.* Vol. 2. Washington, D.C.: American Psychological Association, 1962. Pp. 61–94.
KRIS, E. *Psychoanalytic explorations in art.* New York: International Universities Press, 1952.
KRUMBOLTZ, J. D., & THORESEN, C. E. The effect of behavioral counseling in group and individual settings on information seeking behavior. *J. counsel. Psychol.*, 1964, *11*, 324–335.
KRUMBOLTZ, J. D. Behavioral goals in counseling. *J. counsel. Psychol.*, 1966, *13*, 153–159.

LIEF, A. *The commonsense psychiatry of Dr. Adolph Meyer.* New York: McGraw-Hill, 1948.
LITTLE, Ruby. Diagnostic recording. *J. soc. Casewk.*, 1949, *30*, 15–19.
LLOYD-JONES, E. M., & SMITH, M. R. *A student personnel program for higher education.* New York: McGraw-Hill, 1938.
LOVASS, O. I., SCHAEFER, B., & SIMMONS, J. Q. Experimental studies in childhood schizophrenia: Building social behavior in autistic children by use of electric shock. *J. exp. Res. Pers.*, 1965, *1*, 99–109.

MANN, Nancy A. Free association and preferred defenses. Unpublished doctoral dissertation, Univer. of Michigan, 1965.
MATARAZZO, J. D., WIENS, A. N., MATARAZZO, Ruth G., & SASLOW, G. Speech and silence behavior in clinical psychotherapy and its laboratory correlates. Paper read at third APA sponsored Conference on Research in Psychotherapy, Chicago, 1966.
MEAD, Margaret. *And keep your powder dry.* New York: Morrow, 1943.
MEEHL, P. E., and McCLOSKY, H. Ethical and political aspects of applied psychology. *J. abnorm. soc. Psychol.*, 1947, *42*, 91–98.
MENNINGER, K. A. *Theory of psychoanalytic technique.* New York: Basic Books, 1958.
MENNINGER, K. A., MAYMAN, M., & PRUYSER, P. *The vital balance: the life process in mental health and illness.* New York: Viking, 1963.
MILLER, D. R. Prediction of behavior by means of the Rorschach test. *J. abnorm. soc. Psychol.*, 1953, *48*, 367–375.
MORENO, J. L. *Who shall survive?* Beacon, N. Y.: Beacon House, 1953.

MUNSON, Joan E. Patterns of client resistiveness and counselor response. Unpublished doctoral dissertation, Univer. of Michigan, 1960.

MURRAY, H. A. *Explorations in personality.* New York: Oxford University Press, 1938.

NACHMANN, Barbara. Childhood experience and vocational choice in law, dentistry and social work. *J. counsel. Psychol.*, 1960, 7, 243–250.

OSBURN, H. G. An investigation of the ambiguity dimension of counselor behavior. Unpublished doctoral dissertation, Univer. of Michigan, 1952.

PATERSON, D. G., & DARLEY, J. G. *Men, women and jobs.* Minneapolis: University of Minnesota Press, 1936.

PATERSON, D. G., SCHNEIDLER, Gwendolyn, & WILLIAMSON, E. G. *Student guidance techniques.* New York: McGraw-Hill, 1938.

PATTERSON, C. H. *Counseling and psychotherapy.* New York: Harper, 1954.

PEPINSKY, H. B. The selection and use of diagnostic categories in clinical counseling. *Appl. psychol. Monogr.*, 1948, No. 15.

PIAGET, J. *The origins of intelligence in children.* New York: International Universities Press, 1952.

PIAGET, J. *The construction of reality in the child.* New York: Basic Books, 1954.

PORTER, E. H., Jr. The development and evaluation of a measure of counseling. *Educ. psychol. Measmt.*, 1943, 3, 105–126.

PORTER, E. H., Jr. *An introduction to therapeutic counseling.* Boston: Houghton Mifflin, 1950.

POWDERMAKER, Florence. The techniques of the initial interview and methods of teaching them. *Amer. J. Psychiat.*, 1948, 104, 642–646.

RACKER, H. A contribution to the problem of countertransference. *Int. J. Psychoanal.*, 1953, 34, 313–324.

RAIMY, V. C. (Ed.) *Training in clinical psychology.* New York: Prentice-Hall, 1950.

RAPAPORT, D. *Diagnostic psychological testing.* Chicago: Yearbook Publishers, 1944.

RAPAPORT, D. The theory of ego autonomy: A generalization. *Bull. Menn. Clinic*, 1958, 22, 13–35.

RAPAPORT, D. The structure of psychoanalytic theory: a systematizing attempt. In S. Koch (Ed.), *Psychology: A study of science.* Vol. 3. New York: McGraw-Hill, 1959. Pp. 55–183.

RAUSH, H. L., & BORDIN, E. S. Warmth in personality development and in psychotherapy. *Psychiatry*, 1957, 20, 351–363.

REIK, T. *Listening with the third ear.* New York: Farrar, Strauss, 1949.

RIGLER, D. Some determinants of therapist behavior. Unpublished doctoral dissertation, Univer. of Michigan, 1957.

RIOCH, Margaret, ELKES, C., & FLINT, A. A., Jr. NIMH pilot study in training mental health counselors. *Amer. J. Orthopsychiat.*, 1963, 33, 678–689.

ROBINSON, F. P. *Principles and procedures in student counseling.* New York: Harper, 1950.

ROBINSON, F. P. Modern approaches to counseling "diagnosis." *J. counsel. Psychol.*, 1963, 10, 325–333.

ROE, Anne. Early determinants of vocational choice. *J. counsel. Psychol.*, 1957, *4*, 212–217.

ROGERS, C. R. *Client-centered therapy*. Boston: Houghton Mifflin, 1951.

ROGERS, C. R. Persons or science? A philosophical question. *Amer. Psychol.*, 1955, *10*, 267–279.

ROGERS, C. R. The necessary and sufficient conditions of therapeutic personality change. *J. consult. Psychol.*, 1957, *21*, 95–102.

ROGERS, C. R. Therapy, personality, and interpersonal relationships. In S. Koch (Ed.), *Psychology: A study of a science*. Vol. 3. New York: McGraw-Hill, 1959. Pp. 184–256.

ROTHLISBERGER, F. J., & DICKSON, W. J. *Management and the worker*. Cambridge: Harvard University Press, 1939.

RUDIKOFF, Lynn C., & KIRK, Barbara A. Test interpretation in counseling. *J. counsel. Psychol.*, 1959, *6*, 223–228.

RYAN, T. Antoinette, & KRUMBOLTZ, J. D. Effect of planned reinforcement counseling on client decision-making behavior. *J. counsel. Psychol.*, 1964, *11*, 315–323.

SALZINGER, K., PORTNOY, Stephanie, & FIELDMAN, R. S. Verbal behavior in schizophrenics and some comments toward a theory of schizophrenia. In P. Hoch & J. Zubin (Eds.), *Psychopathology of schizophrenia*. New York: Greene and Stratton, 1966.

SANFORD, F. H. Notes on the future of psychology as a profession. *Amer. Psychologist*, 1951, *6*, 74–76.

SANFORD, F. H. Toward a sociology of psychology. *Amer. Psychologist*, 1952, *7*, 83–85.

SARBIN, T. R. The case record in psychological counseling. *J. appl. Psychol.*, 1940, *24*, 184–197.

SCHAFER, R. *The clinical application of psychological tests*. New York: International Universities Press, 1948.

SEEMAN, J. A study of client self-selection of tests in vocational counseling. *Educ. psychol. Measmt.*, 1948, *8*, 327–346.

SEEMAN, J. A study of the process of nondirective therapy. *J. consult. Psychol.*, 1949, *13*, 157–168.

SEGAL, S. J. A psychoanalytic analysis of personality factors in vocational choice. *J. counsel. Psychol.*, 1961, *8*, 202–210.

SHAFER, L. F. The problem of psychotherapy. *Amer. Psychologist*, 1947, *2*, 459–467.

SKINNER, B. F. *Science and human behavior*. New York: Macmillan, 1953.

SKINNER, B. F. *Verbal behavior*. New York: Appleton-Century-Crofts, 1957.

SNYDER, W. U. "Warmth" in nondirective therapy. *J. abnorm. soc. Psychol.*, 1946, *41*, 491–495.

SNYDER, W. U. *Casebook of nondirective counseling*. Boston: Houghton Mifflin, 1947.

SPEISMAN, J. C. Depth of interpretation and verbal resistance in psychotherapy. *J. consult. Psychol.*, 1959, *23*, 93–99.

SPITZ, R. A., & WOLF, Katherine M. Anaclitic depression. *Psychoanal. Study of the Child*, 1946, *2*, 313–342.

SPITZ, R. Countertransference. *J. Amer. Psychoanal. Assn.*, 1956, *4*, 256–265.

STEAD, W. H., SHARTLE, C. R., *et al. Occupational counseling techniques*. New York: American Book, 1940.

STONE, L. *The psychoanalytic situation.* New York: International University Press, 1961.

STRONG, E. K., Jr. *Vocational interests of men and women.* Stanford: Stanford University Press, 1943.

SULLIVAN, H. S. *The interpersonal theory of psychiatry.* New York: Norton, 1953.

SUPER, D. E. A theory of vocational development. *Amer. Psychol.,* 1953, *8,* 185–190.

SUPER, D. E. Transition: From vocational guidance to counseling psychology. *J. counsel. Psychol.,* 1955, *2,* 3–9.

SUPER, D. E., & CRITES, J. O. *Appraising vocational fitness.* (2nd ed.) New York: Harper, 1962.

SUPER, D. E., STARISHEVSKY, R., MATLIN, N., & JORDAAN, J. P. *Career development: self-concept theory.* New York: College Entrance Examination Board, 1963.

TAFT, Jessie. *A functional approach to family casework.* Philadelphia: University of Pennsylvania Press, 1943.

TEAD, O., & METCALF, H. C. *Personnel administration.* New York: McGraw-Hill, 1953.

THELEN, H., & STOCK, Dorothy. *Emotional dynamics and group culture.* New York: New York University Press, 1958.

THORNE, F. C. *Principles of personality counseling.* Brandon, Vt.: *J. clin. Psychol.,* 1950.

TIEDEMAN, D. V., & O'HARA, R. P. *Career development: choice and adjustment.* New York: College Entrance Examinations Board, 1963.

TITCHENER, E. B. *A textbook of psychology.* New York: Macmillan, 1919.

TOWNSEND, A. H. An empirical measure of ambiguity in the context of psychotherapy. *Mich. Acad. Sci., Arts & Letters,* 1956, *41,* 349–355.

TOWNSEND, A. H. The relationship between parental commitment and certain forms of dependent behavior. Unpublished doctoral dissertation, Univer. of Michigan, 1958.

TRUAX, C. B., & CARKHUFF, R. R. Client and therapist transparency in the psychotherapeutic encounter. *J. counsel. Psychol.,* 1965, *12,* 3–9.

TUMA, A. H., & GUSTAD, J. The effects of client and counselor personality characteristics on client learning in counseling. *J. counsel. Psychol.,* 1957, *4,* 136–143.

TYLER, Leona E. Minimum change therapy. *Pers. Guid. J.,* 1960, *38,* 475–479.

VOILAND, A. L., GRUNDELACH, M. L., & CORNER, M. *Developing insight in initial interviews.* New York: Family Service Association, 1947.

WARMAN, R. E. Differential perceptions of counseling role. *J. counsel. Psychol.,* 1960, *7,* 269–274.

WHITE, R. W. *Ego and reality in psychoanalytic theory.* New York: International Universities Press, 1963.

WILLIAMS, JOAN V. The influence of therapist commitment on progress in psychotherapy. Unpublished doctoral dissertation, University of Michigan, 1959.

WILLIAMSON, E. G. *How to counsel students.* New York: McGraw-Hill, 1939.

WILLIAMSON, E. G. Counseling and the Minnesota point of view. *Educ. psychol. Measmt.*, 1947, 7, 141–155.

WILLIAMSON, E. G. *Counseling adolescents.* New York: McGraw-Hill, 1950.

WILLIAMSON, E. G., & DARLEY, J. G. *Student personnel work.* New York: McGraw-Hill, 1937.

WOLPE, J. *Psychotherapy by reciprocal inhibition.* Stanford, Calif.: Stanford University Press, 1958.

WRENN, C. G. *Student personnel work in college.* New York: Ronald, 1951.

WRENN, C. G. The ethics of counseling. *Educ. psychol. Measmt.*, 1952, *12*, 161–177.

WRENN, C. G. *The counselor in a changing world.* Washington, D.C.: American Personnel and Guidance Association, 1962.

YOUNG, F. C. College freshmen judge their scholastic promise. *Personnel Guid. J.*, 1954, *32*, 399–403.

INDEX

Abt, L. E., 154, 296n
Adler, A., 129–132, 168
Adlerian theory, 129–132
  of psychotherapy, 130
    cognitive factors in, 131–132
    contrasted with psychoanalytic, 132
  role of inferiority in, 130
  social interest in, 130
  style of life, 130
Albee, G. W., 4
Alexander, F., 190
Alexander, L. S., 23
Allen, F. H., 124–129, 167–168
Allen, F. J., 14
Allport-Vernon Study of Values Inventory, 338, 339, 347–350, 356
Ambiguity, 149–164
  in client-centered theory, 157–158
  dangers of, 164–165
  defined, 149–152
  effect on counselor, 163–164
  ego autonomy and response to, 155–156
  functions of, 158–160
  measurement of, 152–153
  in projective tests, 154–155
  in psychoanalytic theory, 156–157
  relationship to anxiety, 155, 160–161
  relationship to client orientation, 162–163
  in treatment of psychotics, 161–162
American Council on Education Psychological Examination, 337, 342
American Psychological Association, 37–38
Ansbacher, H., 130n

Ansbacher, Rowena, 130n
Atkinson, J. W., 193n

Bandura, A., 164
Beall, Lynette, 429, 431
Behavior therapists, 114
Bell, J. E., 296n
Bell Adjustment Inventory, 309
Bellak, L., 154, 296n
Benedek, Theresa, 164
Bennett Mechanical Comprehension Test, 337, 339
  interpretation of, 308
Berdie, R. F., 22
Bettelheim, B., 199
Bindman, A. J., 37
Bixenstine, V. E., 36
Bixler, R. H., 212n, 295n, 305n
Bixler, Virginia H., 305
Black, J. D., 302n
Blos, P., 120
Blum, G. S., 138
Bordin, E. S., 18, 20, 140, 149n, 156, 183n, 220–221, 295n 427, 429, 431
Braatøy, T., 187
Brayfield, A. H., 38
Brewer, J. M., 424
Brody, E. B., 161
Butler, J. M., 207

Cairns, R. B., 190
Cantor, N., 28
Caplan, G., 5
Carkhuff, R. R., 184
Cartwright, D., 5
Case records, 445–454
  accuracy of, 452–454
  agency uses of, 448

467

Case records—*Continued*
  diagnostic recording, 449–452
  form of, 449–454
  functions of, 446–449
  preliminary notes for, 453–454
  process recording, 450–452
  recordings and transcripts, 446, 453
  summaries of, 452
  typescripts of, 451
Clark, K. B., 5n
Centralism in personality theory, 136–137
Client-centered theory, 120–124
  denial to awareness in, 121–122
  of personality, 120–122
  of psychotherapy, 122–124
  role of ambiguity in, 157–158
  of self, 121
  therapist style in, 184
  view of interpretation, 123
  view of transference, 123–124
Client's expectations, 219–222
  faith in counselor, 221
  of counselor commitment, 219–220
Client's needs, responding in initial interviews to, 226–228
Client's task, alternatives in, 225
Cognitive process, in counseling and psychotherapy, 174
  development of, 168–169
  functions in behavior, 169–170
  in interpretation, 170–172
  in neurosis, 169–170
  in play therapy, 172–173
  recommendations regarding, 174–177
  relationships to ambiguity, 172
Colby, K. M., 179–180, 215
College aptitude test scores, interpretation of, 318–322
Commitment in psychotherapy, adaptations to dependency, 195–200
  client expectations, 219–220
  defined, 188
Conation, and empathy, 176–177
  relationship to cognition, 168–170, 176
Cooperative General Culture Test, 337
Correll, P. T., 33

Counseling, cognitive approaches to, 111–114
  definition, 10
  distinguished from education, 24–26
  distinguished from psychotherapy, 18–20
  educational, 21–22
  ethical issues in, 37–46
  family, 16–17
  marital, 22
  placement, 23–24
  religious, 23
  role of informing in, 113–114
  vocational, 14–18
Counseling relationship, cognitive-conative balance in, 177–179
  examples of, 48–105
    active interpretation in, 74–85
    cognitive emphasis in, 48–53
    concentrating on personality in, 53–64
    mutual activity in, 85–97
    responding to resistance in, 97–105
  interruption of, 418–420
  methods of control of, 369–381
    examples of, 370–373, 374–380, 441–444
    pressures toward extending, 368–369
    reasons for limiting, 367–368
    as reflected at start of hour, 382–402
  resistance in, 382, 403–410
  termination of, 410–418, 420–422
Counseling services, factors in accessibility, 33–37
  relation to other personnel agencies, 35–37
Counselor's needs, 222
  in initial interview, 221–222
Covner, B. J., 452
Crawford Small Parts Dexterity Test, 338, 340–341
Crawford Spatial Relations Test, 338
Crites, J. O., 306n
Cutler, R. L., 181–182

Darley, J. G., 15, 28, 113, 425
Dependency
  reaction types, 187–190

origins of, 193–195
Developmental tasks, 139
Diagnosis, Allen's attitude toward, 144
  Bordin's categories of, 145
    Pepinsky's addition, 145n
    Robinson's addition, 145n
  in initial interviews, 228–231
  in psychoanalytic therapy, 143–144
  in a psychological counseling agency, 146
  Roger's position on, 144, 145, 146–147
  and understanding, 143–147
  Williamson's description of, 144–145
Dibner, A. S., 160–161
Dicks, R. L., 23n
Dickson, W. J., 28
Dittmann, A. T., 204
Dreikurs, R., 131
Dressel, P. L., 301–302
Dvorak, Beatrice J., 15
Dynamic defined, 114–115

Eclecticism in psychotherapy, 133–134
Effort to understand, in client-centered therapy, 202
  defined, 188
  in infant development, 200–201
  in psychotherapy, 201, 203
  relation to paranoid defense, 201, 203
Ego, autonomy of, 155–156
  constructive processes of, 143
  defensive processes of, 142–143
  in psychoanalytic theory, 155
  in psychology, 114
  strength of, 170
Elkes, C., 20
Ellis, A., 131
Erikson, E. H., 139, 193n

Feld, Sheila, 7
Feldman, R. S., 113
Fenichel, O., 116, 119, 166, 177, 202, 206
Fiedler, F. E., 109–110
Flescher, J., 184
Flint, A. A., 20

Ford, D. H., 131
Forgy, E. W., 302n
Frank, J. D., 221
Free association
  in counseling, 226
  in psychoanalysis, 118
Freedman, M., 181
Frenkel-Brunswik, Else, 155, 160
Freud, Anna, 116n
Freud, S., 115, 116
Fromm-Reichmann, Freda, 161–162, 179n, 181, 215n

Garrett, Annette, 16
Goldstein, A. P., 221
Gordon, J. E., 12
Greenacre, Phyllis, 175n
Greenspoon, J., 159
Guntrip, H., 193n
Gurin, G., 7
Gustad, J. W., 302n

Hartman, H., 143, 169
Heller, K., 159–160
Hiltner, S., 23n
Holland, J. L., 427
Holt, R. R., 12n
Hull, C. L., 112

Impulse, as used in psychoanalytic theory, 116
Initial interview, developmental problem shown in, 270–294
  diagnostic potentialities of, 228–231
  with emotionally labile client, 232–250
  examples of, 232–294
  in vocational counseling, 250–270
Intake procedures, 215–219
  comparative values of, 216–219
Interpretation, cognitive process in, 170–172
  depth of, 119–120
  influence of counselor's conflicts on, 181–182
  prerequisites for, 223
  techniques of, 179–180
  theorists' attitudes toward, 166–168
  working through, 180–181

Introspection of emotional experiences, 177
Ivey, A. E., 33

Jacobson, Edith, 198, 207
Jahoda, Marie, 9

Kasius, Cora, 129n
Kelley, G. A., 131
Kirk, Barbara, 305n
Krasner, L., 114
Kris, E., 143, 169n
Krumboltz, J. D., 113, 114
Kuder Preference Record, 311, 357

Learning theory's role in counseling and psychotherapy, 112–114
Lief, A., 133
Little, Ruby, 445n
Lipsher, D., 164
Lloyd-Jones, Esther M., 28
Lovass, O. I., 113–114
Lowenstein, R., 169

McClelland, D. C., 193n
McCloskey, H., 26
Mann, Nancy, 156
Mastery drive, 190–193
    anxiety about, 190, 192
Matarazzo, J. D., 159–160
Matarazzo, Ruth G., 159
Matteson, R. W., 301–302
Mayman, M., 4n
Mead, Margaret, 138
Meehl, P. E., 26
Menninger, K. A., 4n, 215
Metcalf, H. C., 28
Meyer, Adolph, 133
Miller, D. R., 154–155
Miller, Paula, 164
Minnesota Multiphasic Inventory, 305, 309, 311, 338, 339, 345–347, 357, 411–412
Minnesota Paper Form Board Test, 337
Minnesota Reading Examinations, 337, 342–344
Minnesota Spatial Relations Test, 338
Moreno, J. L., 205n
Munson, Joan, 164

Murray, H. A., 14

Nachmann, Barbara, 140, 427, 428
Normality, distinguished from abnormality, 9

O'Hara, R. P., 426
Osburn, H. G., 152–153, 161

Parsons, Frank, 14
Paterson, D. G., 15, 425
Patterson, C. H., 18
Pavlov, I., 112
Personality problems, application of group dynamics in, 5
    primary prevention of, 5
    range of, 4
Personality test scores, interpretation of, 309
Personality theory, Adlerian, 130–132
    centralism in, 13–14, 136–137
    client-centered, 120–122
    eclectic, 132–133
    psychoanalytic, 115–117, 137–138
    Rankian, 124–126, 138–139
    relation to therapeutic theory, 135–136
Personnel work, 28–33
    areas concerned with, 30–33
    objectives of, 28–30
Piaget, J. 143
Porter, E. H., Jr., 122, 147n, 215n
Portnay, Stephanie, 113
Powdermaker, Florence, 215n
Psychoanalytic theory, of defense mechanisms, 116
    influence on vocational counseling, 425–426
    of personality, 115–117, 136–138
    of psychotherapy, 117–120
    role of parents in, 117
    therapist style in, 184
    the unconscious in, 117–118
    psychological counseling and, 120
Psychological testing, client withdrawal during, 300–301
Psychological tests, as aid to reality testing, 297–301
    client's ability to forecast results of, 310

client's concentration on, as an obstacle to counseling, 296–297
client's selection of, 299–305
client's evaluation of effect of, 301–302
diagnostic use of, 296
as focus of resistance, 326–333
interest and personality inventories, 355–364
interpretation of, 305–312, 337–354
client resistance to, 307
request for, as resistance, 260–263
role in counseling versus psychotherapy, 295
as a stimulus to self-exploration, 298, 333–334
use of profiles in interpretation of, 310–312
use with test-oriented client, 314–326
Psychotherapy, effect of disliking patient in, 187
modeling in, 186
role of values in, 185–186
Primary prevention, relation to counseling goals, 5–6
Pruyser, P., 4

Racker, H., 184
Raimy, V. C., 18, 20
Rank, O., 124, 190
Rankian theory, 124–129
differentiation in, 124–126
on interpretation, 128
of psychotherapy, 126–129
view of transference and resistance, 127–128
will to health, 124–125
Rapoport, D., 143, 155–156, 296n
Raush, H. L., 183n, 204
Reassurance, 208–212
client-centered view of 208–209
Thorne's attitude toward, 209
Thorne's eight types of, 209–210
Reciprocal inhibition, 113, 114
Redlich, F. C., 161
Reik, T., 176, 202
Resistance, example of responding to, 97–105
in psychoanalysis, 118–119

in psychotherapy, 140–141
at start of hour, 403–410
Rice, Laura M., 207
Rigler, D., 164
Rioch, Margaret, 20
Roe, Anne, 140, 426
Rogers, C. R., 26, 120–124, 158, 167, 184, 190, 202, 208–209, 425
Rorschach test, 309
Rothlisberger, F. J., 28
Rudikof, Lynn C., 305n
Ryan, Antoinette, 114

Salzinger, K., 113
Sanford, F. H., 28–29, 38
Sarbin, T. R., 445n
Saslow, G., 159
Schafer, R., 296n
Schneidler, Gwendolyn, 425
Scholastic Aptitude Test for medical schools, 337, 339
Seeman, J., 157, 301, 304n
Segal, S. J., 140, 427, 429
Shaffer, L. F., 168n
Shartle, W. C., 23
Skinner, B. F., 112, 114
Smith, Margaret, R., 28
Snyder, W. U., 64, 202
Speisman, J. C., 172n, 197
Spitz, R. A., 184, 193n
Spontaneity, defined, 203–204
as a factor in development, 204–205
in psychotherapy, 204–208
defined, 188
Stead, W. H., 23
Stock, Dorothy, 189
Stone, L., 184
Strong, E. K. Jr., 312n
Strong Vocational Interest Blank, 311, 339, 347–349, 357, 359–363, 441
Sullivan, H. S., 205
Super, D. E., 14n, 140, 339n, 426
Support, see reassurance

Taft, Jessie, 124, 129
Tead, O., 28
Thelen, H., 189
Thematic Apperception Test, 309

Therapeutic contract, 215, 218–219
Therapist expressiveness, 207
Thoresen, C. E., 114
Thorne, F. C., 112, 133, 209
   attitude toward reassurance, 209
   eight types of reassurance, 209–210
Tiedeman, D. V., 426
Townsend, A. H., 151n, 194–195
Transference, 117–118
   contrasting views of, 141–143
   in psychological counseling, 120
Transitional stages,
   and location of counseling services, 11–12
   and openness to counseling, 6–9
Truax, C. B., 184
Tyler, Leona E., 17n
Tuma, A. H., 302n

Vocational choice, freedom of impulse expression in, 270–294
Vocational counseling, developmental model of, 426–429
   critical choice point in, 440–441
   exploratory phase in, 430–440
   illustration of, 430–444
   earlier forms of, 424–426

influence of psychoanalytic theory on, 425–426
relation to preventive goals, 423–424
Vocational development, 426–429
   personality development and, 426–427
   self-concept view of, 426
   Super's view, 426
Veroff, J., 7
Voiland, A. L., 215n, 228

Wagstaff, Alice, K., 207
Warman, R. E., 36
Warmth, components of, 187–188
White, R. W., 190n
Wiens, A. N., 159
Williams, Joan V., 197
Williamson, E. G., 18, 28, 112, 113, 298, 425
Wolf, Katherine M., 193n
Wolpe, J., 113, 114
Wrenn, C. G., 20, 28, 37n

Young, F. C., 30

Zander, A., 5